Chinese Statecraft in a Changing World

Jean Dong

Chinese Statecraft in a Changing World

Demystifying Enduring Traditions and Dynamic Constraints

Jean Dong
Centre for Contemporary Chinese Studies
University of Melbourne
Melbourne, VIC, Australia

ISBN 978-981-99-6452-9   ISBN 978-981-99-6453-6 (eBook)
https://doi.org/10.1007/978-981-99-6453-6

© The Editor(s) (if applicable) and The Author(s), under exclusive license to Springer Nature Singapore Pte Ltd. 2023

This work is subject to copyright. All rights are solely and exclusively licensed by the Publisher, whether the whole or part of the material is concerned, specifically the rights of translation, reprinting, reuse of illustrations, recitation, broadcasting, reproduction on microfilms or in any other physical way, and transmission or information storage and retrieval, electronic adaptation, computer software, or by similar or dissimilar methodology now known or hereafter developed.
The use of general descriptive names, registered names, trademarks, service marks, etc. in this publication does not imply, even in the absence of a specific statement, that such names are exempt from the relevant protective laws and regulations and therefore free for general use.
The publisher, the authors, and the editors are safe to assume that the advice and information in this book are believed to be true and accurate at the date of publication. Neither the publisher nor the authors or the editors give a warranty, expressed or implied, with respect to the material contained herein or for any errors or omissions that may have been made. The publisher remains neutral with regard to jurisdictional claims in published maps and institutional affiliations.

This Springer imprint is published by the registered company Springer Nature Singapore Pte Ltd.
The registered company address is: 152 Beach Road, #21-01/04 Gateway East, Singapore 189721, Singapore

Paper in this product is recyclable.

Foreword

We live in an era in which breathless commentary on the likelihood of war with China has become commonplace. Driven by the self-interest of politicians chasing votes, national security specialists seeking relevance, and newspapers pursuing readers, this mounting drumbeat threatens to become a risk to our national security in its own right. As the origins of the First World War graphically demonstrate, the emergence of a belligerent mindset—and all the misinterpretations and miscalculations that typically accompany it—is often the precursor to tragic and avoidable conflict.

Of even greater concern is the fact that this belligerence is often accompanied by profound ignorance of Chinese people, geography, history, and culture. This widespread lack of curiosity about this ancient civilisation that is now seen by some as an existential threat is profoundly disturbing.

I sincerely hope that Australian and Western opinion-leaders read this book. Jean Dong sets out a thorough and dispassionate explanation of the broad contours of Chinese history, specifically targeted at a Western audience. As she shows, there are consistent patterns in Chinese strategic conduct stretching back many centuries, shaped in particular by the implications of geography, that are still highly relevant today. Through detailed analysis of issues such as the long-standing Chinese desire for friendly states on its borders and the impact of China's two major river systems on its economic and political development, Dong provides us with lenses through which the preoccupations of contemporary China can be more clearly understood. And the conclusion that a balanced and fair-minded reader will draw is this: while the dramatic return of China to the pre-eminence it enjoyed in the pre-industrial era inevitably brings with it serious international stresses and tensions, there is no reason to conclude that this makes outright military conflict with the West inevitable or even likely.

So what does China want? Contemporary Western commentary is very threadbare on this question. Although there are numerous answers to this question, all of which need to be weighed up accordingly, in my view there is one theme that is central: China wants to be treated seriously.

Presumptions of Western dominance in global affairs are so deeply embedded in our discourse that we hardly notice them. But after almost two centuries of Western brutality, bullying, and condescension, the Chinese certainly do. Few Australians would be able to give a thorough explanation of the Century of Humiliation, but the savage indignities imposed on a weakened China by an economically and technologically dominant West in the nineteenth and twentieth centuries have not been forgotten by the Chinese. Western assumptions of hegemony and superiority became so dominant that in the early 1950s the major American political parties squabbled over 'who lost China?'—as if the most populous nation on earth were a suitcase absent-mindedly left at a railway station.

Understanding China does not mean we have to agree with it, or avoid standing up to it. Australia has been right to resist attempts to expand Chinese power in the South Pacific and influence domestic Australian politics, for example. Understanding China means we will be infinitely better prepared to navigate our way through the challenges that inevitably accompany the astonishing rise of Chinese economic and military strength.

Many regard German belligerence as the primary cause of the First World War, without even stopping to ask why the Germans were belligerent. The extent of German belligerence relative to the behaviour of other European powers remains a matter of vigorous debate, but examination of the reasons Germany was willing to go to war is revealing. Fear of a rapidly industrialising Russia that had three times its population, and whose industrial and military expansion was in part financed by the French who were eager to regain Alsace-Lorraine that had been ceded after defeat in the Franco-Prussian War of 1870–1871, was a critical factor. The inability of Germany to access adequate food and mineral resources that internal and external colonies delivered in vast quantities to competitor nations like Britain, France, Russia, and the United States was also central. Sadly no political leaders of the time sought to deal with these issues in a way that would diminish the risk of outright military conflict. And once that conflict started, it proved impossible to halt or constrain.

If today's Western leaders believe that China is set on a path that makes major war unavoidable, they have a responsibility to seek to understand why, and develop strategies designed to divert China down a different path. While military deterrence has a role to play in this process, it is a very blunt, risky, costly, and inflexible approach to rely entirely on. Failure to understand China and its aspirations means the risk of drifting into the kind of zero-sum confrontation that triggered the First World War becomes much more likely.

In a dispassionate, balanced, and scholarly contribution, Jean Dong has provided us with an excellent means through which to tackle the challenge of understanding China. Those who study international affairs—and particularly those who shape them—should study this text carefully. If we are to avoid the tragic miscalculations of the past, a clearer understanding of China is absolutely essential.

Melbourne, Australia

Lindsay Tanner
Australian Minister for Finance
2007–2010

Preface

What This Book Is About

Humanity is currently navigating an era of continuous and interconnected disruption, often described as a 'polycrisis'. We find ourselves continuously exposed to warnings that the world is not only a dangerous place, but teetering on the brink of collapse. A permanent sense of crisis has become the 'new normal'.

The list of most commonly addressed challenges goes something like this. There is the accelerating drumbeat of extreme weather events and contested battle over critical resources. There is the deep societal transformations arising from the rapid advancement of technology and artificial intelligence, including their applications to cyber and armed weaponry. There is the intensified geopolitical landscape with its escalated risks of conflicts and wars. And there is the amplified frustrations around inequality, which have fuelled the rise of populism, nationalism, extremism, and terrorism on a global scale.

Against this tumultuous landscape, China's rising economic influence and military expansion add a layer of complexity, amplifying the fragility of our interconnected world and challenging existing global norms. A critical question, of course, is whether 'the China challenge' is to be understood primarily as another disruptive threat endangering precious global norms, or whether—in a historical moment of global reinvention—China could be a positive game-changer for the world. And if the latter, what could be done to amplify this role.

One thing at least is clear: in spite of the unparalleled challenges that China has brought to the global stage, the nation is not fading from the scene. As such, a proactive approach is essential to deal with China's influence effectively. This applies irrespective of the reader's attitude towards China. It is, in fact, all the more important as China is perceived as a potential adversary. Indeed, the first principle of developing strategies and policies towards nations perceived as potential rivals is to grasp the underlying motives behind their actions. This is not about acquiescing to their stance, but being adequately prepared to develop an effective approach in dealing with them.

This book aims to facilitate this objective by unpacking the underlying logic behind China's policy-making and how it has contributed to the shape and content of the country's global ambitions. For this, the book focuses on examining the 'why' beyond the 'what', enabling new questions to be asked about 'how' to deal with China. More specifically, what can be done for China to become a more constructive and accountable participant in the emergence of a prosperous shared world. In this regard, arguably, this book is not just about China or understanding China per se, but forging solutions for common global challenges and avoiding the most catastrophic forms of war—all the while fully acknowledging China's disruptive and problematic violations of global norms and universal categories, as well as its inevitable influence on almost every global issue.

The main contribution of this book is presenting a novel perspective to identify realistic and practical possibilities to increase strategic options, exert influence and effect changes regarding China. I propose to call it 'Dynamic Constraints Analysis'. The approach involves articulating the constraints and flexibility facing Chinese decision-making. By 'constraints', I refer to the enduring structural limitations derived from China's geography and long history that curb China's actions, thereby compelling it to make trade-offs. By contrast, 'flexibility' refers to those elements in China's tradition and material conditions that enable more open-ended decision-making.

As an illustration of constraints, consider China's geographically intricate and occasionally antagonistic borders. These conditions have prompted the nation's search for strategic security, represented by large-scale investment in the modernisation of its military force. Concurrently, contingencies among neighbouring countries could pose significant threats to China's land borders, potentially drawing it into prolonged and costly land-based commitments. Over China's long history, this situation has consistently forced it to make a trade-off between landward security and maritime ambition, a constraint that still largely applies today.

Additionally, China's persistent food security issues, derived from its geographical characteristics, led to a form of 'performance legitimacy' intrinsically linked to economic growth and material welfare. China's primary interest in pursuing economic security and prosperity through growth could result in alterations to market regulations in its own favour or the unilateral dominance of sea lanes. Nonetheless, maintaining economic-driven legitimacy also obliges Chinese policy-makers to uphold the country's position in the global trade system. This necessitates that China strikes a balance between an aggressive stance and functioning as a responsible participant on the global stage.

Although Beijing's vision for China's rise is ambitious, its grand strategy is not just a long list of heterogeneous goals, but a clearly ordered list, with priorities and trade-offs defined by a range of enduring constraints. However, such constraints do not necessitate an unchanging and static approach to global strategy. Instead, they guide tactical and strategic dynamics as circumstances require. Understanding these dynamic flexibilities within the system can broaden the range of strategic choices, expanding the set of potential actions, and thus providing a route to regain control and influence.

To give one example of flexibility, China has been characterised by enduring centralised power, yet there has been a continuous power dynamic between central and local governments. Flexible local implementation across government levels, from provincial to township, enables the piloting of new projects or the formation of counter-powers to influence the central government. This is achieved through spillover effects to other provinces, by generating local 'know-how', and/or by fostering a bottom-up approach to impact the central level. Furthermore, concerning China's highly centralised and opaque decision-making processes, there is an opportunity to influence decisions by offering inputs on the details of implementation. This is because Chinese standard practice typically involves making relatively broad policy decisions initially, with specific details to be refined at the implementation stage through a range of consultative processes.

The application of 'Dynamic Constraints Analysis' serves a dual purpose. First, it aims to equip readers with a tool to distinguish between 'imaginary fears'—perceived threats that China poses stemming from its statements or actions—and 'legitimate fears'—genuine challenges that China's rise presents to our collective future, driven by its core interests. By highlighting the constraints in China's actions, this approach helps in conceptualising imagined fears more constructively while concentrating on addressing real challenges. Second, this analysis seeks to aid readers in realistically evaluating strategic options and alternatives by highlighting the enduring components of China's decision-making and inherent flexibility at play. As a result, readers can more effectively assess the feasibility and potential for success of actionable steps.

It should be acknowledged that the approach articulated above is not exceedingly ambitious or bold. Rather, it is largely about the art of 'doing small things'. This reflects an attempt at finding the right balance. In our age of global fragility and interlinked human security threats, we need a bold agenda to match the magnitude of the challenges at stake. Yet we must also remain humble in the face of the unknown. In a context of radical uncertainty, we should tread carefully, and take considered steps to manage the current transition phase.

This book was written to serve as a tool for sense-making, not persuasion. Rather than attempting to sway readers towards a positive or negative view of China, the book was designed to assist in comprehending the facts and discerning their relevance in a given context. Therefore, this book does not ask readers to accept China's political system or values, nor does it make any predictions regarding China's future actions or instruct readers to adopt a certain course of action. Its more modest but useful aim is to assist readers in developing their understanding, enhance their interpretative frameworks, and strengthen their capacity to deal with China effectively. Like China's ancient oracle, the *I Ching*, or *Book of Changes*, the book is here to help think about problems in a new manner by tapping into the human capacity to make sense of patterns. To this end, the book aspires to achieve three objectives.

Firstly, the book aims to help readers regain historical agency by broadening our understanding of the past, and thus inspiring more ways of imagining the future. While many valuable analyses on China are available, it is worth noting that some studies commonly focus on a relatively recent timeframe, starting with the Opium War or the establishment of the People's Republic of China. Solely relying on these perspectives to comprehend the underlying logic behind Chinese policy-making is likely to result in incomplete understanding. Many answers, explanations and analogies are not to be found in the immediate past, but rather necessitate engaging with greater depths of history. For this reason, the book adopts a long historical timeframe (circa 2000 BCE to present). It specifically examines the dynamics of history as they relate to modern issues. This makes it possible to explore resonances between ancient and contemporary China, especially in terms of governance.

Secondly, this book seeks to illustrate the rich tapestry of global culture by drawing contrasts between the political, economic, and philosophical concepts of Chinese and Western contexts. Emphasising these differences is not a bid to establish a ranking of cultures, but rather to deepen our appreciation for the diverse and complex facets of our interconnected world. Our understandings of the present are profoundly shaped by our individual historical realities and the norms and values we hold. Consequently, we often interpret current events through the lens of our conventional grasp of history. This makes the exploration of diverse historical experiences and cultural contexts vital to bridging cognitive and emotional gaps between different cultures.

Thirdly, this book offers a practical interpretation of key narratives and theories, allowing readers to act upon those insights at their level and in their context. To this end, it consciously embraces a cross-disciplinary approach. The aim is to bring together many intersecting forms of knowledge, ranging from history to macroeconomics, geopolitics, philosophy, and beyond, providing a synthesis. This approach, as well as the wide range of contexts and concepts presented in the book, is a reflection of the intricate and diverse nature of China's own history, politics, and society.

Why I Wrote This Book

My main motivation for writing this book was observing many examples of miscalculation and misjudgement from the West in their interactions with China. On many occasions, those have led to undesired and undesirable results. I was able to follow much of this from the inside over the last decade, as I worked on high-level bilateral engagements between Australia and China, as well as multilateral diplomacy, with large corporations, government bodies, and think tanks.

Was the crisis that led to the First World War caused by German capabilities or German conduct? Henry Kissinger raises this question in his book *On China*. The underlying reference is the 1907 Crowe Memorandum, which influenced the confrontational British stance before the First World War. This Memorandum gives an unambiguous answer: namely, that when assessing the best stance to take when faced with a potential challenger, the decision should be based on its capabilities, not its conduct.

The question raised by Henry Kissinger applied to China then and remains relevant today. As China masters advanced military capabilities, those capabilities may well overshadow China's conduct. This means that the West's trust in Chinese leaders' formal assurance and Chinese policies could wane dangerously, leaving China's military capacity as the only thing shaping the West's approach to China. In other words, we are at risk of seeing an escalation of military responses, in turn fuelling Beijing's assertiveness—a renewed arms race based on China's capabilities only, irrespective of its conduct.

This risk, combined with my personal observations of recurring misperceptions, prompted me to delve into Chinese statecraft, studying patterns and changes rooted in its extensive history and the resonances between ancient and contemporary China. In particular, I sought to identify the enduring geographical and historical constraints that have tempered China's ambitions and compelled it to make measured trade-offs. Such insights, if they were to be heard, could offer a more nuanced perspective, differentiating unwarranted anxieties from genuine concerns about China's influence, resulting in more targeted and effective strategies.

In our era of successive global challenges and pressing collaborative endeavours, dealing with China effectively offers an opportunity of great prosperity for all, while failure to engage productively may bring dire consequences. More importantly, the window of opportunity to engage and impact China effectively is narrowing.

China's assertiveness is often presented as a cause for concern—yet its vulnerability poses a significantly greater risk. A vulnerable China is a less cooperative and capable China, and one less willing and able to seek solutions for shared global challenges. At present, China is experiencing a prevailing sense of insecurity, originating from both internal and external sources. Beijing is increasingly convinced that, regardless of its actions, the United States and the West will perceive and interact with China unfavourably. Paradoxically, this heightened vulnerability may drive China to embrace a riskier stance, particularly in relation to Taiwan, as concerns over its global reputation and military posture recede.

If China were to take a turn towards a left-skewed, inward-looking or aggressive direction, it could take an entire generation to revert to a more positive course of action. Critical time for coordinated efforts to tackle existential challenges—environmental, social, and technological—would be lost in the process. This underscores the urgency to act promptly; seize the window of opportunity while it remains open; and explore innovative, multifaceted approaches to address the challenges presented by China. This sense of urgency has strengthened my commitment to search for practical measures to meet 'the China challenge' in a peaceful and constructive way and build greater understanding to increase the chances of this happening.

How I Wrote This Book

I offer this book with great humility, knowing that the future will inevitably unfold in ways that I have not foreseen. The question I constantly asked myself was 'how do I know if this is true or correct?'

Since I started undertaking the research in 2018, I have immersed myself in a wide range of studies and policy papers, and spoken to many figures in politics, business, and academia around the world. I travelled to Japan, Singapore, Indonesia, South

Korea, Saudi Arabia, and major European countries on work commitments and as part of my role as a taskforce member for the G20 think tank engagement group. During those trips, I visited numerous research institutions and think tanks to identify what issues they were most concerned about regarding China. I also engaged in many conversations and exchanges to draw criticism and feedback from people of various backgrounds, cultures, and positions on the ideas articulated in this book. The goal was to ensure that my analysis was real and objective, with minimal ideological or other bias.

In the second half of 2021, I invested in a six-month field research in China to stress-test my arguments. Over this period, I visited dozens of universities, think tanks, government departments, and companies and had discussions and debates with over one hundred Chinese representatives. I also visited rural villages to get a local view from ordinary citizens. My goal, again, was to understand the current dynamics of intellectual discourse in China with as broad a view as possible, including controversial debates on emerging topics. It was particularly important for me to write with first-hand information and direct experience, against the backdrop of poor information flows and limited person-to-person exchanges during the COVID-19 pandemic.

This process of research taught me to be truly humble. My work builds on the significant academic achievements our society has enabled, in which I found great inspiration and freedom. Therefore, I didn't rush to initiate any new theories, but rather focused on articulating new perspectives from existing theories, striving towards making the presentation most useful to readers. In line with this aim, I chose to organise the book in three parts, as follows.

Part I of the book focuses on the fundamental factors that shaped China's logic of governance and decision-making. It applies historical, political, economic, and philosophical perspectives to provide a framework for identifying, conceptualising, and interpreting the core features of China's governance model. Part I aims to enhance comprehension of a rapidly changing China, specifically how its leaders think, make decisions, and act upon them.

Part II of the book focuses on the trajectories taken by a rising China and its impact on the world. It analyses China's military ambitions, particularly around hot spots like Taiwan and the South China Sea; how China is likely to exert its influence on a global level; and how Xi Jinping's vision, experience, and personality are shaping the direction of China's development. Part II particularly looks at the ongoing constraints that Chinese leaders face, and the trade-offs they have to make. It aims to provide a realistic assessment of the nature and scope of China's ambition and to identify potential leverage points that could expand strategic choices in dealing with China.

Part III of the book opens a discussion about China in an age of exponential change, and provokes the reader to adopt a cyclical view of history as a way to explore different solutions to 'the China challenge'. This final part proposes a possible way forward which calls for two key tasks to be handled simultaneously. One is managing the current period of transition and uncertainty, the other is imagining and building a new future by shifting the paradigm. For this, the book offers a reconceptualisation of two fundamental concepts: growth and security.

This book was written for a broad readership, for those interested in the contemporary China challenge, as well as an audience of senior policy-makers, diplomats, and business leaders who wish to comprehend China's intent and make critical decisions about dealing with China. When engaging with leading figures from around the world, it became increasingly clear that when it comes to China, what is most useful is deep analysis based on a comprehensive and panoramic view that can make sense of current events. That is why I adopted a cross-disciplinary approach to convey a concise logic, with the intention to create a practical framework that can be readily applied in real-world situations. The downside is that the book is not specifically tailored to China specialists who have devoted the majority of their research to China. In the interest of synthesis and applicability, the book is sure to miss some of the details and fine-tuning that come with a focused perspective. Keen readers will certainly benefit from exploring more in-depth research on the topics most relevant to their concerns—many of which are included in the references throughout this book. I hope the specialists will forgive occasional shorthand or simplifications, and readers will turn to their work for further nuance.

I hope that this book can be a contribution to one of the most important topics of our century. Only together can we find an optimal solution. On that note, I encourage readers to challenge and critique my arguments and engage in intellectual debate, as a way of gaining deeper understanding and suggesting new ways of thinking. I thank you all for your efforts in taking action towards a better collective future.

Melbourne, Australia   Jean Dong

Acknowledgements

The journey of writing this book has been an incredibly fulfilling milestone in my life. Thus, I express these acknowledgements with profound appreciation and humility. I didn't get here just by myself, but with people who believed in me, inspired me and supported me throughout the journey.

My heartfelt gratitude goes to Lindsay Tanner, Malcolm Broomhead, Rowan Callick, Colin Heseltine, Mark Allison, and Uri Dadush, who generously devoted their priceless time to review and critique the manuscript, as well as consistently supported me throughout the process. Their ceaseless inspiration and wisdom, coupled with their invaluable feedback, have tremendously enriched my thought process and fine-tuned my perspectives.

My profound gratitude and appreciation also extend to many distinguished experts who generously shared their time and insights, aiding my understanding of specialised subjects and intricate issues about China. Through thought-provoking intellectual exchanges, insightful comments and stimulating questions, they provided important contributions that have greatly influenced and refined my perspectives. In particular, I wish to convey my sincere appreciation to Wang Gungwu, Zhao Tingyang, Bilahari Kausikan, Peter Drysdale, Kishore Mahbubani, Anthony Milner, Danny Quah, Fu Chengyu, Wang Hui, Wang Yiwei, Kerry Brown, Xue Lan, He Baogang, Andrew Robb, Geoff Raby, Li Mingjiang, and Alicia Garcia-Herrero.

In addition, I would also like to express my deep appreciation to my dear friend, Julien Leyre, whose unwavering and invaluable support has been instrumental throughout this process. Serving as the development editor of this book, he became my trusted sounding board and editorial mentor. His insightful feedback and wisdom at every stage of the editorial process have been pivotal in shaping and enhancing this book. Our collaborative effort, a real-world 'East meets West', fused diverse perspectives and values, leading to an enriched shared vision. This process strengthened my belief in the power of trust, humility, and open-mindedness to bridge differences, inspiring hope for inclusivity on a global scale. I am deeply grateful for this enriching experience and our enduring friendship.

Last but not least, I would like to acknowledge the anonymous reviewers of the book, whose constructive feedback during the peer-review process was greatly appreciated.

As a final note, I would like to make a disclaimer that while all the individuals acknowledged above have provided invaluable support in the completion of this book, it does not imply they agree with or endorse the views and arguments presented herein. Responsibility for any criticism rests solely with me.

Praise for *Chinese Statecraft in a Changing World*

"The use of the ideas of dynamics and constraints makes sense to a historian. I imagine international relations experts will find them useful too."
—Wang Gungwu, *University Professor, National University of Singapore*

"This excellent book addresses one of the critical geopolitical questions of our age. Is China's ambition to replace the United States as the dominant power or will it be content to sit as an equal partner on the global stage, and how would the relationship evolve without catastrophic conflict? It provides great insights into the internal systems and thinking of the Chinese leadership both in a historical and current context."
—Malcolm Broomhead, *Chairman of Orica; Non-Executive Director of BHP Group, 2010–2022*

"This book is worthy of great attention. The author shows deep knowledge and understanding of both China and the Western world, making this book an excellent go-between. Articulating the country's long history with appreciation for today's major global challenges, it offers a realistic analysis of what China truly looks like, and how it's likely to react in different scenarios. This book is critical reading for anyone looking to brush off the noise of polarised arguments, and engage in serious sense-making about China's deep-rooted past and flexible futures."
—Zhao Tingyang, *Professor of Philosophy, Chinese Academy of Social Sciences; Author of All Under Heaven: The Tianxia System for a Possible World Order*

"Jean Dong has contributed to the growing literature on elite Chinese politics and economics with an ambitious and intriguing focus on placing contemporary events in the context of ancient and long-standing Chinese trends and traditions. She has succeeded in this while at the same time acknowledging the extent of the ideological shift now under way—one that she suggests may well outlast Xi Jinping—that includes elevating security as a priority. For Xi both vaunts China's 'rejuvenation', incorporating all that has made the country great in past eras, while also seeking to stress as he did at the 20th National Communist Party Congress that 'there is no end to theoretical innovation'."

—Rowan Callick, *Australian Expert and Author on China; Former China Correspondent for The Australian and The Australian Financial Review*

"There is no more crucial question in contemporary international relations than China: the imperatives of its statecraft, its motivations and goals. Too many analyses are ideologically motivated. Jean Dong is a welcome, refreshing and important exception. She offers clear, balanced and realistic insights into China's global role amidst changes in the international environment of an unprecedented speed and scope. Her work will be invaluable to academics and practitioners alike as they struggle to understand a China that often puzzles but can never be ignored."

—Bilahari Kausikan, *Permanent Secretary of the Ministry of Foreign Affairs of Singapore, 2010–2013*

"As a development economist it is impossible for me to have anything but deep respect for China's epochal achievement in reducing poverty and raising the living standard of a large part of humanity. I have long and hard tried to understand it and found in Jean Dong's profoundly serious book an invaluable guide and source of insights. You do not have to be a China expert, nor do you have to agree with all of Jean's scholarly interpretations to recognize the commitment, wisdom and balance that define her work. As a world citizen, I must add: we are living in dangerous times, and Jean's book—if carefully studied by those charting the course of nations—will surely make us safer."

—Uri Dadush, *Research Professor, University of Maryland; Non-Resident Fellow, Bruegel*

"Jean Dong's book offers fundamentally important insights into why China does what it does. Her wide-ranging narrative covers historical and current trends, as well as external and domestic influences. At a time of great global uncertainty, with China at the epicentre, this is an invaluable and necessary contribution. While it is right to focus on China's growing strength and assertiveness, it is China's insecurity and vulnerabilities, she notes, that pose a greater risk. And, as she further writes, miscalculations and misjudgements from the West in their interactions with China can lead to undesirable results. This is an essential message to those who present China in one-dimensional and simplistic terms, and should be absorbed by policy makers, strategic analysts and, indeed, the general public, as they seek to comprehend what is one of the world's greatest challenges."

—Colin Heseltine, *Australian Ambassador to the Republic of Korea, 2001–2005; Deputy Head of Mission in the Australian Embassy in Beijing, 1982–1985 and 1988–1992*

Praise for *Chinese Statecraft in a Changing World*

"In an era of 'polycrisis', the 'China threat' theory and the 'China collapse' theory are like two sides of the same coin, flipping in turn, which to a large extent not only affects public opinion, but even dominates the policy orientation of many countries. Against this background, the author adopts the analytical framework of 'Dynamic Constraints Analysis', which integrates long-term historical perspective, broad geographical relationship, complex policy making process and detailed data, and provides a basis for understanding contemporary China and its policy formation process. This novel perspective is important to help avoid misdirection in strategic options driven by the 'politics of fear' in addressing the China challenge. This is a timely, inspiring, rare and excellent book."

—Wang Hui, *Professor of Literature and History, Tsinghua University; Author of The Rise of Modern Chinese Thought*

"For a world seeking to deal with the 'China Challenge', Jean Dong's book makes an outstanding contribution towards an informed and balanced understanding of today's China. It is written to serve as a tool for 'sense-making, not persuasion'. Jean seeks not to ask the reader to accept China's political system or values, nor make predictions regarding China's future actions, but rather, to better understand how geography and the depths of thousands of years of civilisation very materially shape much of the culture, priorities and actions of contemporary China. The results of Jean's extraordinarily extensive research are fascinating, compelling and scholarly. This book removes ignorance and fosters respect."

—Andrew Robb, *Australian Minister for Trade and Investment, 2013–2016*

"Here is a book, written in Australia, that gives real depth to public debate. It suggests how geography influences the thinking of a nation and then discusses the key institutions, ideas and priorities that make China distinctive. Writing beautifully for the general reader, Jean shows how present-day China emerges from its past–reminding us time and again that a great deal of understanding, together with a certain calmness, can be gained from historical insights. Few issues matter more for Australia than assessing China's future, especially its foreign policy intentions. Not everyone will be convinced by Jean's views–but all will agree that the book should be essential reading."

—Anthony Milner, *Professorial Fellow, University of Melbourne; Former Basham Professor of Asian History, Australian National University*

Contents

Part I China Through the Looking Glass

1 The Grip of Geography: China's Enduring Struggle for Order and Unity 3
    The Nexus of Water and Power 4
    Land of Famine: An Isolated Agrarian Society 6
    Tilling the Throne: The Emperor as 'Farmer in Chief' 8
    Keeping the Land United 11
    References 13

2 Crafting Legitimacy: The Entangling Balancing Act 17
    Mandate of Heaven: Food or Justice? 17
    Big Government or Small Government? 19
    Absurd Decisions or Arbitrary Decisions? 20
    Holding onto the Throne 21
    Bigger Pie or Fairer Distribution? 22
    Living a Better Life: Raising Expectations 23
    Heavenly Mandate Tested 25
    Reinventing Legitimacy 28
    An Ongoing Struggle 29
    References 31

3 Birdcage Economy: Who Holds the Strings of China's Economy? 35
    Avoiding Tyranny or Avoiding Chaos? 35
    Catching the Ant 36
    Businessmen Under Siege 39
    Rule of Law: For Whom? 41
    State-Owned Enterprises: A Mere Legacy of the Past? 42
    Walking a Tightrope: Unity of Opposites 44
    References 48

4	**A Fusion of Worlds: Interplay of Chinese Tradition and Marxism**	51
	The Rule of Ritual: 'Know Your Place'	51
	The Hundred Schools of Thought	54
	The Rule of Law: Enrich the State	55
	Shang Yang's Dilemma	57
	The Rule of Virtue: Strengthening Centralisation	60
	The 'Junzi': A Diversified 'Net-Like' Governance Model	62
	Virtue Politics	62
	China Through the Looking Glass	64
	A Hybrid Model: Blending Marxism with Tradition	65
	References	68
5	**A Contested System: Decision-Making Dynamics in China**	71
	'Students of the Emperor': The Imperial Examination System	71
	Working Your Way Up	74
	Meritocracy in a New Era	75
	The Party-State: A Unifying Force	76
	The People's Liberation Army: Establish CCP Branches at the Level of Companies	77
	Policies from Above, Counter Policies from Below	79
	Fighting for and Sharing the Resources	82
	A Non-unitary Rational Actor: The Dynamics of Upward Accountability	84
	Point of Influence: The 'Consensus Building' Model	86
	The Media as Part of Consensus Building	87
	Picking the Right Stone	88
	References	91

Part II Over the Mountains and Across the Seas

6	**Capability or Intention: Ambition and Restraint in China's Military Build-Up**	97
	China's Geography and Worldview	98
	Neither Cuddly Panda Nor Menacing Dragon	99
	'Unconquerable' Enemies	102
	The War Curse	103
	The Expansion Curse	104
	Secular Pragmatism	106
	China's Core Interest	108
	Buffer States in Modern Terms	111
	Regions Shaping National Prosperity	113
	Increased Offensive Capabilities	115
	Increased Ambition?	117
	Not a Global Power	118
	A Worrying Future?	120

	Intention Versus Capability: Which Matters Most?	122
	References	124
7	**A Cauldron of Anxiety: War or Peace?**	127
	The Grand Gravity Shifts	128
	Symbolic Maritime Power	130
	'You Will Be Beaten Up If You Fall Behind'	132
	Control Over Critical Resources	135
	Hong Kong	136
	The First Island Chain	137
	War Games	139
	Preparing for War in Peacetime	142
	Taiwan	145
	Dilemma of Legitimacy	147
	South China Sea	150
	A Two-Ocean Power: From Hollywood to Bollywood	152
	China's Constraints	155
	References	158
8	**Charting the Path of Influence: Between Force and Soft Power**	163
	Geoeconomics and Statecraft	164
	Tributary System and the 'Tianxia'	165
	Concentric Circles	167
	Symbolic Obedience	169
	Asian Peace Stabiliser or Giant Rogue State?	172
	He Who Has the Gold, Rules?	174
	'Us' and 'Them': China Versus Barbarians	175
	From a Multicultural Empire to a 'Chinese China' Empire	177
	Unifying 'Outer China'	178
	From Cultural Osmosis to Global Assimilation	181
	Taiwan—A Cultural Perspective	184
	A Clash of World Orders?	185
	References	187
9	**The Man and the Times: Xi Jinping and the Intricate Dance of History**	191
	The Longer Telegram	191
	'Founder' Versus 'CEO'	192
	Playing Chess	194
	Did the Man Make the Times?	195
	Did the Times Make the Man?	198
	A Strategic Crossroad: What Does Xi Jinping Want?	203
	A Period of Strategic Opportunities	204
	Gone Is the Favourable External Environment	205
	Not a Temporary Phenomenon	207
	References	208

Part III A Possible Way Forward

10 A World at Stake: Competition, Destruction, or Cooperation? 213
    A Cyclical View of History 215
    Polycrisis: The Most Dangerous Decade 217
    Interlocking Crisis: The Historical Cycle of Technological
    Revolution 219
    An Ambivalent Power 221
    How Does the Cyclical View of History Affect Chinese
    Decision-Making? 227
    Rivalry Partners—The Chanyuan Treaty 230
    References 232

**11 Navigating an Uncertain Future: Redefining Growth
and Security** 235
    A Possible Way Forward: Two Key Tasks 235
    Navigating Uncertainty 236
    Prisoner of Geography 240
    The Impossible Trinity 242
    Imagining 'the End of China' 242
    Points of Influence: Increase Strategic Options 245
    Invent the Future: Solving the China Challenge in a Global Context ... 247
    Why Paradigm Shifts Are Difficult 250
    How Will History Remember Our Century? 252
    References 253

Index 255

List of Charts

Chart 5.1   A top-down approach 80
Chart 5.2   A counter-tactic approach 80
Chart 5.3   A strategic directive cherry-picking approach 81
Chart 8.1   The concentric circles 168

Part I
China Through the Looking Glass

Chapter 1
The Grip of Geography: China's Enduring Struggle for Order and Unity

> *"It [geography] shapes political institutions, power relationships, and historical narratives. No country can fully understand itself or its place in the world without a deep appreciation of its geography."* (Albright, 2006)
> —Madeleine Albright, the 64th U.S. Secretary of State

Abstract Geography exerts a profound influence on a country's dominant narrative, power structures, and political institutions. This chapter aims to explain why and how China's geography has shaped its enduring centralised power structure. The chapter is structured on three crucial factors: China's long history of coping with natural disasters such as large-scale floods, constant and devastating famines due to adverse weather and limited food imports, as well as severe security threats from a vulnerable northwest border. This chapter argues that these factors have influenced the Chinese conception of power. It is seen as a means to prevent collective destruction and promote collective prosperity. They also shaped a pragmatic approach to the role of government and political institutions that prioritise providing food and ensuring survival, as well as impacted the early conceptualisation of 'collective security'. This chapter employs a comparative approach, contrasting the geographical features of Chinese and Western civilisations to illustrate these points.

People come together because of their shared language, values, and stories. Those stories define what people are willing to do together, and how they organise to do so. People also come together because they share the same land where they live and play. These aspects mutually impact one another. The narratives that individuals embrace can shape and constrain their perception of their surroundings, influencing their decisions regarding the utilisation and management of local resources. Conversely, geography impacts the stories people create to forge a unified identity. While recent advancements in communication systems and globalisation have somewhat weakened this connection, its influence persists. For example, like their ancestors 5,000 years ago, the Chinese people continue to confront the challenge of managing devastating floods from the Yellow River today. Egyptian farmers, likewise, remain dependent on the Nile for their water supply. In this way, geography and culture remain intertwined, shaping the lives of individuals and communities across generations.

Those physical features make up a crucial part of today's geopolitical reality. As Napoleon reportedly once said, "To know a nation's geography is to know its foreign policy." In other words, geography significantly influences a country's prevailing narrative and power structure, guiding both short-term and long-term objectives, and determines its global position. For this reason, I have chosen to begin this book by focusing on geography. While geography is not the sole determinant of China's evolution, I modestly suggest that it offers an often-overlooked analytical perspective for a deeper exploration of China's logic of governance and understanding the rationale behind its future trajectory.

The Nexus of Water and Power

Many of the world's great civilisations grew around large rivers—Egypt on the Nile, Babylon between the Tigris and Euphrates, or the Indus Valley Civilisation on the Indus River. The Yellow River, where our story begins, is widely considered the birthplace of ancient Chinese civilisation. Its basin was the most prosperous region in early Chinese history. Today, the Yellow River remains vital to China. As at the end of 2018, more than 420 million people live in the nine provinces and autonomous regions along the Yellow River Basin (Qinghai, Sichuan, Gansu, Ningxia, Inner Mongolia, Shaanxi, Shanxi, Henan, and Shandong), accounting for 30.3% of the country's total population.[1] The regional gross domestic product (GDP) for the Yellow River Basin was 23.9 trillion yuan (USD3.5 trillion), accounting for 26.5% of the country's total GDP.[2]

The Yellow River, originating in Qinghai Province, traverses over 5,464 km before pouring its silt into the Yellow Sea, off the coast of Shandong Province. The river's name and colour are derived from the loess sediment, which enriches the surrounding soil but also causes the riverbed to rise. Currently, the river flows four to six metres above nearby cities and farmland, and even 20 m higher in some parts of Henan Province, earning the nickname 'Hanging River'. Consequently, heavy rains can lead to disastrous floods.

This is not a new phenomenon. From 206 BCE to 1949, nearly biennially or, in other words, over 1,092 times as documented in historical records, the Yellow River has busted its embankments and transformed itself into a raging torrent that swept away entire villages, killing millions of people.[3] The course of the river has also changed significantly, with the mouth of the river moving up to 480 km over the course of history, between south and the north of the Shandong Peninsula. Unlike the other famous flooding river, the Nile, the Yellow River does not have predictable

---

[1] Xi (2019).

[2] Ibid.

[3] Wei et al. (2002).

yearly cycles. It changes course in a dramatic, sudden, unpredictable manner. As a result, the river is also regarded as the 'scourge of the Han people'. This still applies in modern China. In 1933, a significant flood in the Yellow River Basin led to a catastrophe that claimed the lives of 1.83 million people and submerged 850,000 ha of agricultural land.[4]

Unsurprisingly, from early on, the people living in the Yellow River Basin have attempted to control its floods. The central figure in this endeavour was Yu, a mythical king of ancient China, known for establishing the Xia dynasty (2070–1600 BCE). From its origin, the Xia dynasty established a new era in Chinese history which marked the end of primitive tribal alliances and opened the beginning of a sophisticated class-based society. Its mythical founder Yu, according to the legend, achieved this shift by taming the Yellow River and its devastating floods.

To mitigate Yellow River floods, Yu evenly distributed the water across China's eastern plain, carrying out large-scale infrastructure work, dredging canals and waterways. His efforts spanned the entire river basin, extending to the Yangtze River Basin, which also experiences floods.[5] As their basins are contiguous, water management efforts were required for both rivers. Such efforts not only controlled floods, but also generated great benefits for agriculture, enabled people to grow an abundance of food and fostered commerce and trade.[6]

The completion of such large-scale projects required a strong unified power structure for task allocation, and strict prohibition mechanisms to ensure compliance.[7] In other words, the common fight against natural disasters required, but also encouraged, cooperation among the early tribes who lived in the plains of northern China. Up till then, the territory of the Yellow River Basin had been divided among clans connected by blood. Under Yu, that structure was replaced by an administrative division into regions corresponding to the main sections of the Yellow River and Yangtze River basins. With this administrative reorganisation came a great concentration of personal power in the hands of Yu, more than any previous clan leaders.

Although archaeological evidence indicates that there may be some truth to the legend of Yu, he remains a story—but a powerful one, repeatedly told over a few thousand years. This story arguably drives the earliest manifestation and understanding of 'power' in ancient China—building essential infrastructure to avert collective destruction and foster collective means for prosperity. Historical records reveal that, over several thousand years, there have been continuous and enduring efforts to mobilise national resources to build large-scale hydraulic engineering projects for prosperity. From the Spring and Autumn period beginning in 722 BCE to the Tang dynasty (618–906 CE), the average number of hydraulic projects (including repair works) was 12 per century.[8] That number went up to 87 per century during the Tang dynasty and reached the much higher number of 1,206 per century during the Qing

---

[4] Ibid.

[5] Confucius et al. (2012).

[6] Sima (2011).

[7] Wittfogel (1957).

[8] Chi (2019).

dynasty (1644–1912).⁹ Among those projects, a renowned example is the Dujiangyan Irrigation System which was built during the Warring States period (475–221 BCE). This magnificent irrigation system manages water flow from the Longmen Mountains to the Minjiang River in Sichuan Province, forming the foundation of the province's agricultural prosperity and earning it the title of 'Land of Abundance'. Remarkably, the Dujiangyan Irrigation System has endured for over 2,000 years and remains operational today.

Today, the tradition of constructing and maintaining large-scale irrigation and hydraulic engineering projects continues. Since the founding of the People's Republic of China (PRC), over USD 22 billion has been invested in managing the Yellow River alone.[10] Nationwide, more than 87,000 reservoirs/dams and 294,100 km of embankments have been built to control floods, including the famous Three Gorges Dam.[11] As of 2009, the direct economic benefits of flood control and disaster reduction in the country amounted to approximately USD 600 billion.[12]

Indeed, the examination and debate surrounding the impact of persistent floods on China's power structure have long attracted significant academic attention worldwide. Important views include Karl Wittfogel's hydraulic civilisation theory and the collective critique of his *Oriental Despotism* by the Chinese academic community in the 1980s. Other significant alternative perspectives have been offered by French historian Pierre-Étienne Will and American historian Peter C. Perdue.[13] Despite their vastly diverse viewpoints, these studies have highlighted the crucial nexus between hydraulic efforts and their indispensable impact on the nature and character of the power structure in China.

Land of Famine: An Isolated Agrarian Society

Geographically, China is an isolated civilisation. Its territory is enclosed by a range of geographical obstacles. In the west, the high-altitude Tibetan Plateau and the Pamir Mountains separate the Yellow River Basin from South Asia and Central Asia. To the south, towering mountain ranges, such as the Himalayas, have historically limited contact and exchanges with the Indian subcontinent and Southeast Asia. To the east, China is bounded by the East China Sea and the Yellow Sea; their rough waters made navigation difficult, which limited the development of early maritime trade. To the north, vast deserts and expansive steppes separate China from the Siberian Taiga. In the northeast, a series of mountain ranges, including the Changbai Mountains and the Lesser Khingan Range, divide the Chinese plains from the region now

---

[9] Ibid.
[10] Liu et al. (2006).
[11] Xinhua News Agency (2011).
[12] Ibid.
[13] Will (1980); Perdue (1987).

known as Northeast China and the Korean Peninsula. According to American geographer and historian Jared Diamond, this introverted geographical structure guided the development of an isolated agrarian society.[14]

The characteristics of this isolated Chinese civilisation are best understood in contrast with ancient Western civilisation, which developed along the coasts of the Mediterranean. Unlike the plains of China, the Mediterranean presents a large internal sea, allowing easy navigation between numerous coastal plains, each separated and protected from their hinterland by hills and mountains. In this landscape, a network of self-sufficient and interconnected entities developed.

Mediterranean cities had a large number of different food sources available to them, through farming, hunting (in nearby forests), fishing (in relatively gentle seas), and herding cattle and sheep on nearby hills and mountains. In addition, the geography of separated coastal plains and calm seas meant that the inhabitants of more prosperous regions could colonise new lands: other coastal plains, inhabited by less technologically advanced people.[15] Finally, and importantly, food could be obtained from abroad through trade, either with other cities and islands around the Mediterranean, or with the fertile river basins of Mesopotamia and Egypt. Indeed, unlike China, Western civilisation did not emerge in an 'enclosed' geography, but in a landscape that offers the possibility of continuous movement and exchanges all the way from Spain to Bengal. In those conditions, enabling a smooth flow of trade and organising an army for defence and conquest became the primary task of governments.[16]

In contrast, most of the Chinese territory is located far from the sea and its resources. More importantly, China's enclosed geography meant that there was no easy access to external sources of food surplus for import, other than from one region of China to another. This holds significant importance as China is prone to regular droughts alongside floods due to its location in a typical monsoon climate zone. According to Joseph Needham, "The official dynastic histories down to 1911 report that in those 2,117 years no fewer than 1,621 floods and 1,392 droughts were recorded, thus on an average more than one disaster in each year."[17] In addition, it is estimated that from 108 BCE to 1911, an instance of drought- or flood-induced famine occurred in at least one Chinese province every single year, particularly affecting northern China.[18] Famines precipitated by drought contributed to toppling at least five of China's 17 dynasties.[19] From 1876 to 1879, nine million fatalities were caused by the famine in northern China.[20] In modern history, from 1920 to 1921, at least 500,000 people died and over 19.8 million found themselves destitute

---

[14] Diamond (1997).

[15] Kennedy (2017).

[16] Ibid.

[17] Needham (2004).

[18] Zhang and Cheng (2016).

[19] Collins and Reddy (2022).

[20] Zhang and Cheng (2016).

due to famine.[21] In addition, nearly three million died in Henan Province during the devastating famine in 1943.[22] Therefore, China has frequently been referred to as 'a land of famine'.[23]

The vulnerability of Chinese geography reveals the country's enduring struggle for order and unity, driven by a crucial need to maintain collective and focused efforts to counter disruptions from adverse weather that often lead to devastating famines. To secure a continuous food supply to a country with a large population and limited surplus imports, the country must guarantee efficient organised labour in the fields, along with ample food reserves and the ability to distribute grain throughout the Chinese plains to offset local shortages with surpluses from other regions. Accomplishing this task seems less feasible with fragmented local responsibilities, emphasising the need for a unified approach.

Tilling the Throne: The Emperor as 'Farmer in Chief'

The experiences and fear of famine have shaped Chinese people's early perception of the role and purpose of government, prompting a pragmatic approach. That is, political institutions are primarily a means of providing food for the people and guarantee survival. Emperors who could ensure food security would, in exchange, find a population willing to support their rule. In this context, emperors were compelled to prioritise agricultural production and assume a direct leadership role.

China is an agrarian society and prosperity was thus closely related to the country's level of agricultural advancement. In the research undertaken by American historian Albert Feuerwerker, with limited data available, he laid out a number of assumptions which indicated that from the ninth century to the eighteenth century, the agricultural sector provided about 80% of employment to the Chinese population and 70% of the country's national income.[24] An abundance of grain enabled wealth accumulation as it generated surplus that could be channelled into the production of valuable goods such as silk and tea, as well as mining works and other trade commodities. In turn, this served as the basis of China's relative prosperity on a global scale—particularly up until the Industrial Revolution, for as long as agriculture was the primary activity around the globe. According to research, China's economic prosperity (per capita GDP) was on par with Europe (USD 450 vs. USD 550) during the Han dynasty (202 BCE–220 CE) and exceeded Europe (USD 600 vs. USD 576) at the end of the Song dynasty (960–1279).[25] In terms of aggregated GDP, China's GDP has accounted for

---

[21] Ibid.

[22] Ibid.

[23] Mallory (1926).

[24] Feuerwerker (1984).

[25] Maddison (2007).

a reasonably sizeable portion of the world total since the Han dynasty and reached its peak at 32.9% in 1820.[26]

In 221 BCE, when Emperor Qin Shihuang (259–210 BCE), founder of the Qin dynasty, unified China for the first time, one of his first initiatives was agricultural advancement. Bamboo Slips from the Qin Tomb show that Qin Shihuang and his government formulated detailed agricultural management systems to guide farmers, including elements such as the number of seeds to be sown per area of land for each grain type.[27] This focus on agriculture also included legal developments. Qin laws stipulated that local governments must regularly report on the growth of crops in writing.[28] It even provided detailed guidance on how to utilise cattle effectively in the fields, offered rewards to incentivise cattle breeding, and set penalties for practices that would increase cattle mortality.[29] During the Ming dynasty, the emperors encouraged the introduction of new crop varieties, particularly from South America: peanuts (late fifteenth–early sixteenth centuries), corn (sixteenth century), potatoes and sweet potatoes (late sixteenth–early seventeenth centuries), and sunflowers (seventeenth century).[30] The success of those introductions was a major reason for China's significant population growth in the Ming and Qing dynasties.[31]

In order to encourage people to farm effectively, Emperor Yongzheng of the Qing dynasty (1678–1735) personally travelled deep into grain-producing areas, guided agriculture, encouraged land reclamation, and dredged ponds and ditches for irrigation. During his reign, tax revenue from agricultural production constituted the majority of the Qing government's income and the imperial treasury reached one of its highest surpluses.[32] Due to this financial strength, Emperor Yongzheng was also able to quell rebellions in Qinghai, Tibet, and Outer Mongolia, solidifying the Qing dynasty's rule. Similarly, during the Han dynasty, Emperor Wu (156–87 BCE) successfully organised large-scale military forces to repel the nomadic Xiongnu, ultimately leading the Han dynasty through its greatest territorial expansion and opened up the ancient Silk Road. This achievement was only made possible by ample fiscal support, which was derived from robust support for agricultural production under his reign.

After decades of swift industrialisation, modern China has transitioned from an agrarian society into the world's largest industrial nation. The proportion of the population employed in agriculture has decreased to around 30%.[33] And its manufacturing sector rivals the combined size of those in the United States, Japan, and Germany.[34] Nevertheless, the country still faces a potential risk of famine, stemming not only

---

[26] Ibid.
[27] Shuihudi Qin bamboo texts committee (1990).
[28] Ibid.
[29] Ibid.
[30] Zhao (2018).
[31] Ibid.
[32] Rowe (2012); Ma (2013).
[33] Liu (2018).
[34] Wolf (2018).

from food shortages due to diminishing agricultural land, but also from structural imbalances within its system.

In recent years, China has faced significant declines in farmland and worsening conditions. The latest land use survey revealed a drop in China's total arable land from 334 million acres in 2013 to 316 million acres in 2019, a reduction of over 5% within a six-year period.[35] In addition, it is concerning that more than a third of China's remaining arable land faces challenges such as degradation, acidification, and salinisation.[36] Consequently, productivity has suffered; in 2018, fertiliser use in China was 6.4 times higher than in 1978, yet grain yield only increased 2.2 times during the same period.[37] China's anxiety over food security is underscored by a controversial directive from the top in 2023, aimed to guarantee sufficient farmland for grain production. The new directive involves converting some forests into farmland and repurposing land formerly designated for other uses, such as the cultivation of more profitable fruits and vegetables, to instead grow grain.

Further, China continues to rely heavily on imported grain, soybean, oil, and meat from Brazil, the United States, Canada, Australia, New Zealand, and a few other Southeast Asian countries.[38] This trend is expected to rise further as the Chinese population moves towards a diet with increased consumption of meat and protein products. In addition, as climate change exacerbates challenges in feeding its population from domestic sources, China is likely to become more dependent on food imports. Consequently, numerous Chinese companies have begun stockpiling grain, purchasing land in developing countries, and acquiring agricultural firms in both developing and developed nations to ensure a stable supply of essential food items. However, amid the growing rivalry between China and the United States, China is confronting the increased likelihood of trade and supply chain decoupling. Furthermore, Chinese acquisitions of overseas agricultural land and companies are encountering more rigorous scrutiny. These factors amplify China's concerns over food security.

This is why the Chinese Communist Party (CCP) still regards ensuring food security as the most important means to maintain political support. As Xi Jinping stated, "In a big country with a large population, solving the problem of providing enough food is always the top priority for those governing the country."[39] Despite China's rise to prominence as the global manufacturing hub, its primary annual policy paper, known as the No. 1 central document, has consistently focused on food security and the triple concerns of agriculture, rural areas, and farmers. For the same reason, for many Chinese citizens, the understanding of the government's pragmatic role as a guarantor of food and basic living conditions persists. A more detailed discussion on the implications of this issue will be presented in Chap. 2.

---

[35] Liu (2023).

[36] Ibid.

[37] Ibid.

[38] Gale et al. (2015).

[39] The Central People's Government of the People's Republic of China (2013).

Keeping the Land United

China's geographical features not only present significant challenges relating to natural disasters and famine, but they also contribute to serious security risks for the country. China consistently faced threat from nomads on its northwestern borders. In the past 2,000 years, the Chinese Central Plains have been conquered by nomads at least eight times.[40] The northwestern borders are mostly mountainous, cold, and difficult to garrison, and China barely has any buffer states surrounding its territory on those likely invasion routes towards its heartland.[41] In contrast, Europe's geography is characterised by numerous natural barriers, such as mountain ranges, dense forests, and vast seas, which provide protection and create defensible borders for its nations. Additionally, Europe's political landscape, with its many distinct countries and cultures, has historically created a complex web of alliances and rivalries that can deter potential invaders, whereas China's more unified political structure presents a singular target for aggressors.[42]

External invasions have been perceived as one of the greatest disruptions to the stability of life on the Chinese Central Plains. Those invasions often occurred when the country's centre was weak. During the chaotic Warring States period (475–221 BCE), China found itself fractured into seven major states, constantly battling each other for supremacy. As the population swelled and land became scarce, each state aggressively sought to expand its arable land by encroaching on neighbouring territories. This vicious cycle of unending conflict ravaged valuable farmland and severely disrupted agricultural production. In turn, the dwindling population left the region susceptible to nomadic invasions. Additionally, troops from different principalities focused solely on local duties such as constructing a small-scale 'Great Wall' for local protection, rendering a unified defence against external invaders nearly impossible. It was only after Emperor Qin Shihuang unified China and managed to rally a formidable workforce of 300,000 individuals to fortify and extend the Great Wall over 10 years that he successfully drove the nomads back into the steppe.

This historical event arguably led to the early conceptualisation of the notion of 'collective security' in China. It underscored the necessity of uniting disparate forces to achieve a 'critical mass' capable of defending against common adversaries. The concept also promoted the exploration into conditions that could incentivise these separate bodies to agree to unification for their mutual benefit and safeguarding. This theme is central to one of China's most renowned texts, *Romance of the Three Kingdoms*, which can be seen, from one perspective, as a perpetual negotiation among three distinct kingdoms seeking unity and collaboration.

This historical novel tells the story of how the Han empire broke down into three distinct kingdoms. They are the Wei in the northern China plains, roughly corresponding to the basin of the Yellow River; the Shu, centred in Sichuan; and the Wu, covering the rest of the Yangtze Basin. From a geographical standpoint, natural

---

[40] Chen (2013).

[41] Nathan and Scobell (2012).

[42] Ibid.

barriers do not offer solid protection to any of those three regions, against each other or against external enemies. Besides, the droughts and floods mentioned earlier make each of them highly vulnerable to famine. However, their collective capacity can effectively manage water and agricultural production, as well as defend against external invaders, creating the conditions for collective security and prosperity.

Nonetheless, centralisation or unification requires a measure of compromise and balance between different kingdoms. Of the three regions described above, the Wei in the Yellow River Basin has consistently been the largest and strongest. However, it has never been able to overpower a coalition between the other two regions. Consequently, the unity of China could not be accomplished merely through Wei's dominance over the rest of the country: it demanded a certain degree of compromise among the 'Three Kingdoms'. This necessity to maintain a balance of power may be perceived as the foundation for many aspects of China's contemporary decision-making model. These include a general tendency towards consensus and the emergence of the factional governance model which will be further discussed in Chap. 5.

Chinese endeavours to maintain unity and prevent division, separation, and external invasions have persisted throughout history and continue to be relevant today. Many people know about the magnificent Great Wall strengthened by Emperor Qin Shihuang, but fewer know about the massive road-building efforts he undertook to create a strong physical bond among the central regions, and place remote territories more tightly under the control of the newly united country.[43] The scale of that road network is comparable to, perhaps even longer than, the better-known Roman system.[44]

The physical bonds afforded by good roads played a vital role in keeping the land united, not only from a geographical perspective but at an emotional level. That same logic is applied by the Chinese government today. Over the last decades, China has built the world's longest highway system (about 150,000 km), and the world's largest high-speed rail network (about 40,000 km as at the end of 2021, scheduled to grow to 50,000 km by 2025).[45] This network has significantly increased personal and cultural exchanges among people from different provinces and territories, resulting in an sense of emotional connection. The intention to further strengthen the unification of Chinese territories drives two major projects: the Lanzhou–Xinjiang railway (opened in 2014), connecting Ürümqi, the capital of the Xinjiang Uyghur Autonomous Region, via Lanzhou; and the Sichuan–Tibet railway (expected to be completed in 2030), connecting Lhasa, capital of the Tibet Autonomous Region, via Chengdu. The hope is that the transport network will forge physical and personal connections that significantly foster national unity and sustain border stability. Essentially, it is about keeping the land united, especially in the autonomous and relatively remote regions of Tibet and Xinjiang, where separatist movements persist. I will explore this topic more thoroughly in Chaps. 6 and 8.

---

[43] Schuman (2020).

[44] Ibid.

[45] National Railway Administration of the People's Republic of China (2021).

Lee Kuan Yew noted from China's historical records that when the central government is strong, the country experiences peace and prosperity.[46] In contrast, when the centre is weak, provinces and counties are ruled by local warlords, leading to internal divisions and overall weakness in China.[47] This perspective aligns with the prevailing narrative in China today, which inherently posits that unity brings about positive outcomes, while fragmentation breeds negativity. However, an honest historical account must recognise that we simply do not know what life was like for people during periods of weak central control and fragmentation. This is true if only because there is less available evidence as compared to unified victorious states. The latter had ample resources to train historians who would praise their empires or construct impressive infrastructure that would be remembered and revered by future generations.

Nonetheless, Lee Kuan Yew's observation should not be reduced as merely a narrative or a justification of China's centralised power. As highlighted in this chapter, the geographical context of China has significantly influenced the exercise of power, both as a means to prevent collective catastrophe and to advance collective prosperity. Given that this geographical constraint is unlikely to change in the short to medium term, it necessitates the formation of a 'critical mass' to achieve these objectives. This, in turn, encourages disparate forces to seek compromise, culminating in the formation of a unified entity.

When evaluating China's future trajectory, it is vital to recognise the implications of those enduring geographical constraints. Adopting this perspective does not signify endorsement. Instead, the subsequent sections of this book will explore the numerous challenges and drawbacks born of these persistent geographical constraints. The goal is to explore feasible strategic alternatives, acknowledging the reality of our starting point and taking into account systemic inertia. This approach facilitates a comprehensive evaluation of the practicability and potential efficacy of various strategies in tackling the challenges these constraints present.

References

Albright M (2006) The mighty and the almighty: Reflections on America, God, and world affairs. HarperCollins, New York, p.77.

Chen Q (2013) Zhongguo lishishang weihe shuci bei youmu minzu zhengfu? Journal of Translation from Foreign Literature of Economics (2): 66–68.

Chi CT (2019) Key economic areas in Chinese history: As revealed in the development of public works for water-control. Routledge, Abingdon.

Collins G and Reddy G (2022), China's growing water crisis: A Chinese drought would be a global catastrophe. In: Foreign Affairs. Available at: https://www.foreignaffairs.com/china/chinas-growing-water-crisis?utm_medium=newsletters&utm_source=fatoday&utm_campaign=Whenpercent20Tradepercent20Leadspercent20topercent20War&utm_content=20220823&utm_term=FApercent20Todaypercent20-percent20112017. Accessed 31 August 2022.

---

[46] Lee (2018).

[47] Ibid.

Confucius et al (2012) Shang shu (The book of documents). Zhonghua Book Company, Beijing.
Diamond J (1997) Guns, germs and steel. W.W. Norton & Company Inc, New York.
Feuerwerker A (1984) The state and the economy in late imperial China. Theory and Society, 13:297–326. https://doi.org/10.1007/BF00213228.
Gale F et al (2015) China's growing demand for agricultural imports. Economic Information Bulletin 136.
Kennedy P (2017) The rise and fall of the great powers: Economic change and military conflict from 1500 to 2000. Harper Collins Publishers Ltd., London.
Lee KY (2018) Speech by former minister mentor Lee Kuan Yew and current senior advisor to Government of Singapore investment corporation at the Ford Theatre's Abraham Lincoln medal award ceremony. Available at: https://www.mfa.gov.sg/Newsroom/Press-Statements-Transcripts-and-Photos/2014/10/Speech-by-former-MM-Lee-Kuan-Yew. Accessed 15 October 2019.
Liu W (2018) Combining Marxism and China's practices for the development of a socialist political economy with Chinese characteristics. China Political Economy 1(1):30–44. DOI: https://doi.org/10.1108/CPE-09-2018-001.
Liu ZZ (2023) China's farmland is in serious trouble. In: Foreign Policy. Available at: https://foreignpolicy.com/2023/02/27/china-xi-agriculture-tax/. Accessed 2 May 2023.
Liu YH et al (2006) Xiaojian Huanghe xiayou hongzai fengxian. Chinese Science Bulletin 51(July):129–139.
Ma DB (2013) State capacity and great divergence, the case of Qing China (1644–1911). Eurasian Geography and Economics, 54(5-6): 484-499, DOI: https://doi.org/10.1080/15387216.2014.907530.
Maddison A (2007) Chinese economic performance in the long run, second edition, revised and updated 960–2030AD. OECD. DOI: https://doi.org/10.4000/chinaperspectives.4956.
Mallory WH (1926) China: Land of famine. American Geographical Society, New York.
Nathan AJ, Scobell A (2012) China's search for security. Columbia University Press, New York.
National Railway Administration of the People's Republic of China (2021) 2021 nian tiedao tongji gongbao. Available at: http://www.nra.gov.cn/xwzx/xwxx/xwlb/202204/t20220428_326348.shtml. Accessed 12 May 2022.
Needham J (2004) Science & civilization in China. Volume VII:2. Cambridge University Press, Cambridge.
Perdue PC (1987) Exhausting the Earth: State and Peasant in Hunan, 1500–1850. Harvard University Press, Cambridge.
Rowe WT (2012) China's last empire. Harvard University Press, Cambridge.
Schuman M (2020) Superpower interrupted: The Chinese history of the world. Public Affairs, New York.
Shuihudi Qin bamboo texts committee (1990) Shuihudi qinmu zhujian (Shuihudi Qin bamboo texts). Cultural Relics Publishing House, Beijing.
Sima Q (2011) Shi Ji (Records of the Grand Historian). Zhonghua Book Company, Beijing.
The Central People's Government of the People's Republic of China (2013) Xi Jinping zai zhongyang nongcun gongzuo huiyi shang jianghua. Available at: http://www.gov.cn/ldhd/2013-12/24/content_2553842.htm. Accessed 2 July 2019.
Wei YM et al (2002) Hongshui zaihai fengxian guanli lilun (Theory of risk management of flood disaster). China Science Publishing & Media, Beijing.
Will PÉ (1980) Une cycle hydraulique en Chine: La province du Hubei du XVIe au XIXe siècles (A hydraulic cycle in China: The province of Hubei from the sixteenth through nineteenth centuries). Bulletin de l'école Française d'Extreme Orient, 68, 261–288.
Wittfogel K (1957) Oriental despotism: A comparative study of total power. Oxford University Press, London.
Wolf M (2018) How the Beijing elite sees the world. In: Financial Times. Available at: https://www.ft.com/content/c4df31cc-4d26-11e8-97e4-13afc22d86d4. Accessed 1 May 2019.

References

Xi JP (2019) Speech by Xi Jinping at Huanghe liuyu shengtai baohu hegao zhiliang fazhan. In: Qiushi Journal. Available at: http://www.qstheory.cn/dukan/qs/2019-10/15/c_1125102357.htm. Accessed 5 January 2020.

Xinhua News Agency (2011). Zhishui xingbang-xinzhongguo 60 nian shuili shiye gaige fazhan qishilu. 2011. Available at: http://www.gov.cn/jrzg/2011-07/08/content_1902545.htm. Accessed 5 July 2018.

Zhang HZ, Cheng QG (2016) China's food security strategy reform: An emerging global agricultural policy. In Wu F, Zhang HZ (eds) China's global quest for resources: Energy, food and water. Routledge, London, pp.23–42.

Zhao HJ (2018) China's Long-term economic development: How have economy and governance evolved since 500 BC?. Edward Elgar Publishing, Cheltenham.

Chapter 2
Crafting Legitimacy: The Entangling Balancing Act

> *"Everything must be addressed according to its essence, the essence of a country is people, and the essence for people is food."* (Wu, 2021)
> —Emperor Taizong of Tang dynasty (598–649 CE)

Abstract The long Chinese history can be understood as a succession of dynasties, each beginning with a virtuous ruler and ending with an unworthy one. At the core of these cycles lies the enduring political philosophy question: what defines a good ruler? And what legitimises their power? This chapter aims to explore the notion of legitimacy within the Chinese historical context, analysing its impact on the nation's structural political framework and decision-making processes. It also delves into the contemporary implications this concept holds for the CCP. This chapter argues that the economic performance of the CCP serves as a crucial pillar supporting its legitimacy in the short to medium term. However, as we look towards the future, it becomes evident that two distinct factors can potentially instigate shifts in its legitimacy over the long haul. The first stems from domestic challenges, such as rising inequality, changing expectations, substantial debt burden, and demographic transformations. The second factor involves dramatic transformation in the global environment that may prompt the CCP's internal ecology to change and adapt.

Mandate of Heaven: Food or Justice?

As described in Chap. 1, the rise and decline of dynasties in China's extensive history have been closely intertwined with the state of agricultural production. Therefore, one of the most critical criteria to measure the legitimacy of a regime has been its contribution to food security.[1] When food was scarce, the emperor was expected to act like a parent towards his people, that is, ensure that all members of his 'family' were fed. This formed the basis of an implicit agreement between the people and the

---

[1] Zhang and Cheng (2016).

emperors, signifying that emperors who neglected or failed to fulfil their obligations risked losing the 'Mandate of Heaven'—the indisputable right to govern.[2] In other words, under the 'Mandate of Heaven', centralised power must be seen as a means to an end, not an end in itself.

The 'Mandate of Heaven', a concept rooted in ancient and Imperial China, served to legitimise the reign of Chinese emperors. Originally conceived by Chinese philosophers during the Zhou dynasty, commencing circa 1046 BCE, this concept was used to rationalise their triumph over the preceding Shang dynasty (1600–1046 BCE). They asserted that Shang rulers, having abandoned their moral duties and worthiness, consequently forfeited their 'Mandate of Heaven'. This reasoning became standard to model Chinese history, which became understood as a succession of dynasties, each beginning with a virtuous ruler and ending with an unworthy one.[3]

The 'Mandate of Heaven' concept carries two important implications that illustrate fundamental variances in how legitimacy is defined between China and most of the European tradition. Firstly, the legitimacy of the ruler does not come from birth, endorsement by religious figures or a constitutional process, but from their moral character and accomplishments. Secondly, in contrast to the concept of a 'divine right' for kings, the concept of 'Mandate of Heaven' does not confer an unconditional right to rule. On the contrary, it gives people a right to rebel against a ruler who does not fulfil their duties.

Over the course of Chinese history, only two types of forces have consistently restricted the power of the emperor.[4] One was the class of intellectuals and Confucian scholars, who formed the backbone of the bureaucratic system, and the other was peasant rebellions.[5] Whenever the emperor allowed hunger and famine to spread, peasant rebellions could act as a 'volcanic eruption' to force a change of regime.[6] Throughout Chinese history, starting from the Qin dynasty in 221 BCE, peasant uprisings have occurred roughly every 40 to 50 years, causing significant political instability, or even a change of dynasty.[7]

The originality of the Chinese model appears more evident by contrasting with European experiences, especially when examining core responsibilities of the emperor. The role of Chinese emperors was primarily to provide food and look after the people's livelihood. In line with this overarching goal, Chinese emperors were tasked with creating conditions to make this possible, by keeping the land united, taming the floods, and advancing agricultural development. With this came a relative de-emphasis of other aspects of power, such as conflict arbitration. In contrast, this function was considered a central responsibility of European monarchs. This difference cultivates what could be described as a pragmatic perspective on governance

---

[2] Ibid.
[3] Davis and Puett (2015).
[4] Zhao (2018); Qian (2012).
[5] Ibid.
[6] Ibid.
[7] Chen (2012).

in China, where the evaluation of the government's performance is primarily tied to the material well-being of its citizens.

Even Confucius, whose philosophy asserts that the primary function of emperors is to educate and enlighten their people, underscores that if this duty clashes with supplying essential conditions for survival and prosperity, the latter must prevail.[8] This is because moral development can only occur once basic survival needs are met.[9] Mencius, one of Confucius's most renowned successors, further inquired, "if people are not able to support themselves and their family, how can they have spare time to learn and appreciate etiquette?"[10] Therefore, Chinese government policies have been optimised and prioritised for the goal of guaranteeing the material well-being of its citizens—since its early history until today.

Big Government or Small Government?

As discussed in Chap. 1, over the course of 2,117 years in Chinese history, there were at least 1,621 floods and 1,392 droughts, averaging more than one natural disaster per year. Therefore, throughout Chinese history, providing disaster relief and postdisaster reconstruction has been one of the critical functions of the government. In line with this role, building granaries on a national scale to release grain to people who are suffering has been an important political concern in the last two millennia.[11] In fact, in the Qing dynasty, the criminal law clearly stipulated severe punishment for magistrates who could not provide relief to the poor, thus ensuring the victims' 'right to food'.[12] In exchange for those services, the system requires individuals to relinquish a degree of personal freedom in order to establish an effective mechanism for implementing the collective will. In essence, the emphasis on socioeconomic welfare rights often overshadowed the importance of political rights.[13]

As people have come to expect emperors to establish a stable environment that ensures a basic livelihood, they have grown to accept and anticipate a big government—one possessing sufficient power to manage floods, support agricultural production, and protect against foreign invasions. In such a situation, one could argue that, from the citizens' standpoint, discreetly steering the government to achieve their goals may be more effective than attempting to forcefully restrain it. The central issue here leans more towards 'how individuals can most effectively work with the government to achieve the best outcomes for themselves' rather than 'how people can best resist the government'.

---

[8] Duanmu et al. (2022).

[9] Ibid.

[10] Mencius et al. (2022).

[11] Wong et al. (1991).

[12] Daniel (2016).

[13] Lu and Shi (2015).

This is a stark contrast with many commentators in the West discussing 'big' or 'small' government. In many discourses, particularly from the United States, people fear that a government may become tyrannical or at least infringe on individual freedom if it is too powerful. Meanwhile, the role of the government in creating the conditions for collective prosperity is perceived as less prominent. Comparatively, in the United States, people attribute those conditions to a higher degree to the bounty of 'nature' (or God), or as the result of individuals coordinating 'naturally' as part of a free market system.

Absurd Decisions or Arbitrary Decisions?

One interesting reflection here is how varying interpretations of power, and, consequently, the purpose and function of government, result in a distinct political institutional framework. The focus is not necessarily on having 'big' or 'small' government, but rather on the preferred form of power and the degree to which these powers should be divided. In China, executive power takes precedence due to the necessity of effectively governing a vast nation. Conversely, in the West, where concerns about excessive governmental power are more prominent, executive power is typically more limited, with greater emphasis on legislative and judicial power. Furthermore, Western systems are purposefully structured to divide powers, while China favours consolidating them and implementing restrictions through alternative methods, such as the 'Mandate of Heaven', signifying a right to rebel, as well as a range of consensus and deliberative mechanisms embedded within the system (expanded upon in Chap. 5). This distinction calls for deeper reflection on the trade-offs associated with each political institutional framework.

In the words of U.S. Justice Louis Brandeis, the purpose of power separation is "not to promote efficiency, but to preclude the exercise of arbitrary authority".[14] This means that the Western model opens the door to possibly absurd decisions, including the absence of any decision, even in the face of pressing challenges. In contrast, the Chinese political tradition confers greater responsibility to the government, and legitimacy is tied to performance, efficiency, and outcomes. From this perspective, a gridlocked government that lets chaos dominate could cause more harm than a tyrannical government. Here, the worst decision is no decision at all, or an excessively slow, possibly suboptimal decision derived from complex institutional negotiations.

It is important to note that the Chinese model's emphasis on efficiency and outcome comes with two downside risks. Firstly, it opens the door to arbitrary decisions. This means that the government can get away with bad practices—or even obvious injustices—based on the claim that those are necessary conditions to deliver outcomes. A government whose accountability rests solely on its self-justified discipline offers poor assurance of respecting individual rights under all circumstances. The second risk is a simplistic application of the model in other countries, based

---

[14] Allison (2019).

on the naive belief that authoritarian performance legitimacy will itself lead to efficiency and economic prosperity. Developing countries are at risk of seeing their government shift to dictatorship, thus losing the benefits of democratic procedure, without guarantee that the more authoritarian government will in fact achieve better economic outcomes. The second risk is increasingly worrying as China starts to claim the superiority of its political system.

Holding onto the Throne

As discussed in Chap. 1, today, the CCP still considers that providing basic living conditions for the people is one of the most important means to sustain their political support. As Xi Jinping repeatedly asserted that in a vast nation with a sizeable population, addressing the issue of ensuring sufficient food supply remains the foremost concern for those in power.[15] Although the Chinese economic policies formulated to achieve this goal have been dramatically altered on several occasions, in response to major changes in politics and the economy, the goal itself has remained constant. As for the capacity to deliver economic outcomes—or not—it has affected the CCP's legitimacy at various times.

When the CCP took the reins in 1949, it made a declaration that "not even one person shall die of hunger".[16] At the time, this was an ambitious claim: hunger was then endemic. After early successes, a catastrophic failure to meet this promise caused one of the biggest legitimacy challenges to the CCP. From 1958 to 1962, China underwent the most catastrophic famine in human history by absolute numbers of death, with an estimated 45 million deaths resulting from the 'Great Leap Forward' policy.[17] Although the precise number of fatalities remains a subject of debate, the widely accepted estimate is provided by Dutch historian Frank Dikotter, who supports the figure of 45 million.

In 1958, Mao Zedong launched a campaign to reconstruct the country from an agrarian society into an industrialised communist society. To fulfil and exceed unrealistically ambitious quotas, local officials competed to claim 'surpluses' that in fact did not exist, sending scarce food to the cities and leaving farmers to starve. Higher officials, fearful of anti-rightist campaigns, did not dare report the economic disaster caused by these policies, and blamed bad weather for the decline in food output, taking little or no action. After a few years, the Chinese economy was on the brink of collapse, and the CCP authorities faced a more serious legitimacy crisis than ever. To restore legitimacy, they had to interrupt the 'Great Leap Forward' and reorganise people to restore damaged agricultural production systems and the environment.

Since 1978, to further resolve structural food shortage, the government took radical reforms to increase agricultural production, including diversification of the

---

[15] The Central People's Government of the People's Republic of China (2013).

[16] Zhang and Cheng (2016).

[17] People's Daily (2020).

rural economy, crop selection in accordance with regional comparative advantage, production specialisation, expansion of free markets, and a marked rise in state procurement prices.[18] In 1981, the Chinese government endorsed one of the most effective reforms—the 'Household Responsibility System' (HRS) which brought dramatic changes in China's rural areas, and increased agricultural productivity remarkably.[19]

In communist China's early years, collectivised land and the work points system resulted in low labour productivity and insufficient agricultural supply.[20] The HRS transformed incentives by allowing households to contract land, machinery, and other facilities from collective organisations and operate with increased autonomy. Under this system, farmers led production activities and bore responsibility for profits and losses, meaning a peasant's marginal return is the same as the marginal product of their labour.[21] Also the HRS system allowed households to sell their products through a multi-tier pricing system that included the lowest price for payment to the state up to the quota set by the state, a higher rate for above-quota sales to the state, and the market price for crops allowed to be sold at agricultural fairs.[22] After paying taxes and collective commissions, households could retain the remaining income, effectively becoming residual claimants. This change led to increased productivity and better-met consumer demand.

This HRS system is a successful reform. The output value of China's agricultural products increased by 42.23% in constant prices from 1978 to 1984, of which 46.89% was attributed to the introduction of the HRS.[23] As a result of this change, as well as other forms of agricultural development like rural land reform, China's grain production experienced phenomenal growth. Since 1998, China has achieved 95% self-sufficiency in grain.[24] This was portrayed by the Chinese government as a miracle, and significantly increased the CCP's performance legitimacy.

Bigger Pie or Fairer Distribution?

The economic accomplishments of the CCP are extraordinary. Between 1978 and 2018, which spans 40 years since Beijing initiated the 'Reform and Opening Up' policy, the nation saw an average annual GDP growth of 9.5%.[25] Nonetheless, during

---

[18] Lin (1987).

[19] Lin (1988).

[20] Lin (1987). World Bank; Development Research Center of the State Council, the People's Republic of China (2022).

[21] Lin (1987).

[22] Weber (2021).

[23] Lin (1992).

[24] The State Council Information Office of the People's Republic of China (2019).

[25] World Bank; Development Research Center of the State Council, the People's Republic of China (2022).

the same timeframe, income inequality, as represented by the Gini coefficient, consistently rose. It began at 0.16 in 1978, reached its highest point at 0.49 in 2008, and dropped slightly to 0.47 in 2020, still exceeding the 0.4 threshold established by the United Nations.[26]

Since the establishment of the PRC, there have been ongoing debates about balancing the socialist objective of income equalisation and increased political consciousness with industrialisation and economic modernisation. In the 2010s, this debate was reflected in two different economic models. One was known as the 'Guangdong Model' which emphasises that 'the cake must be made bigger before dividing the cake'. The other was known as the 'Chongqing Model' which emphasises that 'if the cake is not distributed fairly, no one wants to bake it'. In 2021, Xi Jinping introduced the concept of 'common prosperity', indicating that China's future development should be equitable and benefit everyone. This perspective marks a significant departure from Deng Xiaoping's earlier suggestion that it was acceptable for some individuals to 'get rich first'. Under the new approach, increasing wealth disparity, where the rich become richer while the poor grow poorer, is no longer considered acceptable. This shift has understandably sparked concerns among China's ultra-wealthy elites and profit-driven private sector, which will be explored in greater detail in the next chapter.

As mentioned earlier, throughout Chinese history, peasant rebellions have been a key challenge to the government in place. It is not uncommon for authoritarian regimes to reduce revolutionary threat by offering public goods to the groups most likely to challenge them. Since the late 1970s, the CCP has spent tens of billions of dollars on poverty reduction. This progress led to nearly 800 million people overcoming poverty which accounts for almost three-quarters of the global reduction in extreme poverty.[27] The driving force behind this substantial commitment to reducing poverty is primarily the pursuit of stability. Chinese leaders have gleaned insights from other countries' experiences, both historical instances like the 1930s and more recent occurrences such as the Arab Spring, recognising the potential risks posed by escalating social inequality.[28]

Living a Better Life: Raising Expectations

The CCP has strengthened its legitimacy based on robust economic performance over the recent decades. However, many Chinese analysts believe that, like revolutionary legitimacy, economic performance legitimacy is finite and bound to be exhausted.[29]

---

[26] Hancock (2021); Wang (2004).
[27] World Bank; Development Research Center of the State Council, the People's Republic of China (2022).
[28] Liu (2013).
[29] Holbig and Gilley (2010).

This model has created its own issues, particularly concerning environmental degradation and increasing inequality.[30] Furthermore, it has inevitably heightened people's expectations, making it increasingly challenging to meet them over time.

Over the last decades, Chinese people's expectations of the government have expanded from a guarantee to provide enough food, to include broader improvements in people's material life and social prospects. As Xi Jinping outlined in a speech following the first plenary meeting of the 18th Central Committee of the Party in November 2012, "Chinese people want better education, more stable work, more satisfactory income, more reliable social security, higher levels of medical and health services, more comfortable living conditions, and a more beautiful environment. To allow children to grow up better, work better and live better."[31] There are two reasons behind the increasing expectations. One is real improvement of living standards which allowed people to look beyond basic living security. The second reason is generational change.

Chinese people born in the 1950s or 1960s were most significantly affected by the Leninist model in their early socialisation, while those born in the 1940s or earlier were more heavily affected by traditional Confucian values.[32] Those value systems, combined with an experience of material hardship, have made them relatively tolerant of unsatisfied social and economic desires. Witness the list of relatively modest items defining what counted as a good life in the '50s and '60s: a watch, a bike, and a radio.

People born in the 1970s were a more conflicted generation. They inherited older values from their parents and lived their early childhood through the Cultural Revolution. However, they grew up in the years of the 'reform and opening up', when Western ideas of democracy and freedom started flooding in. They faced the challenges of dealing with a fast-changing world as young adults, but were also able to benefit more directly from China's rapid economic rise in their formative years. While they may be critical of certain aspects of the Chinese system, they ultimately benefit from it, which makes them more inclined to collaborate with the system.

In contrast, Chinese millennials (born in the 1980s and 1990s) have reaped the benefits of China's economic growth without directly experiencing the negative impacts of the CCP's past policies. They represent both an opportunity and a challenge for the regime. Many Chinese millennials have travelled or studied overseas, acquiring valuable global connections and skills for their country. Yet, more individualistic and concerned with social issues like environmental protection and social justice, their aspirations for a meaningful life may be overshadowed by bleak job prospects, unaffordable housing, and increasingly stringent social control.[33] *The Economist* reported that, as of 2021, average house prices in Beijing and Shanghai were 23 times the median incomes, double the ratio in London.[34] Feelings of disappointment and resentment, combined with limited tolerance for social

---

[30] Ibid.
[31] Xinhua News Agency (2012).
[32] Lu and Shi (2015).
[33] The Economist (2021).
[34] Ibid.

injustice, means they are less willing to accept unsatisfactory governance. With this in mind, although Xi Jinping emphasised during his address at the 20th CCP National Congress in October 2022 that China would intensify its focus on security measures and political objectives, this agenda, heavily influenced by ideological and political matters and centred on nationalist goals, may increasingly face disapproval and opposition from younger generations.

In response to growing dissatisfaction and frustration among Chinese people, China's spending on 'public security', which encompasses controlling speech, social media, and protests, has continued to increase. It reached USD 210 billion in 2020, more than doubling over the past decade.[35] With the CCP tightening social control, it is anticipated that such expenditures will continue to rise, placing additional strain on an already stressed national fiscal budget. This issue will be further explored in the following section.

Heavenly Mandate Tested

There are a number of pressure points challenging the CCP's 'Mandate of Heaven'. First comes a structural difficulty. As basic living conditions are satisfied, people demand more services that tend to be household- or individual-based. Those include affordable medical services, education, housing, and secure retirement benefits. The Chinese central planning system is very experienced in delivering basic public goods and shared services such as water and electricity, public infrastructure, or social order, but it is not so effective at delivering welfare to households or at the individual level.[36]

Secondly, China is heavily indebted. According to figures by the Bank for International Settlements, China's debt has been swelling by about 20% a year since the Global Financial Crisis in 2008, faster than nominal GDP growth.[37] As a result, the country's debt-to-GDP ratio surged from 178% in the first quarter of 2010 to almost 275% in 2022.[38] It is estimated that the local government's hidden debt, including loans and bonds, hit 45 trillion yuan (USD 7 trillion) at the end of 2020, equivalent to 44% of Chinese GDP.[39] Additionally, the extensive stimulus package in response to COVID-19 pushed China's debt level to an unprecedented high.

An increase in debt is not inherently problematic if a reasonable portion is allocated towards productive investments. As China embarked on its reform era in the 1970s, it started with a substantial underinvestment in infrastructure and manufacturing capacity due to years of war and disruption. Consequently, although debt levels surged, its GDP experienced a similarly rapid growth.[40] Until the mid-2000s, the level

---

[35] Nikkei Asia (2022).
[36] Saich (2020).
[37] Choyleva (2020).
[38] Bloomberg News (2022).
[39] Lee (2022).
[40] Pettis (2022).

of investment in the Chinese economy was still relatively low considering the ability of Chinese businesses and workers to efficiently utilise such investment. During this time, China's high debt levels were still productively fuelling economic growth, enabling the country to experience rapid and sustainable expansion.[41] However, around 2006–2008, China appeared to reach overcapacity. From that point on, the rise in debt has not yielded proportional returns in terms of economic growth.

Moreover, in response to the 2008 Global Financial Crisis, the Chinese central government initiated a substantial stimulus package, committing to inject four trillion yuan (USD 579.44 billion) to stimulate economic growth. The four trillion yuan stimulus package that the Chinese government announced was a combination of direct financing from the central government and investments mobilised from other sources, such as local governments, state-owned enterprises, and private entities. Given that the key component of the stimulus package consisted of infrastructure projects spanning both urban and rural areas, it is unsurprising that the majority of investment expenditure was implemented and financed via local governments.[42] Only approximately one trillion out of the four trillion originated from the central government's budget, indicating a financing gap of three trillion yuan.[43]

Moreover, considering the institutional context of the national budget law, local governments were prohibited from borrowing independently at that time.[44] This led them to finance their investment expenditures through off-balance-sheet mechanisms called Local Government Financing Vehicles (LGFVs), the only available avenue.[45]

While this strategy quickly spurred economic growth, it also triggered a surge in local government debt, leading to international worries about China's fiscal risk. It is estimated that almost 2.5 trillion yuan (USD 362.15 billion) of local government debt will fall due in 2021, yet economists estimate that the actual amount outweighs this figure.[46] The off-balance-sheet nature of LGFVs, which adds a layer of opacity, is at the root of this uncertainty, making it a cause for concern in terms of China's macro-financial stability.

Arguably, at present, the primary challenge in China's debt problem is less about the escalating debt levels and more about systemic misallocation of resources. For over 30 years, China has allocated between one-quarter and one-third of its GDP to infrastructure and property investments.[47] In recent years, however, China's infrastructure sector has started to show signs of overcapacity, and its real estate sector has begun facing a debt crisis. A notable example is Evergrande, the world's most indebted developer, which defaulted in December 2021. Other Chinese developers have also started encountering difficulties. The presence of unreported privately placed bonds and undisclosed guarantees for joint ventures, associates, and other

---

[41] Ibid.
[42] Chen et al. (2017).
[43] Ibid.
[44] Ibid.
[45] Ibid.
[46] Choyleva (2020).
[47] Pettis (2022).

third-party borrowings has significantly affected consumer confidence.[48] The CCP has staked its legitimacy on the expansion of the real estate sector, shaping its financial and political institutions to bolster such investments.[49] Confronting this deeply rooted issue is likely to cause upheaval within social, financial, and political systems. Thus, the determination of the CCP to tackle these systemic asset misallocation challenges, as well as the methods they will employ, remains a question of concern.

A third challenge for the CCP's performance legitimacy stems from demographic change. China's births peaked between 1962 and 1972, meaning the retirement-age population will begin to peak in 2022.[50] According to the report produced by the Center for Strategic and International Studies, "By the mid-2020s, China will be adding 10 million elders to its population each year, even as it loses 7 million working-age adults." In addition, "By 2050, there will be 438 million Chinese aged 60 and over, 103 million of whom will be aged 80 or older."[51] This demographic shift will place considerable strain on China's fiscal capacity.

China's two-tier pension system consists of a basic state-provided pension and a mandatory second-tier plan, with both employer and employee making monthly contributions.[52] The pension system primarily covers urban workers, with eligibility for pension based on age, gender, and years of contribution.[53] The basic pension pays one percent of the average of the indexed individual wage and the province-wide average earnings for each year of coverage, subject to a minimum of 15 years of contribution.[54] Employees pay eight percent of wages to the individual account system while the employer pays 16%.[55] Addressing pension payments presents a significant challenge for China. Based on current projections, the national basic pension insurance fund for urban workers is expected to face a deficit of 118.13 billion yuan (USD 18 billion) in 2028.[56] This situation is exacerbated by the strained fiscal capacity across all levels of Chinese government and a slowing economy.[57]

Secondly, there are fewer alternatives for the Chinese government to shift their pension payment liability to other individuals or entities. The falling birth rate means that an increasing number of Chinese elderly will have fewer or even no children to rely on for financial support, as children have traditionally taken up the financial carer role for their parents.[58] By 2025, Chinese rural women turning 65 will on average have 2.2 children, while Chinese urban women will only have 1.3.[59] Further, the

---

[48] Tan (2021)

[49] Ibid.

[50] Luo (2021).

[51] Jackson et al. (2009).

[52] OECD (2019).

[53] Ibid.

[54] Ibid.

[55] Zheng (2020).

[56] Zheng (2019).

[57] Wright (2022).

[58] Jackson et al. (2009).

[59] Ibid.

shrinking working-age population and stagnated growth also mean that state-owned enterprises and private sectors will struggle to shoulder more in the pension scheme, adding pressure to the central fiscal budget.

In a bid to tackle the challenges faced by their pension system, China has embarked on several reforms. For example, in 2022, the Chinese government initiated the development of China's first-ever private pension scheme to address the challenge of an ageing population.[60] The new initiative aimed to expand participation at the individual level by allowing individuals to make voluntary deposits into a pension account and invest their pensions in stable financial products. However, compared to the Western financial market, the current Chinese financial market and personal pension products lack maturity to effectively convert savings into profitable investment and provide satisfactory returns.[61] The ability to manage demographic transformations and meet the material well-being requirements for its ageing population will significantly influence China's long-term prosperity and the CCP's legitimacy.

Reinventing Legitimacy

The CCP is very aware of the fragile nature of performance-based legitimacy. The leadership has therefore sought to establish alternative ways to sustain people's support—and looked at tradition and charisma as an instrument to that end. On the 'tradition' front, the CCP is revitalising a form of nationalism shaped around the narrative of historical humiliation and cultural appropriation. Such an approach is both effective and dangerous. It is effective for mobilising and uniting people domestically against external pressure, by giving them cause to redeem humiliation and restore the glories of the past. However, at the same time, people will compare the current leader and state power with the achievements of the great emperors and dynasties in the past, adding more pressure on the CCP to sustain its legitimacy. This form of legitimacy may prompt more aggressive actions, such as restoring territory perceived as having belonged to 'the great nation' in earlier history. Further, this mentality carries danger in an international landscape characterised by the rising tension between China and the West. Intensifying nationalism and the myth of China's exceptionalism could lead to a self-feeding negative spiral, where China must act assertively or even aggressively to reclaim its lost entitlement, further alienating the West and prompting hawkish voices to push for decoupling or de-risking and the end of engagement with China.

Charisma can be a powerful tool, but its effectiveness may wane over time. Xi Jinping's anti-corruption campaign gained him great popularity among ordinary Chinese people. As early as the late 1990s, the CCP had realised that corruption set a serious challenge to legitimacy based on economic performance, particularly in the context of growing disparity between urban and rural areas. While Beijing

---

[60] The State Council Information Office of the People's Republic of China (2022).
[61] Jackson et al. (2009).

made some efforts to address the issue through campaigns like the 'Harmonious Society' and called for stronger rule of law and virtue, tangible progress was not seen until Xi Jinping's sweeping anti-corruption drive. Survey results regarding government performance during Hu Jintao's tenure (2002–2012) consistently indicated that 'addressing corruption' was the area where people expressed the greatest dissatisfaction.[62] Therefore, this anti-corruption campaign not only garnered substantial support for Xi Jinping, solidifying his concentrated personal power, but also significantly bolstered public confidence in the CCP.

Nonetheless, the extensive campaign has adversely impacted the efficiency and dynamism of the bureaucratic system. On 28 June 2021, Xiao Pei, Deputy Secretary of the Central Commission for Discipline Inspection of the CCP, reported that since the 18th CCP National Congress in 2012, the commission had filed and reviewed 3.85 million cases, investigated 4.089 million individuals, and imposed party discipline and government sanctions on 3.742 million people.[63] As a result, numerous bureaucrats have become overly cautious, hesitant to go above and beyond in their roles. They want to stay on the safe side, and are far from incentivised to initiate new ideas or propose new projects.

However, there appears to be no indication of the campaign concluding. In the work report to the 20th CCP National Congress, Xi Jinping made a strong statement emphasising the continuation of heavy anti-corruption measures. He declared, "Corruption is a cancer to the vitality and ability of the Party, and fighting corruption is the most thorough kind of self-reform there is. As long as the breeding grounds and conditions for corruption still exist, we must keep sounding the bugle and never rest, not even for a minute, in our fight against corruption."[64] While anti-corruption campaigns initially bolstered Xi Jinping's charisma and popularity, China's future growth cannot afford a stagnant bureaucratic system. These campaigns now pose a risk to the nation's economy, and continuing them may ultimately prove counterproductive for maintaining legitimacy.

An Ongoing Struggle

Not only can internal challenges potentially catalyse the emergence of new forms of legitimacy, but the evolving external environment could also exert a significant influence. The foundational theory of communism was influenced by Western industrialisation. To a certain extent, it can be argued that the CCP is a product of the globalisation of ideas. Its very birth stems from the importation of Marxist ideas from Europe to China. As such, throughout its history, significant shifts in the global political landscape have substantially influenced the internal ecology of the CCP. In

---

[62] Saich (2020).
[63] Caixin (2021).
[64] Xi (2022).

response to these changes, the CCP has adapted, resulting in pivotal turning points in the nation's history.

The first instance occurred during the 1939 to 1945 period. The onset of the Second World War altered Moscow's view of the international landscape and the security status of the Union of Soviet Socialist Republics (USSR). This shift in perception, together with the unfolding domestic political dynamics in China, resulted in a policy divide between Moscow and Mao Zedong.[65] The main tension lay around whether the CCP should collaborate with the Kuomintang (KMT) to combat the Japanese, and if the CCP should let the KMT lead them in warfare.[66] Having consistently fought against the KMT, Mao Zedong was cautious of such an alliance. Despite gaining support from both the CCP and Moscow, Mao Zedong faced an internal leadership challenge from Moscow's designated representative, Wang Ming.[67] Mao Zedong capitalised on Moscow's preoccupation with war, which limited their ability to closely monitor the CCP's internal power struggle, and launched the Yan'an Rectification Movement in 1941.[68] This ideological mass movement aimed to eliminate Soviet influence within the CCP. Ultimately, Mao successfully rejected the policy direction set by Wang Ming and Moscow's party line, solidifying his paramount leadership position within the CCP.[69]

The second instance took place during the dramatic transformations in Eastern Europe in the late 1980s and early 1990s. The collapse of the socialist bloc altered the CCP's stance towards the United States and the U.S.-dominated international order.[70] This shift in the global landscape, transitioning from a bipolar U.S.–Soviet rivalry to a more multipolar world, led to the CCP reevaluating its position on the global stage and adopting a 'world multipolarity' strategy.[71] Driven by the urgent need to recover from the economic and social costs of Mao Zedong's Cultural Revolution and adapt to the changing external environment, Deng Xiaoping opened the era of 'reform and opening up', fundamentally altering China's development trajectory for the decades to follow.

It could be argued that the CCP is currently embarking on its possible third significant phase of transformation. This time, the change is driven not only by a rapidly transforming geopolitical landscape, marked by fierce competition among global powers, but also by unprecedented catastrophic risks that extend beyond the control of any single nation. These risks include climate change and the disruptive effects of emerging technologies, such as artificial intelligence. These global phenomena transcend national boundaries and are truly international in their scope.

While there are no clear answers to how the CCP's legitimacy may evolve in this new era, the core principle persists. Rooted in the 'Mandate of Heaven', the emperor's

---

[65] Tian et al. (2007).
[66] Ibid.
[67] Hua et al. (2018).
[68] Ibid.
[69] Ibid.
[70] David (2007).
[71] Ibid.

legitimacy hinges on its ability to address China's most pressing challenges. Historically, these challenges centred around combating natural disasters and feeding the population. More recently, the focus has shifted to sustaining economic growth and enhancing people's well-being. In our current age of interconnected and successive challenges and crises, the most pressing challenge is increasingly intertwined with the imperative of actively contributing to global endeavours aimed at addressing shared challenges. It remains uncertain how the CCP will respond to these challenges and how its internal ecology will adapt. Presently, China's stance is unclear, as it has not explicitly decided whether to engage in a rivalry for global hegemony or act as a collaborative participant in building a multipolar world defined by new shared values. In Chaps. 10 and 11, I will delve deeper into the various potential paths the CCP might pursue and explore the possibilities and constraints China faces in achieving its objectives.

References

Allison G (2019) Destined for war: Can America and China escape Thucydides's trap?. Scribe Publications Pty Ltd, Melbourne. pp.142–43.
Bloomberg News (2022) China's debt to climb to record in 2022, Government Adviser Says. Available at: https://www.bloomberg.com/news/articles/2022-07-06/china-s-debt-to-climb-to-record-in-2022-government-adviser-says#xj4y7vzkg. Accessed 1 October 2022.
Caixin (2021) Zhongyang jiwei fushuji xiaopei: Shibada hou chachu 392 ming gaoguan. Available at: https://china.caixin.com/2021-06-28/101732713.html. Accessed 29 June 2021.
Chen ZW (2012) Financial strategies for nation building. In: Joseph F, Morck R (eds) Capitalizing China. University of Chicago Press, Chicago, pp.313–333.
Chen Z et al. (2017) The financing of local government in the People's Republic of China: Stimulus loan wanes and shadow banking waxes. In: Asian Development Bank Institute. Available at: https://www.adb.org/sites/default/files/publication/396826/adbi-wp800.pdf. Accessed 9 October 2021; Asian Development Bank (2014) Zhongguo difang caizheng guanli: tiaozhan yu jiyu. Available at: https://www.adb.org/sites/default/files/publication/42793/local-public-finance-management-prc-zh.pdf. Accessed 18 May 2020.
Choyleva D (2020) China's local government debts should be the real worry. In: Nikkei Asia. Available at: https://asia.nikkei.com/Opinion/China-s-local-government-debts-should-be-the-real-worry. Accessed 28 December 2020.
Daniel B (2016) Xianneng zhengzhi. CITI Press, Beijing.
David S (2007) China stands up: The PRC and the international system. Routledge, New York.
Davis K, Puett M (2015), Periodization and "the medieval globe": A conversation. The Medieval Globe 2(1): 1–14.
Duanmu C et al (eds) (2022) Lunyu (the Analects of Confucius). Zhonghua Book Company, Beijing.
Hancock T (2021) China needs cut to inequality for common prosperity: PBOC's Cai. In: The Bloomberg. Available at: https://www.bloomberg.com/news/articles/2021-11-29/china-needs-cut-to-inequality-for-common-prosperity-pboc-s-cai?leadSource=uverifypercent20wall. Accessed 8 April 2022.
Holbig H, Gilley B (2010) Reclaiming legitimacy in China. Politics & Policy, 38(3): 395–422.
Hua G et al (2018) How the red sun rose: The origins and development of the Yan'an rectification movement, 1930–1945. The Chinese University of Hong Kong Press, Hongkong.

Jackson R et al (2009) China's long march to retirement reform: The graying of the Middle Kingdom revisited. In: Center for Strategic & International Studies. Available at: https://www.csis.org/analysis/chinas-long-march-retirement-reform. Accessed 15 June 2021.

Lee A (2022) China's hidden debt: how much is it and what is Beijing doing to curb the financial risk? In: South China Morning Post. Available at: https://www.scmp.com/economy/china-economy/article/3165411/chinas-hidden-debt-how-much-it-and-what-beijing-doing-curb. Accessed 1 March 2022.

Lin YF (1988) The household responsibility system in China's agricultural reform: A theoretical and empirical study. Economic Development and Cultural Change, 36(3): 199–224.

Lin YF (1992) Zhidu jishu yu zhongguo nongye fazhan. Shanghai People's Press, Shanghai.

Lin JY (1987) The household responsibility system reform in China: A peasant's institutional choice. Discussion Papers, 534. In: Yale University Elischolar. Available at: https://elischolar.library.yale.edu/egcenter-discussion-paper-series/534. Accessed 12 September 2022.

Liu H (eds) (2013) Liang ci quan qiu da wei ji de bi jiao yan jiu (Comparative study on the two global crisis). China Economic Publishing House, Beijing.

Lu L, Shi TJ (2015) The battle of ideas and discourses before democratic transition: Different conceptions of democracy in authoritarian China. International Political Science Review, 36(1): 20–41. DOI: https://doi.org/10.1177/0192512114551304.

Luo ZH (2021) Caizhen juzhang de fannao: Jinpingheng xiade fuzhong qianxing. In: Caixin Global. Available at:https://opinion.caixin.com/2021-01-05/101646835.html. Accessed 10 January 2021.

Mencius et al (eds) (2022) Mengzi (Mencius). Zhonghua Book Company, Beijing.

Nikkei Asia (2022) China spends more on controlling its 1.4bn people than on defense. Available at: https://asia.nikkei.com/static/vdata/infographics/china-spends-more-on-controlling-its-1-dot-4bn-people-than-on-defense/.

OECD (2019) Pensions at a Glance 2019. Available at: https://doi.org/10.1787/b6d3dcfc-en. Accessed 2 January 2020.

People's Daily (2020) Guanyu jianguo yilai dangde ruogan lishi wenti de jueyi. Available at: http://www.people.com.cn/item/20years/newfiles/b1040.html. Accessed 12 December 2020.

Pettis M (2022) The only five paths China's economy can follow. In: Carnegie Enowment. Available at: https://carnegieendowment.org/chinafinancialmarkets/87007. Accessed 2 July 2022.

Qian M (2012) Zhongguo lidai zhengzhi deshi. SDX Joint Publishing Company, Beijing.

Saich A (2020) Testimony before the U.S.-China economic and security review commission: Year in review. In: U.S. China Economic and Security Review Commission. Available at: https://www.uscc.gov/sites/default/files/2020-09/Saich_Testimony.pdf. Accessed 19 December 2020.

Tan WZ (2021) Fitch says a third of rated Chinese developers would face cash crunch in a scenario where sales fall by 30%. In: CNBC. Available at: https://www.cnbc.com/2021/12/28/fitch-ratings-on-liquidity-of-china-real-estate-developers-debt-crisis.html. Accessed 8 August 2022.

The Central People's Government of the People's Republic of China (2013) Xi Jinping zai zhongyang nongcun gongzuo huiyi shang jianghua. Available at: http://www.gov.cn/ldhd/2013-12/24/content_2553842.htm. Accessed 2 July 2019.

The Economist (2021) Individualism reigns in China—and with it, more social responsibility. Available at: https://www.economist.com/special-report/2021/01/21/individualism-reigns-in-china-and-with-it-more-social-responsibility. Accessed 15 March 2021.

The State Council Information Office of the People's Republic of China (2019) Zhongguo liangshi anquan baipishu. Available from http://www.scio.gov.cn/zfbps/ndhf/39911/Document/1666231/1666231.htm. Accessed 9 January 2020.

The State Council Information Office of the People's Republic of China (2022) China rolls out private pension plan. Available at: https://english.www.gov.cn/policies/latestreleases/202204/21/content_WS62610528c6d02e5335329bbf.html. Accessed 8 August 2022.

Tian ZR et al (2007) 20 shiji 30 niandai de zhongguo zhengzhi shi-zhongguo gongchandang de weiji yu zaisheng. Tianjin Academy of Social Sciences Press, Tianjin.

References

Wang H (2004) Social change and its potential impacts on Chinese population health. Hygiea Internationalis 1(1). DOI:https://doi.org/10.3384/hygiea.1403-8668.0441109.

Weber I (2021) How China escaped shock therapy: The market reform debate. Routledge, Abingdon.

Wong RB et al (1991) Chinese traditions of grain storage. In: Nourish the people: The state civilian granary system in China, 1650–1850. University of Michigan Press, Ann Arbor.

World Bank; Development Research Center of the State Council, the People's Republic of China (2022) Four decades of poverty reduction in China: Drivers, insights for the world, and the way ahead. Available at: https://thedocs.worldbank.org/en/doc/bdadc16a4f5c1c88a839c0f905cde802-0070012022/original/Poverty-Synthesis-Report-final.pdf. Accessed 10 November 2022.

Wright L (2022) China's slow-motion financial crisis is unfolding as expected. In: Center for Strategic & International Studies. Available at: https://www.csis.org/analysis/chinas-slow-motion-financial-crisis-unfolding-expected#:~:text=Thepercent20slowpercent2Dmotionpercent20financialpercent20crisis,technocratspercent20inpercent20containingpercent20systemicpercent20risks. Accessed 19 September 2022.

Wu J (2021) Zhenguan zhengyao (Essentials about politics from the zhenguan reign 629–649AD) Zhonghua book company, Beijing. p.124.

Xi JP (2022) Full text of the report to the 20th national congress of the Communist Party of China. In: Chinese Ministry of Foreign Affairs. Available at: https://www.fmprc.gov.cn/eng/zxxx_662805/202210/t20221025_10791908.html. Accessed 28 October 2022.

Xinhua News Agency (2012) Xi Jinping deng shibajie zhonggong zhongyang zhengzhiju changwei tong zhongwai jizhe jia mian. Available at: http://www.gov.cn/ldhd/2012-11/15/content_2266858.htm. Accessed 18 August 2019.

Zhang HZ, Cheng QG (2016) China's food security strategy reform: An emerging global agricultural policy. In Wu F, Zhang HZ (eds) China's global quest for resources: Energy, food and water. Routledge, London, pp.23–42.

Zhao HJ (2018) China's Long-term economic development: How have economy and governance evolved since 500 BC?. Edward Elgar Publishing, Cheltenham.

Zheng BW (eds) (2019) Zhongguo yanglaojin jingsuan baogao. China Labor and Social Security Publishing House, Beijing.

Zheng GC (2020) Zhongguo yanglaojin: zhidu gaige, wenti qingdan yu gaozhiliang fazhan (Pension in China: Reform, Problem List and High-quality Development). Chinese Social Security Review 4(1):3–18.

Chapter 3
Birdcage Economy: Who Holds the Strings of China's Economy?

> *"The United States treats economic issues from the point of view of the requirements of global growth. China considers the political implications, both domestic and international."*
> (Kissinger, 2011)
> —Henry Kissinger, the 56th U.S. Secretary of State

Abstract The growing tension between the CCP and the Chinese private sector, coupled with the CCP's extensive economic intervention, has sparked concerns both within China and around the world. This chapter aims to unpack the origins of this enduring tension by examining China's unique historical and geographical contexts. It argues that a primary cause of the tension stems from the deep-rooted mistrust towards businessmen and capitalists, who are perceived as rivals to the state in competition for power and the decision-making process of 'who gets what, when, and how'. Consequently, the Chinese regime can only conditionally accept private sector growth and the organic development of market conditions to the extent that it does not jeopardise political and social stability. This chapter contributes to the ongoing debate on state intervention and state-owned enterprises by offering an interpretation through the ancient Chinese concept of Yin-yang, emphasising the importance of incorporating negative feedback loops to achieve equilibrium between opposing ideas, instead of prioritising and optimising one extreme, thereby averting any radical outcomes.

Avoiding Tyranny or Avoiding Chaos?

In the first two chapters, I discussed the influence of geography and history on the development of centralised power in China and the expected roles and functions of the government. In this chapter, I will concentrate on the economic governance principles that have emerged out of China's historical and geographical contexts. Despite the considerable transformation in China's economy since the imperial period, the extensive approach of state intervention has remained constant. This was evident even during the 'reform and opening up' era as well as the period of China's double-digit growth. A starting point to examine the state intervention in China is the distinct core values that various political systems strive to uphold.

Early Americans were "theoretically sceptical of all governments".[1] A fundamental sentiment shaping people's relationship with their government was the fear that granting excessive powers to the authorities could infringe upon individual liberties.[2] Hence, governmental power ought to be restrained, particularly with regard to abstaining from interference in economic activities. In the most clear-cut version of this view, the government should only play the role of a 'night watchman'. This political mentality has remained dominant in the United States, and to a lesser extent, it influences conceptions of government in other Western countries.

This perspective makes perfect sense to the extent that liberty is a core value, and the design of public institutions is optimised to preserve liberty. However, other value systems may result in different governance systems. In China, order has traditionally been the central political value—the much-feared alternative being chaos.[3] According to the Chinese perspective, prioritising liberty could disrupt established order and potentially lead to chaos. To maintain order and limit chaos, many things that would be solved through private individuals freely interacting on the market in the West are considered the government's responsibility in China. These include the operation of state-owned enterprises (SOEs), the implementation of economic planning, and the enforcement of capital controls. This Chinese approach gives rise to a system characterised as 'excessive responsibility'. One consequence is that Chinese people often perceive business and capital through a political and social lens, rather than considering them as an independent domain.

Catching the Ant

The deep intertwining of economy and capital in politics can be particularly observed in China's crackdown on leading private enterprises in recent years. Let us review a recent example. Since 2020, Chinese regulatory authority has tightened its rules in the sectors of internet and e-commerce, technology, private tutoring as well as real estate, reducing the private sector's share of the country's major businesses for the first time in seven years since 2014.[4] This has led to a market selloff that, at its most extreme, erased USD1.5 trillion from Chinese stocks.[5] It is perceived that this crackdown started with Ant Group's suspended initial public offering (IPO).

Before it was suspended on 2 November 2020, the listing of Ant Group (formerly known as Ant Financial and Alipay) was set to be the largest ever IPO in history by

---

[1] Merriam (1984).
[2] Smith (1974).
[3] Allison (2019).
[4] Hancock (2022).
[5] Ibid.

cash raised (USD 34.5 billion), beating the record set by Saudi Aramco in 2019 (USD 29.4 billion).[6] Ant Group, a subsidiary of the Chinese Alibaba Group, was established in 2014 to manage Alipay and other consumer financial services of Alibaba. The company oversees nearly all of Alibaba's consumer payment operations, including the e-commerce platform Taobao, which has over a billion users, and represents one of the world's largest micro-lending enterprises.[7] In its original plan, after the IPO, Ant Group was to offer a wide range of different services, ranging from basic banking loans to asset management, investment consulting, insurance, superannuation, and so on. From a commercial perspective, all this looked exciting and promising. However, it caused worry to the Chinese government from the perspective of social and political stability. Arguably, this is one of the core reasons for the shocking suspension called two days before Ant Group's planned IPO date.

The business model of Ant Group mainly relies on payment services, small and micro-businesses, as well as personal retail lending, asset management, and insurance.[8] The lending arm was most concerning to the Chinese government.[9] In 2019, Ant Group handled 110 trillion yuan (USD 16 trillion) in payments, nearly 25 times more than PayPal which is the biggest online payment platform outside China.[10] Meanwhile, as at June 2020, Ant Group's consumer loan balance reached 1.7 trillion yuan (USD 254 billion), accounting for 21% of the total short-term consumer loans issued by China's deposit-taking financial institutions.[11] It is worth noting that the majority of retail users who take bank loans though the Ant financial platform are ordinary people with shallow pockets.[12]

In China, lending is a very tightly regulated sector. Government regulators are very uncomfortable with banks heavily using micro-lenders or third-party technology platforms like Ant Group for underwriting consumer loans.[13] This was amplified by fears of rising defaults and deteriorating asset quality in a pandemic-hit economy, which is more prone to social unrest and political instability.[14] In addition, Ant Group planned to be listed as a tech company, not a finance company—meaning it would not be subject to the capital contribution ratio that financial institutions have to meet. Prior to the IPO, the capital contribution ratio of Ant Group was only about one to two percent, equivalent to a leverage ratio of 50–100 times, while new regulations require a minimum of 30% for financial institutions.[15]

In order for Ant Group to satisfy the required capital-to-leverage ratios, the company would need to triple the net assets of its micro-lending subsidiaries,

---

[6] Kharpal (2020).
[7] Hongkong Exchange News (2020).
[8] The Economist (2020a, b).
[9] Ibid.
[10] Ibid.
[11] Zhu and Leng (2020).
[12] Aryan (2020).
[13] Zhu and Leng (2020).
[14] Ibid.
[15] China Banking and Insurance Regulatory Commission, People's Bank of China (2020).

amounting to an approximate total of USD 16 billion.[16] While Jack Ma criticised the Chinese state's stringent business regulations, the Chinese government expressed concerns about Ant Group's potential to distort financial market values and encourage excessive debt consumption among ordinary citizens. This was deemed an excessive level of risk exposure for Ant Group itself and for the system at large.

Nonetheless, the halted IPO does not mark the conclusion of the story. Ant Group has been implementing several internal structural changes to comply with regulations set forth by the Chinese government. In 2022, two years after its IPO was derailed, Ant Group is ultimately permitted to raise capital—subject to various constraints, one of which involves the Hangzhou government becoming the second-largest shareholder in the consumer financing business.[17] In July 2023, having confirmed that the majority of the substantial issues plaguing platform companies' financial businesses have been resolved, Chinese authorities wrapped up an extended regulatory scrutiny of Ant Group with a hefty fine of 7.12 billion yuan (USD 984 million).[18] This decision symbolises a major progression towards the end of the country's rigorous crackdown on its internet sector.[19]

The suspended Ant Group IPO is not the only example. In July 2021, only 48 hours after China's largest app-based transportation services company Didi raised USD 4.4 billion through an IPO on the New York Stock Exchange, the Cyberspace Administration of China initiated an investigation into the company and removed its apps from local app stores.[20] This action immediately led to a swift five-percent decline in Didi's share price.[21] In June 2022, Didi delisted from the New York Stock Exchange and is working to meet security regulations for a Hong Kong relisting.[22] By January 2023, Didi had gained approval to resume new user registration in China.

The primary takeaway from the instances of Ant Group and Didi is that the Chinese government does not aim to abolish the market economy or capital markets. Rather, its intent is to establish the parameters and boundaries within which private enterprises and the capital market can operate. In other words, as long as private businesses align with government-approved directions and ensure that their pursuit of wealth also benefits the state, they can continue to operate smoothly.[23] A well-known analogy called the 'birdcage economy', coined by Chen Yun, a prominent Chinese political leader from the 1980s to the 1990s, illustrates this message clearly: the economy is free to soar like a bird, but only within the confines established by central planning.

China's crackdown on private sectors caused no small worry on the global stage. The financial markets have seen large outflows. The cost of capital has risen: Chinese

---

[16] Mak (2020).
[17] Shrivastava (2023).
[18] Zhu and Xu (2023).
[19] Ibid.
[20] The Economist (2021).
[21] Ibid.
[22] Lu (2022).
[23] The Economist (2020a, b).

shares trade at a 45% discount to American ones, making a near-record gap.[24] Venture capitalists say they have changed their decision-making on investment in China from the best ideas to the biggest subsidies.[25] In the past two decades, China has been regarded as the world's largest and one of the most reliable growth engines. However, the rising speculation regarding possible financial profits being restricted by a political party that exhibits distrust towards private wealth and power, along with growing concerns about heightened Chinese government dominance and a more challenging business landscape, have shaken the confidence of international business leaders.[26] Despite the new Chinese leadership's repeated assurances of commitment to 'reform and opening up' and support for private enterprises since taking office in March 2023, there appears to be significant scepticism and caution among international business leaders. The restoration of this damaged confidence requires the concrete implementation of clear, transparent, and consistent policy actions from China's top leadership.

Businessmen Under Siege

The relative lack of trust between the state and businessmen as well as capitalists has a long history in China, and can be traced back at least to the the Warring States period. Here, I use the word 'businessmen' to refer to individuals who primarily engage in commercial activities with the intention of generating profit from the difference between buying and selling prices. This definition does not include farmers who participate in small-scale craft or trade during quieter periods or those who produce goods for the purpose of exchanging them with others. Additionally, the term does not encompass large enterprises and SOEs responsible for developing major infrastructure, tools, consumer products, or minerals.

One fundamental factor behind the enduring mistrust between the state and businessmen is geography. Chapter 1 discussed how China's distinct geography required the emperor to prioritise addressing natural disasters through the construction of large-scale public infrastructure, securing food supply by ensuring an adequate labour force for agriculture, and safeguarding the nation from external threats by establishing a robust military force. All of these tasks demanded significant labour contributions. Consequently, emperors viewed the interests of businessmen and capitalists as being directly at odds with those of the state. If commercial endeavours were too developed, there would be a potential risk of an increasing number of people being drawn to these pursuits, leaving fewer individuals available for agricultural and infrastructure work or military service. Furthermore, it would become more challenging for

---

[24] The Economist (2022).

[25] Ibid.

[26] Ibid.

the state to collect taxes and generate fiscal revenue from agriculture, which constitutes a substantial part of state revenue, thereby presenting significant threats to the stability of the regime.

To delve deeper into the roots of this mistrust, examining the etymology of terms relating to capital and wealth generation in Western and Chinese traditions can provide valuable insights. Such divergent conceptualisations have a profound influence on shaping distinct policy priorities. In English and the majority of European languages, the term 'capital' shares its roots with the word 'cattle'. Initially, 'capital' denoted a herd or flock, which was the main source of wealth for proprietors in a pastoral economy. Capital, perceived as a group of sheep or cattle, has the ability to self-reproduce under the attentive guidance of a skilled shepherd who leads the animals to new grazing lands. By increasing the numbers in its flock through careful animal husbandry, 'cattle-capitalists' can grow the amount of wealth available to all, feed themselves and others, and create abundance.

In contrast, pastoralism held a less significant position in China compared to Europe. Chinese agrarian society prioritised land utilisation for crop cultivation, reducing the availability of pastures and subsequently the prominence of livestock in the economy. Land, particularly land safeguarded from floods, adequately irrigated, and cultivated with grain, was the most critical factor in agricultural production and the main wealth source. The Chinese term for 'capital' bears no connection to livestock; instead, it etymologically links to the seashells that functioned as currency in ancient times, without any connotations of a self-reproducing force.

Those distinct understandings of 'capital' prompt different ways to view how to create abundance. In a Western-pastoral paradigm, opening new pastures for cattle to reproduce is likely to increase the overall number of animals—and therefore wealth. However, in China, merely collecting more seashells does not inherently create value. Instead, it is more effective to improve flood protection through water management, advance agricultural technology for increased grain production, and regulate land acquisition by large landowners who may prioritise more lucrative silk production over essential grain crops, potentially resulting in scarcity and instability for the broader population.

Due to the different approaches of generating prosperity, a long-standing policy tradition of 'promoting agriculture and restricting businesses' emerged in China. This policy was first instituted by Emperor Qin Shihuang and was closely adopted by the Han dynasty, with varying degrees of implementation by subsequent dynasties. Consequently, imperial authority and political priorities were primarily anchored in farmers and the agricultural economy, as opposed to industry and commerce. In accordance with this policy, the emperor elevated the social status of farmers while assigning the lowest social rank to businessmen.

Rule of Law: For Whom?

In international forums, China is often criticised for not upholding the 'rule of law'. There are two ways of understanding the expression of 'rule of law'. On the one hand, it is about the right of individuals not to be accused and arrested arbitrarily. This involves provisions such as 'habeas corpus', due process, or freedom of expression. On the other hand, the expression can also be understood as referring to the rule of 'commercial laws', whereby the state cannot arbitrarily take over private property, raise taxes, or go back on commercial concessions. From the perspective of businessmen, they are more subject to the second aspect, which is the rule of (commercial) law.

In the eyes of Chinese emperors, businessmen and capitalist oligarchs compete with the state for a critical source of power: that of allocating resources, and therefore balancing the interests of different social groups or stakeholders. The Chinese regime can only conditionally tolerate the spontaneous order of the market, to the extent that it does not interrupt social and political stability. Therefore, ensuring that businessmen and capitalists can enjoy the 'rule of law' has not been a high priority throughout Chinese history. At least, it is secondary to the country's political agenda. So, Chinese businessmen and capitalists have had to accept a relative lack of protection for private property and commercial interests, particularly as there was no mechanism that allowed them to negotiate with the government.

In addition, as a side effect of mistrust for businessmen and capitalists, the Chinese state has come to believe that it needs to retain control of essential industry sectors to ensure that the wealth generated goes to government pockets—not so much officials can benefit, but rather so that the government can control wealth redistribution. Consequently, a number of key industries have thus operated under state monopoly for a very long time, including salt, iron, copper, tin, lead, gold, silver, cinnabar, oriental aquamarine, and coal, as well as a number of other lucrative industries such as wine, tobacco, and certain spices.[27] During the Song dynasty, specifically in 997, income from monopoly businesses such as those listed above accounted for approximately 32.66% of total fiscal revenue—the greatest share after land rent. This figure climbed to 50.27% in 1021, and even reached 67.26% in 1085.[28] This trend continued over the following centuries. In the late Qing dynasty in the year of 1911, the revenue from salt alone accounted for 26% of total fiscal revenue.[29]

Through its control of key industries, the Chinese regime was able to set prices as a mechanism to allocate resources and establish a balance among different interest groups especially in times of scarcity. For example, during the reign of Emperor Wu of Han dynasty, the iron industry was managed through a government agency, one of the goals being to protect iron prices from the risk of increases by private businessmen.[30] This was important because iron ploughshares were critical agricultural tools for the

---

[27] Zhao (2018).

[28] Ibid.

[29] Shen (2002).

[30] Zhao (2018).

many farmers who could afford to raise cattle for land cultivation.[31] Nonetheless, due to the steep prices of iron, these farmers, despite being capable of maintaining cattle, found themselves unable to purchase these necessary iron ploughshares.[32]

In the United States, there is a famous saying: 'Where there is a will, there is a way.' This is definitely true in China. Under the strong constraints and pressure put in place by the government, smart businessmen and capitalists have developed all sorts of methods to collude with officials or government agencies to avoid disadvantages.[33] This has been the underlying motivation behind corrupt behaviour in Chinese history. In addition, historically, Chinese bureaucrats receive comparatively low base salaries, making them prone to collusion. The challenges faced by both businessmen and Chinese bureaucrats continue to be relevant today and provide explanations to the ongoing problem of corruption in China, as explored in Chap. 2.

State-Owned Enterprises: A Mere Legacy of the Past?

After the establishment of the PRC in 1949, Chinese leaders opted for a Soviet-inspired planned economy model. One could argue that the motivation behind adopting a planned economy was not just to imitate the USSR's high growth rate, which saw a 27% increase in per capita consumption between 1928 and 1937.[34] While an array of factors influenced this decision, including ideological commitments of the Communist Party, specific developmental objectives, and the broader international political context, one element that strongly resonated was the central concept of the Soviet economic model. This model, which endorsed granting the state exclusive control and authority over economic resource allocation, echoed underlying principles of Imperial China's economic governance. In line with this logic of governance, SOEs were put in place soon after the founding of the PRC.

Today the word 'SOEs' refers both to wholly state-owned enterprises and to state-owned capital holding companies that perform the responsibilities of investors on behalf of the state. SOEs cover almost every essential sector in China, including coal, oil, nonferrous metals, steel, electricity, railway, aerospace, defence, food production and distribution, tobacco and alcohol. By the end of 2019, there was about a total of 13,000 SOEs with 167,000 subsidiaries at all levels of governments (central, provincial, and city).[35] As of July 2022, there were 98 SOEs centrally overseen by the State-Owned Assets Supervision and Administration Commission, the main body managing national-level SOEs.[36] China's top three SOEs (measured by revenue in

---

[31] Ibid.
[32] Ibid.
[33] Wang (2000).
[34] Robert (1998).
[35] Hao (2020).
[36] State-owned Assets Supervision and Administration Commission (2022).

2022) are Sinopec, China National Petroleum, and China State Construction Engineering.[37] Together, according to the World Bank data in 2017, SOEs contribute approximately 23–28% of total GDP, and employ 5–16% of the Chinese workforce.[38] Guotai Junan Securities, a leading Chinese securities company, provided further estimates that SOEs accounted for 12% of urban labour employment in 2020.[39]

Since 1978, the Chinese government has undertaken a major economic reform: "In an effort to awaken a dormant economic giant, it encouraged the formation of rural enterprises and private businesses, liberalised foreign trade and investment, relaxed state control over prices, and invested in industrial production and the education of its workforce."[40] As a result, market forces and capitalism have been incorporated into its system, and the private sector has become more and more prominent. From 1978 till August 2022, the number of Chinese private businesses surged from virtually none to over 47.01 million enterprises, accounting for 93.3% of the total number of enterprises.[41] Chinese private sectors contributed more than 60% of China's GDP, 50% of its tax revenue, 80% of urban labour employment, and 70% of national technology innovation.[42] In this situation, SOEs are often considered remnants of history, seemingly slated for removal. Yet, the present situation proves that SOEs are more than just relics of the past. Three factors are propelling the strengthening of SOEs in China.

Firstly, besides their direct economic function, SOEs are instrumental in accomplishing national strategic priorities, including objectives outlined in the Five-Year Plan.[43] As Xi Jinping stated, "SOEs are an important material and political foundation of socialism with Chinese characteristics, and an important pillar and force for the Party to govern and rejuvenate the country."[44] Over the past decade, Chinese policymakers' expectations of SOEs have shifted according to evolving developmental goals. Previously, SOEs aimed to become strong national champions promoting China's global economic influence. Recently, they have focused on propelling China to the forefront of technological advancements, particularly in areas like 5G, semiconductors, space, and advanced manufacturing.

The importance of SOEs became even clearer whenever the nation faced a state of emergency. When the Global Financial Crisis hit China in 2008, SOEs were immediately used to boost domestic demand and maintain macroeconomic stability by investing more when growth slowed down.[45] During the COVID-19 pandemic, SOEs were required to serve the national emergency "regardless of the cost" and

---

[37] Fortune China (2022).

[38] Zhang (2019).

[39] Guotai Junan Securities (2022).

[40] Hu and Khan (1997).

[41] She (2022).

[42] People's Daily (2023).

[43] Naughton (2018).

[44] Xinhua News Agency (2020).

[45] Ibid.

"with no conditions".[46] Companies such as China State Construction Engineering Corporation and China Railway Construction Corporation gathered their resources to complete the construction and transformation of dedicated hospitals swiftly. In order to solve the shortage of masks, PetroChina, Sinopec, China National Chemical Corporation, and other companies were ordered to quickly switch production lines to produce masks and other medical protective equipment.

Lastly, Chinese SOEs also fulfil government-assigned goals like providing social benefits, which are vital for maintaining national stability and prosperity. SOEs generate substantial capital through their operations and monopolistic advantages. This capital can be utilised, under specific policies and regulations, to address various financial and social objectives of the government. For instance, when addressing China's basic pension insurance funding gap, the government directed SOEs to contribute part of their capital.[47] By September 2020, 67 SOEs and state-owned financial institutions had transferred around 860.1 billion yuan (USD 119 billion) to the National Social Security Fund to bridge this gap.[48]

Since Xi Jinping took power at the end of 2012, the progress of SOEs' reforms has been contradictory. On the one hand, Xi Jinping has called for SOEs' reform to increase efficiency through mixed ownership and better governance, and to adopt net profitability as a key success measure.[49] On the other hand, however, he has increased the CCP's presence in SOEs in recent years, asserting the decisive role of the Party and the government, rather than the market.

Navigating through these ambivalent indications presents a challenge in formulating a conclusive forecast on China's economic trajectory and the role of SOEs in the future. However, based on Chinese historical evidence and rationale discussed in this chapter, it is reasonable to anticipate that state intervention and SOEs will continue to be a significant part of the Chinese economy, particularly in managing core assets and resource allocation to maintain political and social stability. The private sector will thrive until it potentially threatens stability, at which point the balance may shift. Concerns from the international community about the unfair advantages of Chinese SOEs and diminishing private sector dynamics will likely persist in the short to medium term, contributing to the ongoing tension between China and the West.

Walking a Tightrope: Unity of Opposites

China's economic development trajectory is seen as distinct due to its unique blend of 'Chinese characteristics'. These involve a dual approach that combines planned strategies and market forces, allowing for the coexistence of a central plan alongside a certain degree of market influence over resource allocation, product pricing,

---

[46] Xinhua News Agency (2020).
[47] China Daily (2019).
[48] Ibid.
[49] Xi (2013).

and profit distribution. This combination represents both "the negation of Western orthodox economics and the breakthrough of the traditional Marxist theories".[50] To this day, economists within China and globally continue to debate whether the country's economic development can be attributed to the ongoing role of the state in its economy or if it has succeeded in spite of such state intervention. While there is no definitive answer to this question, a fresh perspective rooted in Chinese philosophy may help illuminate the complex and seemingly contradictory economic governance logic employed by China.

This logic of governance draws on the fundamental concept of Yin-yang which can be traced back at least to the third-century BCE. It describes how seemingly opposite or contrary forces are better understood as complementary, interconnected, and interdependent. In the natural world, those forces not only give birth to each other but also interact in a deeply interrelated manner. Examples include female (yin) and male (yang), dark (yin) and light (yang), or old (yin) and young (yang). The concept of Yin-yang is used in all sorts of New Age circles, and therefore carries a sense of mystical vagueness. To bring it back to earth, and prompt more concrete understanding, I would like to propose an analogy from the field of systems engineering, and suggest that the 'Yin-yang' principle is better described as a propensity to insert negative feedback loops.

A negative feedback loop is a mechanism within a system that reduces variation and promotes stability. In the context of Chinese political institutions, this means that a 'Yin' element is intentionally incorporated into the system to balance or counteract the effect of a 'Yang' element. This deliberate contradiction is aimed at balancing opposing ideas, rather than opting for one of two extremes and optimising for it, thus preventing any radical outcome. This logic markedly contrasts with the dominant mindset in Western businesses—especially startups and high-growth technology companies—where systems are designed for exponential growth. To achieve this end, the Western model favours positive feedback loops that accelerate changes.

The 'Yin-yang' principle may offer valuable insights into the ongoing debate surrounding state intervention and SOEs in China, which inherently involves competing objectives and contradictions. The following section will explore several key conundrums presented by this issue.

Firstly, social stability versus economic dynamism. As previously discussed, a dynamic market economy requires private capital and businesses. However, without limits, private capital could grow excessively and pose risks, potentially leading to an oligarchy that negatively impacts national policies and social norms, ultimately harming citizens' interests. The Global Financial Crisis of 2008 serves as an example of how unchecked growth in private capital can pose significant risks. Additionally, large technology oligarchies, such as Facebook and TikTok, can potentially spread misinformation, influence elections, and compromise users' privacy if there are no checks and regulations in place to control their exponential growth. Moreover, there are specific responsibilities and risks the government cannot delegate to the private

---

[50] Liu (2018).

sector, particularly in essential services, where citizens ultimately hold the government accountable for significant shortcomings. For example, in the early 2000s, the city of Cochabamba in Bolivia privatised its water utility, resulting in skyrocketing prices that many citizens could not afford. This led to widespread protests and social unrest, ultimately forcing the government to reverse the privatisation. The government was ultimately held responsible for resolving the crisis and ensuring a more stable price.

Secondly, competition versus investment. In a perfectly competitive sector, we can anticipate lower prices and greater consumer options. However, this may reduce investment incentives, particularly in costly areas such as R&D and infrastructure, due to less appealing returns. Consequently, the long-term interests of end-users like consumers, households, and businesses could be at risk. The telecommunication industry exemplifies this dilemma: although lower prices may benefit users in the short term, it is not in their long-term interest if companies go bankrupt and fail to deliver reliable services. Achieving a balance between competition and investment as well as short-term and long-term end-user interests may necessitate some government intervention.

Thirdly, efficiency versus the interests of citizens. Efficiency is a critical challenge in natural monopoly industries, which are marked by high infrastructure costs and substantial entry barriers. These industries, such as telecommunications, water, postal services, and oil and gas, often have lower total costs when a single firm or a few firms produce the entire output. To promote efficiency, the government may be inclined to create a monopoly or an oligopoly. However, natural monopolies can result in market failures, potentially jeopardising citizens' interests. Therefore, a state leader's economic prowess lies in achieving a balance between these competing concerns.

Last but not least, domestic control versus international interaction. While SOEs offer governments the means to control resources and wealth distribution, they may lack the flexibility and appeal needed for international market engagement compared to private businesses. In China's case, as relations with the West deteriorate, there is a shift towards a more inward-looking economic strategy, with an increased emphasis on state-driven development. However, to ensure its sustainable economic prosperity, China must strike a balance between strengthening the SOEs and empowering the private sectors. Equally important is achieving a balance between governmental intervention in economic activities and maintaining an open and robust macroeconomic environment, which adheres to globally recognised rules and effective law enforcement. It is important to underscore that the above discussion, viewed from the 'Yin-yang' perspective, shares similarities with the Western discourse. Specifically, it aligns with Western debates on the tension between societal and private goals, as well as the role that SOEs play, both subjects that are well explored in Western literature.

Facing those ongoing dilemmas, the 'Yin-yang' principle is useful to hint at a different way of understanding what 'optimising' a system, structure, or institution would look like. On the one hand, it is about identifying a clear goal and aligning all elements of the system towards that goal, inserting positive feedback loops to amplify trends and movements of the different parts. On the other hand, it is about increasing the stability of the system by deliberately inserting contradictions and negative feedback loops.

In the Chinese context, the presence of SOEs and government involvement is not intrinsically problematic. Western scholars also differentiate between the legitimate, sector-specific roles that SOEs can perform, particularly in sectors where free market competition fails to optimise social welfare.[51] Issues arise when there is an excessive overemphasis on one aspect of the equilibrium—SOEs and government intervention—that negatively compromises the other side, disrupting market dynamics and fairness. While Beijing's intent to tackle China's economic challenges, such as monopolies, inequality, debt, and SOEs' reform, is undisputed, the primary approach of achieving these goals through excessive Party control raises doubts and concerns.

When China grapples with major challenges, such as substantial economic or social reform, a pivotal question often emerges: is the solution rooted in the development of a 'stronger system' or the cultivation of a 'stronger leadership'? This question forms the crux of the debate on how to best navigate and manage these multifaceted challenges.

A 'stronger system' emphasises the systemic or structural aspects of a problem, often calling for reforms of robust institutions, creation of new laws, improvements in bureaucracy, assurances of transparency and accountability, or promotion of fair competition. On the other hand, a 'stronger leadership' focuses more on the role of individuals, particularly leaders, in solving the problem. It demands a leader who possesses not only decisiveness and vision but also effectiveness, all vital traits for steering the nation through the prevailing challenges at hand. While the CCP has undertaken systemic reforms in the past few decades, it has simultaneously demonstrated a propensity towards a 'stronger leadership'. This tendency is made clear by the fact that such reforms have been executed under strong and unified leadership and command. A conceivable explanation for this preference lies in the CCP's inherent anxiety regarding the preservation of its power and authority. This is particularly apparent in the CCP's escalating control over the economy and the rising dominance of SOEs, a reaction to mounting economic and technological decoupling stress from the Western world. Consequently, the Chinese system currently possesses limited negative feedback mechanisms, such as restrictions on dissent.

For external parties, directly inserting negative feedback loops within the system to influence China's domestic economic policy is extremely challenging. However, negative feedback loops can be introduced by, in the short term, shaping the strategic environment around China through strategic diversification, strengthening multilateral trade institutions such as the World Trade Organization, as well as setting new standards through bilateral trade and investment agreements to encourage Beijing to comply. In the long term, a more inclusive and bold approach can be explored, which entails facilitating a necessary paradigm shift on the concept of 'growth' at the global level which will be further explored in Chap. 11.

---

[51] Hubbard (2018).

References

Allison G (2019) Destined for War: Can America and China escape Thucydides's trap? Scribe Publications Pty Ltd., Melbourne.

Aryan A (2020) Explained: What is the Ant Group, and why is their IPO suspended? In: The Indian Express. Available at: https://indianexpress.com/article/explained/explained-what-is-the-ant-group-why-is-their-ipo-suspended-6943919/. Accessed 20 November 2020.

China Banking and Insurance Regulatory Commission, People's Bank of China(2020) Zhongguo yinbao jianhui zhongguo renmin yinhang guanyu <wangluo xiaoe daikuan yewu guanli zanxing banfa (zhengqiu yijiangao)>. Available at: http://www.gov.cn/xinwen/2020-11/03/content_5556884.htm 2020/11/03. Accessed 12 December 2022.

China Daily (2019) 67jia yangqi yi huazhuan guoyou ziben yue 8601yi chongshi shebao jijin. Available at: https://china.chinadaily.com.cn/a/201910/11/WS5da0109da31099ab995e4a96.html. Accessed 30 March 2020.

Fortune China (2022) 2022《Cai fu》zhongguo 500qiang paihangbang. Available at: https://www.fortunechina.com/fortune500/c/2022-07/12/content_414336.htm. Accessed 7 November 2022.

Guotai Junan Securities (2022) 2022nian guoqi gaige zhuanti baogao. Guotai Junan Securities, Beijing.

Hancock T (2022) China crackdowns shrink private sector's slice of big business. In: Bloomberg. Available at: https://www.bloomberg.com/news/articles/2022-03-29/china-crackdowns-shrink-private-sector-s-slice-of-big-business?leadSource=uverifypercent20wall. Accessed 9 November 2022.

Hao P (2020) Guowuyuan guanyu 2019 niandu guozi xitong jianguan qiye guoyou zichan guanli qingkuang de zhuanxiang baogao. In: The National People's Congress. Available at: http://www.npc.gov.cn/npc/c30834/202010/92861cc1660044d0b4c1511083bab902.shtml#:~:text=percentE6percent88percentAApercentE8percent87percentB32019percentE5percentB9percentB4percentE5percentBApercent95percentEFpercentBCpercent8CpercentE5percent9BpercentBDpercentE8percentB5percent84percentE7percentB3percentBBpercentE7percentBBpercent9F,percentE6percent9Dpercent83percentE7percent9Bpercent8A47.9percentE4percentB8percent87percentE4percentBApercentBFpercentE5percent85percent83percentE3percent80percent82. Accessed 8 August 2021.

Hongkong Exchange News (2020) Application Proof of the Ant Group Co., Ltd. Available at: https://www1.hkexnews.hk/listedco/listconews/sehk/2020/1026/2020102600165.pdf. Accessed 2 November 2020; Shrivastava M (2023) The continuing saga of China's Ant Group. In: The Diplomat. Available at: https://thediplomat.com/2023/01/the-continuing-saga-of-chinas-ant-group/. Accessed 24 April 2023.

Hu ZL, Khan MS (1997) Why is China growing so fast? In: International Monetary Fund. Available at: https://www.imf.org/EXTERNAL/PUBS/FT/ISSUES8/INDEX.HTM. Accessed 6 September 2020.

Hubbard PC (2018) The nature and performance of China's State-owned Enterprises. In: The Australian National University. Available at: https://openresearch-repository.anu.edu.au/handle/1885/148705. Accessed 11 July 2023.

Kharpal A (2020) Ant Group to raise $34.5 billion, valuing it at over $313 billion, in biggest IPO of all time. In: CNBC. Available at: https://www.cnbc.com/2020/10/26/ant-group-to-raise-tktk-billion-in-biggest-ipo-of-all-time.html#:~:text=Antpercent20Grouppercent20wouldpercent20raisepercent20percent2434.5,Goldmanpercent20Sachspercent20andpercent20Wellspercent20Fargo. Accessed 11 November 2020.

Kissinger H (2011) On China. Penguin Books Ltd., New York. p.495.

Liu W (2018) Combining Marxism and China's practices for the development of a socialist political economy with Chinese characteristics. China Political Economy 1(1):30–44. https://doi.org/10.1108/CPE-09-2018-001. p.37.

References

Lu S (2022) Didi says it will proceed with delisting from NYSE. In: Wall Street Journal. Available at:https://www.wsj.com/articles/didi-says-it-will-proceed-with-delisting-from-nyse-11653310564. Accessed 8 November 2022.

Merriam CE (1984) Meiguo zhengzhi sixiangshi (A History of American Political Theories). The Commercial Press, Beijing.

Naughton B (2018) State enterprise reform today. In: Garnaut R (eds) China's 40 years of reform and development: 1978–2018. ANU Press, Canberra, p.374–384.

People's Daily (2023) Shixian minying jingji jiankang fazhan gaozhiliang fazhan. Available at: https://www.gov.cn/xinwen/2023-03/25/content_5748251.htm. Accessed 4 April 2023.

Robyn M (2020) Beijing puts Ant on a shorter leash. In: Reuters. Available at: https://www.reuters.com/article/us-china-ant-group-breakingviews-idUSKBN27J0D4. Accessed 5 January 2020.

Robert AC (1998) The standard of living in the Soviet Union, 1928–1940. The Journal of Economic History 58(4):1063–1089.

She Y (2022) Woguo minying qiye shuliang 10nian fanliangfan zai qiye zongliang zhong zhanbi chao jiucheng. In: Economic Daily. Available at: https://www.gov.cn/xinwen/2022-10/12/content_5717756.htm. Accessed 9 November 2022.

Shen XF (2002) Qingdai caizheng shouru guimo yu jiegou bianhua shulun. Social Sciences of Beijing, Beijing.

Shrivastava M (2023) The continuing saga of China's Ant Group. In: The Diplomat. Available at: https://thediplomat.com/2023/01/the-continuing-saga-of-chinas-ant-group/. Accessed 24 April 2023.

Smith A (1974) Guo fulun (The wealth of nations). The Commercial Press, Beijing.

State-owned Assets Supervision and Administration Commission (2022) Yang qi ming lu 9 (List of Central SOEs). Available at: http://www.sasac.gov.cn/n4422011/n14158800/n14158998/c14159097/content.html. Accessed 7 November 2022.

The Economist (2020a) What Ant Group's IPO says about the future of finance. Available at: https://www.economist.com/briefing/2020/10/10/what-ant-groups-ipo-says-about-the-future-of-finance. Accessed 12 November 2020.

The Economist (2020b) Xi Jinping is trying to remake the Chinese economy. Available at: https://www.economist.com/briefing/2020/08/15/xi-jinping-is-trying-to-remake-the-chinese-economy. Accessed 10 October 2020.

The Economist (2021) Didi's removal from China's app stores marks a growing crackdown. Available at: https://www.economist.com/business/2021/07/05/didis-removal-from-chinas-app-stores-marks-a-growing-crackdown?utm_campaign=the-economist-today&utm_medium=newsletter&utm_source=salesforce-marketing-cloud&utm_term=2021-07-05&utm_content=article-link-1&etear=nl_today_1. Accessed 8 November 2021.

The Economist (2022) How Xi Jinping is damaging China's economy. Available at: https://www.economist.com/leaders/2022/05/26/how-xi-jinping-is-damaging-chinas-economy?utm_content=ed-picks-article-link-1&etear=nl_weekly_1&utm_campaign=r.the-economist-this-week&utm_medium=email.internal-newsletter.np&utm_source=salesforce-marketing-cloud&utm_term=5/26/2022&utm_id=1181419. Accessed 12 July 2022.

Wang JF (2000)Zhongguo lishi tonglun. East China Normal University Press, Shanghai.

Xi JP (2013) Xi Jinping; guan yu <Zhonggong zhongyang guanyu quanmian shenhua gaige zhongda wenti de jueding> de shuoming. In: Xinhua News Agency. Available at: http://www.xinhuanet.com//politics/2013-11/15/c_118164294.htm. Accessed 8 November 2020.

Xinhua News Agency (2020) Xi Jinping zhuchi zhaokai zhongyang quanmian shenhua gaige weiyuanhui di shisici huiyi. Available at: http://www.xinhuanet.com/politics/leaders/2020-06/30/c_1126179095.htm. Accessed 9 January 2021.

Zhang CL (2019) How much do state-owned enterprises contribute to China's GDP and employment. In: World Bank Group. Available at: http://documents.worldbank.org/curated/en/449701565248091726/How-Much-Do-State-Owned-Enterprises-Contribute-to-China-s-GDP-and-Employment. Accessed 12 April 2020.

Zhao HJ (2018) China's Long-term economic development: How have economy and governance evolved since 500 BC?. Edward Elgar Publishing, Cheltenham.

Zhu LJ, Leng C (2020) China tells Ant to expect scrutiny of credit business ahead of record listing. In: Reuters. Available at: https://www.reuters.com/article/us-ant-group-ipo-china-regulator/china-tells-ant-to-expect-scrutiny-of-credit-business-ahead-of-record-listing-sources-idUKKBN27J14I. Accessed 15 November 2020.

Zhu J, Xu J (2023) China ends Ant Group's regulatory revamp with nearly $1 billion fine. In: Reuters. Available at: https://www.reuters.com/technology/china-end-ant-groups-regulatory-revamp-with-fine-least-11-bln-sources-2023-07-07/. Accessed 9 July 2023.

Chapter 4
A Fusion of Worlds: Interplay of Chinese Tradition and Marxism

> "China seemed to me to have remained essentially Confucian in its belief in a single, universal, generally applicable truth as the standard of individual conduct and social cohesion. What Communism had done, I suggested, was to establish Marxism as the content of that truth." (Kissinger, 2011)
> —Henry Kissinger, the 56th U.S. Secretary of State

Abstract Political philosophy significantly contributes to shaping a country's logic of governance and policy developments. This chapter argues that, although China is defined as a 'communist regime', its traditional political philosophies exert a greater influence on its contemporary logic of governance than Marxism–Leninism. Contemporary China can be regarded as a hybrid model—with Marxism serving as the guiding state ideology and traditional political philosophies, namely, the 'rule of ritual', the 'rule of law', and the 'rule of virtue', forming the underlying logic of governance. This chapter is structured to sequentially explain the origins of these three political philosophies and their influences on modern China's governance and decision-making. Additionally, it delves into the interplay between Chinese traditional political philosophies and Marxism in the contemporary era. The chapter argues that the recent resurgence of Marxism does not intend to replace the foundational governance ethos moulded by traditional political philosophies, nor does it seek to ignite fresh class conflicts. Rather, it serves as an instrument to strengthen the rule of the CCP, reinforce its state economic strategy, and rally the populace under a shared national ideology.

The Rule of Ritual: 'Know Your Place'

Political philosophies are crucial in shaping a country's logic of governance and policy developments. While China is known as a 'communist regime', its long-standing philosophical tradition exerts more influence on its contemporary decision-making model than Marxism–Leninism. Three key political philosophies—the 'rule of ritual', the 'rule of law', and the 'rule of virtue'—have significantly impacted Chinese logic of governance. The contemporary Chinese governance model can be perceived as a synthesis of these elements. This chapter will trace the steps of notable Chinese philosophers and examine the evolution of Chinese political philosophy from the Zhou dynasty to the Han dynasty. It aims to explore how various political philosophies were utilised by Imperial China to govern the country and manage its people, and how these philosophies have collectively shaped the logic of governance and decision-making of contemporary China.

The rule of ritual is the primary tool applied by the Western Zhou dynasty (1046–771 BCE) to govern China. It refers to a normative set of rules and ritual practices that defined the social customs proper to the people of China.[1] This system laid a foundation for fundamental philosophical advancements that became the bedrock of Chinese values and the logic of governance throughout the subsequent history of China. This significant contribution is a primary reason why the Western Zhou dynasty is regarded as the most culturally impactful among the early Chinese dynasties.

According to *The Book of Rites*, a collection of texts describing the social norms, administration, and ceremonial rites of the Western Zhou dynasty, the main purpose of the rule of ritual was to drive the acceptance of hierarchical social relationships: 'know your place' was the guiding principle.[2] This principle was put into practice through a method of standardisation. Under the rule of rituals, myriad facets of human existence were regulated and standardised by prescribed behaviours, encompassing everything from special gestures and specific language mandated for certain situations to the recitation of select texts, the wearing of particular types of clothing, or the consumption of designated food and drink, all founded on a stringent social hierarchy.[3] These rules and norms were uniformly applied across all territories and among all individuals under the regime's jurisdiction. Violation or overstepping of these norms was regarded as a grave offence. From this standpoint, it could be argued that the rule of ritual signifies an early manifestation of law in China.[4]

Two related concepts—or 'moral imperatives'—were central to the rule of ritual: obedience towards social and political superiors (e.g. from the ruled to the rulers), and gratitude towards superior family members (e.g. from child to parent). Both represent hierarchical relationships accompanied by asymmetrical emotional exchanges. In the realm of political relations, attributes such as 'loyalty', 'integrity', and 'righteousness' were necessitated to steer people's behaviour. Concerning blood relations, 'love' is expressed as a sense of gratitude or familial devotion, known in Chinese as 'xiao', which essentially embodies obedience. These character traits continue to be highly esteemed and promoted among the Chinese people today.

If disparities between hierarchical ranks were underscored without emphasising the resulting harmony, society could risk becoming dissonant. Therefore, the other crucial component of the rule of ritual was identified as 'yue'. 'Yue' (乐) is a Chinese term that signifies an ideal state of harmony and joy that comes from living in accordance with moral principles and social order. In practice, 'yue' is often associated

---

[1] Ashton (2017).

[2] Guoxue Collection Series Editorial Committee (2010).

[3] Peng (2012).

[4] Schuman (2020).

with 'music' played during rituals and ceremonies. The aim is to use dance, theatrical performances, and other events as a dynamic sensory platform to shape people's understanding and acceptance of a hierarchically organised society.[5] This permits the expression of emotions in a socially acceptable way, thereby promoting increased harmony and tolerance. In fact, this tradition persists today, with examples ranging from musical group exercises in corporations to New Year's theatrical broadcasts on television, or other collective activities aimed at 'pacifying the emotions' and bringing people together.

Hierarchy is not a foreign concept to Westerners, but its interpretation in political and professional environments often differs from the Chinese perspective. There exist two common metaphors that depict hierarchy in the Western contexts, which are notably absent in China. Investigating the difference can illuminate a unique comprehension of the term 'hierarchy'.

The first metaphor is that of the 'shepherd and the sheep'. As discussed in Chap. 3, the significance of pastoralism in the Western economy is considerable. One subsequent implication is the prevalence of pastoral imagery and references in the Western culture, most prominently in Christianity. Regardless of whether leaders portray themselves as a 'good shepherd', or common people resist those in power by asserting 'I'm not a sheep', the relationship depicted by this metaphor inherently involves a distinction between human and animal that in some way translates to social interactions.

The second recurrent metaphor is the relationship between the master and the slave. This metaphor is extensively represented throughout the Western philosophical and political discourses, deeply rooted in a socioeconomic reality where slavery had a significant role until fairly recent history. For instance, in the United States, the practice was abolished just over 150 years ago, but it continues to influence racial relations in the nation to this day. Once again, this relationship delineates a difference of nature between the master, who is a part of society, and the slave who lacks civic rights, reduced to the status of property, existing somewhere between the human and the animal.

In the Chinese context, there is a recurring distinction between 'Chinese' and 'barbarian'. While 'barbarian' is often associated with occupying a lower position in the hierarchy, it is important to note that the term only implies a perceived cultural inferiority and does not necessarily dehumanise. Quite on the contrary, since hierarchy is central to the organisation of 'civilised' Chinese society, being part of that hierarchy is a fundamental part of being human. In the Chinese context, a 'civilised' human is one belonging to a hierarchically structured collective, where obedience to those in higher positions is expected, and prioritising collective duty over personal interests is the norm. The downside is that social hierarchy has come to be perceived as an objective fact of existence. After a few thousand years of following the rule of ritual, Chinese people within the system are prone to accepting despotism, complying

---

[5] Peng (2012).

with ancestral laws and traditions, often without exercising independent thought, which raises the risk of individual alienation.[6]

The indispensable impact of the rule of ritual on the Chinese society is evident. At the dawn of the twentieth century, Chinese scholar Liao Qichao highlighted the negative impact of the rule of ritual on China's development. He argued that it played a role in the country's lagging behind the West in modern times, the inability of democracy to take root in China, and even the eventual collapse of the Chinese Republic.[7] However, despite decades of modernisation, China remains a hierarchical society. This hierarchical approach is particularly evident within the bureaucratic system, where entitlement to benefits is strictly determined by one's rank. This can be observed in various aspects, ranging from transportation classes and medical benefits to office and housing sizes. The required obedience for hierarchy extends beyond politics and into business environments, where employees are expected to demonstrate deference to their superiors. Adherence to prescribed social etiquette also remains important in contemporary China. For instance, customs, such as specific seating arrangements for public gatherings, are still followed. Consequently, the emphasis on relationships over individuals and responsibilities over rights has perpetuated the enduring presence of hierarchy and authority within Chinese political thought. This has ultimately led to the pervasive notion that everyone must 'know their place' within the system.

The Hundred Schools of Thought

As the Western Zhou dynasty lost its power, the Spring and Autumn period (770–476 BCE) and the Warring States period (475–221 BCE) began. Those periods saw the 'disintegration of rituals': disintegration of the core governing order of the Western Zhou dynasty, and struggle for survival among warring regional lords in competition with each other. Although it was a chaotic period filled with strife and brutal conflicts, it was also a time of significant cultural and intellectual growth. Without a dominant political power in China, philosophers could move from city to city, freely share their political philosophy in public settings, and recruit students. This period becomes known as the 'Contention of a Hundred Schools of Thought'. The situation bore similarities to that prevailing on the other side of Asia between the city-states of classical Greece: a period of political disunity during which philosophical debates flourished.[8]

Amid the numerous intellectual movements vying for prominence since the collapse of the Western Zhou dynasty, diverse approaches to governance, warfare, and diplomacy emerged. However, they share a common objective: discovering the most suitable method to consolidate the fragmented states and restore order to the nation.

---

[6] Schuman (2020).

[7] Ibid.

[8] Davis and Puett (2015).

Legalism and Confucianism stand out as the most notable political philosophies of this time, establishing new principles for Chinese administration after the breakdown of the rule of ritual. The concepts and perspectives debated and honed throughout this period have left an enduring impact on the lifestyles and social awareness of people in East Asian nations and the global East Asian diaspora to this day.

The Rule of Law: Enrich the State

The period of the Hundred Schools of Thought ended with the establishment of the Qin dynasty in 221 BCE, and the subsequent purge of dissent of other political thought. This purge was accompanied by the dominance of a philosophy known as Legalism. It is widely acknowledged that Legalism laid the military, administrative, political, and economic foundations that strengthened the Qin state and eventually enabled the Qin to conquer its six rival states, unifying China into a centralised country for the first time in history.

It should be noted here that Legalism—and its associated logic of governance—is relatively unknown outside China, especially compared to the thought of Confucius. The basic tenets of Legalism evoke arguments made in Hobbes's *Leviathan*. According to Legalism, human nature is inherently evil, necessitating control through the rule of law. This philosophy advocates for centralised state power, which is achieved through a stringent legal system and clear rewards and punishments, to maintain a strong and unified nation. Essentially, Legalism operates on a system of incentives that appeal to human desires, commonly referred to today as the 'carrots and sticks' approach, consistently applied through the utilisation of pain and pleasure as motivators.[9]

The word 'law', as used in the context of Chinese Legalism, has a very different meaning from that usually understood in a Western context. This philosophy would probably be better referred to as 'rule of administration' or 'rule of administrative methods'—the main proposition being that the various standards of administrative operations are formally stipulated in enforceable legal documents.[10] This way of specifying administrative details in textual form can be understood as 'rational administration', and has the characteristics of being computable, predictable, controllable, and logical.[11]

The main thinker behind Legalism was Shang Yang (390–338 BCE), a philosopher and politician from the Qin dynasty. In *The Book of Lord Shang,* a foundational philosophical work for the School of Legalism, he outlined a comprehensive range of strategies for governing the nation, which encompassed the creation and enforcement of laws, the distribution of bureaucratic tasks, and the establishment of a nationwide

---

[9] Schell and Delury (2013).
[10] Goldin (2011).
[11] Garfield and Edelglass (2011).

administrative system.[12] This book provides meticulous instructions on a wide array of governance matters, from reclaiming wasteland to bolster the economy, to the collection of taxes, construction of a formidable military, and recruitment of officials.[13] The approaches suggested in this work are notably more pragmatic than those presented in Confucian texts.

Legalism is often compared to Machiavellianism since it pursues consolidating and strengthening the wealth and power of the state to achieve stability and order. Shang Yang defined the goal of the rule of law in one simple phrase: "Enrich the state and strengthen its military power."[14] Indeed, the legalists considered the rule of law from the standpoint of the ruler, not ordinary people. As for the people, legalists consider that it is most beneficial for them to live in a nation that is powerful, stable, well ordered, and economically thriving.[15] Frankly, this line of thought and narrative continues to be embraced and advocated by the CCP today. Furthermore, legalists even believe that the state and the people have opposite interests. Shang Yang states that the weakness of the people means that the country is strong, and the weakness of the state means that the people are strong.[16] Therefore, a properly governed country will try its best to weaken its people.[17]

It is understandable that Legalism blossomed and established itself as the principal political ideology during the Qin dynasty. This is because the paramount objective of the Qin dynasty was to construct a robust, effective, and economically dependable nation-state that could assert control over the plains of Central China—a goal that was successfully achieved with the endorsement of Legalism. Moreover, as part of the measures to reinforce Legalism as the official governing philosophy, books that were seen as inconsistent with this philosophy were often subjected to censorship or destruction. Additionally, proponents of other philosophies faced significant pressures, and in some cases, severe punishment. The excesses of Legalism made the Qin regime very unpopular with the people of the time. After the Qin were overthrown, Legalism was demoted from its prominent role in favour of Confucianism. Yet, though short-lived, the impact of Legalism endured.

The Qin dynasty holds the distinction of being the first to successfully 'unify' China under a single rule. The Xia dynasty discussed in Chap. 1, and the Shang dynasty discussed in Chap. 2 may be regarded as the inaugural civilisations within the geographical boundaries of what is presently referred to as China. However, they did not 'unify' the country, as their control was restricted to a minor portion of northern China. The Western Zhou dynasty, on the other hand, had an emperor who served primarily as a symbolic link between autonomous regional feudal lords. The emperor's power during this time can be likened to the influence of the Holy Roman

---

[12] Pines (2017).

[13] Ibid.

[14] Schell and Delury (2013).

[15] Pines (2017).

[16] Ibid.

[17] Ibid.

Emperor during Medieval Europe or the Japanese emperor during the Shogunate era—essentially, quite limited.

Emperor Qin Shihuang revolutionised this system, bringing an end to the segmented states and instituting a centralised structure where all lands under the heavens were considered the emperor's domain. These lands could be bestowed upon his officials as gifts, but he also held the power to reclaim them at his discretion. The emperor held direct authority over the core territories of China—the basins of the Yellow and Yangtze Rivers. Symbolically, his dominion was perceived as extending across 'the entire world'. I will return to this point in Chap. 8, when discussing the Chinese model of international relations known as the 'Tianxia' system.

When Emperor Qin Shihuang unified China, he did not claim to be simply creating a new dynasty—one that would presumably decline eventually, and be replaced. Rather, he claimed to be bringing the dynastic cycle to an end, and create an enduring empire: one that would last for ten thousand generations.[18] Supporting this claim, not only did the Qin dynasty unify the land, it also strove to create a shared identity for 'Chinese people'. This involved the introduction of a common script of written characters, a new calendar and a set of standards for weights and measures. Efforts currently conducted by the CCP to strengthen the Chinese identity can be seen as an extension of this enduring tradition. I will further discuss this point in Chap. 8.

The Qin dynasty fell soon thereafter, but the vision of an enduring empire most certainly did not—nor did the sense of shared civilisational belonging. This sense of a shared culture and destiny, and enthusiasm for the idea of establishing an 'enduring empire', inspired numerous subsequent emperors to appreciate the worth of Legalism. Though harsh, the system had proven effective in unifying land and country, and supporting a centralised bureaucratic rule which was able to oversee massive public works. Consequently, over the last two millennia, despite Confucius's rule of virtue emerging as the prevailing political philosophy, Legalism did not vanish. Chinese emperors and politicians often blended elements of Legalism with the Confucian ethos to achieve their objectives, merging legal efficiency and effectiveness with moral benevolence. Hence, it is broadly claimed that Legalism did not fade away but was instead integrated into the Confucian rule of virtue. This concept is typically articulated using the phrase '*Wai ru nei fa*', translating to 'Confucian on the outside, legalist on the inside'. This implies that the Chinese emperor employed the Confucius rule of virtue to harmonise people's mindsets, while resorting to Legalism for the actual administration of the nation.

Shang Yang's Dilemma

A central characteristic of Shang Yang's Legalism lies in its primary goal to support the state's endeavours to strengthen the nation and establish an effective administration. However, Shang Yang recognised a critical dilemma: namely, that the 'rule

---

[18] Davis and Puett (2015).

of law', no matter how well honed, remains vulnerable to the failures of the 'rule of man'. It means that the quality of the country's governance system is only ever equal to the quality of the people who make and execute this system. And there is always the risk that the emperor or other people in positions of power may—for good or bad intentions—issue laws that result in chaos, confusion, contradiction, thereby undermining the rule of law. This dilemma puzzled Shang Yang for all his life and has continued to puzzle China for more than 2,000 years, up until today.

In today's China, the process for issuing laws still reflects, to a certain degree, the ancient model of imperial decrees, where laws were personally issued by the emperor.[19] One could describe China's legal system today as involving three different types of laws: 'general laws' voted by Chinese National People's Congress (NPC), 'policy-laws' (政策法规), and 'law-policies' (批示/指示).[20]

In China, general laws must be ratified by the NPC through a vote. However, this organ cannot be said to function as a legislature, comparable to the U.S. Congress or the British Houses of Parliament.[21] The NPC has a total of about 3,000 members who cannot be accurately labelled as true legislators, given that they are not directly elected by the people, nor do they serve as full-time salaried government representatives.[22] Despite its role in approving laws, the NPC's function tends to be more symbolic than substantial. Instead, the most crucial legislative group in China is the NPC's Standing Committee, consisting of roughly 150 members.[23] This committee actively participates in the creation and amendment of laws.

As discussed above, general laws must be ratified by the NPC through a vote. However, the 3,000 NPC members only convene annually in March, limiting the pace of legal change. The Chinese legal system involves other types of 'law-like' elements that enable it to adapt to change with flexibility, known as 'policy-laws' (政策法规) and 'law-policies' (批示/指示).[24] It should be mentioned here that the legal systems of liberal democracies also include a variety of decrees and regulations in addition to laws passed by National Assemblies—but those are considerably more prominent in China.

Policy-laws are documents formulated by party and government agencies, primarily concerning government affairs.[25] Typically, they encompass methods, guidelines, industry standards, as well as regulations and rules formulated by the Central Committee of the CCP, the State Council, and their respective departments.[26]

On the other hand, 'law-policies' constitute "meetings, notices, instructions, and speeches that are given legal effectiveness because they emanate from high-level

---

[19] Chen (2005).
[20] Ibid.
[21] Saich (2015).
[22] Ibid.
[23] Ibid.
[24] Chen (2005).
[25] Ibid.
[26] Ibid.

government authorities and Party bodies".[27] They can also materialise as decisions, notes, or decrees, termed as 'Pi Shi' (批示) in Chinese, which represent written remarks or directives from a superior in response to subordinate's reports. Alternatively, they might be communicated as instructions or directions, referred to as 'Zhi Shi' (指示), which are usually orally conveyed general guidance from a higher up in reply to inquiries or reports from subordinates.[28] Unsurprisingly, new law-policies appear much more frequently than new policy-laws, because they can be made readily by a senior leader, either in writing or orally.[29]

The 'law-policies' play an important role in the Chinese legal system. Chinese legal authorities can indeed utilise this 'law-policies' mechanism to determine rights and/or responsibilities (i.e. 'law-policies' acting as civil laws), make vital decisions on critical matters like life or death (i.e. 'law-policies' serving as criminal laws), or expedite or slow down the enforcement of existing laws (i.e. 'law-policies' functioning as procedural laws).[30]

To give one example, in a speech delivered at the Central Economic Work Conference on 11 September 2020, Xi Jinping warned leading Chinese technology companies to focus their capital and capacity on improving global innovation competitiveness rather than squeezing traditional small fresh food wholesalers by using subsidies to attract more consumers to order through their mobile delivery apps.[31] This oral statement, which indirectly criticised some technology companies for creating a quasi-monopoly in the fresh food sector and manipulating prices to their advantage, was intended to be promptly adopted as new directives for these enterprises.

Consequently, following Xi Jinping's speech, the General Administration of Market Supervision and the Chinese Ministry of Commerce sprang into action on 22 December 2020, crafting 'policy-laws'—formal rules and rectification requirements—to regulate monopolistic behaviours and unfair competition among technology companies. These regulations were enacted with the intent of "thoroughly learning and implementing the spirit of the Central Economic Work Conference [hosted by Xi Jinping]".[32] By March 2021, the General Administration of Market Supervision imposed fines on five community buying apps, with a total amount of 6.5 million yuan.[33] Between January and May 2021, a total of 1,345 unfair competition cases were investigated and dealt with, with a fine amounting to 122 million yuan.[34]

Although those various law-making mechanisms can serve to increase speed and responsiveness, the coexistence of general laws, policy-laws, and law-policies typically results in a mess of conflicting directions, orders, notes, or speeches,

---

[27] Ibid. p.50.
[28] Ibid.
[29] Ibid.
[30] Ibid.
[31] Xi (2020); Chang (2020).
[32] State Administration for Market Regulation (2020).
[33] State Administration for Market Regulation (2021).
[34] Ibid.

prompting "regulatory and legal cherry-picking".[35] In addition, with policy-laws and law-policies sometimes getting the upper hand over general laws, the dividing line between government administration, judicial system, and the Party become de facto seriously blurred.[36] Indeed, the fact that a simple statement can directly and arbitrarily gain the force as law underscores the dual role the CCP and its administration play as both policy-makers and law-makers, with no proper checks and balances in place.[37] Consequently, this system poses a continuous challenge to the overall confidence in the Chinese government.

The Rule of Virtue: Strengthening Centralisation

Confucian thinking spreads throughout the so-called 'School of Literati' (*ru*). As the word 'literati' implies, the basic goal of Confucianism can be understood as promoting education, more specifically moral education through a shared canon of texts. This canon, known as the Confucian Classics, consists of nine core items: the Four Books and the Five Classics. The Four Books—*The Great Learning, The Doctrine of the Mean, The Analects of Confucius,* and *Mencius*—are fundamental texts by Confucius and his disciples, epitomising Confucianism. The Five Classics—*The Classic of Poetry, The Book of Documents, The Book of Rites, I Ching,* and *The Spring and Autumn Annals*—are pre-Qin works, embodying significant elements of Chinese tradition within the Confucian canon. These texts provided a foundation for establishing the ethical framework of traditional society and formed the central content of the National Civil Service Exam. Chinese emperors utilised Confucianism as a means to foster conformity and a common set of standards, especially among bureaucrats responsible for aiding in national governance.

Confucius's dominant influence in China's logic of governance can be traced back to 134 BCE during the Han dynasty. The Han dynasty has "similarly often been compared with the Roman Empire—a period when eastern Eurasia came to be dominated by a single major empire just as western Eurasia was".[38] During the reign of Emperor Wu of Han dynasty, Dong Zhongshu, a philosopher and politician, formalised the concept of 'displacing a hundred schools of thought and honouring Confucianism exclusively'. This implies that Confucian thought was advanced as the official ideology of the Chinese imperial state. From that point on, Confucianism continued to shape the entire ideological, philosophical, and cultural landscape of Chinese society until the establishment of the Chinese Republic in 1912.

To better understand Confucius as a person and his impact in Chinese history, one could draw a parallel with the foremost Renaissance humanist, Petrarch. Petrarch

---

[35] Chen (2005).
[36] Ibid.
[37] Ibid.
[38] Davis and Puett (2015).

saw the misery around him as the effect of a precipitous decline in morality, particularly among the rulers of prosperous Italian city-states in conflict with each other.[39] The Italy of his time, divided between multiple warring principalities, somehow resembled the China of the Warring States period. In order to improve the elites' morality—and the societies they ruled—Petrarch and his followers began an educational revolution. They took the skeleton of medieval grammatical education, which had been used mostly to train notaries and city officials, and refashioned it into a new form of education, the *studia humanitatis*, what we now call the humanities.[40] The purpose of this pedagogical programme was not professional training, but rather creating a virtuous leadership class in Italian city-states, unified by a common language, common respect for a core set of texts, and a common set of values and virtues.[41] The Confucian perspective and objective, in many ways, align with those of Petrarch.

Understanding the Confucian approach to governance does require understanding the rules of ritual that I described earlier. That is because Confucius took it as his life mission to restore the governing order of the Zhou dynasty. As with the Humanists of the Italian Renaissance, a 'restoration programme' was at play. There are a lot of similarities between the model proposed by Confucius and the rule of ritual. In particular, both focus on 'relationships' as a key mechanism to reduce the difficulty of managing society. However, when it comes to the relationship between the ruler and the ruled, Confucius emphasised reciprocity—rather than the unilateral model of hierarchical relationships articulated under the rule of ritual. This concept is encapsulated in a famous quote from the Confucian philosopher Xun Zi (310–238 BCE), who likened the ruler to a boat and the people to water, stating, "Water can carry the boat, or it can sink it."[42]

Also, unlike Legalism, which enforces obedience through severe punishment, Confucianism aims to strengthen obedience through moral enlightenment. The goal is for people to respect and obey the regime 'from the heart', internalising hierarchy as a stabilising force. Confucius pursued this aim by emphasising morality, leading to the encapsulation of his political philosophy as the 'rule of virtue'. Central to this moral framework is the virtue of 'benevolence'. Ruling with benevolence entails establishing a moral connection between the ruler and the ruled. A 'benevolent' ruler must actively cultivate and fulfil their inherent sense of responsibility towards the well-being of the people. 'Benevolent' people must actively contribute to the harmonious functioning of society, upholding moral values, and fulfilling their roles and duties with sincerity and righteousness.

---

[39] Peters and Hankins (2020).
[40] Ibid.
[41] Ibid.
[42] Xun (2015).

The 'Junzi': A Diversified 'Net-Like' Governance Model

According to *The Records of the Grand Historian*, Imperial China's most famous historical book, Confucius travelled for 14 years among the kingdoms of Wei, Song, Chen, Cai, and Chu in search of an incorrupt ruler.[43] Ruler after ruler failed to appreciate the moral aspect of governance emphasised by Confucius, and his high standards forced him to continue his journey.[44]

Retrospectively, the story underlines how hard it is to find an incorrupt ruler, willing to be bound by morality and responsibility. It also reveals the core challenge for which Confucianism seeks to offer a solution: what force could consistently push rulers to deepen their moral norms and practise their sense of responsibility? By nature, the Chinese governance model works as a one-way, top-down, and linear system. Therefore, it can easily operate as a 'dictatorship', where decisions merely reflect the whims of the ruler. With this comes inherent fragility, and the risk of chaos. By contrast, a solid government requires a diversified 'net-like' governance model, where the diverse interest groups of society exert mutual control and restraint.

Confucianism dealt with this issue by establishing a group of political elites called 'gentlemen' (in Chinese, 'Junzi', from the word 'jun' meaning 'lead'). Their mission was to display exemplary moral behaviours, supervise the work of government alongside the emperor, and safeguard the value of benevolence.[45] The key to the practice of Confucian benevolence was therefore to identify the people with potential to become 'gentlemen', educate them appropriately, and place them in positions to influence governance. Essentially, employing concepts from Western political philosophy, this model could be understood as reducing the risks associated with Chinese governance by incorporating a layer of aristocracy. This aristocratic layer would undergo education in the 'humanities', fostering and refining virtue through their study of the Confucian canon. The standard of being a 'Junzi' is still applied among Party members in China today. There is an implicit judgement that people must meet the moral standards of being a 'Junzi' to join the Party and get promoted. More interestingly, when people find out some officials are corrupt, they call them 'hypocrisy junzi'.

Virtue Politics

The Confucian belief that the state is the moral guardian of the people has had a profound impact on the Chinese logic of governance, laying the foundation for the political idea of 'virtue politics'. The gist of the idea is that political power should be strictly reserved to those who can demonstrate 'virtue'. That notion may not be foreign to a Western reader. In fact, it is as old as the notion of democracy in the

---

[43] Csikszentmihalyi (2020).
[44] Ibid.
[45] Qian (2012).

Virtue Politics

West. Plato defended the ideal of 'virtue politics' in *The Republic*.[46] The founding fathers of the United States and nineteenth-century political theorists such as John Stuart Mill and Alexis de Tocqueville also put forward political proposals to base democratic governance on virtue.[47]

When discussing virtue politics, it is worth noting that the Chinese conception of virtue puts the emphasis on 'virtue from the heart' or 'inner virtue' (i.e. thinking and wanting the good). The Confucian tradition therefore focuses on developing character traits which lead to 'being' a good leader, rather than 'doing good'. In addition, the Chinese tradition recognises that 'virtue' in an ordinary citizen differs from the 'virtue' needed in a leader. The ordinary citizen only needs to look after his or her own interest, while the leader needs to look after a much broader range of interests, including conflicting and contested interests and obligations. When facing such a contested situation, a virtuous leader should extend beyond merely adhering to procedural rules or conducting utilitarian calculations. They should concentrate not solely on a particular action or decision dictated by the situation, but on their own character as the agent of an organisation committed to public good. This engagement requires a direct consideration for others' happiness and well-being, which is expressed through both emotions and actions.

The principle of the 'rule of virtue' continues to be applicable in modern times, particularly in the way that the CCP structures its bureaucracy and governance systems. The CCP explicitly specifies in its *Regulations on the Selection and Appointment of Party and Government Leading Cadres* that the primary criteria for selecting and evaluating cadres are 'virtue' and 'capability'.[48] Among those two, the Party prioritises virtue over capabilities.[49] A person of virtue, even if initially lacking in skills and experience, can be nurtured through comprehensive work experience at all tiers of the government until they are competent enough for promotion. However, developing virtue is not as straightforward. Moreover, a capable leader devoid of virtue might prove more disruptive than a person of average ability but great virtue, with the potential to misuse power and trigger social instability.

To summarise, the selection of Chinese officials does not hinge solely on popular vote or a meritocratic process that prioritises technical proficiency, but significantly weighs their moral qualities. The idea being that the moral qualities will not only enable them to govern, but will also set a moral example that will transform the people.[50] In this model, cultivating morality becomes a political activity in which the state consciously plays a guiding and standardising role of a moral guide. Chapter 5 looks more in depth at those ideas and the mechanisms to put them in practice.

---

[46] Brown (2017).

[47] Devigne (2006); Campagna (2007)

[48] The Central People's Government of the People's Republic of China (2019).

[49] Ibid.

[50] Bell (2016).

China Through the Looking Glass

A famous passage from Montesquieu's *Spirit of the Laws* associates different political regimes to a dominant 'feeling' among the people: each regime is conceived as reliant on a certain type of emotional driver, and recognisable by the dominant feeling among the people. In this model, despotism relies on fear, monarchy on honour, and a republic on virtue. After reviewing China's three dominant political philosophies, the rule of ritual, the rule of law, and the rule of virtue, one may argue that the Chinese logic of governance aims for a balance between the three emotional drivers—ritual, with its insistence on hierarchy, has to do with honour, Legalism with fear, and Confucianism with virtue. Despite the distinctive nature of these emotional drivers, the rule of ritual, the rule of law, and the rule of virtue all share a common goal—strengthening the legitimacy of state power, managing the population, and maintaining social order. For two millennia, Chinese emperors have utilised Confucian values and rituals as the moral foundation, alongside legalist rules and procedures, to implement decisions and policies.[51]

In addition, all three models share a fundamental agreement that people should be divided into two kinds. The rulers who have a quasi-sacred quality must have superior moral attributes, and their mission is to issue the right orders for the subjects to follow; the ruled who are comparatively insignificant, expected to be relatively ignorant, and their duty is to obey the orders of their rulers, acting as the rulers expect.[52] While Legalists advocated for rule of law, expecting impartiality, they insisted that only rulers formulate laws, placing them above the law.[53] The law serves to control the populace, not to limit rulers. Thus, a common loophole in all three Chinese governance models lies in the individual-centric decision-making; the decision quality hinges on the quality of individuals making them. This challenge, persistent throughout China's history, remains today.

The present-day functioning of the CCP highlights this challenge. Although China has evolved into a modern nation governed by law, its highest level of decision-making is controlled by a limited number of individuals within the CCP. This approach has contributed to considerable turmoil in China's past, including events like the 'Great Leap Forward' and the 'Cultural Revolution'. Before the 20th CCP National Congress in October 2022, factions like the Shanghai Clique and the Youth League existed within the top echelons of leadership, providing a certain degree of checks and balances. These factions facilitated alternative political options and necessitated negotiation and compromise among CCP leadership. However, the ascent of Xi Jinping's loyalists to nearly all high-ranking positions has diminished the efficacy of these intra-party checks and balances. As a result, Xi Jinping's personal aims and visions now predominantly influence key decisions. As discussed in Chap. 2, the disadvantages of this method are clear, leading to static bureaucratic dynamics, stifled innovation, and possibly heightened risks in the Taiwan Strait due to a lack of

---

[51] Zhao (2015).

[52] Zhang (2002).

[53] Ibid.

A Hybrid Model: Blending Marxism with Tradition

During the late Qing dynasty and Republican periods, against the background of a collapsing country with wars and chaos, there have been numerous anti-tradition voices among Chinese intellectuals, dismissing traditional Chinese culture as sick and useless. Mao Zedong is one of those. Mao Zedong believed that the Confucian tradition weakened China, and the 'harmony' promoted was a form of slavery.[54] He believed that, by emphasising harmony to such an extent, traditionalists had denied their country the kind of energy, vigour, and innovation that reformers had come to so admire in the West and Japan.[55]

From its establishment in 1921, the CCP has held Marxism as the cornerstone of its ideological framework. In Mao Zedong's words: "From the Opium War in 1840 to the eve of the May 4th Movement in 1919, a total of more than 70 years, the Chinese did not have any ideological weapons to resist imperialism…till the Russian Revolution of 1917 awakened the Chinese, and the Chinese learned something new, which is Marxism-Leninism."[56] This narrative conveys a powerful story: under the guidance of Marxist and Leninist ideology, the CCP triumphed over both the Japanese and the Nationalists, ultimately establishing the People's Republic of China in 1949, overcoming humiliation inflicted by foreign powers.[57]

Indeed, during its first 30 years in power, the CCP transformed China mainly in accordance with Marxist and Leninist principles, regarding them as modern China's state ideology.[58] However, in restoring the economic and social costs caused by Mao Zedong's 'Great Leap Forward' and 'Cultural Revolution', the CCP was forced to adjust its Marxist and Leninist doctrines.[59] In the mid-1970s, Deng Xiaoping introduced 'socialism with Chinese characteristics' to relax the ideological conformity set by Mao Zedong, and let economic development take priority. As a result, class struggle has been replaced by the managed efficiency of economic development.

With the onset of the 'reform and opening up' era, when the CCP introduced market reforms and permitted private sector entrepreneurs into the Party, it has been debated whether Marxism still has any de facto influence on the Party's value system, or if the CCP has in fact rejected orthodox Marxism and Leninism as well as Mao Zedong Thought (or at least basic thought within orthodox thinking).[60] Further down

---

[54] Schell and Delury (2013).
[55] Ibid.
[56] Mao (1991).
[57] Cheek and Ownby (2018).
[58] Ibid.
[59] Sundqvist (2016).
[60] Shambaugh (2008).

the track, under Hu Jintao's administration, the CCP incrementally revived Confucian heritage. Hu Jintao's concepts of harmony and virtuous leadership are seen as signs of Confucian rather than Marxist influence.

China's remarkable economic success produced new challenges for the CCP, primarily in the form of increased social and intellectual diversity.[61] When Xi Jinping assumed power in 2012, he advocated for a reinvigorated commitment to Marxism. This renewed affirmation of Marxism played a critical role in the development of 'Xi Jinping Thought on Socialism with Chinese Characteristics for a New Era', which was incorporated into the CCP's constitution after the 19th CCP National Congress. However, this rejuvenation of Marxism is not intended to spark a new period of class conflict, but rather to function as a tool to address the diverse challenges currently faced by the CCP.

Firstly, Marxism is a tool to strengthen the CCP's legitimacy against liberal democracy.[62] As discussed in Chap. 2, without democratic elections and grappling with the fragile performance legitimacy brought by a slowing economy, the CCP is seeking alternative sources of legitimacy, such as doctrinal legitimacy. Amid the prevailing narrative in China that 'the East is rising, and the West is declining', Marxism underscores the contradictions in capitalist societies and prophesies the eventual rise of a socialist and communist future. This provides the CCP with a theoretical basis to claim its position at the helm of global progression, underscoring the need for powerful leadership and a formidable party for success. Within the Party, a revitalised commitment to Marxism is crucial to uphold CCP party discipline and ensure effective party governance.

Additionally, Marxism functions as a tool to enact the state's economic policies, such as 'regulating disorderly expansion of capital' and promoting 'common prosperity'. As discussed in Chap. 3, the persisting mistrust between the state and businessmen, coupled with fears of capitalists destabilising social harmony, prompted the CCP to take strict measures against the private sector. With its advocacy for a dominant role of public ownership and its emphasis on fairness, Marxism offers an economic theory that supports the CCP's actions in reinforcing SOEs and intervening in the economy.

Last but not least, Marxism acts as a unifying tool to rally the Chinese population behind a shared national ideology. The core DNA of any country's political philosophy and governance logic lies in its own traditional culture, with foreign ideas only supplementing that core. However, as this chapter reveals, there have yet to emerge fully developed modern social theories from the intricate and multi-dimensional realm of traditional Chinese culture. Hence, Marxism is utilised as a guiding framework for interpreting traditional Chinese culture. Xi Jinping has emphasised the need to adapt Marxism to the unique realities of China and merge it with the finer aspects of traditional Chinese culture to ensure its effectiveness.[63] There are three main aspects to consider in this regard.

---

[61] Cheek and Ownby (2018).

[62] Sundqvist (2016).

[63] Ministry of Foreign Affairs of the People's Republic of China (2020).

First of all, Marxism resonates with several governance principles inherent in traditional Chinese culture, enhancing its acceptance by the Chinese people. For instance, the Yin-yang principle, discussed in Chap. 3, exhibits similarities with the Marxist doctrine of dialectical materialism. Also, both Confucianism and Marxism emphasise social equality, fairness, and justice. Secondly, Marxism's modernity compensates for the lack of universality in traditional Chinese culture. The fusion of these two allows for a more extensive application in a global context, thus augmenting the impact of Chinese tradition. Lastly, blending Marxism with traditional Chinese culture strengthens the case against embracing Western-style governance or transitioning towards liberal democracy. It promotes the notion that China can craft a unique political trajectory that builds upon its philosophical heritage, invigorated by Marxist principles.

In conclusion, one can argue that contemporary China is a hybrid model—where Marxism operates as the guiding state ideology, and traditional Chinese political philosophies, integrating the rule of ritual, law, and virtue, shape the nation's fundamental logic of governance. China's logic of governance primarily stems from its geographical and historical roots. This system prioritises stability, centralised power, and the vital role of virtuous leadership. Its economic model focuses on material growth to secure people's survival and welfare, maintains government control over the economy, and imposes restrictions on capitalists and businesspeople to prevent chaos. These elements form the institutional inertia, prevalent throughout Chinese history and currently embraced by the CCP. However, inertia alone is not the only driving force. When these factors are synergistically combined, they are expected to facilitate social and economic equilibrium for China.

One question that naturally arises from the above discussion is: to what extent do we need to tolerate or respect a society with sharply contrasting political outlooks?[64] This question could be overlooked in the past when cultural and political homogeneity was the norm within many societies, reducing the urgency to explore differing political viewpoints. However, in the current global landscape, addressing this question demands thoughtful consideration of unprecedented obstacles such as climate change and the disruptive impact of artificial intelligence. Given that no single nation holds clear and proven solutions to those challenges, to navigate the uncertain and disruptive era, we must engage with divergent political and governance models across various regions of the world.[65] This requires fostering political standards and moral practices that draw insights from a diverse range of political traditions to develop effective solutions. The role of China, due to its influence on significant global matters, becomes critical in this equation. In this era of uncertainty, the aim should not be to approve the Chinese methods unconditionally, but rather to treat it as a provocation for rethinking and retesting established paradigms. Such a viewpoint allows us to interpret the structural components of governance systems as choices rather than immutable norms. In this process, we might discover novel and more effective strategies to tackle the urgent common global issues at hand.

---

[64] Bell (2017).

[65] Ibid.

References

Ashton CH (2017) To rule by ritual: The theorization of ritual psychology in the bamboo texts of guodian. The University of British Columbia. Available at: https://doi.org/10.14288/1.0354456. Accessed 18 August 2020.

Bell D (2016) Xianneng zhengzhi: Weishenme shangxianzhi bi xuanju minzhuzhi geng shihe zhongguo. CITI Press, Beijing.

Bell D (2017) Comparing political values in China and the West: What can be learned and why it matters. Annual Review of Political Science 20(1):93–110, p.95.

Brown E (2017) Plato's ethics and politics in the Republic. In: The Stanford Encyclopedia of Philosophy. Available at: https://plato.stanford.edu/entries/plato-ethics-politics/. Accessed 23 January 2020. One might look at other works of Ancient philosophy, such as Aristotle's *Nichomachean Ethics* or Plutarch's *Life of Solon* as articulating the concepts of virtue and politics.

Campagna N (2007) Virtue in Tocqueville's America. Amerikastudien/American Studies 52(2):169–186.

Chang S (2020) Shequ tuangou zhengyi beihou shidui hulianwang jutou keji chuangxin de gengduo qidai. People's Daily, 11 December 2020.

Cheek T, Ownby D (2018) Make China Marxist again. In: Dissent Magazine. Available at: https://www.dissentmagazine.org/article/making-china-marxist-again-xi-jinping-thought. Accessed 8 January 2020.

Chen LT (2005) Chinese policy laws and separation of powers. East Asia Law Review 1(1):49–73.

Csikszentmihalyi M (2020) Confucius. In: Stanford Encyclopedia of Philosophy. Available at: https://plato.stanford.edu/archives/sum2020/entries/confucius/. Accessed 8 May 2020.

Davis K, Puett M (2015), Periodization and 'the medieval globe': A conversation. The Medieval Globe 2(1): 1–14.

Devigne D (2006) Cultivating the individual and society: J.S. Mill's use of ancient and romantic dialectics. History of Political Thought 27(1):91–121.

Garfield JL, Edelglass W (eds) (2011) The Oxford handbook of world philosophy. Oxford University Press, Cambridge.

Goldin P (2011) Persistent misconceptions about Chinese Legalism. Journal of Chinese Philosophy 38(1):88–104.

Guoxue Collection Series Editorial Committee (2010) Shangshu liji. Jilin Publishing Group, Changchun.

Kissinger H (2011) On China. The Penguin Press, New York, p.298.

Mao ZD (1991) Mao zedong xuanji. Vol 4. People's Publishing House, Beijing, p.1471.

Ministry of Foreign Affairs of the People's Republic of China (2020) Xi Jinping sends a congratulatory letter to the CCP and world Marxist political parties forum. Available at: https://www.fmprc.gov.cn/eng/zxxx_662805/202207/t20220729_10730048.html. Accessed 18 March 2022.

Peng L (2012) Sanli rumen yanjiu. Fudan University Press, Shanghai.

Peters N, Hankins J (2020) On virtue politics. In: Public Discourse: The Journal of the Witherspoon Institute. Available at: https://www.thepublicdiscourse.com/2020/01/59123/. Accessed 19 December 2020.

Pines Y (ed) (2017) The book of lord Shang: Apologetics of state power in early China. Columbia University Press, New York.

Qian M (2012) Zhongguo lidai zhengzhi deshi. SDX Joint Publishing Company, Beijing.

Saich A (2015) The National People's Congress: Functions and membership. In: Ash Center of Harvard Kennedy School. Available at: https://ash.harvard.edu/files/ash/files/the_national_peoples_congress.pdf. Accessed 18 May 2020.

Schell O, Delury J (2013) Wealth and power: China's long march to the twenty-first century. Little, Brown Book Group, London.

Schuman M (2020) Superpower interrupted: The Chinese history of the world. Public Affairs, New York.

References

Shambaugh D (2008) China's Communist Party: Atrophy and adaptation. University of California Press, Sacramento.

State Administration for Market Regulation (2021) Dui dishi sanjie quanguo renda sici huiyi di 5122 hao jianyi de dafu. Available at: https://gkml.samr.gov.cn/nsjg/jjjzj/202110/t20211026_336099.html. Accessed 9 October 2021.

Sundqvist GJ (2016) Marxism still matters: The Chinese Communist Party's ideological description of democracy. Studia Orientalia Electronica 4:89–107.

State Administration for Market Regulation (2020) Shichang jiandu zongju lianhe shangwubu zhaokai guifan shequ tuangou zhixu xingzheng zhidaohui. Available at: https://www.gov.cn/xinwen/2020-12/22/content_5572312.htm. Accessed 28 December 2020.

The Central People's Government of the People's Republic of China (2019) Zhongguo zhongyang yinfa <dangzheng lingdao ganbu xuanba renyong gongzuo tiaoli>. Available at: http://www.gov.cn/zhengce/2019-03/17/content_5374532.htm. Accessed 10 November 2019.

Xi JP (2020) Xi Jinping zhuchi zhaokai kexuejia zuotanhui bing fabiao zhongyao jianghua. In: Xinhua News Agency. Available at: http://www.xinhuanet.com/politics/leaders/2020-09/11/c_1126483955.htm. Accessed 3 March 2021.

Xun K (2015) Wang zhi. In: Xun zi. Zhonghua Book Company, Beijing, p.121.

Zhang XM (2002) On two ancient Chinese administrative ideas: Rule of virtue and rule by law. Culture Mandala: The Bulletin of the Centre for East-West Cultural and Economic Studies 5(1):1–5.

Zhao DX (2015) The Confucian-Legalist state: A new theory of Chinese history. Oxford University Press, Oxford.

Chapter 5
A Contested System: Decision-Making Dynamics in China

> *"It is too easy to mistake China for a monopolistic, centralised state."* (Paulson, 2015)
> —Henry Paulson, the 74th U.S. Secretary of the Treasury

Abstract Absolute autocracy—where central institutions exert a strict monopoly on all aspects of power—exists only in theory. In reality, a state must rely on a network of trusted individuals to implement orders from the centre. This chapter discusses the complex power dynamics between the central and local governments in China, arguing that the policy-making process is a contested one, characterised by inter- and intra-government competition, as opposed to being driven by a unitary rational actor. To understand these dynamics, the chapter proposes examining them through the lenses of 'trust' and 'agent' relationships, as well as 'formal' and 'informal' interactions between the Chinese central and local governments. Additionally, it explores various historical strategies China has adopted to unify norms and values across civilian and military bodies, balance national unity with regional diversity, and how these historical approaches are currently being put into practice. Drawing on this analysis, the chapter offers a practical approach for external parties to engage in more effective advocacy and diplomacy with China by unpacking the core of the Chinese decision-making process and identifying key points of influence to achieve desired outcomes.

'Students of the Emperor': The Imperial Examination System

As discussed in Chap. 1, China's geography and history have led to the formation of a strong centralisation of power. And as discussed in Chap. 4, this centralisation was solidified through the combination of the rule of ritual, the rule of law and the rule of virtue, manifesting as a set of centralised political institutional framework. However, it is too easy to mistake China for a state where central institutions exert a strict monopoly on all aspects of power. Rather, the workings of the Chinese bureaucracy involve complex power dynamics between the central and local governments.

In Imperial China, although the emperor held the highest positions in executive power, legislative authority, judicial appeals, and military command, it was not possible for him to govern such an expansive country entirely on his own. The sheer size of the state meant that he needed to rely on smart and loyal people to keep him abreast of affairs and carry out his policies across the country. Therefore, Chinese emperors developed a strict, hierarchical, and orderly bureaucratic system to ensure that all territories forming the country were closely aligned with the central regime, both politically and ideologically.[1]

To effectively provide public services across the territory and maintain the unity and stability of the regime, emperors need to perform two tasks that are conflicting in nature.[2] On the one hand, they must delegate power to local governments: not only because public service delivery always happens on the ground, but also because local governments are better placed to understand local conditions and preferences for the provision of public services. On the other hand, they must also restrict the power of local governments. As the devolution of authority to subordinate government levels increases, it becomes increasingly difficult to ensure the smooth execution of the central government mandates.[3] This also elevates the risk of local authorities exploiting their granted power.[4] To tackle this dilemma, Chinese emperors structured the relationship between the central and local governments as that of a 'trust' and 'agent'.[5] The central government, as the 'trust', holds the power to make all final decisions, while the local government serves as an 'agent', exclusively executing orders from the centre.[6]

This relationship can be traced back to the Qin dynasty. As discussed in Chap. 4, before the Qin dynasty, China was governed according to a feudal model where vassals had relatively independent oversight of fiscal, military, and economic development. The role of the emperor was mainly to maintain a loose union among vassals. When Emperor Qin Shihuang unified China, he abolished feudalism. Instead, he established a sophisticated system of prefectures and counties ruled by agents of the central government. In this model, all decisions over fiscal, military and economic matters were centralised in the person of the emperor, while agents in the prefectures and counties were in charge of putting those decisions into practice. Since then, a top priority for emperors has been to stabilise the trust and agent relationship. The key mechanism to that end has been the imperial examination system, which created a large group of 'students of the emperor', trusted by the emperor to act as agents on his behalf.

---

[1] Zhou (2022), Jin and Liu (2011).
[2] Zhou (2022).
[3] Ibid.
[4] Ibid.
[5] Zhou (2014).
[6] Ibid.

'Students of the Emperor': The Imperial Examination System

The imperial examination system can be traced to the Han dynasty around 202 BCE and was first formally and widely applied in the Sui dynasty (581–618 CE).[7] After nearly 1,000 years of development, by the time of the Ming dynasty (1368–1644), the imperial examination system had become the sole criterion for bureaucratic selection.[8] The imperial examination system influenced a number of meritocratic selection systems in Europe, including Napoleon's selection of officials in accordance with their knowledge and talent. Throughout Chinese history, the imperial examination system served as a key mechanism to maintain a unified governance system across the country and strengthened the central regime's power.[9] This can be attributed to three main factors.

Firstly, the imperial examination system served as a means to crack down on the feudal system, where power and influence were based on family lineage and local constituencies.[10] This imperial examination system forged an alliance between ordinary citizens and the emperor, which became an endogenous part of the Chinese political governance structure. Over its more than 1,000 years of existence, the imperial examination system has provided many ordinary people with upward mobility, allowing them to become part of the government and lead the country. Based on historical records, from 618 to 1904, among those who successfully passed the imperial examination, 83.1% belonged to lower social classes, including yeomen, tenants, and commoners.[11] Only a small percentage came from other social strata. It should be noted that this percentage still indicates a relative over-representation of children from the upper social strata among successful examinees. Nonetheless, success could be said to be widely accessible across society. Over the course of Chinese history, many renowned politicians and senior officials have come from the lower classes, with no link to established power factions. They called themselves 'students of the emperor' and only obeyed the emperor's orders.

Secondly, the imperial examination system was instrumental in unifying norms and values among individuals entrusted with governing the country.[12] Through uniform training and a shared study of Confucian texts in preparation for a standardised examination, a shared understanding and values were fostered. These shared norms subsequently enhanced the country's stability across successive generations.

Lastly, as explored in Chap. 3, the Chinese state has deeply rooted mistrust towards businessmen and capitalists. The imperial examination system effectively curbed the power and influence of businessmen and capitalists over political and government affairs. This system reserved administrative power to individuals who demonstrated virtue and prescribed values through exam success, as opposed to those who accumulated material wealth through prosperous business ventures.

---

[7] Ichisada (2020).

[8] Ibid.

[9] Ibid.

[10] Zhao (2018).

[11] Ibid.

[12] Ibid.

Working Your Way Up

The rationale and methods of the historical imperial examination system are still evident today. The National Civil Service Exam, established in 1994, mirrors the principles of the imperial examination system. This merit-based exam seeks to cultivate a group of public sector employees and prospective political leaders who adhere to a common set of norms, standards, and ethics. Similar to the imperial examination system, the National Civil Service Exam achieves this objective by mandating standardised study and training materials for the examination. In 2023, about 2.6 million people registered in the National Civil Service Exam, competing for approximately 37,000 positions in the public sector.[13] The most competitive position had about 20,000 applicants.[14] This level of competitiveness is not to be interpreted as an aspiration by Chinese people to enter 'cushy' government positions. Rather, it has to do with the way the Chinese power system operates. In the Chinese political system, there is no distinct separation between 'bureaucrats' and 'elected officials'. Gaining entry into the bureaucracy is the primary route to influential positions across all sectors of the state. Ambitious individuals aspiring for top leadership roles in the country are highly motivated to join the bureaucracy and advance their careers, even if it means starting from the lowest positions.

By contrast, liberal democracies typically distinguish between a public service or bureaucracy that guarantees continuity of government services and administration, and a political class, in charge of decision-making, that operates through a party system. Although top jobs in the bureaucracy are influential, there is also a large body of lower-ranking civil servants with more limited power and career prospects. Those lower-ranking bureaucratic roles may therefore be less appealing than private sector roles, particularly for people of comparatively higher capacity.

Critics of Confucianism have pointed out two challenges that the 'rule of virtue' alone cannot solve. The first is whether wise men of exceptional moral quality actually exist, and whether they can be expected to make no mistakes at important junctures. The second is, if those people do exist, whether they can be identified and placed in the right position to govern the country. Although there is no clear solution to the first question, the competitiveness involved in China's National Civil Service Exam and the cadre selection process might give some assurance as to the second challenge.

I have previously discussed the competitive nature of vying for a limited number of civil service positions through examination. However, once individuals enter the bureaucratic system, the competition becomes even more intense. In China, the average annual rate of cadre promotion is only one percent to 4.4 percent, depending on the level of the position.[15] As a general practice, prospective cadre candidates must meet strict criteria before being eligible for nomination for a promotion. Those criteria include educational qualifications, length and depth of work experience, assessment of previous work performance, as well as compulsory Party education

---

[13] BeiJing News (2023).
[14] CCTV News (2022).
[15] CPC News (2014).

(i.e. knowledge of CCP history, core narratives and internal procedures).[16] To support practical measurement, the complicated assessment criteria used within the bureaucracy boil down to five words: virtue, competency, diligence, work outcomes, and cleanliness.[17]

Before promotion, the CCP personnel departments often form inspection teams to independently assess and validate the candidates' moral performance, work experience, and track record.[18] This is done through surveys, interviews, field visits and anonymous ballots from the people who directly worked with the candidate (both above and under them), or were served by them.[19] Further, the assessment can even extend into a candidate's personal life by observing and assessing candidates' social network interaction.[20] The evaluation becomes increasingly stringent as the ranking gets higher. For the dozens of top-ranking officials in charge of a province or a key government department, Xi Jinping is personally involved in discussing and assessing their performance.

Meritocracy in a New Era

China's 'meritocracy' system, which consists of the competitive National Civil Service Exam and strict cadre assessment, is designed to ensure that only people with an excellent track record of performance and moral quality can rise to the highest level of the government. It is considered an important check and balance mechanism within the one-party system. However, the appointment of the CCP's new standing committees at the 20th CCP National Congress raised questions on the validity and continuity of China's enduring 'meritocracy'. The Western media speculated that the new standing committee members might have been selected based on 'loyalty' rather than 'competence' or 'morality'. Many Western commentators were particularly concerned with the case of Li Qiang who lacks the experience of serving as a Vice Premier, which has been a prerequisite to serve as Premier throughout CCP history.

While the existence of 'meritocracy' at the CCP Standing Committee level is currently a topic of debate in some Western media, evidence indicates an emerging trend of 'meritocracy' at the CCP Central Committee level. Citing statistics from the Brookings Institution, the 20th CCP Central Committee has a total of 81 members with technology and science expertise, an increase of nearly 40% over the previous term.[21] Experts in technology and science from the newly appointed Central Committee members specialise in critical sectors that Beijing considers

---

[16] The Central People's Government of the People's Republic of China (2019).
[17] Ibid.
[18] Ibid.
[19] Ibid.
[20] Ibid.
[21] Hao (2022).

strategic imperatives, such as semiconductors, aerospace, environmental science, and biotechnology.[22] Aerospace specialists secured 20 seats, establishing a group referred to as the 'Aerospace Group' or 'Cosmic Club' within CCP politics. Among the 24 members of the CCP Politburo, the number of science and tech-savvy members increased from two to eight.[23] This move underscores Beijing's ambition to become a dominant force in the realms of science and technology. Among the top seven Standing Committee members, Ding Xuexiang is the only one with a technology and science background, with experience working on materials research. Political-risk research director Tristan Kenderdine suggested that Ding Xuexiang, a political protégé of Xi Jinping with a technology background, can be seen as a bridge between the old-guard bureaucrats and the emerging technocratic elites.[24]

The Party-State: A Unifying Force

To guarantee local governments' alignment with the central regime, besides the imperial examination system, Chinese emperors also established the role of Xunfu, which can be translated as the grand coordinator or inspector-general. The inception of this position dates back to the Northern and Southern dynasties in China (420–589 CE), with its formalisation and widespread application occurring during the Ming and Qing dynasties.[25] A Xunfu is a significant official in Imperial China, appointed by and accountable to the emperor. Their exclusive role is touring and rotating among local provinces to oversee and regulate local governments, ensuring adherence to imperial policies. The Xunfu held various powers in a province, including administration, military, supervision, and judiciary, and served as the highest local official alongside the governor.

In contemporary times, the unifying and supervising function once performed by the 'Xunfu' is now carried out by senior members of the CCP. The Party strategically rotates its trusted senior members across provinces, ministries, and SOEs, where they serve as Party Secretaries. While collaborating with, yet holding a superior leadership position to, provincial governors, ministers, or CEOs of SOEs, they supervise operational tasks and assure ideological alignment with the central regime. This intentional rotation allows central leadership to gain a comprehensive understanding of local conditions while preventing the formation of 'local constituencies'.

At the grassroots level, this unifying role is carried out by Party branches, which routinely monitor the ideological development of individual party members and coordinate activities to reinforce their connection and loyalty to the Party. By the end of 2022, China had 98.04 million Party members and 5.065 million Party branches

---

[22] Ibid.
[23] Ibid.
[24] Ibid.
[25] Dai (2020).

at the grassroots level.[26] Those Party branches are like cells in a human body, with first-hand knowledge of local conditions, and the most direct influence on them. This approach of rooting Party cells at grassroots levels originated from a strategy initiated by Mao Zedong to fight battles in the 1920s. I will return to this point in the next section.

Importantly, the 'unifying' influence extends beyond Chinese government and SOEs to the business sector. Numerous Chinese private companies and even start-ups opt to establish Party branches. Data released by the All-China Federation of Industry and Commerce in 2018 revealed that 48.3% of private enterprises meeting the criteria for housing a Party branch had one, up from 27.4% in 2002.[27] As discussed in Chap. 3, China's private sector is compelled to demonstrate its alignment with the government, and creating a Party branch can help convey this message. In this way, it can be said that the Party branches effectively act as a robust supplementary network for communicating and executing the CCP's objectives and policies across the entire nation and at all levels.

The People's Liberation Army: Establish CCP Branches at the Level of Companies

The trust and agent relationship applies not only to China's civil bureaucracy, but also to its military. China's army, the People's Liberation Army (PLA), is under direct control of the CCP, a common expression being that 'the Party directs the Guns'. The PLA can trace its origins to the communist units of the National Revolutionary Army (NRA) of the Kuomintang (KMT) during the Republican Era.[28] On 1 August 1927, they split and became known as the Chinese Red Army.[29] During the Second Sino-Japanese War, it was reintegrated into the NRA as units of the New Fourth Army and Eighth Route Army to fight against the Japanese.[30] On 10 October 1947, these two communist units were aggregated to constitute the PLA.[31]

Formally, the PLA is under the command of the Chairman of the Central Military Commission (CMC). The CMC is China's top military decision-making body, roughly equivalent to the U.S. Joint Chiefs of Staff which is the highest-ranking military body in the U.S. Department of Defense.[32] Unlike the Department of Defense's relationship with the U.S. military, China's Ministry of National Defense only manages the PLA's interactions with foreign militaries and defence agencies

---

[26] Xinhua News Agency (2023).
[27] Sayari Insights (2021).
[28] Edward et al. (1964).
[29] Ibid.
[30] Ibid.
[31] Ibid.
[32] Campbell (2021).

rather than directly governing it.[33] The Chairman of the CMC also commonly serves as China's President and CCP General Secretary. Xi Jinping has held all three roles since 2012. Cumulating mandates in this manner is one of the ways that China maintains centralised power today. Although functions are officially separate, they are occupied by the same individual, resulting in de facto centralisation and underscoring the significance of individual leaders, as previously explored in Chap. 4.

The centralisation of China's military power has a long tradition. Since the Qin dynasty began in 221 BCE, almost all of China's emperors have kept a strict personal control over the military. Decentralisation of army control remains associated with traumatic memories—the worst being the turmoil of the An Lushan Rebellion in 755 CE. In the second half of the Tang dynasty, Emperor Xuanzong of Tang (713–756 CE) gave greater control over military matters to local governments, as a way to strengthen the regime's hold over border regions inhabited by different ethnic groups. However, this decentralised governing approach brought about a situation known as 'the separatist regime of military governors'.[34] An Lushan was a general of Sogdian-Turkic origins, who rose to prominence by defending the northeastern Tang frontier, and accumulated significant military power. An Lushan leveraged his military strength to instigate a rebellion, proclaiming himself emperor and igniting a devastating civil war that led to millions of casualties across the nation. This conflict signalled the beginning of a decline for the once-flourishing Tang dynasty, which never managed to regain its former glory.[35]

In the modern era, the primary strategy for maintaining a stable trust and agent relationship between the CCP and the military is referred to as 'establish CCP branches at the level of companies'.[36] 'Company' here refers to a military unit—the smallest integral unit in an army—typically consisting of 80–250 soldiers. In response to significant setback incurred from the unsuccessful Nanchang and Autumn Harvest Uprisings in 1927, Mao Zedong implemented this strategy. This was aimed at enhancing the CCP's control over the Red Army and strengthening the unity and loyalty among its soldiers.[37]

Similar to the rationale behind establishing Party branches throughout the grassroots levels of Chinese government, commerce, and society, creating Party branches at the military company level serves as an effective and direct means of overseeing and shaping the ideological adherence and fidelity of soldiers. On the one hand, this strong unifying force ensured loyalty of the armed forces. Throughout the history of the PLA, while minor mutinies have taken place, there has never been an instance of mutiny that reached or surpassed the division level, which typically consists of 6,000–25,000 soldiers. On the other hand, this robust ideological alignment grants the PLA remarkable adaptability. This allows for the seamless disassembly of a large military unit into numerous agile companies and their subsequent reintegration to accommodate diverse battle scenarios. Mao Zedong regarded the strategy of forming Party branches at the company level as pivotal for securing the CCP's remarkable

---

[33] Ibid.
[34] Zhao (2018).
[35] Ibid.
[36] Mao (1991).
[37] Ibid.

success in their battles to seize control of China throughout the 1920s and 1930s.[38] And, for nearly a century till today, this strategy has consistently maintained the CCP's absolute leadership over the PLA.

Policies from Above, Counter Policies from Below

As discussed previously in this chapter, Chinese emperors structured the relationship between the central and local governments as that of a 'trust' and 'agent'. This relationship also encompasses another crucial aspect: the formal and informal dynamics, especially in terms of power sharing between the central and local authorities.[39] It means that the central government gains stability and credibility through the formal system of centralised power, while the prevalence of an informal system provides space for flexible local implementation.[40]

Chinese officials appointed to local positions of responsibility are normally expected to meet two primary types of outcomes. First, they must implement the economic policies of the national five-year plan and ensure that the local economic GDP grows year by year.[41] Secondly, they must avoid large-scale mass incidents, and more generally avoid causing embarrassment to the central government.[42] While these dual objectives generally apply to all officials and form the foundation of their promotions, officials have considerable latitude in how they achieve these outcomes. As Henry Paulson, former U.S. Secretary of the Treasury, observed in his book *Dealing with China*: "Decisions made at the top are frequently muddled by diffuse, uneven execution down below, as provincial, county, municipal, township, and village officials interpret and apply the Party's orders. They do this in a variety of ways. Some imaginative, some not. Many well-thought through, others breathtakingly unsophisticated."[43]

From the 'formal' perspective, the decision-making process followed by local government officials can be described as a simple top-down approach. It means that decisions made by the central government are assessed by local authorities in the context of local circumstances, followed by the development and execution of an implementation plan.[44] This top-down approach is captured in Chart 5.1.

However, local governments do not always carry out the decisions of higher authorities in this manner.[45] They rarely reject the decision of a higher authority directly, but follow a skilful tactic to implement their own plans while seemingly implementing those of the higher authority.[46] This mechanism is captured by a

---

[38] Ibid.
[39] Zhou (2014).
[40] Ibid.
[41] Ibid.
[42] Lieberthal (2012).
[43] Paulson (2015).
[44] Huang et al. (1997).
[45] Ibid.
[46] Ibid.

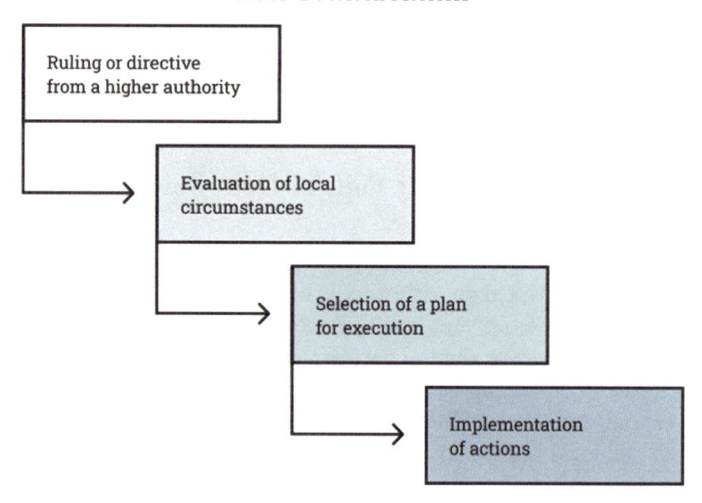

A TOP-DOWN APPROACH

Ruling or directive from a higher authority → **Evaluation of local circumstances** → **Selection of a plan for execution** → **Implementation of actions**

Chart 5.1 A top-down approach

popular saying: 'policies from above, counter policies from below'. This counter-tactic approach is represented in Chart 5.2.

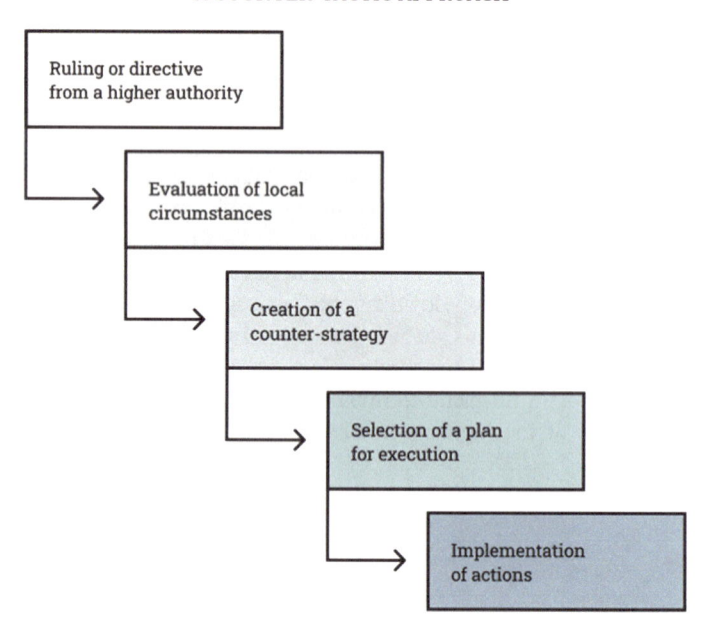

A COUNTER-TACTIC APPROACH

Ruling or directive from a higher authority → **Evaluation of local circumstances** → **Creation of a counter-strategy** → **Selection of a plan for execution** → **Implementation of actions**

Chart 5.2 A counter-tactic approach

Policies from Above, Counter Policies from Below

A STRATEGIC DIRECTIVE CHERRY PICKING APPROACH

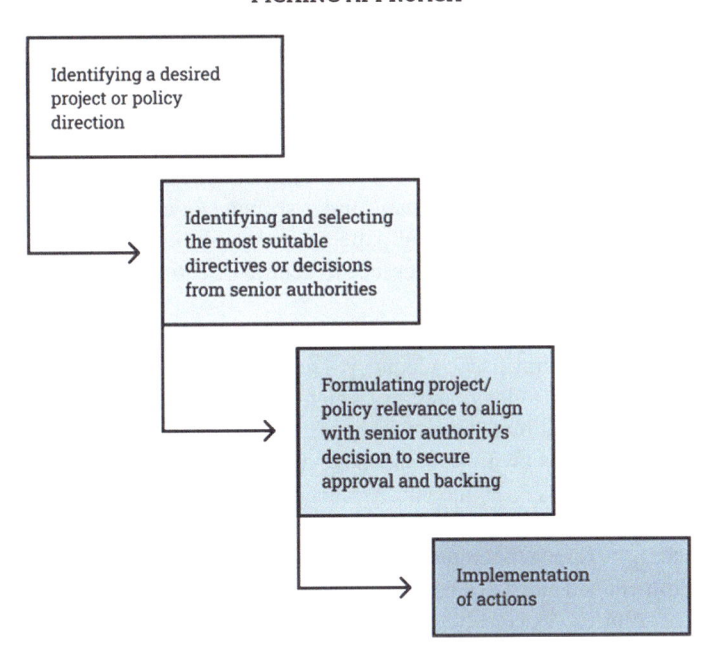

```
┌─────────────────────┐
│ Identifying a desired│
│ project or policy   │
│ direction           │
└──────┬──────────────┘
       │
       └──→ ┌─────────────────────┐
            │ Identifying and selecting│
            │ the most suitable   │
            │ directives or decisions│
            │ from senior authorities│
            └──────┬──────────────┘
                   │
                   └──→ ┌─────────────────────┐
                        │ Formulating project/│
                        │ policy relevance to align│
                        │ with senior authority's│
                        │ decision to secure  │
                        │ approval and backing│
                        └──────┬──────────────┘
                               │
                               └──→ ┌──────────────┐
                                    │ Implementation│
                                    │ of actions   │
                                    └──────────────┘
```

Chart 5.3 TA strategic directive cherry-picking approach

The model can also be reversed. Local government officials with a policy concept or project in mind will pinpoint the most suitable directives from higher authorities and shape an outcome that appears to align with these higher-level instructions. By doing so, they can secure approval and support for their own initiatives. This 'strategic directive cherry-picking' approach is illustrated in Chart 5.3.

In a nation often described as a 'centralised one-party system', the continued existence of informal systems providing flexibility for lower levels of government might appear as a paradox. One might expect that the central government would quickly notice local attempts at skirting its directives and find ways to close the loopholes. This informal flexibility, however, plays an essential role in the central government's capacity to effectively run a large and diverse country. However, it is only allowed to the extent that the informal flexibility will not undermine the formal authority. The following section will further explore this point.

Fighting for and Sharing the Resources

Battling for tax revenue exemplifies the delicate balance between the formal and informal dynamics, and the principle of 'do not undermine the formal authority'. A fundamental feature of the Chinese tax revenue system involves granting exclusive formal rights to tax revenue to the central government, while only permitting a restricted level of autonomy to local authorities. The primary objective is to strengthen the central regime through fiscal sufficiency and to maintain control over local governments. As historical patterns repeatedly indicate, too much local fiscal autonomy may discourage adherence to central directives and potentially lead to fragmentation and instability.

The era of the Republic of China (1912–1949) serves as an example that highlights the significance of central fiscal adequacy. During this period, the KMT allowed provincial governments to levy land tax, which had previously been a vital revenue source for the central administration for more than 1,000 years.[47] In addition, the KMT did not reduce its own fiscal spending in response, causing a weakening of the central government's fiscal income. When combating Japanese aggression in the 1930s and the civil war in the 1940s, the central fiscal deficit made it difficult for the KMT to sustain the regular operations of the country and support the war effort.[48] The KMT government had no choice but to borrow from banks and issue bonds to finance military expenditures. As a result, inflation rose dramatically to unprecedented levels, greatly affecting economic stability and people's livelihoods. This, in turn, weakened the KMT government's popular support and political stability, eroding its legitimacy and governing foundation, ultimately resulting in the KMT government's downfall.[49]

The tax system of the Qing dynasty offers additional perspectives on how the central government skilfully modulates its control over local authorities through these formal and informal dynamics. During the Qing dynasty, the imperial power established a strict formal system to oversee all activities that could yield fiscal revenue, highlighting the absolute power of the emperor and the central regime.[50] Formally, this system allowed provinces to retain a portion of the collected taxes for their local expenses before remitting the remaining funds to the central government. Despite this, local governments frequently faced fiscal deficits. Due to concerns that allowing local governments too much fiscal autonomy might incite disobedience and unrest, the central imperial power was reluctant to grant them greater authority to retain a larger share of the taxes. Instead, the imperial power gave tacit consent for local governments to charge fees and taxes under various names to make up local fiscal revenue deficit.[51] The practice of developing miscellaneous taxes in local areas

---

[47] Zhao (2018).

[48] Ibid.

[49] Ibid.

[50] Zhou (2014), Wang (2008).

[51] Wang (1987).

enhanced the sufficiency of local fiscal revenue without jeopardising the financial adequacy of the central government.[52]

Nonetheless, when those miscellaneous taxes and charges exceeded a certain threshold and started causing social unrest, the emperors would use their formal authority to suppress the harsh taxation of local governments. In other words, when local flexibility undermined central political stability, the central government sacrificed its agents' interests to stabilise the overall situation. Ironically, through this practice, the central government was able to maintain a trusted and positive image among ordinary people. By abolishing miscellaneous taxes, the central government could appear as the protector of the common people, in contrast with a local government which added financial pressure on the people. 'The emperor didn't know' is what people thought was the cause of unfair taxes at the local level.

The 1994 'tax sharing system reform' in China reflects the wisdom gained from historical lessons throughout the nation's past. One of the key functions of this new tax reform was to bolster the central government's fiscal adequacy and enhance its macro-management capabilities.[53] Under this tax sharing system reform, control over revenue is tilted towards the central government, while fiscal expenditure is delegated to local governments (provincial, prefecture, county, and township).[54] In other words, local governments have more responsibility to spend but limited power to raise sufficient revenue. In practice, the fiscal revenue of local governments can rarely support the expenditure responsibilities they bear. In 2019, the central and local governments, respectively, carried approximately 14.7% and 85.3% of general public budget expenditures, but local governments only received about 53.1% of total fiscal revenue.[55] With limited revenue to provide required services, local governments at all levels rely heavily on fee collection and arbitrary charges to finance their expenditures—for instance, by conducting tax audits and charging fines. It is important to note that the power to impose arbitrary fees increases with the level of the local government.

The 1994 tax sharing system reform follows the logic of 'collect first (via the majority of tax revenue), then distribute (through transfer payments)'. It means the central government regularly subsidises local government expenditures through 'transfer payments'. This approach has two purposes. Firstly, this approach facilitates revenue redistribution across the nation, effectively employing centralised taxation to shift wealth from affluent provinces on the eastern seaboard to less prosperous central and western regions, promoting fairness and efficiency.[56] Moreover, it also serves to enhance the central government's macro-management capabilities, enabling it to maintain a degree of control over how the funds are utilised and ensuring that they are used in line with national priorities.[57]

---

[52] Zhou (2014).

[53] Asian Development Bank (2014).

[54] Liu (2020).

[55] Ibid.

[56] Lin (2000).

[57] Asian Development Bank (2014).

However, the conflict between the central government's goal of achieving a balance among provinces and thus stability and local authorities' aim of receiving more subsidies, makes the situation more challenging than it appears. As a common practice, transfer payments from the central government are often intercepted by local governments at various levels, typically resulting in minimal funds reaching the grassroots level of governments. One interesting consequence is that the financial disparity between districts and counties within a single province frequently surpasses that between provinces.[58]

This contested conflict is intensified during times of crisis. Amid the COVID-19 pandemic, grassroots governments at the county and township levels encountered the most severe financial difficulties. Tasked with overseeing COVID-19 testing, implementing quarantine measures, and providing daily essentials like food and medicine to the community, these grassroots-level governments faced unprecedented pressure. A lack of adequate funding could restrict the resources and personnel available, possibly jeopardising public safety and escalating the likelihood of social unrest. To ensure the speedy arrival of funds and avoid misappropriation by higher levels of government (e.g. the province and prefecture), the central government issued special treasury bonds of 2 trillion yuan (USD 289.72 billion) directly to local governments at the county level, thus circumventing higher government interception.[59] The examples examined from a tax revenue perspective reveal that the Chinese system does not operate as a unitary and rational entity. Instead, it represents a complex terrain marked by diverging interests and strategies employed to attain equilibrium.

A Non-unitary Rational Actor: The Dynamics of Upward Accountability

On the surface, many characteristics of China's bureaucracy, such as preferential admission, hierarchical structure, and red tape, are very similar to the Western bureaucracies described by Max Weber. However, under the trust and agent relationship, there is one key difference, namely personal attachment to imperial power. Throughout Chinese history, the recruitment, promotion, mobility, removal of officials—even the life or death of bureaucratic agents—all fell under imperial power.[60] Today, this feature still exists. After individuals enter the civil service, their promotion occurs mainly through the decisions made by the Organization Departments of CCP at a higher level, with ultimate decisions made by the Organization Department of the CCP at the central level.[61] The consequence of this process is known as 'upward accountability'.[62] It means that local governments are accountable to

---

[58] Li and Xu (2008).

[59] The Central People's Government of the People's Republic of China (2020).

[60] Zhou (2013).

[61] The Central People's Government of the People's Republic of China (2019).

[62] Zhou (2013).

the government level directly above them rather than to the citizens. This chain of accountability extends all the way up to the central power, indicating that all levels of government are ultimately accountable to the central authorities.[63]

Four significant implications stem from this system of 'upward accountability'. Firstly, 'upward accountability' may hinder dynamics and innovation within bureaucratic systems. The repeated cycles of purges and promotions mould the nature of the bureaucracy, progressively aligning it with the leader's overarching vision.[64] Consequently, bureaucrats at every level are motivated to discern the top leader's perspective prior to acting, rather than depending on independent rational analysis. On the one hand, when a clear signal is sent from the top, bureaucrats race to adopt and respond: the competition to demonstrate loyalty can lead to excessive and exaggerated actions.[65] On the other hand, when there is no clear signal from the top, bureaucrats are either reluctant to take action, or if they must take action, they tend to favour left-leaning initiatives. The general wisdom shared among Chinese bureaucrats is that 'red fervour will get you further than expertise'.[66]

Secondly, under 'upward accountability', all subordinate governments need to compete for attention and resources from the top, making cooperation between them difficult. The recognition of Chinese policy-making as a contested process characterised by inter- and intra-government competitions may appear as a paradox, since many consider China as a unitary rational actor conducting a coherent calculation of its interests.[67] In the actual implementation of national policies, the competition and conflict of interest, implicit or explicit, can make different layers of governments reluctant to cooperate with each other and share credit.

For instance, as China began adopting a more proactive stance in climate change negotiations, competition among Chinese ministries, such as the Ministry of Ecology and Environment, the National Development and Reform Commission, and the Ministry of Foreign Affairs, has escalated. Each ministry aims to assume a pivotal role in influencing China's climate change policies as this would allow them to draw greater attention from top leaders, leading to increased funding and resources for their respective ministry. Furthermore, when a ministry is anticipated to have only a minor role in a cross-ministry project, they might be reluctant to dedicate their full effort, as they will not obtain the main credit. As a result, they tend to establish separate platforms to independently conduct activities that showcase their effectiveness and accomplishments, thereby fostering competition rather than cooperation.

The third implication of the 'upward accountability' is unclear or overlapping orders of responsibility which may lead to political interference and inconsistent enforcement. For example, a provincial department of commerce is mainly tasked to foster trade and investment. However, this department has to report to both the provincial government, which is responsible for the department's personnel appointments,

---

[63] Ibid.

[64] Blanchette (2022).

[65] Ibid.

[66] The Economist (2022).

[67] Sun (2016).

and the Ministry of Commerce in Beijing, which supervises its actual operations. At times, these two entities may have divergent priorities and interests. This dual upward accountability creates ambiguity and conflicting directives, which in turn hinder the consistent formulation and execution of policies. A provincial department of commerce might expend considerable resources coordinating and balancing diverse directives from higher authority, subsequently diverting the focus from its primary responsibility of promoting commerce and investment.

Last but not least, 'upward accountability' may stimulate short-term profit-seeking behaviour among bureaucratic agents. For example, in order to meet the GDP growth targets set by the central government, local governments may be incentivised to launch a large number of construction projects to boost short-term GDP and employment, even if a long-term analysis of pros and cons would not warrant them. It is worth noting here that Western democracies are often criticised for structural government incentives to think short-term, in line with short election cycles, while China is credited with its capacity to think long-term. This is true to some extent, but the 'upward accountability' of China's bureaucratic often stands in the way of long-term thinking.

Point of Influence: The 'Consensus Building' Model

The need to stabilise and sustain the relationship between the central and local governments gives rise to the 'consensus building' model. This model is a deliberate consultative process for identifying common ground between the interests of the central government and those of all subordinate groups, including competing factions. This 'consensus building' model allows subordinate groups to influence policy by participating in deliberative processes rather than engaging in direct power struggles.[68] At the same time, it enables the central government to anticipate and manage conflicts proactively, hence maintaining stability.

This 'consensus building' model, commonly referred as 'consultative democracy' by the CCP, is widely applied at all levels across China. The ideology of 'consultative democracy' was officially endorsed during the 18th CCP National Congress. The CCP applies 'consultative democracy' as a problem-solving mechanism for addressing social conflicts and preserving stability by integrating citizens' perspectives into decision-making and policy formulation processes.[69]

In general, when formulating important policies, deliberative consultations are conducted with political representatives, business leaders, experts, and ordinary citizens at all levels. Information is gathered through a variety of channels, such as public or private meetings, hearing sessions organised by the government, invitations to contribute to draft documents, online suggestion boxes, and more. These consultations take place year-round and across the country as needed, with the most

---

[68] He (2018).
[69] Zheng (2013).

concentrated period occurring prior to the annual 'Two Sessions' meeting in March. Topics typically encompass economic development prospects and major industry policies.

The process of the 'consensus building' model appears as follows. Information and feedback received are deliberated, negotiated, and finalised through different levels of the formal party-state political structure.[70] The resulting decisions and policies are then executed through the various tiers of the bureaucratic system.[71] Any policy failures or defects during implementation are typically identified by research teams or inspection groups from relevant government departments, as well as through submissions from industry experts.[72] These issues are then addressed through a new cycle of review and evaluation within the political system.[73] This deliberative governance allows the government to take the pulse of public opinion, alleviate the intensity of disputes, and make decisions that are less likely to cause societal chaos.[74]

While this consensus-building model exhibits commendable elements in its design and purpose, it is crucial to note that it is primarily a top-down process. This suggests that the agenda is largely predetermined at the top levels of government and cascades down to the local levels. As a result, this approach could potentially curtail innovation and limit the exploration of alternative solutions. Also, it may not adequately incorporate feedback from local levels and account for regional specifics in the decision-making process. Moreover, public input, when sought, is typically controlled and filtered, potentially not capturing the full spectrum of public perspectives. This could lead to the muting or marginalisation of dissenting views, which could, in turn, compromise the legitimacy and responsiveness of the policies to the actual needs of the public.

The Media as Part of Consensus Building

Besides direct consultation, the media serves as another critical source of input for the deliberation process. This perspective may appear as a paradox. It is widely recognised that the Chinese government directly manages its state media and indirectly controls all other media outlets in China. As a result, media is often viewed as the mouthpiece of the CCP, disseminating official messages to shape public opinion. However, in the context of 'consensus building', it is equally important to consider the media as the ear of the CCP. This perspective acknowledges the crucial role media plays in bringing potential areas of social tension and intellectual disagreements to the attention of party members within the framework of deliberative governance.

---

[70] Li (2017).

[71] Ibid.

[72] Ibid.

[73] Ibid.

[74] He (2018).

To understand why and how this actually works in practice, it is important to understand the relationships between Chinese journalists and the state. In contrast to the 'watchdog' model prevalent in the West, Chinese journalists are expected to collaborate with the regime in the development of social governance.[75] For the Chinese central regime, adopting a proactive approach to their engagement with the media is actually to their advantage. By inviting some critical journalists to observe the inner workings of the government, involving them in policy-setting forums and allowing the media to bring issues and concerns to the Party early on, issues can be solved in their emerging stage, before they lead to large unrest and cause embarrassment.[76]

The primary means the media use to channel important messages into the ears of Chinese senior leadership is by publishing articles on the most prominent pages in newspapers. For more sensitive and critical matters, 'Neican'—restricted reports available only to senior officials in the government and a channel exclusive to the state media—serves as the communication pathway. Although 'Neican' allows for more direct and candid communication, addressing issues through prominent newspapers typically requires concentrating on matters considered solvable. Constructive criticism is the customary approach for framing these issues and challenges, with a mildly critical tone that emphasises solutions and aims to foster a sense of optimism.[77] Although the communication style may be more subtle compared to Western journalism, an attentive ear can still discern these important messages.

From the standpoint of voicing concerns and issues to the CCP, the earlier discussion about the relationship between the state and journalists in China makes clear why Chinese academics and businesspeople see writing impactful opinion pieces for state-owned media or contributing to 'Neican' as an influential means to shape policy decisions and amplify their voices.

Picking the Right Stone

In the face of complex inter- and intra-government dynamics, together with opaque informal behaviours, foreign businesses and governments seeking to enhance their advocacy and diplomacy efforts with China must grapple with a crucial question: what is the optimal strategy for an external party to influence China's decision-making processes? To address this question, it is important to review the core feature of China's decision-making model. To understand this better, I propose the following Table 5.1, which captures contrasting decision-making logics in China and in Western liberal democracies. To succinctly illustrate the logic, the table below simplifies the decision-making process into three primary 'phases': making the decision, announcing it, and implementing it.

---

[75] Repnikova (2017).
[76] Ibid.
[77] Ibid.

Table 5.1 Comparing decision-making processes in China and the West

	Making decision stage	Announcing decision stage	Implementing decision stage
China A relatively opaque decision-making model requiring interpretation	Engagement through a formal and informal deliberative consultation model, offering limited avenues for direct influence	Decision is firm but decision and implementation details are usually worded in vague terms and require interpretation and further clarification	Limited possibility to 'revoke' a decision but great possibility to affect plan significantly through inputs to details of implementation
Western countries A relatively linear and transparent decision-making model	A standard and direct model for input through formal submission, lobbying, media, etc.	Decision is worded clearly in detail, but execution depends on government continuity	Possibility to 'revoke' decisions entirely by challenging government through election or media

In general, Chinese decision-making tends to be somewhat opaque, offering limited opportunities for direct influence beyond participating in consultative processes. While external input is possible, the ultimate decision is made by the top leaders, heavily relying on personal judgement. Even when faced with strong opposition, it is highly unlikely that a decision will be directly revoked; instead, the leaders may seek ways to justify their choice.

The wording of decisions is often intentionally vague, especially regarding implementation details. This approach can be attributed to the pragmatic nature of Chinese decision-making which emphasises experience over assumption. While setting a clear goal, the specifics are left open-ended, allowing the plans to adapt to evolving circumstances and real-world feedback. This approach, as articulated by Deng Xiaoping during the reform and opening up period, is encapsulated by the phrase 'crossing the river by feeling the stones'. To summarise, for external actors, it is more pragmatic and realistic to focus on shaping the specifics of policy implementation, rather than attempting to sway a decision before it is finalised or reversing it once it has been made.

I will examine this point in greater detail. Upon Deng Xiaoping announcing the critical decision to reform and open up China in 1979, the 'what' aspect had already been decided through a non-transparent internal decision-making procedure: China will liberalise its economy. However, the specifics—how, when, where, and who—remained undecided. In the analogy of crossing the river, the goal of traversing the river is set, while the means of accomplishing it are left open, requiring the testing of stones along the way.

In June 1979, a group of prominent Chinese scholars and economists were convened by the central leadership to conduct a nationwide field research. They focused on key economic issues, such as economic theories and methods, economic management systems, and enterprise modernisation.[78] The purpose of this research

---

[78] Liu (2010).

was not to validate whether embarking on the 'reform and opening up' was the correct path.[79] Rather, it aimed to determine the most suitable 'stones' to initiate the reform, the number of 'stones' required to achieve the reform process, and the direction these 'stones' would guide, that is, the anticipated outcomes of the reform.[80]

By contrast, Western decision-making typically follows a linear and scientific logic. The primary distinction between Chinese and Western decision-making lies in setting the objective. While the Chinese thought process starts with a pre-set goal—for instance, crossing the river—the Western approach's initial goal involves deciding whether to cross the river at all and considering alternative options, such as taking different road routes. Following this, information is gathered, analysed, and evaluated to reach a decision, complete with detailed plans for implementation.

Arguably, China currently confronts a situation akin to the early stages of its 'reform and opening up': while the country has set a clear goal of advancing towards a prosperous future, the methods for achieving this and the precise reforms required remain undefined. This uncertainty can be attributed partly to the unprecedented transformations in the geopolitical landscape, driven by climate change, emerging technologies, and inequality, which lack easily applicable experiences or solutions. Additionally, it stems from China's ongoing search for a path that harmoniously aligns with its historical values while simultaneously leading towards a prosperous future.

In the face of the fragile global environment, marked by successive and interlocking risks, effective engagement with China can present an opportunity for collective prosperity. Failure to engage effectively may bring dire consequences for all parties. However, the window of opportunity is narrowing. China currently faces insecurity from internal and external factors, with Beijing perceiving that the West views it negatively regardless of its actions. As stated by Xi Jinping at the 20th CCP National Congress, China must prepare for increasing uncertainties, risks, and worst-case scenarios.[81]

While there is some validity to Beijing's increasingly pessimistic perspective on the external environment, this outlook is also magnified by a self-reinforcing mindset among the top leadership. As Xi Jinping has amassed unparalleled personal power since Mao Zedong at the 20th CCP National Congress, he has simultaneously grown more distant and isolated, consequently affecting his ability to make sound decisions. The voices within the system are likely to exhibit more sycophancy than honest critique, and the people who remain at the table to give him advice tend to display absolute loyalty rather than challenge his views.[82] This small, rigid and self-reinforcing group seems to harbour an increasingly bleak view of the external environment, making for a potentially volatile period ahead.[83]

---

[79] Ibid.

[80] Ibid.

[81] Lin and Wuthnow (2022).

[82] Blanchette (2022).

[83] Ibid.

Should China veer towards a more left-leaning, introspective, or hostile path, it might require a whole generation to redirect towards a more positive trajectory. This shift could result in the loss of crucial time needed for coordinated efforts to address catastrophic global challenges. Therefore, proactive and effective measures are imperative. For the heads of states around the world, especially leaders of the West, they must make efforts to maintain a direct communication with Xi Jinping to allow alternative ideas to puncture his leadership bubble.[84] They are in the rare position to be able to exert some direct influence on China's decision-making at the formation stage. For business leaders, experts and bureaucrats outside of China, they can gain some influence by engaging China at the policy formational stage by establishing and maintaining formal consultative channels to actively share their perspectives with the Chinese government. However, given the prevailing political environment, it is possible that their opinions may be filtered or dismissed by Party loyalists before reaching top decision-makers. Consequently, focusing on the implementation phase and collaborating on the finer details may be a more practical and effective approach to significantly influence the outcome. This can be achieved by sharing expertise to foster better results through cooperation.

In order to successfully navigate and exert influence in the complex landscape of China, it is imperative to possess a deep and nuanced understanding of the factors that inform its decision-making processes. This understanding has been systematically explored in the first five chapters of this book, which delve into China's geography, extensive history, and traditional philosophy. Moreover, it is essential to grasp the nature and extent of China's global ambitions, its historical interactions with the international community, and its potential future impact. These critical questions form the foundation of the second part of the book, which emphasises the significance of a comprehensive understanding of China's multifaceted identity for effective engagement with this global powerhouse.

References

Asian Development Bank (2014) Zhongguo difang caizheng guanli: tiaozhan yu jiyu. Available at: https://www.adb.org/sites/default/files/publication/42793/local-public-finance-management-prc-zh.pdf. Accessed 18 May 2020.

BeiJing News (2023) 6000 duoge ren jingzheng yige gangwei, kaogong yuelaiyuenan le ma? Available at: https://news.ycwb.com/2023-04/02/content_51859121.htm. Accessed 31 May 2023.

Blanchette J (2022) Xi Jinping's faltering foreign policy: The war in Ukraine and the perils of strongman rule. In: Foreign Affairs. Available at: https://www.foreignaffairs.com/articles/china/2022-03-16/xi-jinpings-faltering-foreign-policy?utm_medium=newsletters&utm_source=fatoday&utm_campaign=Xipercent20JinpingpercentE2percent80percent99spercent20Falteringpercent20Foreignpercent20Policy&utm_content=20220316&utm_term=FApercent20Todaypercent20-percent20112017. Accessed 18 June 2022.

---

[84] Ibid.

Campbell C (2021) China's military: The People's Liberation Army (PLA). In: Congressional research services. Available at: https://crsreports.congress.gov/product/pdf/R/R46808. Accessed 12 December 2021.

CCTV News (2022) 2022 nian guokao baoming renshu shouci tupo 200wan xizang yizhiwei jingzhengbi da 2000:1. Available at: https://news.cctv.com/2021/10/25/ARTIMerUMvxFdOUVOOxCt7IL211025.shtml. Accessed 12 December 2022.

CPC News (2014) Dashuju jiedu zhenshi jiceng gongwuyuan jiucheng shi keji yixia ganbu. Available at: http://theory.people.com.cn/n/2014/0415/c40531-24895856.html. Accessed 16 December 2022.

Dai WJ (2020) Songdai xunfushi chutan. Huizhou Academy Journal 40(1):55–61.

Edward R et al (1964) The Chinese Red Army, 1927–1963: An annotated bibliography. Harvard University Asia Center, Cambridge.

Hao K (2022) China's Xi stacks government with science and tech experts amid rivalry with U.S. In: Wall Street Journal. Available at: https://www.wsj.com/articles/chinas-xi-stacks-government-with-science-and-tech-experts-amid-rivalry-with-u-s-11668772682. Accessed 13 December 2022.

He BG (2018) Deliberative citizenship and deliberative governance: A case study of one deliberative experimental in China, Citizenship Studies, 22(3):294–311, DOI: https://doi.org/10.1080/13621025.2018.1424800.

Huang QY et al (1997) Business decision making. The Haworth Press, New York.

Ichisada M (2020) Keju shi. Elephant Press, Beijing.

Jin GT, Liu QF (2011) Zhongguo xiandai sixiang de qiyuan: chaowending jiegou yu zhongguo zhengzhi wenhua de yanbian. Law Press, Beijing.

Li X (2017) The endgame or resilience of the Chinese Communist Party's rule in China: A Gramscian approach. Journal of Chinese Political Science 23(1):83–104.

Li ST, Xu ZY (2008) The trend of regional income disparity in the People's Republic of China. In: Asian Development Bank. Available at: http://www.adbi.org/discussionpaper/2008/01/25/2468.regional.income.disparity.prc/. Accessed 22 June 2020.

Lieberthal K (2012) Managing the China challenge. In: Brookings. Available at: https://www.brookings.edu/on-the-record/managing-the-china-challenge/. Accessed 5 May 2020.

Lin SL (2000) The decline of China's budgetary revenue: Reasons and consequences. Contemporary Economic Policy 27(4):477–490.

Lin B, Wuthnow J (2022) The weakness behind China's strong façade. In: Foreign Affairs. Available at: https://www.foreignaffairs.com/china/weakness-behind-china-strong-facade. Accessed 15 January 2023.

Liu H (2010) 80 niandai: zhongguo jingji xueren de guangrong yu mengxiang. Guangxi Normal University Press, Guilin.

Liu K (2020) Woguo de zhongyang he difang caizheng guanxi. In: The National People's Congress of the People's Republic of China. Available at: http://www.npc.gov.cn/npc/c30834/202008/08bd6bb3168e4916a2da92ac68771386.shtml#:~:text=percentE4percentB8percentBBpercentE8percentA6percent81percentE6percent98percentAFpercentE5percentAEpercent9EpercentE6percent96percentBDpercentE5percentA2percent9EpercentE5percent80percentBCpercentE7percentA8percent8E,percentE6percent89percent93percentE5percentA5percentBDpercentE6percentB1percentA1percentE6percent9Fpercent93percentE9percent98percentB2percentE6percentB2percentBBpercentE6percent94percentBBpercentE5percent9Dpercent9ApercentE6percent88percent98percentE3percent80percent82. Accessed 15 November 2021.

Mao ZD (1991) Mao Zedong xuanji. Vol 4. People's Publishing House, Beijing.

Paulson H (2015) Dealing with China. Hachette, London, pp.363–364.

Repnikova M (2017) Media politics in China: Improvising power under authoritarianism. Cambridge University Press, Cambridge.

Sayari Insights (2021) Chinese Communist Party cells in private companies: Though not yet universal, increasingly situated to play greater roles in corporate governance. Available at:

References

https://sayari.com/resources/chinese-communist-party-cells-in-private-companies-though-not-yet-universal-increasingly-situated-to-play-greater-roles-in-corporate-governance/. Accessed 14 December 2022.

Sun J (2016) Growing diplomacy, retreating diplomats—how the Chinese foreign ministry has been marginalized in foreign policymaking. Journal of Contemporary China 26(105):419–433.

The Central People's Government of the People's Republic of China (2019) Zhongguo zhongyang yinfa <Dangzheng lingdao ganbu xuanba renyong gongzuo tiaoli>. Available at: http://www.gov.cn/zhengce/2019-03/17/content_5374532.htm. Accessed 10 November 2019.

The Central People's Government of the People's Republic of China (2020) 2wanji yuan zhongyang caizheng zijin zhida jiceng shuaxin xinzhongguo caizheng jilu. Available at: http://www.gov.cn/xinwen/2020-11/09/content_5560047.htm. Accessed 9 March 2020.

The Economist (2022) China's martial rhetoric will not help it defeat covid. Available at: https://www.economist.com/leaders/2022/04/30/chinas-martial-rhetoric-will-not-help-it-defeat-covid. Accessed 18 June 2022.

Wang YN (1987) Zhongguo guanliao zhengzhi yanjiu. China Social Sciences Press, Beijing.

Wang YJ (2008) Qingdai tianfu zoulun (1750–1911). People's Publishing House, Beijing.

Xinhua News Agency (2023) Dangyuan 9804.1wanming, jiceng dangzuzhi 506.5 wange. Available at: http://www.news.cn/mrdx/2023-07/01/c_1310730431.htm. Accessed 1 July 2023.

Zhao HJ (2018) China's long-term economic development: How have economy and governance evolved since 500 BC?. Edward Elgar Publishing, Cheltenham.

Zheng WT (2013) Guanche luoshi zhonggong shibada jingshen jianquan shehui zhuyi xieshang minzhu zhidu. In: Chinese People's Political Consultative Conference. Available at: http://www.cppcc.gov.cn/zxww/2013/04/19/ARTI1366362429482826.shtml. Accessed 12 May 2020.

Zhou XG (2013) Guojia zhili luoji yu zhongguo guanliao tizhi: Yige weibo lilun shijiao. Kaifang shidai (Open times):5–28.

Zhou XG (2014) Cong "Huangzongxi dinglu" dao diguo de luoji: Zhongguo guojia zhili luoji de lishi xiansuo. Kaifang shidai (Open times) 4:108–132.

Zhou XG (2022) The logic of governance in China: An organisational approach. Cambridge University Press, Cambridge.

Part II
Over the Mountains and Across the Seas

Chapter 6
Capability or Intention: Ambition and Restraint in China's Military Build-Up

"The highest victory is to defeat the enemy without ever fighting." (Sun, 2022)
—Sun Tzu, The Art of War

Abstract As China's global influence expands, what will be the shape and content of its global ambitions? Will China seek to expand its power through territorial acquisition, co-opting client states, or trade? Most crucially, under what circumstances will China regard as situations where it has no choice but to threaten, or even use military force? To answer those questions, this chapter aims to provide a framework through which to view changes and continuities of China's intent behind its military build-up. The argument is that China's 'invasion-prone' geography, conservative worldview, pragmatic military strategy and historical lessons demonstrate that war and territorial expansion do not assure enduring security, and may even lead to a decline in central power. This has fostered a Chinese strategic tradition that leans more towards defence than offence, and coexistence rather than aggression. The primary motive behind strengthening China's military capability is to build a deterrent force. The intended outcome is to induce any potential rivals to reconsider their presumptions of assured victory when intervening in China's peripheral regions, thereby fostering conflict resolution through non-military or soft-power approaches.

The swift emergence of Chinese military supremacy has produced 'a cauldron of anxiety' worldwide, leading to heated debate about the potential for power transition from the United States to China and its impact on the global order, including the likelihood of Chinese hegemony.[1] As China's global influence expands, questions arise about the shape and content of its global ambitions. Will China attempt to increase its power through territorial conquest, co-opting client states, or trade? Most crucially, under what circumstances will China regard as situations where it has no choice but to threaten, or even use military force?

---
[1] Zhang and Buzan (2012).

This book began by discussing the significance of China's geography and its impact on China's logic of governance and decision-making. It is important to note that the collective decisions made by people, spanning the past to the present and extending into the future, are hardly separate from the physical context where those choices are made.[2] For this reason, the second part of this book will begin by revisiting geography and examining its influence on the fundamental interests and rationale of China's military strategy and foreign policy. This will provide readers with a framework to examine changes and continuities in China's military strategy, as well as support foreign policy-makers and business leaders in formulating more robust strategies based on a deeper comprehension of China's real motives and intent.

China's Geography and Worldview

As discussed in Chap. 1, like many of the world's great civilisations that grew around large rivers—Egypt on the Nile or Babylon between the Tigris and the Euphrates—Chinese civilisation emerged along the Yellow River. Abundant water resources were beneficial for agricultural development, enabling China to develop into an agrarian society. The character of the agrarian society is stability, which stems from the need for people to settle near farmland, ensuring the continuity of growth cycles across generations through their labour. Further, Chap. 1 also emphasised that China's isolated geography and restricted imports for goods necessitate a primary focus on self-sufficiency in agriculture. As wealth accumulated through agriculture and through cities developed over time, the Chinese were able to cultivate a comparatively sophisticated culture. This, in turn, resulted in advancement in engineering, mathematics, medicine, and other technological fields. Owing to this degree of technological progress, China stood among the most advanced of all premodern civilisations.

China's vast size, agricultural self-reliance, technological advancement and cultural sophistication have enabled its people to feel satisfied with what they possess. Consequently, there has been less demand or desire for products, raw materials, or inexpensive labour from other economies. The Italian traveller and merchant Francesco Carletti (1573–1636), one of the early Europeans to come in contact with China, noted: "they [the Han Chinese] believe themselves to be full of all knowledge, to have an abundance of everything good, and to have no need of anything", and "for that reason they have no desire to acquire other regions, but are content with their own".[3]

By contrast, Western civilisation originated from the sea-trading, colony-building cities of Greece, and later the Mediterranean Empire of Rome. Geographical features made foreign expansion core to the Greco-Roman era.[4] As discussed in Chap. 1, the

---

[2] Marshall (2015a).
[3] David (2007).
[4] Fairbank and Frank (1974).

prosperity and security of Greek city-states could not be just based on local agriculture, but depended on extensive trade networks. The Mediterranean offered easy navigation along the coast for large parts of the year. The inhabitants of more prosperous regions could colonise other coastal plains inhabited by less technologically advanced people, and exploit those regions for gold, silver and precious metals, or agricultural resources.[5] In addition, geography enabled long-distance trade networks for bulk and exotic products, extending down through Egypt and the Maghreb to Africa, and through the Middle East to India and the Far East.[6] Along those trade routes, precious metals, spices and incense, silk and slaves circulated between Roman Europe and the rest of the world—and taxes on those items contributed no small part to the Empire's treasury.[7]

Nineteenth-century European imperialism inherited the expansive nature of Greco-Roman civilisation, finally leading to world hegemony. In the words of Paul Kennedy, author of *The Rise and Fall of the Great Powers*, "All this generated a continual interaction—of further European expansion, bringing fresh discoveries and thus trade opportunities, resulting in additional gains, which stimulated still more expansion."[8] Therefore, the European worldview, shaped by geography, was very different from that developed in China. Looking at the outside world, the Europeans perceived it as a vast territory that, if explored, could greatly benefit the motherland. By contrast, the Chinese worldview mainly defaulted to perceiving the conquest of faraway lands as suspicious, disruptive and potentially dangerous for the stable and prosperous living environment that had already been built in the motherland.

Neither Cuddly Panda Nor Menacing Dragon

The Chinese conservative worldview shaped its core interests with the aim of protecting their stable, self-sufficient, and advanced society from disruptions. There are three types of disruptions that were feared: natural disasters, domestic turmoil, and disruptions from the outside. Part I of the book discussed how the Chinese built a strong centralised power and a sophisticated bureaucratic system to tackle natural disasters such as floods and droughts and manage domestic disruption. Here, this chapter will focus on discussing the military strategy developed by China to avoid external disruptions.

The lessons of history have instilled in the Chinese a deep appreciation for peace and stability, recognising the detrimental impact of wars on their well-being and prosperity. Nevertheless, this does not imply that the Chinese are perpetually pacifistic or consistently adopt a non-threatening demeanour. In fact, over the past two

---

[5] Kennedy (2017).
[6] Ibid.
[7] Ibid.
[8] Ibid. p 28.

millennia, they have fought numerous wars with external adversaries. Thus, considering their historical experiences, under what circumstances do the Chinese perceive it necessary to resort to threats or military action? The recurring patterns indicate that the Chinese resort to military action when confronted with external disturbances that pose an existential threat to their society's security and stability, to an extent that prosperity would be unattainable if the threat materialised. This scenario has unfolded many times throughout Chinese history.

Indeed, external invasions have long been viewed as one of the most severe threats to the stability of life in the Chinese Central Plains. These lands have fallen prey to nomadic incursions no fewer than eight times.[9] The first transpired in 771 BCE, marking the demise of the Western Zhou dynasty, a development in which the Quan Rong tribes, an active ethnic group from the northwestern region of China, played a pivotal role.[10] Assisting the Shen, a vassal of the Zhou, the Quan Rong tribes were instrumental in the rebellion that dismantled the Western Zhou regime. In the aftermath of these events, the Quan Rong tribes successfully invaded and occupied the Western Zhou capital, compelling the surviving heir of the Western Zhou to relocate to Luoyang. There, he reasserted his rule, marking the inception of what is now retrospectively referred to as the Eastern Zhou dynasty, a term distinguishing this period from the earlier Western Zhou era. The most recent nomadic conquest took place in 1644, when the Ming dynasty was conquered by the Manchus, and the history of the Han Chinese wearing the Manchu pigtail began until the Republic of China was established in 1912.[11]

During ancient and early Imperial China, connections with the world beyond Chinese borders were very limited. Although the Chinese knew of a powerful Roman Empire during the Han dynasty, it was never a threat to China's status due to the vast distance between them. China's vulnerability to invasions lies in its immediate northwestern borders. Over the course of China's extensive history, ceaseless nomadic tribes, such as the Mongols and the Xiongnu, have inhabited the territories to the northwest of China. The nation's northwestern borders, characterised by mountainous and cold terrain that is challenging to defend, lack buffer states along potential invasion routes to the heartland, which intensifies the threat posed by nomadic tribes in the bordering regions.[12]

The distinct geographical conditions have had a significant influence on the recurrent conflicts between the settled Chinese and the nomadic tribes throughout history. Nomads have been described as 'living with the grass' in early Chinese literature.[13] The dryness and scarce rainfall combined with harsh winter temperatures render most

---

[9] Chen (2013).
[10] Ibid.
[11] Ibid.
[12] Nathan and Scobell (2012).
[13] Sima (2011).

of their regions unsuitable for agricultural development. Therefore, the primary livelihood of the inhabitants relied on vast herds of sheep, horses, and cattle that grazed on open grasslands, even though the frost-free grazing season was quite brief.[14]

According to research, nomadic attacks on China were closely related to the monsoon climate of East Asia.[15] When the summer monsoon is strong and brings heavy rainfall to the grasslands north of China, the nomads could live and work in peace.[16] However, when the summer monsoon was weak and the rain could not reach the northern grasslands, drought would make the nomads' lives difficult. To survive, they will either harass farmers, rob Chinese caravans and settlements, or launch large-scale attacks on the Chinese heartland.[17] It is noteworthy that the dynamic of conflict between settled farmers and nomadic pastoralists along China's northwest frontier shares some similarities with the modern-day situation in the Sahel region of Africa. A key factor driving conflicts in places like Darfur can be attributed to struggles over diminishing resources for survival, particularly water and fertile land, exacerbated by environmental shifts such as desertification.

The contrasting geography and living conditions influenced military preparedness as well. For China, the primary focus was on maintaining internal stability. As discussed in Chap. 4, individual Chinese were encouraged to cultivate virtue and prepare for the imperial examination from a young age, in order to join the bureaucracy. Conversely, for the nomads, survival in a harsh and unpredictable environment took precedence. As raids and plundering were frequently the sole means of survival, individuals honed their combat skills from an early age. This way, "their tribal leaders could rapidly mobilise a large part of the male population and summon several hundred thousand warriors to fight".[18] Furthermore, the utilisation of war horses made the nomads' attacks highly adaptable. They fought as "highly mobile mounted archers who could move quickly to encircle and attack columns of infantry, or cut-off crucial enemy supply lines".[19] This made them "an exceptionally dangerous and elusive enemy" for the Chinese.[20]

To better understand the difference in military strategy between the Chinese and the nomads, it is important to understand the concept of offence-defence balance. The key idea here is that exogenous factors, such as geography, can influence the relative value of attacking or defending a territory.[21] The Xiongnu's geography, the use of war horses, and their flexible military style, provided them with an offensive advantage. This means it was easier to penetrate the enemy's land, destroy its army and take over its territory, rather than defend their own. In contrast, the Chinese advantage was essentially defensive. The Chinese inhabit a closed-off geographical

---

[14] McLaughlin (2016).
[15] Chen (2013).
[16] Ibid.
[17] Zhao (2012).
[18] McLaughlin (2016).
[19] Ibid. p38.
[20] Ibid. p38.
[21] Fearon (1997); Jervis (1978).

environment with established cities and fortifications, a long distance away from the centres of other civilisations, and even limited access from the sea. This means it was easier for China to protect and hold its own territory than move forward, destroy, and take over. As a result, defence has come to be China's default military strategy.

In addition, according to Confucian values, warfare itself is a deplorable activity and armed forces were only necessary to ward off barbarian attacks or internal revolts. Therefore, although the Chinese had already mastered advanced technologies such as gunpowder, compass and bronze smelting, they did not apply them to make weapons, lead offensive wars and penetrate their enemy's land. Instead, they spent most of their military budget building a purely defensive weapon: the Great Wall, a well-known series of border fortifications, described in Chap. 1.

'Unconquerable' Enemies

As described earlier, China's border has presented the country with many enemies, most of which are 'unconquerable'. The adjective 'unconquerable' does not mean that the enemies are too strong to be conquered, but that they can never be eliminated entirely. When heavy summer monsoon yielded abundance over the grasslands, the nomads lived in peace with the Chinese. However, those bountiful times also encouraged population growth—causing an even bigger threat at the next drought. One of the key ways to temper this risk was to establish and maintain buffer states: the greater the distance between states, the more the offence-defence balance favours the defence.[22] Once the buffer state was gone, the balance of power between China and the nomadic enemy shifted, benefiting the attacker.

I will examine the 'buffer-state strategy' in further detail. During the Han dynasty, the Xiongnu attacked a buffer state called Yuezhi. This friendly nomadic steppe neighbour inhabited crucial lands to the west of China, including a strategic gateway to the ancient Silk Road. With this buffer state out of the way, the Xiongnu gained greater access to the Chinese Central Plains and blocked off the Han's commercial ties with countries along the Silk Road.[23] In order to protect border security and commercial ties, the Han dynasty fought many wars with the Xiongnu. The goal is not for a complete annihilation of the Xiongnu, but to control, or at least neutralise, buffer states on their borders to prevent the Xiongnu's aggression. In this context, even though China's core military position is defensive, sometimes an 'active defence' or even offensive action, was the only way to achieve the defensive goal.[24]

The significance of geography cannot be understated, as conflicts arising from the vulnerable northwestern border were not solely a concern for the Han regime. Indeed, as soon as the nomads successfully attacked the northwestern border and ascended to the position of emperor in Beijing, they were confronted with the same

---

[22] Fearon (1997).

[23] McLaughlin (2016).

[24] Jervis (1978); Fravel (2019).

issue.[25] For example, during the Manchu-ruled Qing dynasty, a nomadic group called the Dzungar Khanate, an Inner Asian group of Mongol origin based in Xinjiang and Western Mongolia, began to rise and move eastward. Growing increasingly powerful, the Dzungar Khanate began to target the Khalkha Mongols and other Mongolian tribes, which served as a buffer between the Qing dynasty and themselves, in their quest to unify Mongolia. In order to prevent the Dzungar Khanate's efforts to unify Mongolia and exploit it as a pathway to penetrate the Chinese Central Plains, the Qing dynasty launched a fight against the Dzungar Khanate, spanning nearly seven decades (1688–1758).[26] Ironically, it is through this 'active defence' against the Dzungar Khanate—the intention of which was to avoid disruption—that the Qing dynasty brought Mongolia and Tibet under its rule. Similarly, earlier in China's history, Tang China asserted control over the Mongolian Plateau region while defending against the Turks, who posed a significant military threat to the Tang dynasty.

The question, however, is whether China can ever achieve a reliable and lasting sense of security through active defence or offensive actions, such as those of the Tang and Qing dynasties, leading to the conquest of nearby territories. For this sense of security to be complete, China would need to conquer an extent of territory that reaches impenetrable barriers, like oceans and mountain ranges, to sufficiently prevent external invasion. To the west, it means China must control Tibet, so that the Pamirs and the Himalayas can serve as a natural protection. To the east, China would need to include Japan, the Philippines and maritime Malaysia to form a circle of protection over the sea. To the south, it would need to extend at least into North Vietnam, possibly including the entire coast of Vietnam along the Annamese Range. To the north and northwest, where China has historically faced the most threats, even if China was to include Xinjiang and most of Siberia, it would still face many potential enemies around a distant western border. Clearly, the ambition to reach complete security appears impossible for China. And this is a very dangerous goal, beyond the self-evident geopolitical implications of China pursuing territorial control over Japan, Vietnam or Siberia. From China's own historical records, the pursuit of excessive territorial control through warfare has typically led to decline.

The War Curse

Engaging in wars with external aggressors poses a risk of depleting the nation's wealth and ultimately leads to decline. China's history classic, the *Book of Han*, records that the costs involved in the military expeditions against the Xiongnu were beyond calculation.[27] Those costs were not just monetary, but also included labour. In 200 BCE, Emperor Gaozu of Han (256–195 BCE) mobilised a force of 320,000

---

[25] Fairbank (1969).
[26] Cang (2014).
[27] McLaughlin (2016).

soldiers in the frontier zone to fight against the mounted warriors of the Xiongnu.[28] Many of those soldiers were recruited among ordinary male peasants. The extensive mobilisation significantly disrupted the agricultural labour force, which had repercussions on the nation's well-being, as both population growth and national fiscal revenue were closely tied to farming productivity. Those domestic challenges, together with the strain of external conflicts, collectively contributed to the downfall of the Han dynasty.

Another example is the decline of the Sui regime. In the sixth and seventh centuries, the Korean Kingdom of Goguryeo refused to submit to the Sui regime and launched continual raids into the northern borders of the Sui. Additionally, it established strong military alliances with the Turks, thus posing a more significant threat along the Sui frontier. To counter the threat, the Sui regime waged a number of wars with Goguryeo between 598 and 614.[29] Those wars exhausted the national treasury, causing hundreds of thousands of deaths and great suffering among the people.[30] As a result, the Sui regime faced uprisings from various groups, including peasants, farmers, soldiers, and even aristocrats and military officers.[31] These revolts rapidly spread across the nation, culminating in the fall of the Sui dynasty in 618.

The Expansion Curse

In general, invading nearby nations carries a higher chance of success, as the closer the battlefields the easier it is for troops to receive supplies and defend the conquered land. Nonetheless, the sheer magnitude of China makes frontier expansion a highly expensive endeavour. According to *The Art of War*, before the military arrived at the border, at least 50% of the supplies would be exhausted, and many soldiers would have died along the march.[32] The chances of success were therefore also relatively low. Large-scale military mobilisation, as well as maintaining long-distance provisions and supply lines also bring severe pressure on the Chinese regime.[33]

The founding Emperor of Ming dynasty, Hongwu, warned his successor to never target small island nations or remote small nations with punitive military expeditions.[34] That is based on the calculation that those nations would not be able to provide China with the needed supply of land and people to offset the costs of invasion, and were therefore not worth the military investment.[35] He even listed fifteen

---

[28] Ibid.
[29] Lee (1984).
[30] Ibid.
[31] Wei et al. (1973).
[32] Sun (2022).
[33] McLaughlin (2016 ionRef>).
[34] Farmer (2021).
[35] Ibid.

countries that should never be targeted, including Japan, Korea and Cambodia.[36] This advice from Emperor Hongwu did not come lightly. As the founder of the Ming dynasty, he was not short of ambition. However, the lessons of history made him believe that expansionism was ultimately dangerous to his regime.[37]

This piece of geostrategic wisdom greatly contrasts with the benefits that the Spanish, the Dutch, and later the English derived from expansion. One important reason for this difference is that Chinese military endeavours were not linked with businessmen, or commercial expansion.[38] As discussed in Chap. 3, Chinese rulers have a tradition of distrusting businessmen and private capitalists, so they never allowed merchants to link with the military for commercial expansion. Chinese rulers only allowed the military to link with the bureaucracy as an auxiliary means of governance.[39] By comparison, in Europe, the military has been associated with exploration, commodity trading, colony establishment and overseas empires from at least as early as the Greek city-states.[40] The connection between military expansion and commercial interest has brought huge profits to the European motherland and further encouraged European expansion. In fact, the colonisation of Indonesia was initially led by the Dutch East India Company, rather than the Dutch Republic itself; while British India, as well as other Asian colonies of Britain including Hong Kong, was originally under the control of the (British) East India Company, rather than the Crown.

Last but not least, expansion and colonisation increase a country's relative vulnerability. For example, Britain had a relatively secure position as an island. However, once it took over India, it had to consider Russia as a neighbour and potential direct enemy.[41] Considering China's already complicated border situation, territorial expansion has historically been a challenge to China's security. Since many of the areas surrounding China are inhabited by people of different ethnic groups, colonising them and keeping them under control would require considerable resources, inevitably weakening central power and threatening internal stability. Once central power is weakened, maintaining control over conquered territories becomes increasingly challenging for the ruling regime. This often triggers rebellions among the conquered populations, particularly those with distinct values and beliefs.[42]

To give one example, towards the end of the Tang dynasty, most of the areas conquered by the Tang regime claimed independence and fought against China. As a result, the Tang territory was reduced to about three-million square kilometres, down from 10.76 million square kilometres at its peak.[43] Another example is the Mongol-led Eurasian continental empire which "ranged from the shores of the China Sea

---

[36] Ibid.

[37] Ibid.

[38] Fairbank and Frank (1974).

[39] Ibid.

[40] Ibid.

[41] Robert (1978).

[42] Ibid.

[43] Song (1994).

to Anatolia in Asia Minor and to Central Europe".[44] The extent of this territory remained unmatched in terms of centralised control over a contiguous area until the peak of the Stalinist Sino-Soviet bloc.[45] However, the Mongol Empire eventually became too large to manage and control from one single central point. In the end, it divided into several self-sufficient parts, which promoted faster local assimilation, and accelerated disintegration.[46]

This pattern of excessive expansion leading to decline applies beyond Chinese history. During the heyday of the Roman Empire, it had a large armed force with no less than 300,000 troops deployed overseas.[47] Rome's advantage in military strength and armament played a crucial role in facilitating its expansion. However, it eventually became too large to be ruled from a single centre. Division into western and eastern halves weakened the monopolistic character of its power.[48] The Chinese emperors have been well aware of this danger. As discussed in Chap. 1, their core mission was to hold the land united, not expand the territory to the greatest extent. Therefore, the ambitions of Chinese rulers to expand their territory were constrained by the fundamental requirement to preserve the nation's internal stability, which underpins the stability of their regime.

Secular Pragmatism

Ancient Chinese strategists developed a highly pragmatic way of deciding whether, when, and how to attack adversaries.[49] This decision is not based on achieving complete annihilation of the adversaries—let alone personal glory—but rather competing for relative gains to support the country's core interests. The principal idea is that victory without fighting is the supreme victory.[50] In practice, it means acknowledging that enemies at the border were inexhaustible and warfare could not provide reliable and enduring security, potentially even contributing to the central power's decline. It also means that Chinese strategists have employed various strategies to deter, weaken, or even coexist with foreign entities to halt aggression, rather than conquering them, maintaining a permanent military presence, or seeking their total destruction. This approach explains why Chinese rulers would not give military command to pure 'warrior' types.[51] This is because the training received by warriors

---

[44] Brzezinski (1998).
[45] Ibid.
[46] Ibid.
[47] Ibid.
[48] Ibid.
[49] Allison (2019).
[50] Sun (2022).
[51] Fairbank and Frank (1974).

Secular Pragmatism   107

tends to be overly focused on forceful attack, limiting their ability to effectively coordinate complex strategies to adeptly avoid external threats.[52]

The concept of 'Shi' (势), as articulated in Sun Tzu's *Art of War*, provides further nuance to Chinese strategic thinking. 'Shi' means 'strategic advantage', a concept that comprises many elements, including geography, natural conditions, and the balance of forces and morale.[53] It suggests a comprehension of the dynamics and possibilities inherent in a specific scenario, and the skilful adaptation required to secure comparative advantages. For example, Ban Gu, author of the *Book of Han*, described the best strategy for managing the nomads as "neither forming alliance with them nor waging wars against them".[54] Because "alliance costs gifts and results in financial deficit and war exhausts the troops and invites invasion".[55] A ruler shall "punish and defend against them when they come; prepare and guard against them when they go".[56] However, "If they admire righteousness and pay tribute, treat them pursuant to the rituals, befriend them unceasingly, thus making them in the wrong [when conflicts occur]."[57]

In translating this timeless wisdom to a modern understanding, U.S. General Mark Milley's observations offer great insights. Much like how the Chinese historically acknowledged the nature of the 'unconquerable enemy' around its borders, Mark Milley observed that the Chinese also fully understand 'how powerful the United States is', regardless of their diplomatic rhetoric.[58] He further brings to light the practical nature of China's military approach, explaining, "they [China] are very realist in the sense that they are keenly aware of cost, benefit, and risks…They want to achieve their national objectives, but they want to actually do it without armed conflict".[59] Similar to ancient Chinese military wisdom, he suggested that deterrence, achieved through formidable and skilled militaries, diplomatic endeavours, and the explicit communication of resolve to an adversary, have proven to be successful strategies.[60]

Chinese pragmatic military strategy was further reinforced by China's highly secular culture. Overall, the Chinese believe that there is only one world, namely 'this present world'.[61] As a result, their general concern has been to find out how humans could live in harmony with the cosmic and natural forces associated with 'this present world'.[62] This view has prompted a kind of conservative attitude.[63]

---

[52] Ibid.
[53] Mott and Kim (2006).
[54] Schuman (2020).
[55] Ibid.
[56] Ibid.
[57] Ibid.
[58] Milley (2023).
[59] Ibid.
[60] Ibid.
[61] Fang (2015).
[62] Ibid.
[63] Ibid.

China has generally lacked enthusiasm for external aggression and conquest, out of a belief that it would create a vicious cycle of retaliation, so that long-term harmony and prosperity in 'this present world' would be threatened. Coexistence or, ideally, cooperation and even convergence, are what the Chinese wish for. I will return to further discussion on how the Chinese cultivate cooperation and convergence in Chap. 8.

China's Core Interest

In the recent decade, with unprecedented military build-up and rising Chinese nationalism, China's responses to territorial disputes and conflicts with other countries have become more and more assertive. People around the world have become concerned that under Xi Jinping's leadership, China's military stance has changed from a defensive to an offensive one, and from an approach of coexistence to one of dominance —that the 'cuddly panda' has finally become the 'menacing dragon'. Some commentators even warn that, in an extreme case, a Third World War, emerging from the Sino-U.S. conflict, is unavoidable. Instead of projecting anxieties on the potential conflicts and paying too much attention to over-enthusiastic expressions of nationalism within China, it is more useful to analyse the core interests of China's military build-up. An insightful analysis of this cannot be achieved by merely considering factors such as Chinese defence spending or the size of their armed forces.[64]

As discussed in Chap. 5, the PLA is under strict control of the CCP. This unwavering authority over the PLA ensures that PLA military strategies align with China's overarching political goals. In other words, China's grand political objectives define the intent, essential purpose and use of Chinese military power, including nuclear weapons.[65] China's grand political objectives are largely influenced by its geography. As Henry Kissinger stated, "America has never had a powerful threatening neighbour; China has never been without a powerful adversary on its borders."[66] Indeed, the United States only shares a land border with the comparatively less powerful and friendly nations of Mexico and Canada, whereas China has consistently dealt with complex and occasionally hostile borders throughout its history.

China currently shares borders with 22 neighbouring countries. The country has constantly faced external threats and territorial disputes with its neighbours. Research shows that there were at least 23 major territorial conflicts since 1949.[67] There have also been periods of sustained threats to Chinese security when China squared off against the Soviet Union during the Cold War.[68] During some periods, China even

---

[64] Fravel (2019).

[65] Campbell (2021).

[66] Kissinger (2014).

[67] Fravel (2019).

[68] Ibid.

faced imminent attack. This includes Taiwan mobilising forces to return to the mainland in 1962, clashes with the Soviet Union over the Zhenbao Island in 1969, and the Soviet Union deploying hundreds of troops on China's northern frontier in the 1970s.[69]

More importantly, the United States' geographically secure and remote position affords it greater latitude for trial and error without facing severe military repercussions. On the other hand, China's complex border challenges leave little margin for strategic errors, thereby fostering a more cautious approach. China's complex borders means it seldom has the luxury of dealing with any of its neighbours in a purely bilateral context, giving rise to the *Third Ring* of Chinese security concerns.[70] The *Third Ring* refers to the political and security concerns relating to six distinct multistate regional systems, each comprising a group of states with interconnected foreign policy interests: Northeast Asia, Oceania, continental Southeast Asia, maritime Southeast Asia, South Asia, and Central Asia.[71] China is the only country in the world that is physically part of such a large number of regional systems. Russia and the United States may engage in even larger numbers, but it is by choice rather than the constraint of geography.[72]

China's unique and vulnerable geography has defined its core interest as the instinctive pursuit of survival and managing its surroundings to maintain stability. China's instinctive pursuit of survival inherent in its geography constrains the top leaders of the country, giving them fewer choices and less room to manoeuvre than external observers might think.[73] The criteria for situations in which China feels compelled to threaten or employ military force have persisted for a few thousand years: if external disturbances or aggression intensify to the extent that they present an existential risk to China's security and social stability, the country will resort to active defence or even offensive actions, irrespective of the opponents' strength.

A recent example is the Korean War (1950–1953). When U.S. troops advanced towards the Yalu River, the border between North Korea and China, Beijing was concerned about a perceived existential threat posed by the possibility of U.S. troops crossing the Yalu River and threatening China's border. In Beijing's eyes, had U.S. and United Nations forces successfully occupied North Korea and installed a pro-West government during the Korean War, it could have resulted in U.S. troops and their allies being stationed directly along China's border. This would have posed a significant threat to China's security and independence. In response, even though possessing significantly less military power than the United States, Mao Zedong deployed approximately three million soldiers during the three-year war, with 600,000 casualties.[74] From China's viewpoint, this action served as a caution

---

[69] Ibid.
[70] Nathan and Scobell (2012).
[71] Ibid.
[72] Ibid.
[73] Marshall (2015b).
[74] Park (2013).

to the United States to maintain a distance from the Yalu border or risk engaging in a full-scale conflict. The conflict inflicted a deep wound in Sino-U.S. relations, which took over 20 years to repair.[75]

From 1949 to 1956, in response to considerable external threats, the defence expenditure of the PRC constituted an average of 35% of its total fiscal expenditures.[76] In recent times, as China has undergone rapid double-digit growth, defence spending has declined as a percentage of GDP, yet it has risen in absolute terms.[77] This means although China's defence expenditure as a percentage of GDP has hovered at or below two percent since 1999, its actual budget amount has risen from 107.6 billion yuan (USD 15.73 billion) in 1999 to 1.554 trillion yuan (USD 224.79 billion) in 2023.[78] Currently, China's defence budget is the second-largest military expenditure in the world, after the United States. In 2023, China marks its 29th consecutive year of increasing its defence budget, which is the longest uninterrupted streak by any country in the world.

In the eyes of Americans, the growth of China's military power is interpreted as an attempt to gain status as a superpower, not just a pursuit of its own defence goals.[79] The question often asked is: if China has no world-class obligations, why would it need a world-class military?[80] Various U.S. analysts and commentators worry that China's increasing military power is not only aimed at expelling the United States from its hegemonic sea-power status and seeking hegemony in Asia, but also replacing the United States in the world.[81]

The Chinese views the situation differently. In *Cooperation Under the Security Dilemma*, American political scientist Robert Jervis explained an important game-theory. When State A believes that State B knows that State A only wants to preserve the status quo and that State A's arms are meant only for self-preservation, then any military expansion by State B would likely be viewed as an indication of aggressive ambitions by State A.[82] Moreover, State A might consider State B's objections to its own military build-up as unjustified, given that State B is not facing any imminent danger.[83] As a result, State A may conclude that State B's protests reveal its aggressive motives.[84] According to the logic articulated above, from China's perspective, the country may think that it is developing its military capability from a purely defensive intent, out of concern for national security due to its vulnerable geography. The fact that the United States objected to China's military build-up so strongly only proves

---

[75] Hao and Zhai (1990).

[76] The State Council Information Office of the People's Republic of China (2009).

[77] Ibid.

[78] The State Council Information Office of the People's Republic of China (2009); The State Council Information Office of the People's Republic of China (2023).

[79] The Paper (2019).

[80] Ibid.

[81] Ibid.

[82] Jervis (1978).

[83] Ibid.

[84] Ibid.

its aggressive intentions. And indeed, data shows that the growth of China's military spending is positively affected by the growth of U.S. military spending.[85]

Buffer States in Modern Terms

As discussed earlier, maintaining buffer states has long been strategically important to safeguard China's homeland security and deter against external aggression. This remains true today, although the most important buffer states are not foreign entities, but the two autonomous provinces of Xinjiang and Tibet. Understanding this role is important to make sense of CCP policy in those territories, particularly in relation to separatist movements.

The historical status of Xinjiang, specifically whether it has always been an integral part of China, is indeed a significant point of contention between the Chinese government and many Western scholars. Xinjiang has a complex history marked by shifting boundaries and changing political affiliations. Over centuries, it has been under the control of various entities, including Chinese dynasties, Mongol empires, and Turkic kingdoms. China often emphasises periods of Chinese control, such as the Protectorate of the Western Regions during the Han dynasty, to assert its historical claim over Xinjiang. Meanwhile, some Western scholars may contend that during the Protectorate of the Western Regions, China's influence was more of a military presence than comprehensive control, and it was not until the Qing dynasty that the region was formally conquered and incorporated into China's provincial system. They also highlight periods of non-Chinese rule or autonomy to argue that Xinjiang has not always been an integral part of China.

Today, a variety of ethnic groups reside in both Xinjiang and Tibet, each with their unique cultural identities. Xinjiang is populated by Uyghurs, who are majority Muslim and speak a language related to Turkish, while Tibet is historically home to Tibetan people and a range of other minority ethnic groups—including the Monpa, Tamang, Qiang, Sherpa, and Lhoba.

From a geostrategic perspective, Tibet and Xinjiang both serve as a protective buffer state for the Chinese heartland. Tibet, located in the Himalayas with an average elevation of 4,380 m above sea level, is the highest region on Earth, and offers natural protection, particularly against its powerful Indian neighbour. Xinjiang shares an extensive 5,600 km land border with eight countries: Russia, Mongolia, Kazakhstan, Kyrgyzstan, Tajikistan, Afghanistan, Pakistan and India. Furthermore, the Belt and Road Initiative land routes go straight through Xinjiang, and connect southwards to the deep-water port of Gwadar in Pakistan, offering an alternative access to the sea beyond the South China Sea and the Strait of Malacca.[86] More importantly, Xinjiang is also home to China's nuclear weapons testing sites.

---

[85] Zhang et al. (2021).
[86] Marshall (2015b).

Given the geostrategic importance of Xinjiang and Tibet, not only does China want to control them, but other countries may be motivated to control them too, prompting a geopolitics of fear.[87] From the Chinese perspective, if China does not control Tibet, India may attempt to command the high ground, and use it as a base to penetrate the Chinese mainland.[88] Tibet meets northern India in the Himalayas, and the precise definition of the border has been a source of territorial disputes, sparking a war in 1962 and clashes in 1967.[89] More recently, in 2020, another armed clash along the border resulted in the first combat-related deaths since 1975.[90] Similarly, China also fears that if it does not control Xinjiang, the region may become a gateway for foreign influence, threatening China's security right on its doorstep. In other words, in framing the issues of Xinjiang and Tibet, Beijing often emphasises geopolitical security over human rights.[91] The Chinese government expresses concerns not necessarily over the regions' autonomy, but over potential threats to national unity and stability, including the possibility of these areas aligning with China's geopolitical rivals. The historical contexts include Tibet's attempt to establish independence in 1913, and the protests and violence in Xinjiang and Tibet during the 2000s have contributed to Beijing's intensifying efforts to suppress cultural, linguistic, and religious differences in these regions.

In order to defend and maintain control over these two critical buffer states, there have been continuous efforts to integrate and assimilate the territory and populations of Xinjiang and Tibet into the Han mainstream. Since the Han dynasty, the regime has introduced a mechanism called 'tuntian' (屯田) meaning 'a strategy of military farms'. This state-supported approach merged military and agricultural functions, permitting soldiers, landless farmers, and refugees to cultivate the Western frontier lands with the purpose of guarding frontier areas against nomad aggression.[92] This system guaranteed adequate agricultural production to sustain a military presence on the frontier, providing defence against potential incursions and promoting the growth of the Han population in these regions. In turn, this ensured that the Western border regions would be reliably attached to Chinese interests.

Both the Tang and Ming dynasties significantly upheld and implemented the 'tuntian' system. Since the Qing regime brought Xinjiang under its control in the 1750s, it has borrowed the Han tuntian model and implemented it on a large scale. By 1840, there were more than 110,000 people in various scion fields in Xinjiang, covering a total cultivated arable land of nearly 200,000 hectares.[93] By the end of the Qing dynasty in 1911, there were nearly 704,000 hectares of cultivated arable land in Xinjiang mostly held by Han farmers.[94]

---

[87] Ibid.

[88] Ibid.

[89] Campbell (2021).

[90] Ibid.

[91] Marshall (2015b).

[92] Luo et al (2017).

[93] History Compilation Committee of Xinjiang Production and Construction Corps (1986).

[94] Ibid.

In the Republican era, for the same purpose of defending national borders, Han Chinese were encouraged to move to Xinjiang and Tibet, with an explicit intent to dilute the local population. This was echoed by the Head of the KMT Government Chiang Kai-shek. In his book *China's Destiny,* he wrote that "if even one area is occupied by a different race, then the entire nation and entire state loses the natural barriers for self-defence. Therefore Taiwan, Penghu, the four northeast provinces, inner and outer Mongolia, Xinjiang and Tibet are all strongholds for the protection of the nation's survival".[95] In line with this statement, he proactively encouraged Han settlement in border regions.

The CCP continued this process. In 1954, it established a modern tuntian system, under the name 'Xinjiang Production and Construction Corps' (XPCC). According to the Chinese government description, this is a unique state-owned economic and paramilitary organisation, with the purpose of consolidating border defence, promoting economic development and strengthening connection and integration between Han people and Uyghurs. By the end of 2022, the total population of the XPCC was over 3.6 million.[96] The XPCC was sanctioned by the United States in 2020, citing alleged human rights abuses. I will return to this point in Chap. 8.

Furthermore, with railway and road network connection, the state-sponsored resettlement of Han people in Xinjiang, Inner Mongolia and Tibet has risen rapidly. The Han population in Xinjiang has increased from four percent in 1949 to 42% in 2020.[97] Although the Han population remains relatively small in Tibet itself given its harsh climate conditions, it has grown quickly in the better-connected, historically Tibetan-populated areas of Qinghai and Sichuan, accounting for 50.53% and 93.2% of total permanent residents respectively as of 2021.[98]

Regions Shaping National Prosperity

Xinjiang and Tibet not only matter to China's geo-security, but also its economic prosperity. Xinjiang is China's biggest province-level division. With a size of 1.67 million square kilometres, it covers approximately one-sixth of the Chinese territory. To put the size of Xinjiang in context, it is big enough to fit the United Kingdom, Switzerland, France, Germany, the Netherlands, Austria and Belgium and still have room for Luxembourg and Liechtenstein.[99] In Imperial China, from an economic perspective, the dry desert basin and rugged mountains that make up most of Xinjiang were not of interest to the Chinese regime. However, today, with advanced energy exploration technology, this territory has become the oil and natural gas tank for China.

---

[95] Hayton (2022).

[96] Statistics Bureau of Xinjiang Production and Construction Corps (2022).

[97] The Economist (2016).

[98] The People's Government of Sichuan Province (2021); People's Daily (2021).

[99] Marshall (2015b).

Xinjiang's abundant natural resources play a key role in securing prosperity for China and its surrounding regions. Xinjiang is rich in energy resources, with coal, oil, natural gas, wind energy and solar energy ranking among the top in the country. As of 2014, Xinjiang held 5.6 billion tonnes of oil and 1.4 trillion cubic metres of natural gas reserves, crucial for powering industries like steel, building materials, petrochemicals, and electricity in China.[100] The West–East Gas Pipeline, operational since 2004, transports natural gas from Xinjiang's Tarim Basin to eastern China. By 2015, it had delivered 284.6 billion cubic metres of natural gas, meeting 50% of China's consumption, benefiting over 140 cities, 3,000 enterprises, and nearly 400 million people.[101] This quantity of gas equates to 370 million tonnes of standard coal, preventing 17.35 million tonnes of harmful substances and 1.252 billion tonnes of carbon emissions.[102]

Besides energy, water can also cause turmoil.[103] The Tibetan Plateau holds the third-largest store of ice in the world, after Antarctica and the Arctic. Melted ice from Tibet feeds into ten of Asia's largest rivers, including the Yellow River, Yangtze, Mekong, Sutlej and Brahmaputra. More than 20% of the world's population live in downstream watersheds of the Tibetan Plateau.[104] With Asia becoming the new global economic centre of gravity, one can appreciate the importance of controlling access to water sources.

The Tibetan Plateau, known as 'China's Water Tower', is also pivotal to China's energy generation, and achieving its 2060 carbon-neutral target. Hydropower is China's second-largest energy source, which constitutes 16% of the country's energy output.[105] The Chinese 14th five-year plan revealed that China will construct the world's largest hydroelectric dam on Tibet's Yarlung Tsangpo River, holding 113 gigawatts of hydropower, or 17% of China's total.[106] Once finished, this dam will generate over twice the power of the Three Gorges Dam.[107]

India fears China's upstream dam developments could impact its security, while Beijing is concerned that India's infrastructure expansion in disputed areas like South Tibet/Arunachal Pradesh could reduce Chinese territorial influence. This geopolitics of fear has led China to intensify control over upstream rivers, fuelling India's anxieties. Due to the geostrategic and economic importance of Xinjiang and Tibet, along with associated geopolitical fear, Beijing is anticipated to sustain or potentially increase its stringent policies in these areas. With the international community becoming increasingly alarmed over human rights conditions in these regions, the strain between China and the West is likely to endure. Further discussion on this subject will be provided in Chap. 8.

---

[100] The State Council Information Office of the People's Republic of China (2015).

[101] PetroChina (2015).

[102] Ibid.

[103] Marshall (2015b).

[104] Wilson and Smith (2015).

[105] China Renewable Energy Engineering Institute (2021).

[106] Xu et al. (2002).

[107] Ibid.

Increased Offensive Capabilities

Since 1949, China has adopted a comprehensive military strategy, with 'active defence' as its core principle.[108] The principle of 'active defence' assumes that China is the weaker, more vulnerable side, and should mainly pursue defensive goals.[109] The focus is on counterattacking once an attack on China occurs. Nonetheless, among those 23 territorial conflicts, China has only employed military force for six of them.[110]

Ironically, the PLA's primary focus on defence has led to doubts about its capabilities among U.S. military analysts.[111] Unlike the United States, which has been involved in numerous conflicts since the end of the Cold War—including Iraq, Afghanistan, the Balkans, Syria, and Libya—the PLA has limited recent combat experience, as China's last war occurred in 1979. The absence of recent combat experience, often referred to as the 'peace disease', poses challenges. It may result in inflated military spending and heightened anxiety among China's top leadership, often leading to disproportionate actions. The war in Ukraine may have further intensified Beijing's concerns, as Russia's inexperience—having not fought a large-scale war against a strong organised force since capturing Manchuria from Japan in 1945—is considered a contributing factor to its failures.[112]

Since the foundation of the PRC, changes in the global conduct of warfare and in the international security environment have brought new challenges for this country. In order to maintain its capability to deter and prevent further aggression, China has adopted three major responses to them potential threats, most of them involving an increase in its offensive capabilities.

The first case was a direct response to the United States' first nuclear threat during the Korean War in 1950.[113] Consequently, Chinese leaders developed nuclear weapons to deter attacks through assured retaliation.[114] While China has emphasised retaliation capabilities over nuclear parity, maintaining a 'no-first-use' policy since 1964 and limiting nuclear capabilities to minimum effective levels, its offensive capabilities have still made substantial advancements. The U.S. Department of Defense estimates that China had a total of 400 nuclear warheads as of 2022.[115] Although the U.S. Department of Defense assessed that China is "on a trajectory to exceed the size of a 'minimum deterrent' as described in the PLA's own writings", China's current estimated arsenal amounts to a much smaller and less diverse nuclear posture than

---

[108] The State Council Information Office of the People's Republic of China (2019).
[109] Fravel (2019).
[110] Fravel (2007).
[111] Heath (2018).
[112] The Economist (2022).
[113] Fravel (2019).
[114] Ibid.
[115] U.S. Department of Defense (2022).

that of the United States or Russia, which together account for 90% of total nuclear weapons in the world.[116]

The second trigger for China to change its military strategy was the Gulf War in 1991. Iraq's rapid defeat, prompted by the use of precision missiles by the United States, made Chinese senior military officers realise the enormous advantage that a high-technology force has over less technologically advanced adversaries.[117] This realisation came closer to home during the 1990s, first with the U.S. deployment of two aircraft carrier strike groups to protect Taiwan in 1996, and then with the United States' accidental bombing of China's embassy in Belgrade in 1999.[118] Since then, China has focused on transforming the PLA from an infantry-heavy, low-technology, ground-forces-centric military into a high-technology networked force with an increasing emphasis on joint operations and naval and air power projection.[119] China's rapid economic growth since the 'reform and opening up' period have created the fiscal conditions for the PLA's modernisation.

This strategic transition has three significant effects. First, extra resources have been allocated to the Chinese naval and air forces, and the General Armaments Department was formed in 1998 to bolster the design and procurement of weapons.[120] Second, the defensive emphasis has widened from focusing solely on China's homeland territory to include its periphery, such as the contested Indian border, the East China Sea and South China Sea, and Taiwan.[121] Third, the PLA's modernisation has transitioned China from merely defending against superior forces to taking pre-emptive measures against possible threats.[122]

The third major change in military strategy occurred between 2004 and 2014. It was driven by the rapid development of information technology and its application in warfare, from the Gulf War to subsequent operations in Kosovo, Afghanistan, and Iraq.[123] China began to understand that, similar to how nuclear warfare defined the strategic landscape in the twentieth century, cyber warfare is becoming the strategic battleground in the era of information.[124] As a result, China shifted its military strategy to focus on its capability to transmit, process, and receive information as a vital enabler in an 'integrated joint operations'.[125] According to *Made in China 2025*, China is actively seeking to be a leader in the development of various advanced cyber technologies, such as high-tech chips, artificial intelligence and quantum computing.[126] The deep interconnection between military and civilian technology

---

[116] Campbell (2021), p. 20; U.S. Department of Defense (2022).
[117] Fravel (2019).
[118] Ibid.
[119] Campbell (2021).
[120] Fravel (2019).
[121] Ibid.
[122] Ibid.
[123] Ibid.
[124] Libicki (2009).
[125] Fravel (2019).
[126] State Council of the People's Republic of China (n.d.).

in China means that many advancements in the civilian field have potential military applications. New military technologies provide the benefits of pre-emptive attacks, which could substantially shift the balance between defence and offence. So, will new military advancements within China (as opposed to external threats that triggered the previous changes) become the spark for another shift in military strategy towards utilising these emerging capabilities?

Increased Ambition?

A crucial part of Xi Jinping's dream of a great rejuvenation of the Chinese nation is to build strong armed forces. That means upgrading the PLA into a 'world-class' military by 2049.[127] In line with this vision, Xi Jinping initiated the most ambitious reform and reorganisation of the PLA since the 1950s.

The lack of a clear definition as to what would qualify as a 'world-class' military is a cause of increasing fear, given China is no longer in a position of economic or technological inferiority.[128] This new expression provided no clear insights, but raised many concerns about a potential change in the status quo, including on all of the following points: China's strategic opponent (who will China fight?); primary strategic direction (where will China fight?); basis of preparations for military struggle (what are the characteristics of the wars that China will fight?); and basic guiding principles for operations (how will China fight these wars?).[129]

Earlier, this chapter discussed how Imperial China faced an expansion constraint. However, expansion in modern terms does not necessarily require conquering territory. It can be done through economic influence. As China's economic power has grown, it has also 'expanded' beyond Asia through massive overseas investments. China is building ports in Kenya, railway lines in Angola, and a hydroelectric dam in Ethiopia, with Chinese companies and workers spread out across the world.[130]

Although homeland security and the defence of China's territorial claims remain the core mission of the Chinese military force, this mission has begun to expand as China's economic power has surged. This was reflected in China's most recent defence white paper, *China's National Defense in the New Era*, published in July 2019. The paper stated that the mission of the PLA was to safeguard China's overseas interests, and to support the sustainable development of the country.[131] With this comes increasing worry that peacetime logistical systems and commercial infrastructure can be leveraged to facilitate access and support Chinese military operations during conflicts.[132] Futhermore, China has established a permanent base in Djibouti

---

[127] Xinhua News Agency (2018).

[128] Fravel (2020).

[129] Ibid.

[130] Marshall (2015b).

[131] The State Council Information Office of the People's Republic of China (2019).

[132] Campbell (2021).

in 2017, which can be used to secure support for China's forward-deployed forces.[133] Concerns are also being raised that China is seeking more potential bases for the same purpose, from the South Pacific to the east coast of Africa.[134] So, the question now is, will China further expand its military force across the globe?

Not a Global Power

While China has firmly positioned itself as a titan in the global economy, it has yet to attain the status of a global military superpower. There are three constraints to China's aspiration.

Firstly, China's complex and frequently contentious borders limit its aspiration of achieving worldwide military influence. In recent years, despite the growing evidence of China actively expanding its naval presence in both the Pacific and Indian Oceans, the challenges posed by its 22 neighbouring countries could potentially involve China in prolonged and costly land-based operations. Historically, this predicament has consistently forced China to strike a balance between landward security and maritime aspirations, a constraint that remains largely relevant today. An in-depth analysis of this point will be presented in Chap. 7.

China's vulnerable landward security results in a security priority that is closely tied to its immediate doorstep—in Asia. It is anticipated that, for the short to medium term, the bulk of Chinese military strategic planning will largely centre on resolving long-standing major disputes over its sovereignty, particularly over Taiwan, the South China Sea, and the China-India border.[135] All those issues have the potential to erupt into armed conflicts and none of them can be easily resolved, which will distract China from other security issues. Before China can achieve a level of military dominance in those major disputes such that opposing states are deterred from challenging Beijing, it will be a big stretch for the Chinese military force to expand its ambitions beyond Asia.[136]

Secondly, as the world's economic centre of gravity and strategic focus continue to shift towards Asia, the region has become a focus for competition among major powers. This means that Asia will be a focal point for future military competition between China and the United States, a situation that is further exacerbated by the security interests of the United States' most loyal allies in the region. Japan has increased joint U.S.-Japan military exercises, with the eventual goal of developing an integrated plan to defend Taiwan.[137] South Korea has called for the expansion of the deployment of the U.S. anti-ballistic missile defence system, Terminal High

---

[133] The U.S.-China Economic and Security Review Commission (2020).
[134] Wortzel (2014).
[135] Fravel (2020).
[136] Ibid.
[137] Yeo (2021).

Altitude Area Defense (THAAD), which Beijing perceived to present a significant threat to its security.

Further, the formation of AUKUS between Australia, the United Kingdom, and the United States in 2021 will empower Australia to acquire nuclear-powered submarines. These submarines can be integrated with U.S. and Japanese naval assets to form a defensive patrol line stretching from the South China Sea to the Taiwan Strait.[138] Moreover, India has partnered with the United States, Japan, and Australia to establish the Quadrilateral Security Dialogue (Quad) in order to counterbalance China's influence. Although the Quad does not constitute a formal military alliance, its member nations participate in joint naval exercises and closely collaborate on security matters. These intensified focuses on security efforts around China's periphery further limit China's ability to expand its influence beyond its regional boundaries.

Although Xi Jinping has an ambitious vision for China, his grand strategy is not just a long list of goals, but an ordered list, with clear priorities.[139] The constraints surrounding China's borders have shaped its perception of the likelihood of war, which is primarily focused on territorial security and highly regional in nature. An authoritative source, the 2013 Science of Military Strategy, outlines four potential categories of war that China could face. Those are (1) a "large-scale, high-intensity defensive war" against a "hegemonic nation"; (2) a "relatively large-scale, relatively high-intensity anti-separatist war" in order to "safeguard the reunification of the nation"; (3) a "small- to medium-scale, low- to medium-intensity self-defence and counterattack operation" against "main opponents on the periphery"; and (4) a "small-scale, low-intensity anti-terrorist, stability-maintenance, and rights-defending war" of "a relatively lower level".[140]

Thirdly, in recent years, caught in the escalating competition between the United States and China, countries across Asia are pulled in opposite directions. This could potentially lead to a division between Security Asia (with countries aligning around U.S. strategic commitments) and Economic Asia (where China serves as the primary trade and investment partner).[141] China's fear of claustrophobia and containment makes it almost impossible to accept another dominant power in the region, particularly if that other power perceives China as a rival. In China's eyes, should another nation dominate the rest of the Asian region, it could then turn its attention to dominating China itself.[142] In short, China's regional foreign policy in Asia can be summarised as seeking to "prevent the domination of the Asian region by others while expanding Chinese influence among neighbours".[143] This emphasis will further confine China's military concentration within the Asian region.

---

[138] Ou (2021).
[139] Erickson (2019).
[140] Campbell (2021), p. 25; Shou (2013).
[141] Rudd (2015).
[142] Nathan and Scobell (2012).
[143] Ibid. p33.

Given China's core security concerns lie in Asia, China often takes a tough stance on security issues within the region. Many international commentators have interpreted this assertive posture as a worldwide message, symbolising an excessively ambitious and aggressive projection of Chinese power. However, it is quite likely that this message is principally directed at Asian countries, particularly those closely aligned with the United States. The objective is not to embody an aggressive global ambition or to challenge the world order, but rather to deter smaller neighbouring nations from aligning with the opposition's camp and thus posing a threat to China's regional security. Historical evidence supports this rationale.

In 104 BCE, Emperor Wu of Han responded to an aggression from the Central Asian state of Ferghana by dispatching a large force of Chinese soldiers to attack it.[144] The first attempt was not successful because the long-distance march exhausted troops and supplies.[145] Emperor Wu deemed this failure unacceptable, fearing it would lead neighbouring states to view China with contempt.[146] To rectify the situation, he mobilised with command over 60,000 fresh soldiers for a second mission. These subsequent endeavours involved better planning and more resources to avoid supply depletion, ultimately achieving success.[147] The victory over Ferghana demonstrated that the Chinese could launch large-scale wars across the entire expanse of the Tarim Basin.[148] After this success, dozens of Tarim kingdoms submitted to Chinese protection and renounced their obligations to the nomadic Xiongnu, providing China safer access to the Silk Road.[149] The tough position held by China in Asia today can be viewed as a measure to deter disrespect and establish a credible deterrent. However, it could also inadvertently give rise to a security dilemma, a topic that will be further explored in Chap. 7.

A Worrying Future?

Napoleon allegedly said, "China is a sleeping lion. When it wakes, the world will tremble."[150] The true meaning of this statement remains elusive, and many have interpreted it as a reference to China's economic ascent. However, it is conceivable that Napoleon was actually contemplating the prospect of war.[151] He well understood that when a country is challenged militarily, it responds with military innovation.[152]

---

[144] McLaughlin (2016).
[145] Ibid.
[146] Ibid.
[147] Ibid.
[148] Ibid.
[149] Ibid.
[150] Andrade (2016).
[151] Ibid.
[152] Ibid.

By the mid-eighteenth century, the Qing dynasty had effectively defeated its most formidable nomadic adversaries, including the Mongols and the Turks of Central and North Asia, and even intimidated the Russians.[153] It means that the Qing dynasty was no longer threatened by significant external disruptions from the northwestern border and the Qing regime experienced a period of relative peace between 1760 and 1839. As a result, the Qing military innovation slowed, and hands-on combat experience dwindled.[154] Meanwhile, warfare in Europe was intensifying, spurring military advancements. This disparity is one of the factors that contributed to China's eventual decline. Viewed from this angle, one might argue that fostering a relatively peaceful global environment is the most prudent strategy, as it could mitigate the need for China to adopt more aggressive military strategies.

Chinese history shows that existential threats can prompt China to take aggressive actions irrespective of the opponent's strength. It has done so under the Han regime, when it fought many wars with the Xiongnu to prevent them from taking over buffer states, penetrating the Chinese Central Plains and cutting the Han regime's commercial ties. The Sui regime also waged multiple wars with Goguryeo to prevent it from building up military alliances with the Turks on China's border. Similarly, the Korean War was fought to deter a potential U.S. threat on the Chinese border.

The current deteriorating relationship with the United States and its severe consequences on Chinese economy may eventually be perceived as threatening China's very survival (both from an economic and a security perspective). This perception may lead Chinese leaders to conclude that China's security environment can no longer be characterised as peaceful and thus prompting a change of military stance. In fact, the recent report that Xi Jinping presented at the 20th CCP National Congress in October 2022 depicted a China under threat. In comparison with the assessment made in the 19th CCP National Congress Report in 2017, which saw the country continuing to enjoy a favourable external environment for development, the later report stated, "Risks and challenges are concurrent and uncertainties and unforeseen factors are rising."[155] It implies a changing view of China's external security environment, meaning Beijing must prepare for worst-case scenarios.[156] If this was to happen, a major change in the Chinese military strategy would be likely, particularly as China no longer maintains an intrinsically weaker position. Three factors could potentially trigger this transformation.

Firstly, some analysts have argued that pressure from economic and technological decoupling or de-risking with China may deter China's aggressive military behaviour. However, there are counterarguments that China's large domestic market makes it less reliant on international trade. Following this logic, economic decoupling and de-risking could encourage China's quest for self-sufficiency, thereby lessening its concerns about international community pressures on its military manoeuvres.[157] As

---

[153] Ibid.

[154] Ibid.

[155] Lin and Wuthnow (2022).

[156] Ibid.

[157] Mastro (2021).

a result, China might be more prone to taking riskier actions towards contentious areas such as Taiwan.

Additionally, beneath China's growing hard-line stance towards the United States, there lies more profound factors. Those who have studied the history of foreign occupation in China will understand that Chinese people have a heavy psychological shadow on any attempt to invade or split the Chinese territory. This always triggers a deep sense of humiliation and anger. Although one might argue that the 'victim narrative' is strongly promoted by the CCP, it is grounded, at least in part, in historical reality. As Prime Minister of Singapore Lee Hsien Loong observed, contemporary Chinese citizens sincerely believe that they have been downtrodden in recent history.[158] They remember that past and are determined to move on from it.[159]

Some Western observers may not fully appreciate the significance of these historical factors for the Chinese people, and how profoundly these factors mould their interpretations of Washington's actions. Despite the United States' continual assurances that it has no intentions to constrain China, its actions, especially those relating to sensitive subjects like Taiwan, are seen as attempts to divide China and obstruct its growth. More critically, these public opinions are increasingly incorporated into the nation's internal feedback mechanism, significantly influencing China's military and foreign policy.[160] Consequently, although they may be biased and filtered, these views could incite the Chinese leadership to pursue a more assertive strategy.

Thirdly, as discussed earlier, Chinese military force is under unwavering control of the CCP, which has ultimate power over its military strategy setting. For a significant shift in Chinese military strategy, it necessitates consensus among the CCP top leadership concerning fundamental policies and authority structures.[161] This cohesion aids in a smooth transition and effective implementation of new strategies. At the 20th CCP National Congress, Xi Jinping fortified his control, with all roles within the Central Military Commission—which oversees the PLA—occupied by his loyalists. Xi Jinping's unprecedented consolidation of military power and the comprehensive removal of adversaries within the military have set the stage for China to adjust its military strategy if deemed necessary.

Intention Versus Capability: Which Matters Most?

This chapter highlights that the rationale behind China's military build-up lies in its instinctive pursuit of survival and the establishment of credible deterrence to maintain the stability of its periphery. Such deterrence can compel the United States and other potential foes to reassess any certainty of success when meddling with China's

---

[158] Lee (2021).
[159] Ibid.
[160] Zhao (2023).
[161] Fravel (2019).

border affairs.[162] With these deterrent capabilities, China can resort to soft-power means to resolve conflicts, minimising domestic disturbances. This stance is deeply rooted in China's complex geographical border issues, conservative worldview, pragmatic military strategy, and historical lessons showing that war and expansion do not guarantee lasting security and may even lead to decline.

Till now, China has actively sought a greater global role, revised its military strategy three times, and integrated revised military innovations. Even so, its military strategy continues to uphold the principle of 'active defence'.[163] At the 20th CCP National Congress in 2022, the report underscored hastening the PLA's modernisation, with a key part of this process being the enhancement of the PLA's 'strategic deterrence system'.[164] This focus on deterrence underscores that China's military strategy still leans more towards defence rather than aggression.[165]

However, from the perspective of the international community, and particularly the Western countries, once China has mastered more advanced military capabilities, its 'intention' matters less. Historical lessons relating to strategic posture may be relevant here. One example is Israel's surprise at being attacked in the Yom Kippur War in 1973. Upon reflection and investigation, Israeli experts concluded that they made a mistake in misreading Egypt and Syria. What matters is not the enemy's intentions, which are difficult to read and can change in a flash, but its capabilities.[166] This shift in focus to capabilities over intentions has been a significant aspect of Israel's strategic thinking since the Yom Kippur War. Similarly, Henry Kissinger paraphrased the core argument in *The Crowe Memorandum*, asking, "Was the crisis [that led to the First World War] caused by German capabilities or German conduct?"[167] The unambiguous answer provided by Eyre Crowe highlighted that capability matters most.

In this context, the fear of China will inevitably intensify as China's military capability increases, regardless of its 'intention' or 'conduct'. Such fears may lead to an interpretation of any reasonable action from the Chinese side as antagonistic and aggressive. In turn, this can play into Beijing's fear and promote further aggressive actions. This creates a dangerous spiral, prompting China to become a 'menacing dragon'. The most precarious geopolitical flashpoint in this scenario is Taiwan. A thorough examination of this geopolitical flashpoint is essential for understanding the complexities of the issue and will be discussed in depth in the next chapter.

---

[162] Rudd (2015).

[163] U.S. Department of Defense (2022).

[164] Ibid.

[165] Ibid.

[166] Michman and Mizrahi-Arnaud (2017).

[167] Kissinger (2012).

References

Allison G (2019) Destined for War: Can America and China escape Thucydides's trap?. Scribe Publications Pty Ltd, Melbourne.
Andrade T (2016) The gunpowder age: China, military innovation, and the rise of the West in world history. Princeton University Press, Princeton.
Brzezinski Z (1998) The grand chessboard: American primacy and its geostrategic imperatives. Basis Books, New York, p.16.
Campbell C (2021) China's military: The People's Liberation Army (PLA). In: Congressional research services. Available at: https://crsreports.congress.gov/product/pdf/R/R46808. Accessed 12 December 2021.
Cang M (ed) (2014) Minzushi yanjiu. Vol 9. China Minzu University Press, Beijing.
Chen Q (2013) Zhongguo Lishishang weihe shuci bei youmu minzu zhengfu? Journal of Translation from Foreign Literature of Economics (2): 66–68.
China Renewable Energy Engineering Institute (2021). Zhong guo ke zai sheng neng yuan bao gao (China renewable energy development report). China Water&Power Press, Beijing.
David S (2007) China stands up: The PRC and the international system. Routledge, New York, p.8.
Erickson AS (2019) China. In: Balzacq T et al (eds) Comparative grand strategy: A framework and cases. Oxford University Press, Oxford, UK, pp.73–98.
Fairbank J (1969) China's foreign policy in historical perspective. Foreign Affairs 47(3): 449–463.
Fairbank J, Frank K (ed) (1974) Chinese ways in warfare. Harvard University Press, Cambridge.
Fang ZH (2015) Cong wenhua wenlixue jiaodu kan shijie wenming zhongxin de xingcheng. Renmin Luntan, 495: 15–19.
Farmer EL (2021) Zhu Yuanzhang and early Ming legislation: The reordering of Chinese society following the era of Mongol rule. Brill Publishers, Leiden.
Fearon JD (1997) The offense-defense balance and war since 1648 (draft paper). In: The University of Stanford. Available at: https://web.stanford.edu/group/fearon-research/cgi-bin/wordpress/wp-content/uploads/2013/10/The-Offense-Defense-Balance-and-War-Since-1648.pdf. Accessed 20 February 2019.
Fravel M (2007) Power shifts and escalation: Explaining China's use of force in territorial disputes. International Security 32 (3): 44–83.
Fravel M (2019) Active defense: China's military strategy since 1949. Princeton University Press, Princeton.
Fravel T (2020) China's "world-class military" ambitions: Origins and implications, The Washington Quarterly, 43(1):85–99, DOI: https://doi.org/10.1080/0163660X.2020.1735850.
Hao YF, Zhai ZH (1990) China's decision to enter the Korean War: History revisited. The China Quarterly 121: 94–115.
Hayton B (2022) The invention of China. Yale University Press, New Haven. p.306.
Heath T (2018) China's military has no combat experience: Does it matter? In: The RAND Blog. Available at: https://www.rand.org/blog/2018/11/chinas-military-has-no-combat-experience-does-it-matter.html. Accessed 03 March 2020.
History Compilation Committee of Xinjiang Production and Construction Corps (1986) Xinjiang shengchan jianshe bingtuan nianjian (Xinjiang Production and Construction Corps Yearbook). Xinjiang University Publishing House, Urumqi.
Jervis R (1978) Cooperation under the security dilemma. World Politics 30(2):167–214.
Kennedy P (2017) The rise and fall of the great powers: Economic change and military conflict from 1500-2000. Harper Collins Publishers Ltd., London.
Kissinger H (2012) On China. Penguins Books, New York, p.518.
Kissinger H (2014) World order. Penguin Press, New York, p.226.
Lee KB (1984) A new history of Korea. Harvard University Press, Boston.
Lee HL (2021) PM Lee Hsien Loong at the Aspen Security Forum. In: Prime Minister's Office Singapore. Available at: https://www.pmo.gov.sg/Newsroom/PM-Lee-Hsien-Loong-at-the-Aspen-Security-Forum. Accessed 15 October 2021.

References

Libicki MC (2009) Cyber deterrence and cyber war. Rand Corporation. Santa Monica.

Lin B, Wuthnow J (2022) The weakness behind China's strong façade-Xi's reach exceeds his military's grasp. In: Foreign Affairs. Available at: https://www.foreignaffairs.com/china/weakness-behind-china-strong-facade?check_logged_in=1. Accessed 15 November 2022.

Luo L et al (2017) Uncovering the ancient canal-based tuntian agricultural landscape at China's northwestern frontiers. Journal of Cultural Heritage 23(Supplement): 79–88. https://doi.org/10.1016/j.culher.2016.04.013.

Marshall T (2015a) The power of geography. Elliott & Thompson, London.

Marshall T (2015b) Prisoners of geography: Ten maps that tell you everything you need to know about global politics. Elliott & Thompson, London.

Mastro O (2021) The Taiwan temptation: Why Beijing might resort to force. In: Foreign Affairs: Available at: https://www.foreignaffairs.com/articles/china/2021-06-03/china-taiwan-war-temptation. Accessed 19 October 2021.

McLaughlin R (2016) The Roman Empire and the silk routes: The ancient world economy & the Empires of Parthia, Central Asia & Han China. Pen & Sword Books Ltd, Barnsley.

Michman D, Mizrahi-Arnaud Y (2017) The fog of certainty: Learning from the intelligence failures of the 1973 war. In: Brookings. Available at: https://www.brookings.edu/blog/markaz/2017/10/23/the-fog-of-certainty-learning-from-the-intelligence-failures-of-the-1973-war/. Accessed 15 August 2022.

Milley M (2023) How to avoid a great-power war: A conversation with General Mark Milley. In: Foreign Affairs. Available at: https://www.foreignaffairs.com/podcasts/how-to-avoid-great-power-war-mark-milley. Accessed 10 May 2023.

Mott WH, Kim JC (2006) The philosophy of Chinese military culture. Palgrave Macmillan, New York.

Nathan AJ, Scobell A (2012) China's search for security. Columbia University Press, New York.

Ou WC (2021) The impact of AUKUS on Taiwan. In: Taipei Times. Available at: https://www.taipeitimes.com/News/editorials/archives/2021/10/09/2003765773. Accessed 03 February 2022.

The Paper (2019) Meizhong duikang? Shi wen Rui Xiaojian. Available at: https://www.thepaper.cn/newsDetail_forward_4425338. Accessed 9 March 2020.

Park M (2013) Why the Korean War still matters. In: CNN. Available at: https://edition.cnn.com/2013/03/07/world/asia/korean-war-explainer/index.html. Accessed 12 February 2018.

People's Daily (2021) Jinshinian Qinghai changzhu renkou cheng disu zengzhang taishi. Available at: http://qh.people.com.cn/n2/2021/0615/c378418-34777631.html. Accessed 12 July 2021.

PetroChina (2015) Xiqi dongshu guandao gongsi jieshao. Available from http://www.cnpc.com.cn/cnpc/zgsyqhjs/201509/41319d24d56742c7947b2653a84cd140.shtml. Accessed 03 March 2018.

Rudd K (2015) U.S.-China 21: The future of U.S.-China relations under Xi Jinping. In: Belfer Center for Science and International Affairs. Available at: https://www.belfercenter.org/sites/default/files/legacy/files/Summary%20Report%20US-China%2021.pdf. Accessed 21 September 2022.

Schuman M (2020) Superpower interrupted: The Chinese history of the world. Public Affairs, New York, p.36.

Shou XS (ed) (2013) The science of military strategy. China: Military Science Press, Beijing.

Sima Q (2011) Shi Ji (Records of the Grand Historia), Zhonghua Book Company, Beijing.

Song Y (1994) Zhongguo lishishang jige chaodai de jiangyu mianji gusuan. Historiography Bimonthly. 3:149–150.

The State Council of the People's Republic of China (n.d.) Made in China 2025. Available at: http://www.gov.cn/zhuanti/2016/MadeinChina2025-plan/index.htm. Accessed 9 February 2020.

Statistics Bureau of Xinjiang Production and Construction Corps (2022) Xinjiang shengchan jianshe bingtuan 2021nian guomin jingji he shehui fazhan tongji gongbao. Available at:https://tjgb.hongheiku.com/sjtjgb/38225.html . Accessed 15 May 2023.

Sun W (2022) Sunzi bingfa (the Art of War). Zhonghua Book Company, Beijing, p.89.

The Economist (2016) The upper Han. Available at: https://www.economist.com/briefing/2016/11/19/the-upper-han. Accessed 22 May 2021.

The Economist (2022) Russia's army is in a woeful state. Available at: https://www.economist.com/briefing/how-deep-does-the-rot-in-the-russian-army-go/21808989. Accessed 03 June 2022.

The People's Government of Sichuan Province (2021) Sichuansheng diqici quanguo renkou puchan zhuyao shuju jieguo xinwen fabuhui. Available at: https://www.sc.gov.cn/10462/10705/10707/2021/5/27/3ef3323416694f98a236021554b82406.shtml. Accessed 12 July 2021.

The State Council Information Office of the People's Republic of China (2019) China's national defense in the new era. Foreign Languages Press Co. Ltd, Beijing.

The State Council Information Office of the People's Republic of China (2009) Xin zhongguo linian junfei zhichu fenxi. Available at: http://www.scio.gov.cn/zggk/gqbg/2009/Document/426589/426589.htm. Accessed 11 August 2020.

The State Council Information Office of the People's Republic of China (2015) Xinjiang yi tanming shiyou tianranqi chuliang junju quanguo shouwei. Available at: http://www.scio.gov.cn/zhzc/8/2/Document/1439917/1439917.htm. Accessed 01 February 2020.

The State Council Information Office of the People's Republic of China (2023) China's 2023 defense budget to rise by 7.2 percent, remaining single-digit for 8th year. Available at: http://english.scio.gov.cn/chinavoices/2023-03/06/content_85146919.htm. Accessed 2 May 2023.

The U.S.-China Economic and Security Review Commission (2020) 2020 Report to Congress of the U.S.-China Economic and Security Review Commission. Available at: https://www.uscc.gov/annual-report/2020-annual-report-congress. Accessed 9 August 2021.

U.S. Department of Defense (2022) Military and security developments involving the People's Republic of China. Available at: https://www.defense.gov/CMPR/. Accessed 5 January 2023.

Wei Z et al (1973) Sui Shu (Book of Sui). Di Ji Vol 3. Zhonghua Book Company, Beijing.

Wilson MC, Smith AT (2015) The pika and the watershed: The impact of small mammal poisoning on the ecohydrology of the Qinghai-Tibetan Plateau. AMBIO 44:16–22. DOI: https://doi.org/10.1007/s13280-014-0568-x.

Wortzel LM (2014) China's military modernization and cyber activities: Testimony of Dr. Larry M. Wortzel before the House Armed Services Committee. Strategic Studies Quarterly 8(1):3–22.

Xinhua News Agency (2018) Qiangjun zhengcheng qi xinhang. Available at: http://www.gov.cn/xinwen/2018-10/20/content_5332982.htm. Accessed 19 August 2019.

Xu DM et al (2002) Yaluzangbujiang shuineng kaifa (Hydro Power Development at the Yalu Tsangpo River). Engineering Science, 4(12):47–52.

Yeo M (2021) Japan's new defense whitepaper issues warnings over Taiwan's security, climate change. In: Defense News. Available at: https://www.defensenews.com/smr/energy-and-environment/2021/07/13/japans-new-defense-whitepaper-issues-warnings-over-taiwans-security-climate-change/, 13 July 2021.

Zhang YJ, Buzan B (2012) The tributary system as international society in theory and practice. The Chinese Journal of International Politics 5:3–36.

Zhang C et al (2021) Jiedu 2021 nian zhongguo junfei. In: AVIC Securities. Available at: https://pdf.dfcfw.com/pdf/H3_AP202103071469464988_1.pdf?1615196741000.pdf. Accessed 2 December 2021.

Zhao HJ (2012) Qihou bianhua sh fou yingxiang le woguo guoqu liangqiannian jiande nongye wending? (Did climate change affect the social stability of Chinese agrarian economy in the past 2000 years?). China Economic Quarterly, 11(2): 691–722.

Zhao T (2023) How China's echo chamber threatens Taiwan. In: Foreign Affairs. Available at: https://www.foreignaffairs.com/taiwan/-china-echo-chamber-threatens-taiwan. Accessed 12 May 2023.

Chapter 7
A Cauldron of Anxiety: War or Peace?

> *"For whosoever commands the sea commands the trade;*
> *whosoever commands the trade of the world commands the*
> *riches of the world, and consequently the world itself."*
> (Ratcliffe, 2017)
> —Walter Raleigh, British explorer (1552–1618)

Abstract The future of the global order is anticipated to be determined less by conflicts in Europe and more by geopolitical rivalry and possible confrontations in maritime Asia, with Taiwan at the centre of attention. This chapter examines the central flashpoints in maritime Asia, with a particular focus on Taiwan's status and the South China Sea. It seeks to unpack the critical geostrategic, economic, and political complexities that underpin these issues. This chapter argues that the crux of the conflict between China and the United States lies in China's prospective rise as a significant naval power. This prominence is anticipated to span both the Pacific and Indian Oceans and is likely to be reinforced with credible maritime deterrence capacities. To better understand the motives behind China's naval power expansion, the chapter delves into the history of Chinese naval development, contrasting it with European and U.S. experiences. Finally, it identifies the constraints that hinder China's ability to extend its maritime influence and engage in potential conflicts or wars.

The future of the global order is anticipated to be determined less by conflicts in Europe and more by geopolitical rivalry and possible confrontations in maritime Asia, with Taiwan at the centre of attention. This scenario prompts inquiries about the potential possibility of an armed confrontation in the Taiwan Strait, the rationale behind China's unwavering expansion of naval military capabilities, and the possibility of China evolving into a global sea power. To tackle these questions, this chapter will investigate the history of Chinese naval development, explore its fundamental interests and objectives, and examine the constraints that hinder its capacity to grow and engage in potential conflicts or wars.

The Grand Gravity Shifts

Inherently, land powers tend to have a regional focus, with their primary interests centred on their immediate borders. On the other hand, sea powers naturally embody a more global nature. This is due to their dependence on open sea lanes and their need for access to ports worldwide, both of which are vital for their trade and prosperity. The mastery of the seas has played a pivotal role in the history of Europe. The evolution of European civilisation unfolded around the Mediterranean banks, bringing together a multitude of city-states situated along coastal expanses. More than 2,000 years ago, when the Greeks defeated the Persians, they laid the foundation for the establishment of a maritime empire, bringing prosperity through trade between colonies and allies across a pacified Mediterranean.[1] In the early Roman Republic, one of the primary conflicts was the struggle for maritime supremacy against the Phoenician city-state of Carthage.[2] After the defeat of Carthage, Rome reigned as a maritime hegemon over the whole Mediterranean, heralding a period of prosperity called Pax Romana.

More recently, in the modern period, sea power has been the basis of European prosperity and power. Portugal, Spain, the Netherlands, and the United Kingdom all achieved a measure of hegemony by establishing sea power—this time over the oceans connecting Europe, Africa, Asia and America.[3] Those countries mastered maritime trade by building a global network of sea bases through colonies and allies, as well as a strong navy to control critical shipping lines, strategic channels and ports.[4]

In the twentieth century, global dominance of the seas shifted to the United States, becoming one of the key pillars of U.S. hegemonic power. In *The Influence of Sea Power upon History*, the U.S. naval officer and historian Alfred Mahan wrote: "if a nation be so situated that it is neither forced to defend itself by land nor induced to seek extension of its territory by way of the land, it has, by the very unity of its aim directed upon the sea, an advantage as compared with a people one of whose boundaries is continental."[5] Indeed, the geography of the United States, featuring an extensive coastline bordering the Atlantic Ocean, Pacific Ocean, Arctic Ocean, Gulf of Mexico, and Southern Caribbean Sea, is conducive to the formation of a sea power. This geography, combined with a wealth of natural resources and a relatively mild climate, furnishes the United States with favourable conditions to cultivate maritime strength, and employ this power in its competition or containment strategies against other formidable nations.

In the world of sea-power theory, national greatness was inextricably associated with the sea—its commercial use in peacetime and the control of it during wartime.[6]

---

[1] Stavridis (2019).
[2] Scullard (2021).
[3] Stavridis (2019).
[4] Ibid.
[5] Mahan (1890), p.51.
[6] Ibid.

This perspective asserted the role of sea power in determining the destiny of the country, and even the global order. Therefore, China's potential rise as a prominent naval power poses a considerable challenge to the United States' dominance.

As discussed in Chap. 6, China, by default, is a land power. Historically, China's military prowess was primarily manifested in its land combat capabilities, which were crucial for fighting against nomadic invaders and safeguarding land trade routes along the ancient Silk Road.[7] Naval pursuits, however, received comparatively less emphasis. The Han dynasty established the first naval force in Chinese history, referred to as the 'Tower Ship Navy'.[8] However, it was mainly used in internal riverine warfare. During the Han and Tang dynasties, large-scale naval operations continued to play a role in Chinese warfare, but China rarely used its navy for outward-bound expeditions or conquests. An explanation for this, as discussed in Chap. 6, is that China's main external threat has consistently originated from the northwestern nomads. This persistent threat led the Han and Tang regimes to concentrate their political, economic, and military resources in the northwest to combat adversaries like the Xiongnu, all of which took place far from the coastal frontier.[9]

During the Song dynasty, there was a major shift in that regard. The focus of China's foreign trade shifted from the ancient overland Silk Road to the maritime Silk Road which stretched over the seas.[10] Two main factors played a role in this shift. The first was a change in China's demographic centre of gravity. With long periods of unstable political environment and repeated wars in the northwest, combined with better climate and water conditions for double cropping in the southeast, a large proportion of the Chinese population migrated from the northwest to the southeast.[11] Consequently, China's demographic centre of gravity gradually moved from the northwest to the coastal southeast, where numerous seaports allowed maritime trade to gain increasing importance.

The second reason was the increasing pressure from the nomads. In 1127, a nomadic tribe, the Jurchen, overran the northern half of the Song territory, forcing the Song regime to relocate its capital to southeastern Hangzhou, and the whole country to recentre around this region. Meanwhile, the Jurchen effectively blocked off Chinese access to trade with the external world via land routes. The Song dynasty therefore adopted an active policy to explore trade opportunities by sea.[12] This policy shift brought a major change in taxation, with maritime trade tax and tonnage tax becoming an important fiscal revenue source to the Song regime.[13] Consequently, the Song regime became increasingly invested in bolstering maritime commerce along the southeastern coasts and safeguarding the sea lanes.[14] By the end of the

---

[7] Huang (2017).

[8] Sima (2011), China Institute of Navigation (1988).

[9] Huang (2017).

[10] Ibid.

[11] Ibid.

[12] Fairbank (1969).

[13] Xu (2009).

[14] Ibid.

Song dynasty, the GDP of the southeastern coastal region has overtaken that of the northwest, and it has remained the economic heartland of China until today. It can therefore be said that, by the end of the Song dynasty, China had transformed from a purely continental country to one with both land and maritime attributes.

The ramification of this transformation is significant because it altered China's security status. Given the emerging importance of maritime trade and its significant contribution to the Song regime's fiscal income and the nation's overall stability, any potential blockades or invasion by sea became a growing concern for the Song regime. To protect the country's maritime trade and escort merchant fleets through the Southeast Pacific and Indian Oceans on long trade missions to the Hindu, Islamic, and East African regions, in 1131, the Song regime established the first permanent standing navy in Chinese history.[15] The invention of the magnetic compass and advanced shipbuilding techniques quickly allowed the Song's naval power to become globally prominent.

The Chinese navy reached its peak in the early Ming dynasty which claimed the lead in global maritime power. In 1420, the Ming navy counted 1,350 combat vessels, including 400 floating fortresses and 250 long-range cruising ships.[16] The Ming naval force even had "naval bases with large garrisons on coastal islands, and a system of communication by means of dispatch boats and beacon fires".[17] The Ming dynasty's advanced naval power enabled the well-known expeditions led by Zheng He.

Symbolic Maritime Power

Almost one hundred years before Columbus sailed to the New World, Ming Admiral Zheng He had led seven long-distance expeditions between 1405 and 1433.[18] All seven fleets went to India, three of which reached Hormuz on the Persian Gulf, two reached Aden, and the furthest ventured as far as Kenya.[19] Those expeditions involved more than 115,000 soldiers and over 600 large ships.[20] However, the purpose of those extraordinary expeditions was not for conquest, but to promote the symbolic prestige of China and a sense of awe for the Ming dynasty.[21]

The purpose of those expeditions could be described as building a defensive mechanism on the seas through trade for the Ming regime. Zheng He very generously gifted countries, clans and tribes along his journey with prestigious Chinese products to show off the wealth and advancement of the Ming regime. By demonstrating the

---

[15] Needham (1978).
[16] Kennedy (2017).
[17] Fairbank (1969), p.454.
[18] Gronewald (2021).
[19] Marshall (2015).
[20] Ibid.
[21] Kennedy (2017).

regime's power and supremacy, the Ming Empire hoped it could deter potential aggressors from the seas. By including some of the nations along the sea routes in the Chinese tributary system, it could also reduce the risk of external aggression by proactively offering exchange of products. That is why Zheng He's expeditions did not seek to conquer new territory beyond its region, nor create forward bases that could be used to support military operations to control the great sea lanes of the Pacific, Atlantic, and Indian Oceans, or even establish colonies along those.[22] By contrast, as British historian Paul Kennedy described: "Unlike the fleeting visits paid by Cheng Ho [Zheng He], the actions of the Portuguese and Spanish explorers symbolised a commitment to alter the world's political and economic balances. With their ship-borne cannon and musket-bearing soldiers, they did precisely that."[23]

In 1433, while the Portuguese ships of Prince Henry the Navigator had not yet reached the bulge of West Africa, and future great explorers Christopher Columbus, Vasco da Gama and Afonso de Albuquerque had not yet been born, China already held a dominant position in global sea power.[24] However, Zheng He's expeditions ended, and his great fleets were left to rot away. From that point on, for the next five centuries, China shifted its attention primarily to domestic matters. Over this period, despite attacks by Japanese pirates along the Chinese coastline and cities near the Yangtze River, as well as the recurring presence of Portuguese vessels off the Chinese coast, the Chinese regime did not undertake significant efforts to reestablish a formidable navy. There are at least three factors that contributed to this shift in focus.

First, unlike the United States and Britain, a continental geography and the associated border vulnerability did not allow the Chinese to fully develop their maritime power. With continuous menace from land-based nomadic tribes, the navy was always seen as an adjunct rather than the core of China's military focus. During the Ming dynasty, the northern frontiers of China were under pressure again from the Mongols, and the regime needed to concentrate its national resources in this vulnerable area. According to historical records, the cost of Zheng He's expeditions had been an enormous burden for the Ming regime. In addition to gifts to foreign tributaries and states, the salaries and rewards paid to the thousands of soldiers involved in those expeditions were beyond calculation.[25] The Vice-Minister of the Ming Ministry of War criticised Zheng He's expeditions for having "wasted tens of myriads of money and grain and moreover the people who met their deaths may be counted in the myriads".[26] He further questioned, "Although he [Zheng He] returned with wonderful precious things, what benefit was it to the state?"[27] The overriding demand of land security compelled a potentially powerful but superficial pursuit of sea power to be sacrificed.[28]

---

[22] Marshall (2015).

[23] Kennedy (2017), pp.26–27.

[24] Fairbank (1969).

[25] Wang (2019a).

[26] Gronewald (2021).

[27] Ibid.

[28] Kennedy (2017).

Secondly, the Ming dynasty was immersed in an atmosphere of 'restoration' following the Mongol-ruled Yuan dynasty. This led to a period characterised by introspective and conservative policies. The conservative Ming bureaucracy was more concerned with restoring the glory of China's past, not create a possibly greater future built on overseas expansion and trade.[29] In addition, natural disasters like the severe floods of the Yellow River in 1448 caused millions to be homeless and destroyed thousands of acres of arable land, leading to severe famines in Shandong and Hunan.[30] The Ming regime thus kept their attention on addressing internal affairs.

Thirdly, as discussed in Chap. 3, Chinese rulers have traditionally distrusted private capital and merchants. They did not allow much freedom for businessmen to conduct independent maritime trade. Therefore, during the Ming dynasty, China could not develop a mature and strong maritime merchant group that could make expeditions profitable, and pressure the regime to further expand its maritime power. Whereas both Dutch and English colonial expansion in East Asia were led by private merchant companies—the Dutch East India Company and the (British) East India Company. In sum, for the Ming emperors, the return on maritime expeditions was not proportional to the money and resources invested.

Later, in 1644, when the Manchu established the Qing dynasty in Beijing, their focus and efforts were tied to building their continental empire, and fighting with the nomads, such as the Dzungar Khanate in Central Asia—so they continued to ignore the sea.[31]

The disappearance of the Ming oceangoing fleets brought an abrupt end to previously established links between China and the countries to the west—India, Africa, the Middle East, even Europe—leaving a void.[32] Europeans gradually replaced the Chinese on overseas trade markets in the Indian Ocean and the Asian side of the Pacific Ocean. At the same time, the opening of new sea routes to the Indian Ocean and the discovery of America sparked a wave of ocean navigation in Western Europe. The profits from nautical trade directly accelerated the primitive accumulation of capital in Europe, and can be identified as one of the main early reasons for Europe's later global dominance.[33]

'You Will Be Beaten Up If You Fall Behind'

With Europe's ascendance to dominance, threats and disruptions to China's security and prosperity began to emerge predominantly from its maritime borders. Since the early nineteenth century, China's primary security concerns shifted from its northwestern frontier to its maritime periphery. Such a threat culminated in the

---

[29] Ibid.
[30] Gronewald (2021).
[31] Fairbank (1969).
[32] Kennedy (2017).
[33] Ibid.

'You Will Be Beaten Up If You Fall Behind' 133

Second Opium War in 1860, when European troops overcame the Qing regime's navy, marched to the capital, and burned down the Yuanmingyuan (Old Summer Palace) reputed as 'The Garden of Gardens'. On this occasion, Chinese supremacy and pride were obliterated. What the Chinese learnt from it is that 'you will be beaten up if you fall behind'.

Since then, the Qing regime started attaching greater importance to the navy by establishing the modernised imperial Chinese navy, with four fleets based in Tianjin, Shanghai, Fuzhou and Guangzhou.[34] The Beiyang Fleet, based in Tianjin, garnered more resources than all other Chinese fleets, owning two German-built battleships, each with a displacement of 7,500 tonnes.[35] However, due to a poor industrial base, corrupt bureaucracy and weak treasury support, the Beiyang Fleet was totally defeated during the First Sino-Japanese War in 1894, while the French destroyed the Fuzhou fleet in a matter of minutes in 1884 as part of a war for control over Vietnam.[36] Consequently, China's sea power was eclipsed once again. In the first half of the twentieth century, the Republic of China established the Republican Chinese Navy. However, in the wars with Japan and throughout the Second World War, this navy concentrated mainly on riverine warfare, as it lacked equipment, training and a strong industrial base to compete with the Japanese Navy over the open seas.[37]

Coming out of decades of invasions from its maritime periphery, the PRC came to believe that a secure China must have a strong navy. In 1949, the PRC established the People's Liberation Army Navy (PLAN). Committed to never repeating the experience of its 'Century of Humiliation', the PRC developed the concept of 'maritime security', emphasising territorial sovereignty over the seas. This concept was embodied in Mao Zedong's 1949 declaration to "defend our coasts and rivers".[38] This declaration signified that the primary purpose of the PLAN was to defend the national territory and maintain sovereign security, rather than project power globally.[39]

Over the last decades, the PLAN's capability has increased significantly. According to the U.S. Department of Defense and the U.S. Office of Naval Intelligence, China reportedly had a total battle force of around 340 surface ships and submarines in 2022, comprising 125 major surface combatants, and this is projected to grow to 440 ships by 2030.[40] In comparison, the U.S. Navy's battle force counts approximately 293 ships, making the PLAN the world's largest naval force by number of ships.[41] In addition, China has consistently increased its military expenditure for a continuous span of 29 years. Although there is no detailed breakdown of the Chinese

---

[34] Cole (2014).

[35] Ibid.

[36] Fairbank (1969).

[37] Academy of Ocean of China (2018).

[38] Wen and Zhang (2018).

[39] Academy of Ocean of China (2018).

[40] U.S. Department of Defense (2022), O'Rourke (2022).

[41] Ibid.

defence budget allocation, according to Chinese expert analysis, the recent defence spendings continued to focus on developing and optimising the scale and structure of weapons and equipment, with naval power and air force being the main focus.[42] The United States assessed that China's naval modernisation effort is aimed at developing capabilities for addressing the situation with Taiwan militarily if need be, for a greater degree of control or domination over China's near-seas region as well as for defending China's commercial sea lanes.[43]

Beyond conventional naval capabilities, China has significantly concentrated its efforts on enhancing its space and cyberspace proficiencies. Much like the decisive role that railways, telegraphs, quick-firing guns, steam propulsion, and armoured warships played in determining military strength in the latter half of the nineteenth century, satellites, digital and cyber networks, undersea cables, space systems, and unmanned systems are expected to significantly influence sea power competition in the future.[44] In fact, space and cyberspace have already become important components of China's comprehensive national power and a critical element of its strategic competition with the United States.[45]

The 2015 Chinese defence white paper referred to space and cyberspace as the new commanding heights in strategic competition.[46] In the same year, the PLA established the Strategic Support Force to comprehensively integrate space and cyberspace into PLA operations.[47] The most recent defence white paper, *China's National Defense in the New Era*, published in 2019, strengthened the mandate for the PLA to safeguard China's security interests in outer space, electromagnetic space and cyberspace.[48] In this context, if Alfred Mahan were alive, he would certainly remind the United States to pay close attention to China's emerging naval strength.[49] This concern arises not only from the increasing capabilities of the Chinese navy which could challenge U.S. naval dominance, but also from the possibility of a single country mastering new technology ahead of others. This could consequently create 'offensive advantages' that shift the offence-defence equilibrium in favour of aggressive strategies.[50]

---

[42] Zhang et al. (2021).

[43] O'Rourke (2022).

[44] Stavridis (2019).

[45] Wortzel (2014).

[46] Campbell (2021).

[47] Ibid.

[48] The State Council Information Office of the People's Republic of China (2019).

[49] Stavridis (2019).

[50] Fearon (1997).

Control Over Critical Resources

In a highly competitive global environment, consistent access to critical maritime resources is vital for any country's prosperity. This involves not only control over any relevant extent of water, but also control of critical channels, ports and transportation lines—many of those lying beyond the national territory.[51] The fear of losing access, in itself, can lead to war. A typical historical example is Japan. Japan is an island country with a narrow territory and insufficient resources. The attempt to remedy those shortcomings and ensure continued essential supplies was part of the reason for Japan's expansion into China and Southeast Asia before the Second World War.[52] When the United States imposed a strategic material embargo against Japan in 1940, it directly played into Japan's fears. This escalating fear has been proposed as one of the causes for Japan's attack on Pearl Harbor in 1941.[53]

To give another example, during the mid- to late seventeenth century, as the Age of Exploration dawned, the Dutch and the British both intended to seek markets and profits overseas in the Americas. According to the mantra of sixteenth-century British explorer Sir Walter Raleigh, "For whosoever commands the sea commands the trade; whosoever commands the trade of the world commands the riches of the world, and consequently the world itself."[54] In order to gain access to critical resources and establish economic primacy, England challenged the Dutch's established trade networks over the seas. This was an existential matter for both countries' survival and their prosperity.[55] To resolve issues regarding freedom of navigation and commercial regulation, the two countries fought three major wars from 1652 to 1674, and in the eighteenth century a fourth one was fought again, eventually resulting in the establishment of England's dominant naval might in Europe.[56]

Since Deng Xiaoping's reform and opening-up policy in 1978, China's maritime trade and economic interactions with the outside world have increased substantially. China's sea-borne trade accounted for 95% of its total trade and 45% of national GDP, compared with the U.S. figures of 85% and 20% respectively.[57] China's heavy economic dependence on maritime trade and foreign resources is feeding Chinese anxiety about its maritime economic security.[58] Consequently, the concept of 'maritime security' has been reinterpreted to mean not only territorial sovereignty over maritime areas and coastal defence, but also China's economic security.[59] This means that China has started to focus on ensuring the smooth flow of critical resources by building capacity to intervene in potential blockades and interference from hostile

---

[51] Jervis (1978).

[52] Ibid.

[53] United States Department of State, Office of the Historian (2021).

[54] Ratcliffe (2017).

[55] Allison (2019).

[56] Ibid.

[57] Gompert (2013).

[58] Ibid.

[59] Academy of Ocean of China (2018).

forces.⁶⁰ Capturing this shift, China's 2015 defence white paper asserted, "the traditional mentality that land outweighs sea must be abandoned, and great importance has to be attached to managing the seas and oceans and protecting maritime rights and interests." ⁶¹ In short, China's 2015 defence white paper articulated the shift in the PLA's mission from "offshore water defence" to a dual focus of "offshore water defence" and "open-seas protection".⁶²

From the perspective of economic security, China's interest in strengthening its naval power should come as no surprise. The United States clearly understood the necessity of securing maritime trade to fuel economic growth, which has prompted the development of a strong U.S. Navy, and the emergence of the United States as a prominent sea power by the end of the nineteenth century.⁶³ Yet ironically, the United States seems disinclined to allow China the same measure of influence over East Asian waters that it insisted on for its own neighbouring waters a century ago.⁶⁴

Hong Kong

The maritime economic interest perspective discussed above may provide an important angle to better understand China's policy towards Hong Kong. When it comes to the status of Hong Kong, what is most often discussed is its history: China ceded the island of Hong Kong to Britain in perpetuity after being defeated during the First Opium War in 1840, which marked the first defeat of China to Western powers and opened the 'Century of Humiliation'. Therefore, in the Chinese official narrative, Hong Kong's distinct status is a result of that humiliation, and the recovery of Hong Kong in July 1997 represented a 'redemption' of the national humiliation.⁶⁵ As former Chinese President Jiang Zemin asserted, "the occupation of Hong Kong is an epitome of the humiliation China suffered in modern history... the return of Hong Kong marks an end to the one hundred year national humiliation of China."⁶⁶ This grandiose claim is more than mere political rhetoric: from a realpolitik perspective, Hong Kong's strategic location makes it critical to China's maritime economic security.

Hong Kong, one of the world's busiest trading warehouses and shipping centres, significantly facilitates smooth trade flow between China and the rest of the world. In 2022, the value of goods reexported from and to the mainland through Hong Kong was USD487.4 billion, accounting for 85.4% of Hong Kong's total reexport trade

---

[60] Ibid.
[61] Campbell (2021).
[62] Ibid. p. 29.
[63] Gompert (2013).
[64] Ibid.
[65] David (2007).
[66] Ibid.

value.[67] Because of its geostrategic importance, Beijing tends to frame the status of Hong Kong through the lens of national security, and associated societal control.[68]

Hong Kong is also part of China's periphery challenge. However, its situation is clearly distinct from that of Tibet and Xinjiang as discussed in Chap. 6. Tibet and Xinjiang have never been governed by foreign forces generally regarded as advanced in the international community for an extended period of time since the Industrial Revolution, while Hong Kong has had this direct and comprehensive experience as a British colony. Hong Kong was the first part of China that entered the torrent of modernisation in many aspects. Under British colonial rule, Hong Kong experienced advancement in a range of domains: property rights protection, human rights protection, freedom of speech, freedom of the press and freedom of religious belief and more.[69] The majority of Hong Kong residents today were born and raised in an environment shaped by these experiences. With this historical experience as background, although most of Hong Kong residents are Han Chinese, the challenge faced by Beijing in controlling Hong Kong may well exceed that of controlling Tibet and Xinjiang.[70]

Tibet and Xinjiang have long been under strict control, with the Chinese government implementing restrictive measures such as pervasive surveillance, restrictions on religious practices, and the establishment of 'reeducation camps'. In contrast, Hong Kong's vibrant civil society and well-established legal system, shaped by its colonial past, have fostered a culture of activism and resistance against perceived encroachments on the city's autonomy. This resistance is demonstrated by numerous pro-democracy protests against Beijing's limited concessions on freedom, notably the Umbrella Movement of 2014, and the anti-extradition protests from 2019 to 2020. As a response to this resistance, the Chinese government enacted the National Security Law which has significantly curtailed civil liberties, suppressed dissent, and led to the arrest of many pro-democracy activists and politicians, ultimately undermining Hong Kong's autonomy and freedoms. This action has escalated worries not only among local Hong Kong residents but also people from Taiwan. It also cast doubt over the possibility of a peaceful resolution for Taiwan's status under the 'One Country, Two Systems' framework. I will revisit this topic later in this chapter.

The First Island Chain

China's core interest in safeguarding access to essential maritime resources and concerns over potential blockades frequently give rise to critical discussions surrounding the concept of island chains. As discussed in Chap. 6, Emperor Hongwu

---

[67] Trade and Industry Department, The Government of the Hong Kong Special Administrative Region (2022).
[68] Hans (2020).
[69] Ding (2015).
[70] Ibid.

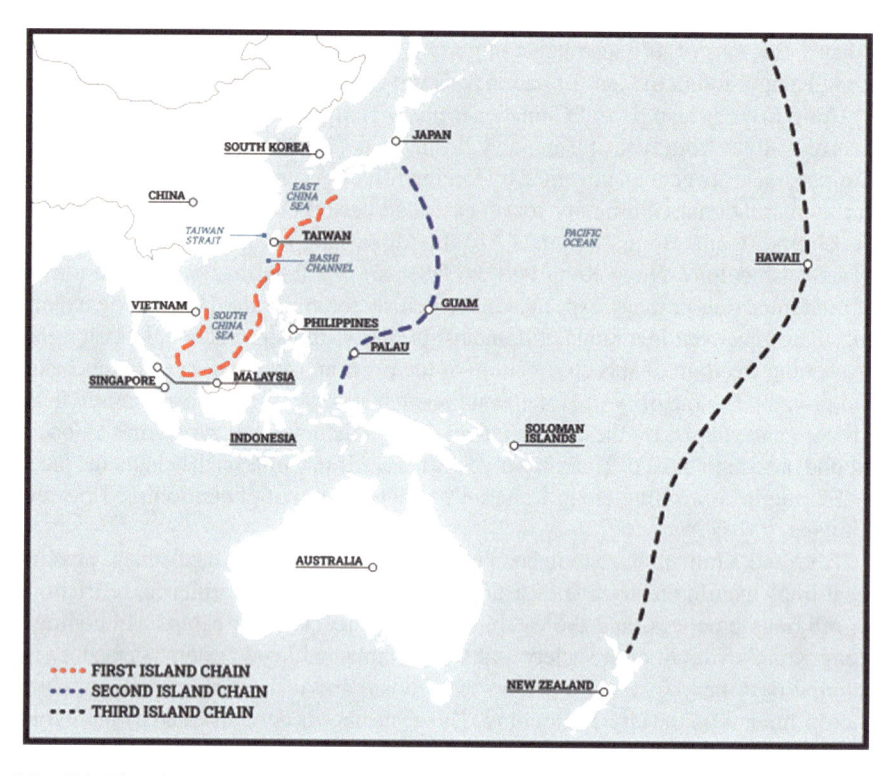

Map 7.1 The Island Chains

of the Ming dynasty warned his successor never to target small island nations remote from China for punitive military expeditions, such as Korea, Japan, and Java, as those countries could not provide returns worth the military investment in terms of land and people. However, the situation has changed considerably since then. Some of the 'small islands' have since become independent countries with a position along transportation lines critical to China's sovereignty and prosperity.

Several of these 'small islands' are situated along what is referred to as the 'First Island Chain', a term denoting a series of archipelagos stretching along the East Asian coastline that were a defensive barrier for the United States during the Cold War. It is important to note that interpretations of the First Island Chain vary, and the idea has evolved over time. Currently, the most commonly accepted concept includes the Kuril Islands, the Japanese archipelago, the Ryukyu Islands, Taiwan, parts of the Philippines, and Indonesia.[71] Additionally, in its annual reports on China's military power, the Pentagon has also incorporated Vietnam into the map of the First Island Chain.[72] Please refer to Map 7.1.

---

[71] Erickson and Wuthnow (2016).

[72] U.S. Department of Defense (2022).

There are several strategically significant chokepoints along the First Island Chain, in areas where the United States has established military bases and advanced anti-ship and anti-air defence systems. These chokepoints could form a series of overlapping 'fortresses' at sea, making China particularly vulnerable to blockades of strategic access points. Thus, the First Island Chain can be compared to an invisible chain enclosing a giant dragon. Although the dragon has a lot of strength, it cannot unleash any of it as long as the chain is there. From a strategic point of view, by maintaining a network of alliances and military presence along the First Island Chain, the United States could potentially pose challenges to the operational freedom of the PLAN in the West Pacific. This strategic position could potentially offer the United States the ability to monitor and anticipate some movements of the Chinese Navy. Furthermore, in a more extreme case, this strategic position could potentially block off China's international trade, and particularly affect the oil transportation line which is China's lifeline. Therefore, for China, the First Island Chain "is a hostile fortification to be punctured, not a friendly fortification to be defended".[73]

In peacetime, the threat of a 'blockade' is a mere prospect. However, the fact that the PLAN can regularly and freely transit through the First Island Chain in peacetime does not imply it can do so in wartime or that Beijing can prevent the United States from crossing that First Island Chain during a war.[74] In wartime, China's ability to break through a blockade around the First Island Chain would depend on the strength of its Anti-Access/Area Denial (A2/AD) military capabilities within the First Island Chain, and its capacity to project firepower beyond it to weaken any counterattack force. According to the U.S. Department of Defense report to Congress in 2022, the PLAN's A2/AD capabilities targeting the First Island Chain are the most robust, while those aimed at areas beyond the chain are comparatively modest.[75] Meanwhile, some U.S. security experts assessed that "Five years from now, the PLA still will have a very limited ability to launch conventional attacks beyond locations in the 'Second Island Chain' in the Pacific; namely, Guam and Palau."[76] Hence, the First Island Chain is considered the most effective point to counter any Chinese maritime aggression.[77]

War Games

Taiwan claimed the most strategic point on the First Island Chain. If China were to seize Taiwan, it could potentially establish Chinese-controlled military facilities, such as ports on the east coast of Taiwan.[78] This development would potentially enable

---

[73] Molan (2022), p.85.
[74] Heginbotham (2021).
[75] U.S. Department of Defense (2022).
[76] Pettyjohn and Wasser (2022).
[77] Ibid.
[78] Cavas (2016).

China to break out of the constraints of the First Island Chain conclusively, resulting in a significant shift in the balance of power within the Asian region and beyond.[79] Against this background, numerous war games have been conducted around the First Island Chain, particularly focusing on Taiwan. The outcomes of these simulations are varied, demonstrating that neither China nor the United States holds a definitive advantage. In addition, regardless which side ultimately prevails, both China and the United States would likely experience substantial losses in fighter planes, warships, and even aircraft carriers, along with thousands of casualties.[80] Some war games suggest that for China to succeed in such a conflict, it must exploit asymmetrical advantages in timing (e.g., sudden attack) and space (e.g., leveraging range advantage through missiles, anti-ship missiles, air-to-air missiles, etc.), while also decisively employing its conventional and, if necessary, nuclear weapons in the most extreme situation.[81] However, in the short to medium term, these asymmetrical advantages may not be a feasible option for China. There are a number of key challenges that remain.

Firstly, a prospective sudden attack on Taiwan would necessitate a robust, precise, and integrated collaboration across various facets of the Chinese military. This could include cyber-attacks, space cyber-attacks, air and missile strikes, a naval blockade, amphibious invasion, and special operations.[82] The narrow window available for such a sudden strike poses challenges for achieving precise coordination among the various military branches.

Secondly, the perception of the Taiwan situation as merely a geographically contained conflict between China and Taiwan eerily mirrors the West's underestimation of Japan prior to the Second World War.[83] The key for China to launch a sudden attack hinges on its ability to inhibit a counter-strike. If China were to attack Taiwan while leaving these U.S. air and naval assets in the West Pacific untouched, it could face a significant and sustained military response from the United States and allied bases in the region, causing enormous costs to its military and its infrastructure on the mainland.[84] Hence, China might concurrently target critical infrastructure and military installations in countries that are potential sources of retaliatory strikes against it. In particular, potential targets include U.S. naval and air bases in Japan, South Korea and Guam.[85] However, this strategy of removing the regional ability of the United States to use force against China in itself is extremely dangerous and could lead to rapid and disastrous escalation of wars.

Thirdly, in a hypothetical wartime scenario, the freedom of movement of Chinese fleets across the Taiwan Strait and the security of its airspace could face substantial

---

[79] Ibid.
[80] Lendon and Liebermann (2023), NBC (2022), Pettyjohn and Wasser (2022).
[81] Ibid.
[82] Ibid.
[83] Molan (2022).
[84] Ibid.
[85] Ibid.

challenges.[86] As discussed earlier, the comprehensive surveillance systems around the First Island Chain, combined with the strong U.S. military presence in the region, make it challenging for the PLAN to cross the Taiwan Strait. The United States or other allies might attempt to block the Taiwan Strait to deter a Chinese naval assault on Taiwan, prevent the transport of Chinese ground forces to Taiwan and allow reinforcing forces to arrive from outside the region.[87] This strategy would likely involve the deployment of a variety of naval vessels, including aircraft carriers, destroyers, and submarines, along with supporting aircraft. The presence of these forces would serve as a signal to China that any attempt to move military forces through the Taiwan Strait would be met with resistance.

The Taiwanese naval force, although considerably smaller than the PLAN, nevertheless contributes to the multi-layered defence dynamics in the region. Additionally, the Japan Maritime Self-Defense Force stands as one of the globe's most technologically advanced navies, with particular expertise in anti-submarine warfare.[88] Its fleet consists of highly sophisticated vessels, manned by a crew renowned for their rigorous training and professionalism.[89] In practice, Japan's post-Second World War constitution enforces a policy of pacifism, implying that any decision to deploy the Japanese Maritime Self-Defense Force would necessitate considerable political and legal adjustments. However, Japan's attitude towards the constraints of Article 9 of its postwar constitution, which only permits military action in self-defence, is evolving. The country is now at least engaging in discussions regarding pre-emptive strikes on potential enemy bases posing threats.[90]

Fourthly, capturing Taiwan would ultimately necessitate ground troops to occupy and control the island. Although the Chinese PLAN Marine Corps' capabilities have improved, especially in areas of amphibious assault, securing beachheads, and rapidly advancing to capture key locations, Taiwan's rugged terrain and coastline present significant challenges for amphibious landings and rapid troop deployment.[91] Some argue that a scenario involving China invading Taiwan would be akin to the D-Day landing, given that both situations envisage an amphibious assault on a heavily fortified territory across a relatively narrow strait. However, realities might prove otherwise. Unlike D-Day, which saw landings across a wide front on relatively flat, open beaches, Taiwan's geographical landscape is considerably different. It offers only 14 small potential invasion beaches, hemmed in by steep cliffs and dense urban environments, heavily defended by armed troops.[92] Additionally, Taiwan's outer islands are bristling with defences, including missiles, rockets, and artillery weapons, and their granite hillsides are extensively crisscrossed with tunnels and bunker systems.[93]

---

[86] Ibid.

[87] Ibid.

[88] Yoshihara and Holmes (2014).

[89] Ibid.

[90] Molan (2022).

[91] U.S. Department of Defense (2022).

[92] Easton (2021).

[93] Ibid.

Navigating these narrow landing zones under heavy fire would make a wide-scale, simultaneous landing akin to D-Day not just highly risky but also logistically challenging. In such a scenario, the considerable troop strength of the PLA might not necessarily offer a tactical advantage. Furthermore, unlike the D-Day landing, China would not be able to gather forces for an assault in nearby friendly nations, and its troops would be under threat of attack during the crossing of the Taiwan Strait as previously discussed.

Lastly but most crucially, in a hypothetical conflict scenario, China's most critical challenge would be executing its strategies effectively without triggering a nuclear response from the United States.[94] Although the United States maintains a policy of nuclear no-first-use, drastic circumstances could potentially modify this posture. If the United States encounters a significant threat or a substantial defeat, the prospect of employing nuclear weapons as a retaliatory action could become a consideration.[95] This underscores the extremely delicate and potentially catastrophic balance of power that exists in any conflict scenario involving nuclear-armed powers. However, many analysts continue to perceive nuclear warfare as a remote possibility.

Given all the challenges discussed above, the feasibility of a sudden strike as an option for China to triumph in a potential war over Taiwan appears less plausible, at least in the immediate timeframe. Consequently, a blockade around the First Island Chain continues to pose a realistic threat to China. In this situation, China has shown a tendency to employ an incremental approach—taking smaller, seemingly unrelated steps towards achieving its objectives without sparking a full-scale war, if feasible.[96] A recent example of this approach includes expanding its grey-zone activities over time, akin to its recent actions in which it frequently sent numerous attack aircraft across the median line of the Air Defence Identification Zone (ADIZ) between Taiwan and China, as part of an intimidation campaign.[97] Over a longer period, China might adopt an incremental approach to set the stage for a sudden attack if the incremental approach does not lead to its goal.[98]

Preparing for War in Peacetime

All nations spend peacetime preparing for the day war breaks out, which may account for some of China's present military actions.[99] Guided by the objective to alleviate concerns of strategic encirclement along the First Island Chain, China has been

---

[94] Molan (2022).

[95] Ibid.

[96] Molan (2022).

[97] Ibid.

[98] Ibid.

[99] Marshall (2015).

pursuing three objectives: building up a 'blue water' navy, establishing overseas bases, and developing a real-time global surveillance system.[100]

As discussed earlier, China's 'blue water' navy is becoming increasingly formidable in terms of numbers and combat capability. In recent decades, China has also been concentrating on enhancing its maritime nuclear capabilities, with an aim to strengthen its sea-based nuclear deterrence.[101] Since 2002, China has been building a variety of nuclear-powered submarines.[102] By 2022, China possessed six Jin-class (Type 094) submarines armed with submarine-launched ballistic missiles.[103] In November 2022, the U.S. Pacific Fleet commander disclosed at a conference that these Chinese nuclear submarines are "equipped with JL-3 intercontinental ballistic missiles", possessing a range exceeding 10,000 km (6,200 miles).[104] This means that these missiles could potentially reach the United States while remaining under the protection of their South China Sea naval base. According to the Pentagon, those Jin-class submarines represent "China's first credible maritime nuclear deterrence".[105]

Simultaneously, China has been working to secure a presence in the South Pacific, with the aim of overcoming the limitations set by the Second Island Chain and the Third Island Chain, as well as expanding its A2/AD military capabilities past the First Island Chain. The Second Island Chain consists of the islands of Japan stretching to Guam and the islands of Micronesia. The Third Island Chain, which has been referred to by Beijing as a "strategic rear area" of the U.S. military, runs from the Aleutian Islands to the Hawaiian Islands, then to the Line Islands, and down to Tonga and New Zealand.[106] Please refer to Map 7.1.

A recent example of China's efforts in the South Pacific is the unprecedented security pact signed between China and the Solomon Islands in March 2020, which granted permission for the Chinese navy to dock and replenish in the Solomon Islands. This security pact sparked regional concerns that a future Chinese military base could be developed over time.[107] The Solomon Islands are strategically located between Vanuatu and Papua New Guinea (PNG). During the Second World War, all three countries housed crucial U.S. or allied naval bases that supported the allied effort in the Pacific.[108] China's action is thus interpreted by the West as a parallel to Imperial Japan's establishment of military bases in the region during its imperial expansion before the Second World War.[109]

---

[100] Fallon (2020).
[101] Paul (2018).
[102] Ibid.
[103] Capaccio (2022).
[104] Ibid.
[105] Ibid.
[106] Ibid.
[107] Harding and Pohle-Anderson (2022).
[108] Ibid.
[109] Ibid.

Viewed from this standpoint, the implications of a possible Chinese military establishment in the South Pacific understandably raise concerns. Firstly, a potential establishment of a Chinese military forward operating base and logistical support networks in the South Pacific could facilitate Beijing's ability to extend its military reach and influence deeper into the Pacific Ocean. This development could pose challenges for the United States and its allies operating within the region, while also potentially challenging the balance of power in the West Pacific. Secondly, Chinese military assets in the South Pacific can bolster their A2/AD capabilities targeted at the Second Island Chain and the Third Island Chain, effectively mitigating the constraints imposed by the First Island Chain. Thirdly, the increased proximity of Chinese military assets in the South Pacific may jeopardise the U.S. military installations in Guam and Hawaii. This increased presence could potentially allow China to secure a strategic advantage in a potential conflict with the United States and pose a direct threat to U.S. territory.[110]

The Prime Minister of the Solomon Islands has publicly denied the possibility of a Chinese military base being built on the territory. However, given the geostrategic importance of this region, it is probable that China will persist in its endeavours with the Solomon Islands in the future, and may reevaluate engagement with Vanuatu and PNG.[111] It is important to note that a common and severe challenge facing Pacific Island nations is climate change. Should other nations fail to provide support in addressing this existential threat, it could present China with an opportunity to expand its influence by assisting these countries in fortifying their coastlines against erosion through financial, technological, and infrastructural aid. This development has the potential to lead to an increased Chinese influence in the region and potentially reshape the power dynamics in the future.

Last but not least, China has been developing a comprehensive and uninterrupted global monitoring system, which includes an expanding array of Chinese satellites, remote sensing assets, and advanced over-the-horizon radars. This development is still in its early stages and faces growing challenges due to technological decoupling from the West. Yet, should China successfully develop advanced surveillance technology in the future, it could potentially 'break through' the island chains. This would be achieved by obtaining real-time information about the deployment of U.S. and allied vessels.[112] Furthermore, China's use of space-based surveillance satellites and over-the-horizon radars could enable it to accurately target significant U.S. fleet assets, including aircraft carriers, helicopter carriers, and destroyers equipped with the Aegis system.[113] By causing substantial damage to these key assets, China could reduce the operational efficacy of the United States in the region, thereby destabilising the United States' standing in the West Pacific.

---

[110] Ibid.
[111] Ibid.
[112] Fallon (2020).
[113] Molan (2022).

Taiwan

With the discussion of the First Island Chain and its crucial impact on the balance of power in the Asia–Pacific and beyond, we come to one of the most critical issues in the world today: the status of Taiwan. It could be argued that the status of Taiwan is influenced by the evolving triangular relationship among China, Taiwan, and the United States. This dynamic is primarily driven by the changing global geopolitical landscape and Taiwan's comparative significance to the United States. To understand the issue better, we will travel back through time.

Taiwan's geostrategic position has made it a long-standing flashpoint. Since the early 1590s, Japan aimed to control the island, with leader Toyotomi Hideyoshi planning to use it as a springboard for overseas expansion.[114] On 17 April 1895, the Treaty of Shimonoseki granted Japan control over Taiwan and the Penghu Islands, ending the First Sino-Japanese War. Since then, Taiwan remained under Japanese rule for 50 years until Japan's defeat in the Second World War.

Before 1942, both the KMT and the CCP supported Taiwan's independence from Japanese colonisation, while placing less focus on reintegrating Taiwan into mainland China. This CCP view was elaborated by Mao Zedong in an interview with American journalist Edgar Snow in 1936. Mao Zedong said, "It is the immediate task of China to regain all our lost territories…. This means that Manchuria must be regained. We do not, however, include Korea, …and if the Koreans wish to break away from the chains of Japanese imperialism, we will extend them our enthusiastic help in their struggle for independence. The same thing applies for Taiwan [Formosa]."[115] As for the KMT, Chiang Kai-Shek's diary entry on 31 July 1941 showed that regarding border and territorial issues, his top two priorities were Outer Mongolia and Xinjiang, with no mention of Taiwan.[116]

Yet, in 1942, the stance of the KMT towards Taiwan underwent a change. Three factors influenced their decision. First, the entry of the United States into the Second World War marked a turning point in the trajectory of the war. This development incited the KMT to contemplate the postwar implications for their territorial claims, which included considerations of reclaiming Taiwan from a potentially vanquished Japan.[117] Second, the KMT aimed to incite unrest in Japanese-controlled territories such as Taiwan to undermine Japanese rule and foster resistance, paving the way for potential postwar territorial claims.[118] Lastly, exiled Taiwanese individuals lobbied the KMT to consider Taiwan a part of China.[119]

1949 marked another critical year, when the CCP ousted the KMT government, and all three parties—CCP, KMT, and the United States—changed their positions on Taiwan. The defeated KMT treated Taiwan as a final stronghold to regroup,

---

[114] Turnbull (2016), Swope (2016).
[115] Snow (2017), p.110.
[116] Duan (2012).
[117] Hayton (2020).
[118] Ibid.
[119] Ibid.

claiming its control over Taiwan based on shared Han Chinese heritage and historical sovereignty.[120] From the CCP's perspective, the defeat of the KMT meant that the PRC became China's sole legal government. This claim included Taiwan, which they deemed needed to be 'liberated' by means of force.[121] Meanwhile, the Truman administration had "ruled out a military defence of Taiwan".[122] Just a few weeks after Beijing had begun to plan for a cross-strait war, Dean Acheson, the then U.S. Secretary of State, on 12 January 1950, elaborated that the U.S. military security in the Pacific was dependent on a defensive perimeter that "runs along the Aleutians to Japan and then goes to the Ryukyus".[123] Importantly, Taiwan was not mentioned as part of this defensive line.[124]

Nevertheless, the U.S. position on Taiwan saw an about-turn just a few months later in June 1950, when the Korean War broke out. Facing threats from both the Soviet and China during the Korean War, the United States saw Taiwan as an "unsinkable aircraft carrier" and "submarine tender" for its military force.[125] As a result, Taiwan's importance was reestablished. On 27 June 1950, Truman introduced the 'Theory of the Undetermined Status of Taiwan' which stated, "The determination of the future status of Formosa (Taiwan) must await the restoration of security in the Pacific, a peace settlement with Japan, or consideration by the United Nations."[126] Further, as a landmark progress, the 1954 Mutual Defense Treaty was signed between the United States and the Republic of China which aimed to prevent the CCP from taking over Taiwan.[127] Consequently, in 1954, 1959, 1963, and 1978, the United States successfully countered mainland China's claim over Taiwan through military actions.[128]

Following 1971, the United States altered its strategy to "allying with China to counterbalance the Soviet Union".[129] As a result, from 1971 to 1982, Sino-U.S. relations were normalised, and Taiwan's geostrategic significance decreased accordingly. In January 1979, the United States formally recognised the PRC and established diplomatic relations with it as the sole legitimate government of China, while terminating diplomatic relations with the Republic of China.[130] Since then, the United States tactically accepted the possibility of peaceful unification of China with "a high degree of autonomy" for Taiwan.[131] However, as U.S.-Soviet ties normalised in the late 1980s, Sino-U.S. cooperation targeting the Soviet Union lost strategic

---

[120] Ibid.
[121] Hickey (1997).
[122] Lin and Zhou (2018).
[123] Time Magzine (1951).
[124] Ibid.
[125] Ibid.
[126] The Truman Library (1950).
[127] Lin and Zhou (2018).
[128] Ibid.
[129] Ibid, p.180.
[130] Carter (1979).
[131] Lin and Zhou (2018).

importance. As a result, China's core interests, including unification with Taiwan, became less significant for U.S. foreign policy.[132]

The geostrategic significance of Taiwan continues to be crucial in today's world. From the perspective of the United States and its allies and partners in Asia, if Taiwan is incorporated into mainland China, this 'unsinkable aircraft carrier' will undoubtedly become a strategic Chinese naval base for potential military conflict in East Asia.[133] By controlling the Taiwan Strait, mainland China could easily extend its sovereignty claim over the South China Sea, control foreign ships navigating the Taiwan Strait, and exclude other foreign military forces from this area.[134] Moreover, it could pose additional threats to the U.S. military bases in the Philippines, Guam, and even Hawaii, as well as to the south of Japan.[135]

The above discussions show although the United States does hold a high moral commitment to Taiwanese democracy and security, the policy response to the status of Taiwan largely depends on the evolving geopolitical landscape, and in particular, the dynamics of Sino-U.S. relations.[136] In other words, how the Taiwan issue will unfold in the future will depend on Taiwan's comparative value and significance for the United States over time.[137]

Dilemma of Legitimacy

Taiwan is a flashpoint. Beyond the geostrategic perspective, there are more complicated political reasons playing in the background. Those political dimensions have varied implications for the legitimacy of the key stakeholders involved in the Taiwan issue, adding political pressure and complexity to potential armed conflicts.

For the CCP, the Taiwan issue is central to the CCP's legitimacy as it represents their "unfinished civil war".[138] The CCP achieved a decisive victory against the KMT during the civil war, establishing itself as the sole legitimate ruling party for all of China, a definition they believe encompasses Taiwan. However, the unresolved status of Taiwan signals a divided China, meaning their civil war never reached a conclusive end.[139] For the CCP, Taiwan's reunification with the mainland is viewed as redressing a historical wrong. Consequently, they believe that accomplishing this reunification would reinforce their power and legitimacy, further solidifying their authority.

---

[132] Ibid.
[133] Ibid.
[134] Ibid.
[135] Ibid.
[136] Ibid.
[137] Ibid.
[138] Eckholm (n.d.).
[139] Ibid.

For the KMT, they rejected Beijing's claim that the Republic of China ceased to exist in 1949, asserting its continuous sovereignty since 1912. From the KMT's perspective, Taiwan has served and continues to serve as the KMT's base for maintaining its claim as the legitimate successor of the China Empire and preserving the status quo under the Constitution of the Republic of China.

For the Democratic Progressive Party (DPP) of Taiwan, their legitimacy is tied to safeguarding the new identity and greater autonomy of Taiwan. Taiwan's turbulent history, which involves continuous struggle to achieve independence—from the Dutch, the Spanish, the Ming regime, the Ming loyalists in exile, the Qing regime, and the Japanese—has fostered a strong desire for democracy and independence among its people.[140] The Taiwanese democratic movement in the 1980s led to heated debates on their identity, eventually resulting in a focus on Taiwanese civic values and a separate identity from China.[141] This new identify was solidified by the 2007 'normal country' resolution passed by the DPP. The DPP's legitimacy centred on Taiwan's distinct identity and greater autonomy may be challenged by the potential unification with mainland China.

For the United States, the status of Taiwan formed the rancorous and divisive debate over the question of 'who lost China' following the CCP's triumph in 1949. This debate triggered a political backlash against the Truman administration and played a part in fuelling the emergence of McCarthyism. With the hope to create a pro-U.S. democratic power and prevent Soviet influence, the United States had provided USD 2 billion worth of aid to the KMT since 1945. This amount represents "more than 50% of the monetary expenditures of the Chinese Government and of proportionately greater magnitude in relation to the budget of that Government than the United States has provided to any nation of Western Europe since the end of the war".[142] Historical narratives and ongoing commitments to Taiwan's security render the status of Taiwan as a crucial and delicate matter in contemporary U.S. politics.

Clearly, all major stakeholders in the Taiwan issue possess intricate political motives tied to the matter, which exacerbate and intensify the pressure concerning potential conflicts. This implication holds particular significance for China and the United States.

Today, the United States' unambiguous position on defending Taiwan is not only important to domestic politics but has a larger meaning. In 2022, Japan's annual defence white paper explicitly stated that "the stability of the situation surrounding Taiwan is also critical for Japan's security".[143] As one of the most important allies of the United States in Asia, the stated importance of Taiwan to Japan calls for the United States' attention to the Taiwan issue. From the perspective of U.S. allies in Asia, if the United States fails to respond to a possible forceful attack on Taiwan, they will view it as the United States pulling back from the region and conclude

---

[140] Lin (2018).

[141] Ibid.

[142] Acheson (1949).

[143] Ministry of Defense, Japan (2022).

that the United States cannot be relied upon anymore.[144] The consequence is "these Asian allies would then either accommodate China, leading to the dissolution of the U.S. alliances and the crumbling of the balance of power, or they would seek nuclear weapons in a bid to become strategically self-reliant".[145] Both scenarios would significantly undermine U.S. influence within the Asian region and create adverse consequences on a global scale.

On the other hand, the CCP deems any outcome that negates the possibility of unification as an issue of war and peace.[146] Following years of unsuccessful attempts to reintegrate Taiwan through economic means, Beijing's decision to use force to conclude the 'unfinished civil war' will depend on their evaluation of the feasibility of accomplishing their objectives through alternative approaches—whether the opportunity is expanding, diminishing, or standing still.[147] Today, the status of Taiwan is a legitimacy question that matters not only to the CCP but also to Xi Jinping personally. It is believed that Xi Jinping views that reuniting Taiwan with mainland China will help cement his place in history.

2022 was a critical year in that regard. The impact of Russia's invasion of Ukraine was felt keenly in Taiwan and Beijing. Vladimir Putin's description of attempts to restore the 'historical unity' between Russia and Ukraine as a kind of spiritual mission is similar to how Xi Jinping speaks of Taiwan, highlighting blood ties and historical ties.[148] Still, for now, no outsider has a clear answer to the million-dollar question: What has Beijing learnt from the war in Ukraine? It is certain that China has gleaned substantial lessons from the situation. One could argue that the Ukraine conflict may have signalled to China the advent of an increasingly challenging era necessitating preparations for the heightened likelihood of conflict, thus underscoring the urgency to augment their military capacities. Specifically, this could entail understanding the pivotal role of sophisticated electronic warfare, the utility of hypersonic weapons, the need for a substantial yet manageable arsenal, the importance of a technologically sophisticated military industry, and the value of credible nuclear deterrence.[149]

Furthermore, one could also argue that China has meticulously studied the Western-led sanctions campaign, seeking strategies to mitigate its own susceptibility to similar measures in the future. Yet, ultimately, Beijing's decision on whether to employ force over Taiwan remains a largely independent political judgement, minimally swayed by Moscow's actions in Ukraine and the subsequent unfolding of the conflict.[150] The decision is fundamentally grounded in China's long-standing policy of reunification with Taiwan, influenced by the geostrategic importance and the legitimacy factors, as well as an assessment of the feasibility of alternative methods to achieve this goal. The timing of such a potential conflict could hinge not only on

---

[144] Haass and Sacks (2020).

[145] Ibid.

[146] Bush (2017).

[147] Ibid.

[148] Sacks (2022).

[149] Buckley (2023).

[150] Sacks (2022).

China's state of readiness but also on its perception of the lack of preparedness and potential vulnerabilities of the United States and Taiwan.[151]

Ultimately, the Taiwan issue comes down to the geopolitics of fear, which means concern that the other party may exploit Taiwan's strategic significance for their own gain and all stakeholders are motivated to proactively assert influence over the circumstances. As mentioned earlier, in the event of a conflict over the Taiwan Strait, neither China nor the United States possesses a clear-cut advantage, with both parties expecting significant casualties and losses. Nevertheless, as the situation involving Taiwan escalates, both China and the United States have significantly bolstered their military investments. This could be perceived as an emerging arms race, as each country prepares for the most severe potential scenarios. This is illustrated by the United States' 2023 defence budget proposal, a historic high of USD 857.9 billion, which continues to identify strategic rivalry with China as a key defence concern.[152] Accordingly, China has increased its 2023 defence budget by 7.2%, reaching USD 225 billion.[153]

History demonstrates that the inability to prosper while engaging in an arms race has been a recurring pattern, with examples such as Philip II's Spain, Nicholas II's Russia, Hitler's Germany, Japan during the Second World War, and the Soviet Union during the Cold War.[154] Furthermore, maintaining financial support for an arms race places a significant strain on both China and the United States, particularly in light of their limited financial resources amid slower economic growth and rising domestic social issues. These internal challenges could prompt both countries to use conflict as a way to alleviate internal pressures, leading to a dangerous downward spiral. In this context, it is essential to consider potential constraints that could restrain China's actions towards Taiwan, which will be discussed later in this chapter.

South China Sea

The South China Sea is considered another flashpoint in Asia, although its magnitude and impact is far less than Taiwan. Although people today regard globalisation as a modern phenomenon, the South China Sea could be described as one of the early key points in the meeting of global civilisations.[155] From the first century to the tenth century, the South China Sea has been the meeting point of ancient China and ancient India.[156] In addition, trade between China and the Arab region through the South China Sea appears around 1,000 CE.[157] There is even sporadic evidence that

---

[151] Molan (2022).
[152] United States Senate Committee on Armed Services (2023).
[153] Zhao (2023).
[154] Kennedy (2017), Huang (2015).
[155] Stavridis (2019).
[156] Ibid.
[157] Ibid.

there was trade between the ancient civilisations of the Mediterranean and the South China Sea.[158] Some settlements in ancient southern China, as well as the Mekong Delta State of Funan (today part of Thailand, Cambodia and Vietnam), were early trading sites in the region.[159]

The South China Sea remains a bustling and thriving hub for global trade today, with roughly half of the world's maritime commerce and liquefied natural gas as well as about one-third of crude oil passing through its waters annually.[160] Meanwhile, the South China Sea has also become an exceedingly sensitive region, significantly influencing geopolitical developments in Asia.

All major economies of the South China Sea region have competing claims over tracts of the South China Sea, leading to potential disputes. Due to limited land resources and dependence on coastal economic centres for trade and economic development, Southeast Asian nations consider the abundant resources and strategic sea lanes of the South China Sea crucial for their prosperity. Therefore, they actively seek to defend 'marine land' areas, manage maritime traffic, and build military power to protect their interests.

For China, the South China Sea is a lifeline, transporting critical resources and handling over 80% of Chinese outbound trade. Beijing currently claims 'indisputable sovereignty' over 62% of the region, encompassing the Paracel Island chain, the Spratly Island chain, and Scarborough Shoal, as well as the adjacent maritime waters surrounding these features.[161] China's claim is visually represented by the nine-dash line. This ambitious self-proclaimed area has been publicly rejected by Indonesia, Malaysia, the Philippines, and Vietnam, with these countries invoking international law to support their maritime sovereignty rights.[162]

Since 2014, China has substantially expanded its power projection and monitoring capabilities in the disputed Spratly and Paracel Islands by constructing dual-use infrastructures, including radar, airstrips, as well as mobile surface-to-air and anti-ship cruise missile systems.[163] However, merely citing economic security is inadequate in explaining China's endeavours to assert dominance over the South China Sea, extending beyond the preservation of freedom of navigation. A more significant factor at play is the vital role of the South China Sea in safeguarding the viability of China's nuclear weapons and increasing nuclear deterrence.[164] In general, land-based nuclear weapon systems are more easily spotted, which reduces their survivability and second-strike capability. In contrast, in the event of an attack, sea-based nuclear weapons systems can better meet the two criteria for greater survivability, namely redundancy and diversification.[165]

---

[158] Ibid.

[159] Ibid.

[160] Ibid.

[161] Campbell (2021).

[162] U.S. Department of Defense (2022).

[163] Center for Strategic & International Studies (n.d.).

[164] Paul (2018).

[165] Ibid.

Since 1958, China has been building submarines to carry nuclear weapons, and the South China Sea offers effective natural protection for them.[166] The South China Sea is very large—larger than the Caribbean Sea. As the largest and deepest marginal sea, South China Sea's average depth is 1,200 m, with the southern Manila Trench reaching over 5,000 m.[167] In comparison, the shallower Yellow Sea has an average depth of only 46 m.[168] Thus, the South China Sea serves as a natural bastion for China's nuclear weapons and strategic submarines. Given its strategic importance, it is likely that Beijing will continue heighten its military dominance over the South China Sea. Further discussion on the strategic importance of the South China Sea to China can be found in the next section.

To the United States, the South China Sea is important for it to continue exerting its influence in this emerging economic centre of the world. Given the growth potential in Asia over the next decades, the focal point of major economies, including the United States and Europe, will most likely shift to Asia. The ongoing conflict between China's continuous ambition to be a dominating force in the South China Sea, the economic and security interests of Southeast Asian countries, and the desire of the United States to maintain its influence, is unlikely to be resolved without difficulty.

A Two-Ocean Power: From Hollywood to Bollywood

In recent years, increasing evidence shows that China is intending to develop into a two-ocean power—focusing on both the Pacific and Indian oceans. According to Alfred Mahan, "Whoever controls the Indian Ocean, dominates Asia. This ocean is the key to the seven seas. In the Twenty-First century, the destiny of the world will be decided on its waters."[169]

The Indian Ocean is a natural maritime transportation channel, with favourable climate and excellent waterway conditions that can be passed year-round. To the west, the Indian Ocean serves as a crucial pathway for both the Suez and Cape of Good Hope routes. To the east, there is an increasingly significant route connecting East Asia to the Indian Ocean through the Strait of Malacca. Further, stretching from the Malacca Strait, along the Indochina Peninsula, the South Asian subcontinent coastline, the Arabian Sea, and finally reaching the Red Sea, the northern arc of the Indian Ocean forms the core of the broader Indian Ocean region. This region, being a substantial part of the world's crucial straits and sea lanes, plays a pivotal role in enabling global trade and maritime connectivity.

The Indian Ocean region is characterised by a multitude of cultural, religious, ethnic, and territorial conflicts, which contribute to its delicate and fragile nature.[170]

---

[166] Ibid.
[167] Ibid.
[168] Ibid.
[169] Mahan (1987).
[170] Wang (2010).

Moreover, a power vacuum currently exists in the region, with no single country occupying a truly dominant position.[171] With the United States implementing its Indo-Pacific strategy to counterbalance China's rise and the increasing involvement of its allies in the region, combined with India's emergence as a major power, the overlapping interests of these nations significantly increase the likelihood of great-power competition and conflicts in this region.

The Indian Ocean region holds tremendous strategic value for China. Not only does it act as a critical transit route for a significant portion of its energy imports, but it also houses key coastal nations that function as essential trading partners.[172] During the Cold War, ideological differences led to tensions between China and some nations within the Indian Ocean region.[173] Yet, driven by mounting energy demands and geopolitical changes, China has notably strengthened its ties in this area in recent years. In the last decade, China has increased its investments in countries with strategic importance in the broader Indian Ocean region and those hold strategic access to this region, including Oman, Bangladesh, Myanmar, Pakistan, and Djibouti.[174] This strategic approach is designed to increase Chinese influence in the region and mitigate China's substantial reliance on the Strait of Malacca for delivery of crucial resources. An emblematic example of this strategy is the establishment of oil and gas pipelines from the western coastline of Myanmar. These infrastructure projects effectively link the Bay of Bengal with Southwest China, thereby circumventing the Strait of Malacca.[175]

As the geopolitical and economic significance of the Indian Ocean escalates, coupled with heightened competition in the Pacific Ocean, China's aspiration to become a two-ocean power and extend the PLAN's presence in the Indian Ocean becomes increasingly clear. Indeed, the PLAN, with its frigates, has been a constant presence in the Indian Ocean's international waters, conducting operations as far as Africa's east coast for up to seven to eight months annually.[176] This enhancement of China's naval capabilities stirs concerns about a possible shift in the balance of power in the Indo-Pacific region, which could "forcibly change the status quo in the region".[177] Additionally, the United States' unease over China's ambitions to expand into both the Indian and Pacific Oceans may be linked to its own historical journey. After fortifying its control over its mainland, the United States asserted its dominance over both the Atlantic and Pacific Oceans.[178] This led to an expansion of its influence over adjacent seas and eventually resulted in the ousting of the Spanish from Cuba.[179]

---

[171] Ibid.

[172] Wang (2009).

[173] Yenigun et al. (2020).

[174] Marshall (2015).

[175] Ibid.

[176] The U.S.-China Economic and Security Review Commission (2020).

[177] Campbell (2021), p.2.

[178] Marshall (2015).

[179] Ibid.

Importantly, the significance of the Indian Ocean underscores the strategic value of the South China Sea to China. Drawing from geopolitical expert Robert Kaplan's views, the South China Sea is as integral to China's ambitions of becoming a two-ocean power in the twenty-first century, as the Caribbean Sea was and remains for the United States since the early twentieth century.[180] In this light, the Indo-Pacific might be seen as a vast Mediterranean, with the South China Sea at its strategic heart.[181] While China faces challenges from staunch U.S. allies and partners like Japan, South Korea, and Taiwan in the east, the less antagonistic Southeast Asia offers China potential avenues to the Indian and Pacific oceans for both economic and defence purposes.[182]

As the only region that faces both the Pacific and Indian oceans, Southeast Asia's strategic value is of utmost importance in the current geopolitical landscape.[183] With the shifting world order amid rising great-power competition, Southeast Asian countries find themselves with amplified opportunities to assert their significance, as these great powers seek alliances and partnerships with smaller nations.[184] Historically, Southeast Asian nations have harboured sentiments of scepticism towards great powers, remembering the rising influence of Japan in the twentieth century.[185] Many Southeast Asian nations have been vassal states of Imperial China or, more recently, client states of the United States. Their past encounters with superpowers have instilled a sense of caution, making them hesitant to unequivocally align with either side.

In addition, both China and the United States present complex choices for these countries.[186] The prospect of a China-centric economic order incites fears of diminished sovereignty and ideological clashes. Simultaneously, there are questions around the motives of the United States in the region. If the U.S. rivalry with China, pressuring Southeast Asian countries to sever ties with China, appears to serve solely American interests rather than fostering a broader balance of power, it will invariably lead regional nations to question the benefits for them.[187]

Over the past century, the Southeast Asian region's principal foreign policy focus has been managing interactions with major global powers. Southeast Asian nations have largely maintained their independence by strategically balancing relations between these major powers while leveraging globalisation to broaden their options.[188] Consequently, these nations view the U.S.-China rivalry in the region as a complex interplay rather than a simple straightforward zero-sum contest, with their decisions rooted more in regional interests than in ideological affiliations. Most

---

[180] Ibid.
[181] Wang (2019b).
[182] The Economist (2021a).
[183] Ibid.
[184] Ibid.
[185] Cho and Park (2013).
[186] The Economist (2021b).
[187] The Economist (2021c).
[188] Cho and Park (2013).

importantly, if Southeast Asian countries can find common ground on critical issues and amplify their collective voice in global foreign policy, they could serve as pivotal connectors, transforming polarised alliances into more harmonious and constructive ones, rather than feeling pressured to align unequivocally with one side.[189]

China's Constraints

In the contemporary global landscape, China is ascending as a formidable maritime power. Showcasing impressive naval strengths, the country is proactively asserting its two primary interests. First, it seeks strategic security due to its geography, represented by large-scale investment in the modernisation of its military force. Second is its quest for economic security represented by growth-driven national prosperity and increased outputs. These dual aspirations are critical for China's enduring stability, and they also impose constraints on the country's maritime and global ambitions. I will start by exploring start by exploring the geographical constraints.

- **A two-front security threat**

As soon as China develops into a strong power on both land and sea, it starts to face a two-front security threat—squeezed between rivals on land and at sea.[190] The ultimate test for Beijing lies in how to effectively handle its vulnerable landward security while expanding its maritime influence.[191] As discussed in Chap. 6, China still faces a highly fragile land security situation. China's recent skirmishes with India along the Himalayan border show how territorial disputes could stoke great-power animosities in unexpected ways.[192] Other contingencies, such as the resumption of the conflict on the Korean Peninsula or the security vacuum caused by political upheaval in a neighbouring Central or South Asian country, could severely threaten China's land border and drag it into a prolonged and costly landward commitment.[193]

The lesson from the 1960s, when China concurrently stood against the United States and the Soviet Union under Mao Zedong's 'dual adversary' strategy, has taught his successors the potentially existential risk of picking two fights at the same time.[194] China's extensive land borders present an ongoing security concern, potentially affecting its ability to fully commit resources to its maritime ambitions. This delicate balance illustrates the trade-offs countries often face in geopolitical strategy. This delicate equilibrium between its land and maritime commitments compels China to temper its maritime ambitions and encourages China to work towards maintaining regional peace for as long as feasible.

---

[189] Ibid.
[190] Yoshihara and Bianchi (2021).
[191] Ibid.
[192] Ibid.
[193] Ibid.
[194] Ibid.

Further, strategists from the PLA have expressed long-standing concerns about the potential for chain-reaction warfare. Despite the growing nationalist sentiment in China advocating for the forceful unification with Taiwan, launching a war over Taiwan necessitates Beijing to prepare for an unexpected chain-reaction warfare. This could deviate from the previously discussed contingencies. If China is consumed with a conflict around Taiwan, tension in one theatre could ignite conflicts with other countries, pushing their territorial claims, potentially leading to situations beyond China's control.[195]

In this context, one may question if China could overcome these geographical constraints by bolstering its military investments. This query naturally leads to the next topic of discussion—economic constraints.

- **The difficult balancing act**

In *The Fall and Rise of Great Powers*, Paul Kennedy indicated that most of the world's governing bodies generally pursue three parallel goals: "to provide military security (or some viable alternative) to protect national interests, to satisfy the socio-economic needs of its citizenry, and ensure sustained growth".[196] However, Kennedy cautioned that striking a perfect balance among these objectives can be challenging, with progress in one area often coming at the expense of the others.[197]

If a nation manages to achieve only the first two objectives, or any single one of them, without accomplishing the third, it will inevitably experience a relative decline over time.[198] This has been a recurring pattern among societies with slower growth that failed to adapt to changing global power dynamics.[199] As Kennedy pointed out, "It is hard to imagine, but a country whose productivity growth lags 1 per cent behind other countries over one century can turn, as England did, from the world's undisputed industrial leader into the mediocre economy it is today."[200] The conclusion from this is that in the existing paradigm, if a substantial country cannot strike a balanced approach towards the conflicting demands of defence, consumption, and investment, it may struggle to sustain its leading position in the long term.[201]

Yet, one of the biggest threats to the balance between defence, consumption and investment is military conflicts. A 2016 RAND study found: "After just one year of a severe non-nuclear war, American GDP could decline by up to 10% and Chinese GDP by as much as 35%—setbacks on par with the Great Depression."[202]

Throughout history, the most significant challenge for Chinese emperors has been the balancing act of maintaining enough military power to ward off external threats, while simultaneously ensuring economic growth to sustain a large populace. This

---

[195] Lin and Wuthnow (2022).
[196] Kennedy (2017), p.445.
[197] Ibid.
[198] Ibid.
[199] Ibid.
[200] Ibid.
[201] Ibid.
[202] Allison (2019), p.155.

challenge remains critical for the CCP today. The 20th CCP National Congress showed an increasing trend of Beijing prioritising national security concerns, potentially at the expense of economic growth. As previously discussed, this strategy could lead to detrimental outcomes, as evident in historical cases such as Philip II's Spain, Nicholas II's Russia, Hitler's Germany, Japan during the Second World War, and the Soviet Union in the Cold War. In contrast, China's rapid growth in recent decades was largely fuelled by trade and economic strategies reminiscent of the post-1945 resurgences of Germany and Japan, rather than their pre-1914 imperial systems.[203] In both scenarios, economic prosperity and geopolitical influence were achieved without resorting to warfare.[204]

Looking into the future, whether China can continue to rise peacefully will not depend so much on the narrow political issue of rising nationalism, but on the kind of status quo that China's core economic interest requires the country to strive for. China's continued economic development requires China to compete with the United States for investment and trade opportunities, but it fundamentally requires this competition to happen in a peaceful and healthy environment. China's long-term domestic stability hinges on steady employment for its workforce of 746 million, and the provision of affordable housing, education, and healthcare for its lower-income earners and the middle class, who make up over 93% of the nation's population.[205] It is clear that there is a pressing need for increased government expenditure on public services. However, data suggests that heightened military expenditure is detracting from these essential services. Furthermore, the substantial financial strain induced by large military expenditures in an economy experiencing slowdown could potentially disrupt societal order and, in turn, threaten China's stability and the CCP's rule.

In conclusion, even with China's concerns about geostrategic encirclement along the First Island Chain, its need to secure strategic maritime resources, and Xi Jinping's personal ambitions for Taiwan, these geographical and economic constraints may moderate China's aspirations and actions. Although China might continue to significantly enhance its military capabilities and expand its global influence, this would also increase the potential for a disastrous showdown with the United States. In an era of nuclear weapons, the potentially catastrophic global ramifications of such a conflict would compel China to reevaluate its stance.

To mitigate the likelihood of conflicts, leaders of the world must manage two key tasks simultaneously. First, the immediate-to-medium-term focus should be on the creation of robust strategies and the strengthening of capabilities to deter any potential Chinese hostility towards Taiwan by escalating the repercussions associated with conflict engagement for China. Second, for the long term, it is crucial to acknowledge that the future shape of the global new equilibrium will depend not only on the interests and ambitions of individual nation-states, but also on emerging

---

[203] Harari (2018).

[204] Ibid.

[205] National Bureau of Statistics (2022), National Development and Reform Commission (2021), Ministry of Human Resources and Social Security of the People's Republic of China (2022).

global risks that are beyond the control of any single country, ranging from artificial intelligence to environmental challenges. Addressing these emergent challenges may necessitate more than just an arms race in response to a delicate threat; it may demand a fundamental shift in our approach to global security and diplomacy. I will explore this perspective in more detail in Chap. 11.

References

Academy of Ocean of China (2018) Haiyang wenhua dailai "haiyangguan" de genben zhuanbian. Available at: http://aoc.ouc.edu.cn/2018/0925/c9824a211289/page.htm. Accessed 8 September 2021.

Acheson DG (1949) Acheson, Statement On China, 1949. In: USC US-China Institute. Available at: https://china.usc.edu/acheson-statement-china-1949. Accessed 5 March 2021.

Allison G (2019) Destined for War: Can America and China escape Thucydides's trap? Scribe Publications Pty Ltd, Melbourne.

Buckley C (2023) China draws lessons from Russia's losses in Ukraine, and its gains. In: New York Time. Available at: https://www.nytimes.com/2023/04/01/world/asia/china-russia-ukraine-war.html. Accessed 28 April 2023.

Bush RC (2017) A one China policy premier. In: Brookings. Available at: https://www.brookings.edu/wp-content/uploads/2017/03/one-china-policy-primer-web-final.pdf. Accessed 3 March 2021.

Campbell C (2021) China's military: The People's Liberation Army (PLA). In: Congressional research services. Available at: https://crsreports.congress.gov/product/pdf/R/R46808. Accessed 12 December 2021.

Capaccio A (2022) China has put longer-range ICBMs on its nuclear subs, U.S. says. In: Bloomberg. Available at: https://www.bloomberg.com/news/articles/2022-11-18/us-says-china-s-subs-armed-with-longer-range-ballistic-missiles#xj4y7vzkg. Accessed 12 January 2023.

Carter J (1979) Establishment of diplomatic relations between the United States and the People's Republic of China. Case Western Reserve Journal of International Law 11(2):227–229.

Cavas CP (2016) Powers jockey for Pacific Island Chain influence. In: Defense News. Available at: https://www.defensenews.com/global/asia-pacific/2016/02/01/powers-jockey-for-pacific-island-chain-influence/. Accessed 19 February 2021.

Center for Strategic & International Studies (n.d.) Chinese power projection capabilities in the South China Sea. Available at: https://amti.csis.org/chinese-power-projection/?lang=zh-hans. Accessed 10 March 2021.

China Institute of Navigation (1988) Gudai hanghaishi. In: Zhongguo hanghaishi. China Communication Press, Beijing.

Cho IH, Park SH (2013) The rise of China and varying sentiments in Southeast Asia toward great powers. Strategic Studies Quarterly 7(2):69–92.

Cole BD (2014) The history of the twenty-first-century Chinese navy. Naval War College Review 67(3):43–62.

David S (2007) China stands up: The PRC and the international system. Routledge, New York.

Ding XL (2015) Xianggang jinru "xinchangtai." In: Financial Times. Available at: https://www.ftchinese.com/story/001060453?archive. Accessed 13 February 2021.

Duan RC (2012) Taipingyang zhanzheng qianqi Jiang Jieshi de zhanhou gouxiang. Bulletin of Academia Historica (32):121–152.

Easton I (2021) Why a Taiwan invasion would look nothing Like D-Day. In: The Diplomat. Available at: https://thediplomat.com/2021/05/why-a-taiwan-invasion-would-look-nothing-like-d-day/. Accessed 12 December 2022.

References

Eckholm E (n.d.) Interview with Erik Eckholm. In: Frontline. Available at: https://www.pbs.org/wgbh/pages/frontline/shows/china/interviews/eckholm.html. Accessed 4 March 2021.

Erickson AS, Wuthnow J (2016) Barriers, springboards and benchmarks: China conceptualizes the Pacific 'Island Chains'. The China Quarterly 225 (2016):1–22.

Fairbank JK (1969) China's foreign policy in historical perspective. Foreign Affairs 47(3):449–463.

Fallon J (2020) Breaking the island chains. In: Defense Viewpoints. Available at: https://www.defenceviewpoints.co.uk/articles-and-analysis/breaking-the-island-chains. Accessed 19 October 2022.

Fearon JD (1997) The offense-defense balance and war since 1648 (draft paper). In: The University of Stanford. Available at: https://web.stanford.edu/group/fearon-research/cgi-bin/wordpress/wp-content/uploads/2013/10/The-Offense-Defense-Balance-and-War-Since-1648.pdf. Accessed 20 February 2019.

Gompert DC (2013) U.S. and Chinese interests and sea power in the Western Pacific. Rand Corporation, Santa Monica.

Gronewald S (2021) The Ming voyages. In: Asia for Educators. Available at: http://afe.easia.columbia.edu/special/china_1000ce_mingvoyages.htm. Accessed 10 October 2021.

Haass R, Sacks D (2020) American support for Taiwan must be unambiguous. In: Foreign Affairs. Available at: https://www.foreignaffairs.com/articles/united-states/american-support-taiwan-must-be-unambiguous?utm_medium=newsletters&utm_source=fatoday&utm_campaign=Howpercent20topercent20Preparepercent20forpercent20thepercent20Nextpercent20Ukraine&utm_content=20220523&utm_term=FApercent20Todaypercent20-percent20112017. Accessed 23 August 2022.

Hans R (2020) Why now? understanding Beijing's new assertiveness in Hong Kong. In: Brookings. Available at: https://www.brookings.edu/blog/order-from-chaos/2020/07/17/why-now-understanding-beijings-new-assertiveness-in-hong-kong/. Accessed 18 March 2021.

Harari YH (2018) 21 Lessons for the 21st Century. Random House, New York.

Harding B, Pohle-Anderson C (2022) China's search for a permanent military presence in the Pacific Islands. In: United States Institute of Peace. Available at: https://www.usip.org/publications/2022/07/chinas-search-permanent-military-presence-pacific-islands. Accessed 19 January 2023.

Hayton B (2020) The invention of China. Yale University Press, New Haven.

Heginbotham E (2021) China maritime report No. 14: Chinese views of the military balance in the Western Pacific. In: U.S. Naval War College. Available at: https://digital-commons.usnwc.edu/cmsi-maritime-reports/14/. Accessed 2 December 2022.

Hickey DV (1997) U.S. policy and Taiwan's bid to rejoin the United Nations. Asian Survey 37(11):1031–1043. DOI: https://doi.org/10.2307/2645739.

Huang RW (2015) Houqi daguo yu shoucheng daguo hudong de lishi yu xianshi. Journal of International Relations 1(1).

Huang CY (2017) Biange yu yansheng: songdai haishang silu de xingeju. South China Quarterly 7(1):46–61.

Jervis R (1978) Cooperation under the security dilemma. World Politics 30(2):167–214.

Kennedy P (2017) The rise and fall of the great powers: Economic change and military conflict from 1500-2000. Harper Collins Publishers Ltd., London.

Lendon B, Liebermann O (2023) War game suggests Chinese invasion of Taiwan would fail at a huge cost to US, Chinese and Taiwanese militaries. In: CNN. Available at: https://edition.cnn.com/2023/01/09/politics/taiwan-invasion-war-game-intl-hnk-ml/index.html. Accessed 19 January 2023.

Lin B, Wuthnow J (2022) The weakness behind China's strong façade-Xi's reach exceeds his military's grasp. In: Foreign Affairs. Available at: https://www.foreignaffairs.com/china/weakness-behind-china-strong-facade?check_logged_in=1. Accessed 15 November 2022.

Lin G, Zhou WX (2018) Does Taiwan matter to the United States? Policy debates on Taiwan abandonment and beyond. China Review 18(3):177–206.

Lin SS (2018) Analyzing the relationship between identity and democratization in Taiwan and Hong Kong in the shadow of China. In: The Asan Forum. Available at: https://theasanforum.org/analyzing-the-relationship-between-identity-and-democratization-in-taiwan-and-hong-kong-in-the-shadow-of-china/. Accessed 4 March 2021.

Mahan AT (1890) The influence of sea power upon history 1660–1783. Little, Brown Book Group, Boston, p.51.

Mahan AT (1987) The Indian Ocean in world politics: Reflections on its future by Prasanta Sen Gupta. India Quarterly 43(3–4):195–212.

Marshall T (2015) Prisoners of geography: Ten maps that tell you everything you need to know about global politics. Elliott & Thompson, London.

Ministry of Defense, Japan (2022) Defense of Japan 2022. Available at: https://www.mod.go.jp/en/publ/w_paper/index.html. Accessed 6 January 2023.

Ministry of Human Resources and Social Security of the People's Republic of China (2022) 2021niandu renli ziyuan he shehui baozhang shiye fazhan tongji gongbao. Available at: http://www.mohrss.gov.cn/SYrlzyhshbzb/zwgk/szrs/tjgb/202206/t20220607_452104.html. Accessed 12 December 2022.

Molan J (2022) Danger on our doorstep. HarperCollins, Sydney.

National Bureau of Statistics (2022) 2021nian jumin shouru he xiaofei zhichu qingkuang. Available at: http://www.stats.gov.cn/tjsj/zxfb/202201/t20220117_1826403.html. Accessed 9 October 2022.

National Development and Reform Commission (2021) Zhongguo zhongdeng shouru renqun yi chao 4yi zhongdeng shouru dajun ruhe "kuoqun." Available at: https://www.ndrc.gov.cn/fggz/jyysr/jysrsbxf/202109/t20210924_1297381_ext.html.

NBC (2022) War Game: What would a battle for Taiwan look like? Available at: https://www.nbc.com/meet-the-press/video/war-game-what-would-a-battle-for-taiwan-look-like/NBCN142309777. Accessed 18 October 2022.

Needham J (1978) Physics and physical technology: Civil engineering and nautics Vol IV:3. In: Science and Civilization in China. Cambridge University Press, Cambridge.

O'Rourke R (2022) China naval modernization: Implications for U.S. Navy capabilities—background and issues for Congress. In: Congressional Research Service. Available at: https://crsreports.congress.gov/product/details?prodcode=RL33153. Accessed 12 January 2023.

Paul M (2018) Maritime nuclear deterrence. In: Stiftung Wissenschaft und Politik. Available at: https://www.swp-berlin.org/publikation/maritime-nuclear-deterrence. Accessed 12 January 2023.

Pettyjohn SL, Wasser B (2022) A fight over Taiwan could go nuclear. In: Foreign Affairs. Available at: https://www.foreignaffairs.com/articles/china/2022-05-20/fight-over-taiwan-could-go-nuclear. Accessed 18 October 2022.

Ratcliffe S (ed) (2017) Oxford essential quotation, 6th edn. Oxford University Press, Oxford.

Sacks D (2022) What is China learning from Russia's war in Ukraine? In: Foreign Affairs. Available at: https://www.foreignaffairs.com/articles/china/2022-05-16/what-china-learning-russias-war-ukraine?utm_medium=newsletters&utm_source=fatoday&utm_campaign=Whatpercent20Ispercent20Chinapercent20Learningpercent20Frompercent20RussiapercentE2percent80percent99spercent20Warpercent20inpercent20Ukraine?&utm_content=20220516&utm_term=FApercent20Todaypercent20-percent20112017. Accessed 18 August 2022.

Scullard HH (2021) From the Gracchi to Nero: A history of Rome 133 BC to AD 68. Routledge, London.

Sima Q (2011) Shi Ji (The Records of the Grand Historian). Zhonghua Book Company, Beijing.

Snow E (2017) Red star over China: The classic account of the birth of Chinese communism. Grove Press, London, p.110.

Stavridis J (2019) Hai quan (Sea power). CITI Press, Beijing.

Swope KM (2016) A dragon's head and a serpent's tail: Ming China and the first great East Asian war, 1592–1598. In: Campaigns and Commanders. University of Oklahoma Press, Norman.

The Economist (2021a) The rivalry between America and China will hinge on South-East Asia. Available at: https://www.economist.com/leaders/2021/02/27/the-rivalry-between-america-and-china-will-hinge-on-south-east-asia?utm_campaign=the-economist-27. Accessed

5 April 2021.

The Economist (2021b) In its rivalry with China, America should not make Asians pick sides. Available at: https://www.economist.com/leaders/2021/01/28/in-its-rivalry-with-china-america-should-not-make-asians-pick-sides. Accessed 10 March 2021.

The Economist (2021c) Biden's new China doctrine. Available at: https://www.economist.com/leaders/2021/07/17/bidens-new-china-doctrine?utm_campaign=the-economist-this-week&utm_medium=newsletter&utm_source=salesforce-marketing-cloud. Accessed 19 October 2021.

The State Council Information Office of the People's Republic of China (2019) Full text: China's national defense in the new era. Available at: https://english.www.gov.cn/archive/whitepaper/201907/24/content_WS5d3941ddc6d08408f502283d.html. Accessed 8 September 2020.

The Truman Library (1950) Statement by the President on the situation in Korea. Available at: https://www.trumanlibrary.gov/library/public-papers/173/statement-president-situation-korea. Accessed 3 March 2021.

The U.S.-China Economic and Security Review Commission (2020) 2020 Report to Congress of the U.S.-China Economic and Security Review Commission. Available at: https://www.uscc.gov/annual-report/2020-annual-report-congress. Accessed 9 August 2021.

Time Magzine (1951) National affairs: An unsinkable aircraft carrier. Available at: https://web.archive.org/web/20091125150338/http://www.time.com/time/magazine/article/0,9171,856644,00.html. Accessed 3 March 2021.

Trade and Industry Department, The Government of the Hong Kong Special Administrative Region (2022) Hong Kong and mainland of China: Some important facts. Available at: https://www.tid.gov.hk/english/aboutus/publications/factsheet/china.html. Accessed 5 January 2023.

Turnbull S (2016) Wars and rumours of wars: Japanese plans to invade the Philippines, 1593–1637. Naval War College Review 69(4):107–121.

U.S. Department of Defense (2022) Military and security developments involving the People's Republic of China. Available at: https://www.defense.gov/CMPR/. Accessed 5 January 2023.

United States Department of State, Office of the Historian (2021) Japan, China, the United States and the road to Pearl Harbor, 1937–41. Available at: https://history.state.gov/milestones/1937-1945/pearl-harbor. Accessed 8 February 2021.

United States Senate Committee on Armed Services (2023) United States Senate Committee on armed services summary of the fiscal year 2023 National Defense Authorization Act. Available at: https://www.armed-services.senate.gov/imo/media/doc/fy23_ndaa_agreement_summary.pdf. Accessed 16 February 2023.

Wang GW (2019a) Guang zhi yi, Vol I. Shanghai People's Publishing House, Shanghai.

Wang SX (2019b) China reconnects: Joining a deep-rooted past to a new world order. World Scientific Publishing Company, Singapore.

Wang XL (2009) Suomali haidao dui woguo haishang anquan de yingxiang. Journal of University of International Relations (5):19–27.

Wang Y (2010) Qianxi zhongguo haiquan fazhan de ruogan wenti. Pacific Journal 18(5):90–98.

Wen Y, Zhang YM (2018) Lun Mao Zedong haifang zhanlue sixiang. In: Party History Research Center of the CCP Central Committee. Available at: http://www.dswxyjy.org.cn/n1/2019/0228/c423718-30948528.html. Accessed 22 September 2021.

Wortzel LM (2014) China's military modernization and cyber activities: Testimony of Dr. Larry M. Wortzel before the House Armed Services Committee. Strategic Studies Quarterly 8(1):3–22.

Xu S (2009) Zhi guan. In: Songhui yaoji gao. Shanghai Guji Press, Shanghai.

Yenigun C et al. (2020) China's military strategy in the Indian Ocean region. Adalya Journal 9(12):255–271. Doi: https://doi.org/10.37896/aj9.12/02.

Yoshihara T, Bianchi J (2021) Seizing on weakness: Allied strategy for competing with China's globalizing military. In: Center for Strategic and Budgetary Assessments. Available at: https://csbaonline.org/research/publications/seizing-on-weakness-allied-strategy-for-competing-with-chinas-globalizing-military. Accessed 5 April 2021.

Yoshihara T, Holmes JR (2014) The next arms race—APAC 2020, the decade ahead. In: The Diplomat. Available at: https://apac2020.thediplomat.com/feature/the-next-arms-race/.

Accessed 12 January 2020.

Zhang C et al (2021) Jiedu 2021 nian zhongguo junfei. In: AVIC Securities. Available at: https://pdf.dfcfw.com/pdf/H3_AP202103071469464988_1.pdf?1615196741000.pdf. Accessed 2 December 2021.

Zhao L (2023) Govt proposes 7.2% rise in defense budget to $225b. In: China Daily. Available at: https://www.chinadaily.com.cn/a/202303/05/WS6403faa3a31057c47ebb23e1.html. Accessed 03 April 2023.

Chapter 8
Charting the Path of Influence: Between Force and Soft Power

> *"A government must have not only the economic heft but also the skill to wield economic instruments effectively. China has demonstrated a unique mastery in using hard instruments of 'soft power'."* (Allison, 2017)
> —Graham Allison, Author of Destined for War

Abstract As China's comprehensive national power grows, how will China exert its global influence? This chapter argues that China is most likely to continue to wield soft power tools, such as economic interests and cultural impact. It also posits that China's military strength serves primarily as a deterrent, a prerequisite that enables the country to predominantly use its soft power tools. This chapter is structured to explore how China has historically and contemporarily employed economic interest and cultural influence as instruments of soft power. Regarding economic soft power, the chapter explores the underlying logic behind China's approach, paying particular attention to its execution through the tributary system. It highlights the emerging obstacles tied to China's strategy of positioning economic soft power as a primary means of attaining global influence. In terms of cultural soft power, the chapter delves into how China has traditionally defined its own identity in contrast to the non-Chinese world, and the evolution of this perspective over time. It also explores how this evolving conception of identity has shaped varying strategies to exert cultural influence, both domestically and internationally.

Chapters 6 and 7 examined the crucial factors that have shaped China's strategic military choices. As those chapters explained, confronted with vulnerable borders and potential flashpoints such as Taiwan, China may be inclined to adopt more aggressive measures. However, certain constraints may deter China from using force as the primary means of expanding its global influence. Firstly, striking a balance between landward security and maritime ambitions demands compromises. Moreover, excessive military spending amid a slowing economy risks undermining social cohesion within the nation, ultimately threatening the regime's stability. Further, it hardly needs to be said that China's growing military might and worldwide expansion would possibly culminate in a catastrophic showdown with the United States in this age of nuclear weapons. Recognising these risks, China opts to focus on soft power initiatives as its main approach to enhance its global standing, with military strength serving as a necessary prerequisite to make this possible.

Throughout its history, China has wielded economic and cultural influence as principal tools in the conduct of its international affairs. Its unique interpretation of 'world order' has shaped the deployment of diverse soft power strategies. These perspectives offer meaningful insights into China's potential methods of global influence exertion in the future, and their impact on the existing international order. This chapter commences with an exploration from an economic viewpoint.

Geoeconomics and Statecraft

China's strategy of utilising economic soft power to navigate its foreign relations can be traced back to its extensive historical experiences in dealing with nomadic communities. Chapter 6 highlights that nomadic invasions in China correlated with East Asia's monsoon climate. During weak summer monsoons, droughts in the north led to nomads struggling for survival, resulting in raids on Chinese farmers, caravans, and large-scale attacks on the heartland. As Robert Jervis argued in *Cooperation Under the Security Dilemma*, "a state can reduce the incentives for another state to attack it, by not being a threat to the latter, and by providing goods and services that would be lost if the other was to attempt exploitation."[1] During the reign of Emperor Jing of the Han dynasty (188–141 BCE), China set up a series of large border markets near the heavily fortified entrances of the Great Wall. The border markets allowed the exchange of Chinese goods with the nomadic communities, helping to prevent disturbances along the borders.[2] The *Records of the Grand Historian* confirmed that the strategy was successful. During the reign of Emperor Jing, although the Xiongnu became bolder, they did not carry out any major invasions.[3]

As Graham Allison stated in *Destined for War*, "A government must have not only the economic heft but also the skills to wield economic instruments effectively. Indeed, China has demonstrated a unique mastery in using economic instruments of 'soft power'."[4] In the Han dynasty example, China recognised the Xiongnu's dire need for Chinese goods, and strategically used border markets to cultivate their economic dependence. When Emperor Wu of the Han dynasty (159–87 BCE) planned surprise counterattacks on the Xiongnu, he dispatched 40,000 cavalries to disrupt the vital border markets.[5] During the 98 BCE peace talks initiated by the Xiongnu, their primary request was reopening the border markets and ensuring continuous access. These border markets thus served as a strategic negotiating tool to prevent and

---

[1] Jervis (1978).
[2] McLaughlin (2016).
[3] Ibid.
[4] Allison (2017).
[5] McLaughlin (2016).

manage armed conflicts, enabling the Han regime to capitalise on their advantageous bargaining position and adopt a conciliatory approach to reduce external pressure.[6]

Further, economic soft power can not only settle direct external aggression by satisfying the aggressor's demand for goods, but it can also weaken a formidable opponent. For instance, to counter the Xiongnu, Emperor Wu of Han formed alliances with the Oasis States in the Tarim Basin, located on the northwestern border.[7] The Han regime sought support from these kingdoms by offering them substantial amounts of valuable goods in exchange for ongoing assistance and political assurances.[8] A number of Tarim rulers favoured this arrangement over paying tributes to the Xiongnu, subsequently renouncing their alliance with the Xiongnu and consequently diminishing the Xiongnu's influence.[9]

The logic embedded in the above examples can be understood as geoeconomics in modern terms. It means the use of economic instruments, which include trade and investment policy, sanctions, and foreign aid, to achieve geopolitical goals.[10] In *Way by Other Means: Geoeconomics and Statecraft*, Robert Blackwill and Jennifer Harris argued that China is the world's leading practitioner of geoeconomics.[11] Indeed, recent years have seen an increasingly assertive China, frequently leveraging its economic prowess to exert influence in international geopolitics or pressurise nations expressing political views that it finds unfavourable. The case of Australia serves as a potent example of this tactic. Amid political discord between the two nations, China has responded by enforcing a series of trade restrictions on an array of Australian commodities, including coal, wine, barley, and beef. However, this strategy has not yielded the desired results. A similar strategy was deployed in 2016 when China initiated a boycott of South Korean goods and curtailed Chinese tourism to South Korea, in reaction to South Korea's installation of the THAAD missile defence system.

Tributary System and the 'Tianxia'

The tributary system served as a broad application of geoeconomic logic. This system, a diplomatic and commercial framework guiding relationships between China and its neighbouring East Asian states, originated in the third century and reached its peak during the Ming dynasty. In John King Fairbank's classic summary, "the Chinese tended to think of their foreign relations as giving expression externally to the same

---

[6] Ibid.

[7] Ibid.

[8] Ibid.

[9] Ibid.

[10] Blackwill and Harris (2016).

[11] Ibid.

principles of social and political order that were manifested internally."[12] The principles and architecture of the tributary system derive from the Chinese philosophical heritage known as the 'Tianxia' system, which places China at the centre, surrounded by tributary states at various degrees of proximity based on their 'civilised' status. To fully grasp the tributary system, it is crucial to understand the 'Tianxia' system.

The term 'Tianxia' directly translates to 'all under heaven' and symbolises an ideal moral and political order without borders, where all entities 'under heaven' are governed by principles of ritual and virtue.[13] This concept emerged from the governance system established by the Zhou dynasty after the Duke of Zhou, along with his allies, overthrew the immoral Shang dynasty around 1046 BCE.[14] For the victorious Duke of Zhou, the real challenge arose postvictory. With a smaller population and relatively weaker military strength, governing the vast lands and the large population once controlled by the Shang dynasty required the Zhou dynasty to create a political system prioritising institutionalised cooperation rather than forceful deterrence. Thus, the 'Tianxia' system came into existence.

In practice, the concept of 'Tianxia' was realised through the 'enfeoffment' model. This model involved the King of Zhou distributing lands to enfeoffed states, which reciprocated with military support, labour assistance, and loyalty to the king.[15] According to historical documents, over 1,200 existing clans and newly enfeoffed states joined this 'Tianxia' network.[16] To maintain this vast and intricate system, the King of Zhou had to preserve a 'higher order value', foster persistent shared interests among enfeoffed states, and commit to a credible and implicit contract that promised not to exploit these states.[17] This resulted in a decentralised social structure, forming a confederation-like government composed of numerous autonomous states.[18]

Like the 'Tianxia' system, the primary objective of the tributary system was to nurture and sustain peaceful relations among nations and regions, favouring commerce as the conduit rather than resorting to force. It could be argued that the tributary system functioned as a defensive mechanism for Imperial China.[19] It allowed foreign populations to access Chinese products through trade, thus dissuading the use of force to procure these goods, as demonstrated by the example of border markets. At the same time, the system recognised states as rational actors motivated by material incentives in their strategic actions and interactions.[20] Motivated by the substantial economic benefits offered by the tributary system, foreign countries and merchants became more invested in production and growth rather than conflict. As a result, the

---

[12] Fairbank (1968).
[13] Zhao (2004).
[14] Sima (2011).
[15] Ye (2005).
[16] Lu et al. (eds.) (2022).
[17] Ibid.
[18] Fairbank and Goldman (1998).
[19] Zhang and Buzan (2012), Zhou (2011).
[20] Ibid.

tributary system efficiently fostered positive international relations while preserving China's preeminent status.

Further, akin to how the King of Zhou must uphold enduring shared values and commit to a credible promise not to exploit these states, the tributary system also involved a commitment from China not to exploit participating states that accepted its authority. That commitment was indeed kept, at least to the extent that Chinese gifts were of more value than the tribute paid by tribute states, and trade with China was beneficial to the economy of those states. This perspective is supported by many examples that participating states actually demanded to pay tribute before the tribute was due. For example, at the beginning of the Ming dynasty, Korea was only required to offer tribute triennially, yet it insisted on increasing this to thrice annually.[21] When it came to the Qing dynasty, Korea was required to pay one tribute per year. In fact, in the 256 years from 1637 to 1893, Korea sent a total of 514 tribute envoys to the Qing regime, an average of two per year, not taking into account informal tributes.[22] Another example is Japan. Although Japan withdrew from the tributary system after Toyotomi Hideyoshi invaded Korea, it required the Ryukyu Kingdom under its control to maintain tributary relations with China for a long time, in order to profit from it.[23]

Concentric Circles

To comprehend how the Chinese notion of 'Tianxia' informs its approach to external relations in practical terms, it is necessary to understand the 'Tianxia' structure in greater detail. This structure is most effectively represented in the following Chart 8.1.

In the historical Chinese interpretation of the world, there are two elements: the Chinese empire, and lands outside of civilisation.

Within the 'Chinese empire', there are three elements:

- The emperor is at the centre of a series of concentric circles.[24]
- 'China proper' forms an immediate circle surrounding the emperor. It consists of the Han people—inhabitants of the Chinese heartlands—who are directly controlled by the central administrative bureaucracy.[25]
- 'Outer China' or 'China dependencies' consist of ethnic minorities recognised by the emperor and under the influence or control of the central Chinese regime (e.g. small clans or cities along the Tarim desert oasis in what are Xinjiang and Tibet today).[26] In traditional Chinese worldviews, they are considered an integral part

---

[21] Ren (1995)

[22] Ibid.

[23] Ibid.

[24] Zhang and Buzan (2012).

[25] Harding (1993).

[26] Ibid.

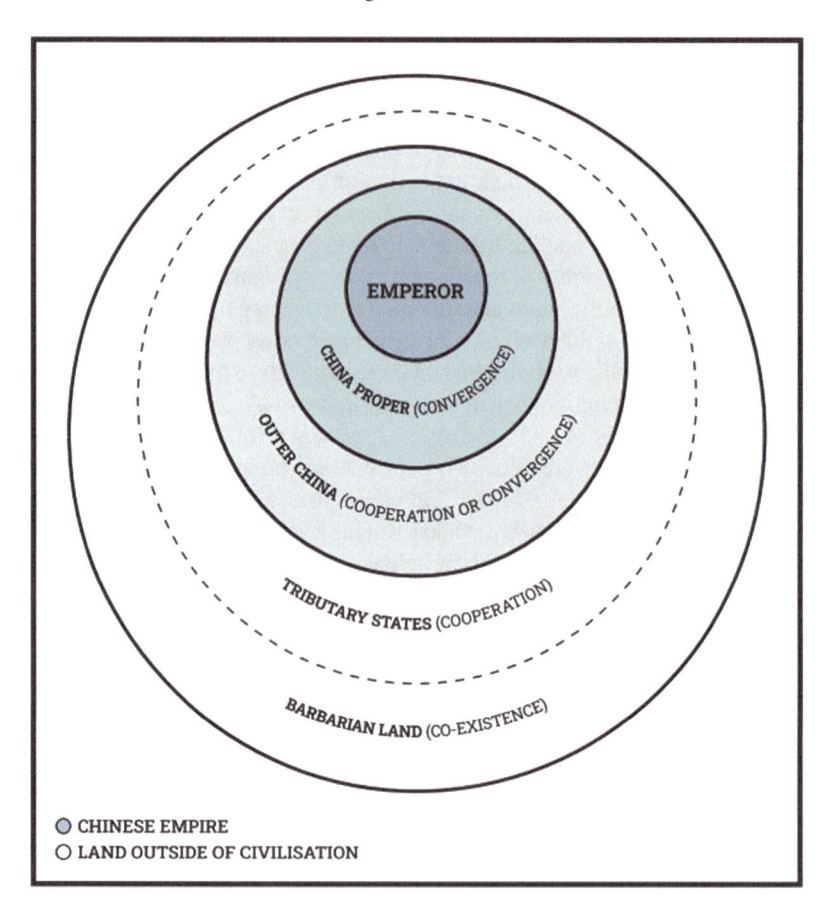

Chart 8.1 The concentric circles

of China. Their subordination is ensured by various means, which could include the use of force if deemed necessary.

Lands outside of civilisation are made up of two elements:

- Tributary states, such as Korea, the Ryukyu Kingdom, Vietnam, and other independent Asian countries, offer tributes and recognise the Chinese central regime, but are not part of China.[27]
- Barbarian lands—that is, areas not under Chinese influence—for example, certain territories occupied by Central Asian and Southeast Asian nomads, or Europeans from across the sea.[28] China has little interest in converting those to Chinese ways.[29]

---

[27] Fairbank (1969).
[28] Liu et al. (eds.) (2017).
[29] Kissinger (2011).

There are two important points to understand the concentric circles. Firstly, the concentric circles are a hierarchical structure. The emperor and the 'Chinese Empire' are not only at the centre but hold the most power. Such power marks the dominance of Imperial China—particularly its cultural dominance—and establishes different levels of autonomy among other participants, based on their cultural proximity with China.[30] The practical implementation of the tributary system is modelled in this hierarchical fashion. Here, China is situated at the centre of this system, while the participating states are arranged in a hierarchy according to their level of investiture in the tributary status.

The second, and arguably more critical component, is the structural configuration of these circles. This varies from a basic coexistence in the outer circles to potential cooperation and convergence in the innermost ones.[31] The underlying principle is that the proximity of a circle to the centre corresponds to its relevance to China's fundamental interests. Consequently, the intent to foster cooperation and convergence in terms of key values and shared perspectives increases as a circle moves closer to the centre. On the contrary, as a circle moves further from the centre, its impact on China's core interests diminishes, leading to reduced expectations of the relationship and less effort being exerted to maintain cohesion. This point will be further explored later in the chapter.

Symbolic Obedience

The notion of 'Tianxia' and the tributary system may sound terrifying to Westerners who are used to value strict freedom of thought and religion within sovereign borders defined by the Westphalian model of international relations. It may well seem that China is an aggressive empire, expanding from its centre, and imposing subordinate status upon proudly independent states, some of whom had fought wars to be free of foreign domination back home.[32] More generally, the idea of a global world order that is hierarchically structured, and where China lies at the centre, is emotionally challenging to many, particularly Europeans and Americans. Europeans and Americans—or 'Westerners'—are used to thinking of themselves as civilised, and at the centre of the world: this is the definition of Eurocentrism, or Western-centrism. It is therefore a stretch to willingly acknowledge China—or even Asia—as being the centre of the world. This difficulty calls for greater understanding of the tributary systems as a symbolic order, and what a symbolic order means.

At the core, the tributary model involves a different notion of sovereignty from the Westphalian system, on which the current world order is based. The Westphalian system is a model inherited from Europe, based on the principle of strict equality between sovereign states, and mutual non-interference. In the seventeenth century,

---

[30] Fairbank (1969).
[31] Zhang and Buzan (2012).
[32] Hayton (2020).

religious, political, and geopolitical factors sparked dynastic disputes among the Holy Roman Empire's German members, escalating into a devastating Europe-wide conflict. The war, with debated casualties between 4 and 12 million, ended after 30 years when European powers established a non-interference principle in the Treaty of Westphalia, setting a new standard for inter-state relationships. Although respected within Europe itself, it should be noted here that this system did not prevent European states from intervening in the affairs of countries on other continents, or even taking over their territories as colonies all through the nineteenth and early twentieth centuries.

Now, how exactly did the Chinese tributary system differ from this model? The tributary system has often been incorrectly portrayed as a suzerain-vassal relationship, similar to that which existed in the Ottoman Empire, where participating states had limited sovereignty over their internal governance and foreign policies. While the tributary system demanded symbolic deference to China, marked by a kowtow (complete prostration) by ambassadors to the emperor, symbolising a distinction in status and the acceptance of China as a symbolic centre, it typically did not mandate political subservience.[33]

Firstly, the tributary system exhibits considerable flexibility, as the Chinese did not assign a precise definition to what a tributary status entailed.[34] Likely, the Chinese astutely left this matter ambiguous and adaptable, granting participating states some latitude to interpret the system's rules and norms without contesting the legitimacy of the tributary system.[35] As part of this flexibility, when required, Imperial China did not hesitate to pay tribute in reverse, while maintaining its nominal status as the receiver of tribute.[36] For example, Emperor Gaozu of Han purchased peace by agreeing to give regular tribute to the Xiongnu in the form of food stocks and large quantities of silk.[37] The silk payment alone may have included up to 10,000 pi (four tonnes) per annum.[38] Within such a flexible framework, these occurrences could transpire without significantly disrupting the entire tributary system, thereby fostering increased overall stability.

In addition, even on the fundamental assumption of Chinese moral and cultural superiority, there seems to have been flexibility in practice.[39] For example, the Xiongnu chief demanded to be acknowledged as a political equal, or as a 'Brother State', by the Han regime.[40] To signify this, he requested the Han emperor to present a Han princess to join his wives. In 200 BCE, Emperor Gaozu of Han did offer a Han princess in marriage to the Xiongnu chief, which meant that the Han regime

---

[33] Lee (2017).
[34] Wang (2013).
[35] Zhang and Buzan (2012).
[36] Ibid.
[37] McLaughlin (2016).
[38] Ibid.
[39] Wang (2013).
[40] McLaughlin (2016).

acknowledged an equal relation with the Xiongnu.[41] Maintaining an equal relation with Lhasa, Kokand, or Moscow under the tributary system was not an exception to the Chinese.[42] In certain extreme instances, the Chinese even accepted a quasi-tribute state status—for instance, the Song regime did so in relation to the Jin regime of Jurchen descent from 1141 to 1164 under the Treaty of Shaoxing, during which time the Jin regime replaced the Song as the centre of the tributary system.[43]

Last but not least, within the tributary system, China largely followed the rule of non-interference.[44] For example, during the Qing dynasty, the Qing regime repeatedly stated in the negotiations between China and Japan on the Korean issue that political and religious decisions would be left to Korea's independent decision, and China would never question or interfere in those decisions.[45] Occasionally, when there was a severe threat to security, China changed its standing and intervened. For example, although the Chinese regime largely left Vietnam's internal affairs to their own, they intervened on one notable occasion in order to prevent a change of power.[46] In 1788, the Qing military launched a military expedition to intervene in Vietnam's internal rebellion against the reigning Le family, who had been loyal tributaries for more than a century.[47]

In summary, although the tributary system was hierarchical, it remained a system involving autonomous actors, which, in almost all cases, were virtually independent. Therefore, the political sacrifice of participating states was mainly 'symbolic obedience'.

China's contemporary economic interactions with the world bear some resemblance to its historical tributary system. Firstly, China does not demand political obedience from other nations, nor does it exploit them, but it does insist on 'tribute' and symbolic adherence. In today's context, this translates to a political assurance that does not directly oppose China's core interests, coupled with a tacit understanding to not disrupt or alter China's internal political system. If these expectations are not met, China may employ economic instruments as a form of corrective action as previously discussed.

Secondly, China continues to support the principle of non-interference in its interactions with other countries. However, it is crucial to recognise a level of ambivalence in China's commitment to non-interference in contemporary terms. China typically refrains from meddling in the internal affairs of other countries, and it perceives any attempt at imposing values as an act of interference and attack of its sovereignty.[48] This strong assertion of sovereignty above all else also serves to maintain its domestic

---

[41] Ban (2003).

[42] Zhang and Buzan (2012).

[43] Jia and Han (eds.).

[44] Shinobu (1982).

[45] Wang (1979).

[46] Amer (1993).

[47] Ibid.

[48] McDonagh (2021).

legitimacy.[49] Hence, China seems to favour a non-Westphalian model and seeks to amend the existing order to better suit its interests. Yet, at the same time, it remains a strong advocate for (Westphalian) sovereignty within the United Nations, using this principle to combat 'interference' or external influence on matters like human rights.

Asian Peace Stabiliser or Giant Rogue State?

Drawing evidence from history, how is China likely to exercise its influence over the world in the future? Two characteristics at least are signs of hope—particularly as they find echoes in the overarching strategy of China today: the traditional pursuit of harmony, and insistence on shifting the focus of regional or global power projection from political-military engagements back to economic activities.[50]

The tributary system reached its peak during the Ming and early Qing dynasties, during which time the economic prosperity and regional security of East Asia reached one of its highest points in history. For close to 500 years, from 1368 to 1840, a long era of peace, known as Pax Sinica, prevailed across regions encompassing present-day China, Japan, Korea, and Vietnam.[51] In the words of political scientist David Kang: "these four major territorial and centralised states developed and maintained peaceful and long-lasting relationships with one another, and the more powerful these states became, the more stable were their relations."[52] Over the same period, Europe, covering a much smaller territory and hosting a much smaller population, saw war on average at least once every four years.

However, the situation has changed considerably since then. At present, Asia could arguably be viewed as one of the regions most fraught with potential triggers for conflict. Numerous territorial disputes over land and sea have prompted many Asian nations to attempt to establish buffer zones. These actions, however, often incite worries among neighbouring countries with stakes in the same territory, who fear it could set an unfavourable precedent or augment their vulnerability.[53] This scenario is often referred to as a 'security dilemma' in which escalating fears among the more vulnerable nations lead them to accumulate more weapons, thereby reducing the potential for cooperation.[54]

Japan has announced it would increase its 2023 defence spending by more than a quarter to 6.82 trillion yen (USD 51.4 billion) amid rising threats from China, North Korea, and Russia.[55] India has slated a defence budget of 5.94 trillion rupees (USD 72.6 billion) for the fiscal year 2023–2024, a 13% increase from the original estimates

---

[49] Hayton (2020).
[50] Blackwill and Harris (2016).
[51] Kang (2010).
[52] Ibid.
[53] Jervis (1978).
[54] Ibid.
[55] Reynolds (2022).

of the prior period, amid tensions with China.[56] Southeast Asian countries increased their military spending by 5.2% to USD 45.5 billion in 2020, with a 36% increase in the region over the 2011–2020 decade.[57] However, those elevated defence spendings are not matched by greater military cooperation.[58] As the primary recipient of foreign investment and the global manufacturing centre, Asia's trade and economic growth would stagnate, and investments would vanish in the event of severe conflict or war.

China, as the most significant economic powerhouse in Asia, has a substantial incentive to foster and maintain peace and stability in the region, at least for its own security and economic well-being. Historically, China has seen trade as a pivotal tool in fostering regional stability. The vast economic benefits derived from its tributary system not only provided a platform for countries to address their demand through commerce rather than conflict, but it also motivated them to focus on production and economic growth. Many nations, wary of missing out on the shared wealth that regional trade brings, have shifted their focus towards enhancing economic activities, and have set their sights on long-term strategies for growth instead of engaging in disputes over scarce resources. However, while China's persistence in using trade to foster regional security has its positive impacts, it can also lead to negative outcomes in the current environment.

Firstly, the burgeoning Asian economy might paradoxically be one of the factors contributing to its escalating political volatility. Although economic growth in Asia, mainly powered by trade, is usually seen as a positive development, it could inadvertently foster political turbulence. As countries grow more prosperous, they might experience rising societal expectations, amplified national ambitions, and intensified nationalism, which could potentially instigate conflicts over resources and territories.[59] In this context, Zbigniew Brzezinski characterised the interplay among Asian nations as a state of meta-stability, a term denoting an externally rigid but internally volatile system.[60] Essentially, this implies that under the stress of maintaining economic growth and increasing nationalism, the dynamics among Asian nations could be prone to abrupt disruptions or fractures.

Secondly, the trade benefits extended by China might inadvertently heighten the security dilemma in Asia. As Robert Jervis has noted, "Statesmen realise that the growth of positive interdependence can provide others with new levers of influence over them. They may resist such developments more than would be expected from theories that stress the advantages of cooperation."[61] The severity of the dilemma is mitigated when two states harbour similar ideologies and values.[62] Conversely, when a significant discrepancy in ideologies and values is perceived, the dilemma's intensity amplifies. Hence, "Extreme differences in values and ideologies exacerbate

---

[56] Kumar (2023).

[57] Da silva et al. (2021).

[58] Frahar and Mathieson (2016).

[59] Brzezinski (1998).

[60] Ibid.

[61] Jervis (1978).

[62] Ibid.

international conflicts."[63] A pivotal question thus arises among democratic countries in Asia: will the integration into a communist-ruled Chinese economic framework necessitate a compromise in sovereignty, and pose an ideological challenge for the involved parties?

He Who Has the Gold, Rules?

China's economic soft power triumph is not only confronted with challenges within Asia, but also on a global scale. Firstly, to keep its economic soft power effective, China must maintain the attractiveness of its own market. Specifically, it needs to leverage the force of domestic consumption to enhance imports, in addition to government-level purchases. However, issues such as income disparity, the need for significant precautionary savings, and elevated housing prices present substantial long-term obstacles to attaining the expenditure level the government aims for.[64] While the Chinese central government has committed to tackling these problems through a range of policies, including income redistribution via tax reform, increased welfare spending, and initiatives to make housing more affordable like a property tax, these efforts may still be inadequate.[65] To motivate consumers to spend more and save less, the government needs to invest more in public services to ease individuals' financial pressures. However, as stated in Chap. 2, high debt levels at both national and local government tiers could impede the Chinese government's capacity to accomplish this.

Secondly, it seems that the era of globalisation based on rational economic calculation is passing. It is now being replaced by a far more complex systemic rivalry between entangled nations, in which security and values are prioritised over commercial gains. This change brings a significant alteration in the frameworks we use to perceive and analyse the world. Traditionally, markets and economic elements were the prime drivers of politics—that is, decisions were largely made and could be interpreted based on economic rationalism.

However, in contemporary times, economic decisions have become increasingly intertwined with national security considerations, crafting a new geopolitical landscape. The current global economic environment is viewed as skewing markets by ramping up the application of trade restrictions and domestic market regulations due to security concerns, while also disrupting the global supply chain by controlling the export of data, crucial resources, and strategic supplies. In the West, manifestations of this can be seen in actions such as the ban on 5G, semiconductors, and TikTok. This trend is not unilateral. China has also been adopting protectionist measures, balancing economic interests against perceived threats to its sovereignty or security. For example, China announced to limit the exports of gallium and germanium,

---

[63] Ibid. p. 174.
[64] Guo (2021).
[65] Ibid.

two essential metals used in the production of certain semiconductors and electric vehicles in July 2023.

Last but not least, from an ecological and environmental viewpoint, the Chinese philosophy of prioritising economic growth as the catalyst for stability and prosperity warrants reconsideration. Economic strategies solely centred on material growth could destabilise societies in the medium to long term, exacerbating inequality and potentially intensifying geopolitical conflicts over scarce resources, which contribute to climate risks and a blame game for deteriorating conditions. With its emerging policy focus on high-quality growth and advancements in green technology, China has substantial potential to establish and implement sustainable growth models that foster regenerative economies. However, transitioning to such models presents significant hurdles, particularly given China's profound reliance on fossil fuels and the substantial transition costs towards a more sustainable economy. A further discussion on this topic will be featured in Chap. 10.

In summary, China boasts a lengthy historical record of employing economic soft power to curb external hostility and navigate regional and international affairs, achieving remarkable success. Yet, amid a shifting geopolitical landscape and domestic economic challenges, coupled with global issues like climate change, China's capacity to use economic soft power for political and geopolitical ends is increasingly restrained. This development effectively renders any concerns regarding a resurgence of the tributary system outdated. This paves the way for the second part of our discussion in this chapter, focusing on how China utilised culture to exert influence.

'Us' and 'Them': China Versus Barbarians

To comprehend how China has harnessed culture as a soft power tool to exert influence and orchestrate its foreign relations, it is crucial to commence with an introspection of how China has traditionally framed its own identity vis-à-vis the non-Chinese world. To establish the backdrop, this section will begin with an investigation of China's own identity and its evolution over time. The aforementioned concept of concentric circles shows that there are three essential components: 'China proper', 'Outer China', and tributary states. In a bid to exert cultural influence, China utilised a range of strategies and efforts to interact with each of these circles. These spanned significant initiatives aimed at promoting cultural and identity assimilation with those nearest to the centre of the concentric circles—'China proper' and 'Outer China'—to facilitating cultural permeation for tributary states.

The long-standing discourse about the differences between the Chinese and the barbarians is a well-known topic. Hence, it may seem paradoxical that the original concept of the Chinese 'Tianxia' does not clearly demarcate between 'us' and 'them'.[66] As previously discussed, the relatively weak Zhou regime, faced with the

---

[66] Zhao (2004).

task of governing a large and diverse populace comprising various clans, found it necessary to institute an inclusive system. The objective was to bring together everyone, ensuring the regime's security and stability. In this regard, no one was considered an unacceptable outsider.[67] This perception began to shift when China first achieved unity under the Qin dynasty. For the first time, China identified itself as a 'unified' entity, distinguishing itself from the non-Chinese, particularly the nomadic groups.[68] Over time, this distinction was further entrenched by the Great Wall, which served as a physical barrier between the nomadic groups and the Chinese Central Plains.

It is important to note that, even though the 'Chinese' were defined in opposition to the 'barbarians', those identities were cultural rather than ethnic.[69] The Chinese traditionally believed that barbarians could be assimilated to become Chinese by accepting the influence of ritual and virtue.[70] From this perspective, the Chinese thought of themselves as a cultural civilisation rather than as a nation. It means descent, ethnicity, class, and national boundaries were not the defining factors for being Chinese. As long as people adopted and upheld core Chinese values and culture, they had a chance to become 'Chinese' and join the ruling classes of China.

Historical documents reveal that during the Tang dynasty, many foreigners who had been assimilated into Chinese culture were designated as high-ranking officials by the Tang administration. These individuals originated from various backgrounds, including Japanese, Turkish, Persian, and Korean, among others. To give one example, Abe no Nakamaro (698–770) served as a Japanese envoy to the Tang regime and later studied in China. He became proficient in Chinese culture and language, and was appointed to various senior positions, such as Director of National Library and National Archives, and even Tang Duhu, or protectorate governor, for Annam (North Vietnam today).[71] Furthermore, according to *The New Book of Tang: The Genealogy Table of Senior Ministers*, among the 369 senior ministers of the Tang dynasty, 23 were of 'barbarian' origin (most of them descendants of the Xiongnu and Xianbei people) who had been deeply sinicised.[72]

Additionally, successive people from the north, such as the Mongols, Manchus, Xianbei, and Jurchens, even reigned over the Chinese Central Plains with varying degrees of success. As a result, the 'borders' of Chinese culture/civilisation varied over time. Clans and tribes from adjacent lands were sometimes part of 'China'—when they took over and established a dynasty—and their people became 'Chinese'. The history of Chinese dynasties is interesting in that regard, and calls for reflection on two ways to read Chinese history and its continuity.

From the perspective of dominant Chinese historiography today—as reflected in standard textbooks—those 'invaders' became 'Chinese', and formed 'Chinese'

---

[67] Ibid.
[68] Schuman (2020).
[69] Ibid.
[70] Ibid.
[71] Liu et al. (eds.) (2017).
[72] Ouyang et al. (eds.) (2015).

dynasties. As long as the capital was based in the Chinese Central Plains and barbarians adopted Han Chinese values, culture, language, and governance models, the Han Chinese conceded their rule and internalised the newcomers as an indispensable part of China. However, this is a reflection of history as told by China today. Other accounts indicate, for instance, that the Manchus mostly maintained their identity in Beijing, and that 'China' was just one conquered province of their Manchu empire.[73] While they largely adopted Han governance models and the Manchu rulers all learned to speak Mandarin in order to rule the country more effectively, they kept their own language, with its own script, as the official language of the court, right up until the fall of the dynasty in 1912.[74] As for the Yuan, it is likely that 'China' was considered just one significant part of their Eurasian empire. No matter how the history is read, under the Yuan and Qing dynasties, different definitions of 'China' emerged. China was a de facto multi-ethnic empire, one that incorporated both the Chinese Central Plains and territories beyond, traditionally run by nomads, as well as people living in desert oases along the Silk Road.

From a Multicultural Empire to a 'Chinese China' Empire

Entering the twentieth century, China found itself carrying a dual legacy, one of the empires as a diverse collective derived from the 'Tianxia' system, and another of China as a community resembling a nation-state—though one grounded in shared culture rather than ethnicity. A third strand was introduced in the late nineteenth and early twentieth centuries when the establishment of the Republic of China upended the old empire completely. These three distinct legacies of Chinese identity are intertwined, yet do not always fit together. This tension impacts all Chinese people.

The Republic of China came into existence during a period when China had been enduring decades of humiliation, compounded by recurrent invasions from Japan and Western imperialists. In such circumstances, merely being a 'cultured China' was insufficient to fortify the nation against foreign aggression. As a response, Chinese nationalist intellectuals fostered the racial notion of a 'Chinese ethnicity'—a concept that sought to unite and incorporate individuals of diverse cultural and ethnic backgrounds into the defence of the homeland.[75]

The Republic of China applied the concept of 'Chinese ethnicity' as a central organising principle in creating an overarching rationale for the Chinese nation-state. This involved a deliberate unification of identity—a 'flattening' of differences within the new country in order to emphasise differences from people outside.[76] Importantly, this new articulation of Chinese identity involved two distinct and parallel forms of unification. The first is to unify 'China proper'—people from the Chinese Central

---

[73] Hayton (2020).
[74] Ibid.
[75] Ibid.
[76] Ibid.

Plains into the Han ethnicity. The other is to unify the Han, Manchu, Mongol and other groups living on territories controlled by the Republic of China, into one single 'Chinese' identity.

In the former case, people traditionally inhabiting the Chinese Central Plains, as well as their descendants living in other regions, ranging from Hebei in the north to Guangdong in the south, were ultimately consolidated into a single, predominant ethnic group known as the 'Han'. At the time, this group accounted for more than 90% of China's population—a proportion that has remained roughly stable to this day. The term 'Han', however, had never been used previously for ethnic self-definition by the inhabitants of the Chinese Central Plains. Instead, they would identify as subjects of a ruling dynasty, for example, 'people of the Great Tang'. 'Han' as an ethnic marker was first used by nomad rulers—the Mongols and later the Manchus—who used it to describe their newly conquered subjects.[77]

The 'Han' embodies a remarkably diverse group, marked by a vast array of distinctive local identities, each with its own set of traditions and languages or dialects. For example, in a region of Guangdong Province, the distinctions between the Hakka people, often referred to as the 'guest' people, and the Punti, also known as the 'native' people, are so significant that they exceed the differences between the Serbs and the Croats in the Balkans.[78] However, under the narrative of 'Han' unification, the distinct characteristics of several hundreds of such local ethnic identities were 'flattened'. The process is based on a narrative stating that those people share the same roots, ancestors and origins.[79] This commonality is traced back to a Neolithic confederation of agricultural tribes, the Hua and the Xia, who settled around the middle and lower reaches of the Yellow River, and gave birth to Chinese civilisation. Such flattening of differences has made an important impact on the Chinese people. Surveys indicate that over 90% of the Han Chinese today think of themselves as forming one ethnic group.[80]

Unifying 'Outer China'

The above discussion tackled the cultural consolidation efforts aimed at 'China proper'. The endeavour to unify and assimilate ethnicities beyond the Han—referred to as 'Outer China'—is a crucial component of the nation-building efforts initiated by the Republic of China. The Republican government considered itself the legitimate successor of the Qing dynasty, thus assigning it rightful authority across the Chinese Central Plains as well as Tibet, Xinjiang, Mongolia, and Manchuria, regions formerly under Qing control. This perceived legitimacy also endowed the Republican government with the right to redefine who was 'Chinese' and to guide the

---

[77] Ibid.
[78] Ibid.
[79] Ibid. p.134.
[80] The Economist (2016).

collective political fate of all groups involved. In the words of Sun Yat-sen, founding father of the Republic of China: "The unification of the Han, Manchu, Mongol, Hui and Tibetan territories into a single country also means the unification of the Han, Manchu, Mongol, Hui, Tibetan and other lineages into a single 'Chinese identity'."[81]

Under the Nationalist ideology, non-Han ethnic minorities had to submit to a government system dominated by the Han. This Nationalist ideology makes it difficult for ethnic minorities to adapt, especially when they perceive themselves as having a separate culture and identity. This dynamic underlies an uneasy relationship between the Han majority and China's ethnic minority groups. When people refer to 'Chinese' today, it generally means the 1.2 billion Han Chinese, rather than the country's 110 million people who belong to ethnic minorities.[82] With this comes the risk of cultural insensitivity turning into ethnic clashes.[83]

Moreover, under this single 'Chinese' identity, the usage of local languages, including Tibetan and Uyghur, has experienced limitations. Although there is no official claim that languages other than Mandarin Chinese should be eliminated, there is a general sentiment that unifying the language is a necessity.[84] More than a sentiment, unification appears to be a political goal, as indicated by the CCP's efforts to unify Mandarin—from the simplification of characters to the adoption of a language law, limiting airtime or schooling in regional languages and local dialects.[85]

The Chinese efforts of unifying language can be traced back to the Qin dynasty. When Qin Shihuang unified China, he called for the unification and standardisation of the Chinese language, specifically in regard to its written characters. This process transformed the Chinese language into a powerful tool for communication and governance.[86] First of all, it facilitated the transference of a wealth of historical experience, encapsulated in written classics, across generations, thereby reinforcing national unity and cultural identification. It could be argued that this aspect significantly contributed to China's distinction of having the world's longest unbroken historical record. Additionally, the unification and standardisation of Chinese written language fostered the expansion and dissemination of Chinese cultural influence through its broad application and distribution. In fact, Chinese characters were adopted in other East Asian languages, and still remain a key component of the Japanese writing system today, where they are known as kanji.

Language, being integral to every aspect of society, can be deemed a vital component of nation-building.[87] Dominant nations often utilise it as a soft power tool for control. Conversely, countries that perceive foreign cultural influences as a threat may employ linguistic measures to reinforce their own national identity. Not only

---

[81] Hayton (2020).

[82] The Economist (2016).

[83] Ibid.

[84] Bewick (2009).

[85] Ibid.

[86] Ibid.

[87] Ibid.

in China, but this phenomenon was also observed in Japan and South Korea. Influenced by German language theorists during his studies in Berlin and Leipzig in the 1890s, Ueda Kazutoshi, a Japanese moderniser, emphasised the significance of the 'mother tongue' in cultivating "the internalised spirit of the nation".[88] In 1898, he led a national language programme under Japan's Special Education Bureau. This involved curbing the use of traditional Chinese characters, setting the Tokyo upper-class dialect as the national standard, and promoting its use in written literature.[89] Similar instances can be found in South Korea as well. After the end of Japanese colonial rule in 1945, the South Korean government initiated a language reform to restore and standardise the Korean language, known as Hangul.[90] This process included establishing the Seoul dialect as the standard language, reducing the use of Sino-Korean words (words of Chinese origin), and promoting the use of purely Korean words.[91] The effort was essential not only for reestablishing Korean cultural identity after years of forced Japanese assimilation policies but also for nation-building following the end of Japanese colonial rule.[92]

The examples mentioned above indicate that genuine nation-building efforts can, even unintentionally, coincide with restrictions on the cultural expressions of certain minority groups. In extreme cases, this can extend all the way to genocide. Chinese interventions in Xinjiang, which limit the expression of Uyghur culture through a range of measures, some of which involve threat and force, have occasionally been described as a genocide by members of the international community. Striking a balance between genuine nation-building and civil liberties has historically been a substantial challenge for many countries, liberal democracies included, and indeed China. To address this, numerous political structures, including forms of political decentralisation or federal systems, have been experimented with across the globe, from Europe to India, offering increased freedom to minority groups. However, it is unlikely that those models would be adopted by China, at least in any predictable future.

As elaborated in Chap. 6, considering Xinjiang's geostrategic significance to national security and economic prosperity, it seems improbable that China will ease the measures implemented in the region as long as it senses a threat to its dominance there. In fact, the more insecure China becomes, the more likely it is to enforce stricter measures in Xinjiang, as a response to bolster its own security against external pressures, including sanctions from the United States. Therefore, it is crucial to understand that relying solely on unilateral sanctions and confrontational language may not only be insufficient but also potentially counterproductive in addressing the concerns about Xinjiang. Realistically, any improvements in Xinjiang are expected to occur slowly.[93] This implies that persuading China's leadership to

---

[88] Hayton (2020), p.245.

[89] Ibid.

[90] Ho et al. (2004).

[91] Ibid.

[92] Ibid.

[93] Lehr and Bechrakis (2020).

alter its strategy will necessitate multilateral, multifaceted, and persistent efforts over an extended period.[94]

Today, the global reaction to the situation in Xinjiang has been varied and influenced by different strategic considerations. While some Western nations, including the United States, Canada, and European Union members, have taken vocal stances against the issue and implemented actions to address it, other countries, particularly those in the Asia-Pacific region or developing economies with substantial economic dependencies on China, have been more cautious in their response. Notably, China has been successful in garnering support from some Muslim-majority nations and emerging economies regarding its policies in Xinjiang.[95] The crucial question remains: How can an ongoing and expanded international consensus be fostered to address the Xinjiang situation constructively over a sustained duration? Or will this matter remain confined and entangled in a larger geopolitical rivalry between China and the West, thereby becoming increasingly intensified as the competition heats up?

From Cultural Osmosis to Global Assimilation

As discussed earlier, China has consistently applied great efforts to build cultural and identity convergence with people close to the centre of the concentric circles— 'China proper' and 'Outer China'. However, when dealing with tributary states, China typically did not actively impose its own ideals and values, but used its advanced civilisation and splendid culture to gain admiration and attraction. As Henry Kissinger summarised, "China expanded by cultural osmosis, not missionary zeal."[96]

Hegemony is "a relation, not of domination by means of force, but of consent by means of political and ideological leadership. It is the organisation of consent".[97] For tributary states, China did not enforce a strong adoption of Chinese culture and values. Rather, it permitted these states to modify and adapt Chinese rituals, virtues, and values in alignment with their own objectives. Chinese leaders were convinced that only through an extended societal process involving proposition, contestation, rejection, adaptation, acquiescence, and acceptance by the participating states, could the ideas, beliefs, norms, and values that were at the core of Imperial China become compatible with those of others.[98] They believed that such a process was the only way to establish a stable and resilient relationship between Imperial China and other countries.[99]

---

[94] Ibid.
[95] Ibid.
[96] Kissinger (2011).
[97] Repnikova (2017).
[98] Zhang and Buzan (2012).
[99] Ibid.

Indeed, for many centuries, the durability of the tributary system was demonstrated. Even as China's national power weakened and could not maintain its dominant stance in East Asia, and as China lost its supremacy to other emerging nations, no alternative institutional frameworks arose to supplant the tributary system in the region.[100] The tributary system's influence was such that it was replicated, rather than challenged, in managing East Asia's bilateral relations, as seen in the tributary systems centred around Japan and Annam in the south.[101]

During the imperial era, Chinese exceptionalism was self-consciously cultural, focused on China's immediate doorstep, and demonstrated little interest in extending its influence beyond the tributary states. However, the advent of modern technologies, such as the internet and transportation, has reshaped this pattern. Geographical limitations no longer strictly confine China's cultural influence. Instead, China is leveraging its increasing national power to promote its values and worldviews as an alternative global model.[102] This is evident in China's annual expenditure of USD 10 billion on promoting and marketing its soft power in the past decade.[103] As one well-known example, by the end of 2018, the Chinese government had set up 549 Confucius Institutes in 154 countries to offer language classes and host cultural events.[104] They also set up 1,193 'Confucius Classroom' arrangements with foreign schools, providing them with teachers, materials, and funding to help children learn Mandarin, reaching a total number of 1.87 million students.[105]

In addition, the 14th five-year plan, published in 2021, revealed China's aspiration to transform into a nation with robust domains in culture, education, talent, sports, and health by 2035.[106] The fact that culture has been prioritised as a primary objective for the first time underscores its significance. In the upcoming decade, a notable surge in films, music, literature, art, and television that incorporate unique Chinese cultural traits is expected. China is poised to devote an unprecedented amount of resources and efforts towards improving its image and soft power through cultural osmosis, much like how the South Korean government fostered the Korean Wave in the 1990s to become a top global exporter of culture alongside the United States, Japan, and the United Kingdom. With the world's economic centre of gravity shifting to Asia, the growing cultural influence of other Asian countries, especially Japan and South Korea, will also contribute to enhancing the influence of Chinese culture as it rides the Asian wave.

An intriguing trend that has emerged from the Chinese government's global cultural dissemination efforts is that the expectation of loyalty and backing for the country's endeavours has broadened, reaching beyond just those living in China or holding a Chinese passport. A speech made by Xi Jinping at the celebration of the

---

[100] Ibid.

[101] Ibid.

[102] Callahan (2008).

[103] The Economist (2017).

[104] Xinhua News Agency (2018).

[105] Ibid.

[106] The National Development and Reform Commission (2021).

100th anniversary of the founding of the CCP in 2021 confirmed this: "the patriotic united front is an important means for the Communist Party of China to unite all Chinese sons and daughters at home and abroad to realise the great rejuvenation of the Chinese nation."[107] This message calls for further reflection.

There are currently about 60 million people of the Chinese diaspora living abroad.[108] They can be found in almost every country in the world. Many have tremendous intellectual, technological, and financial resources, and make significant economic, social, and political impacts in the countries where they live. Xi Jinping's statement implies that these people, perceived to be intrinsically 'Chinese' on the basis of their ethnicity and cultural ties, are expected to support China's rejuvenation efforts. Amid increasing nationalism, this expectation originates not only from the Chinese government but also from a large segment of ordinary citizens, thereby intensifying the pressure. As a result, many in the Chinese diaspora express feeling compelled to advocate on behalf of China, as if it were their obligation.[109]

On the flip side, in many countries around the world, there have been increasing concerns and allegations that the Chinese diaspora was 'weaponised' by the CCP to act in conjunction with the CCP's interests. Some media claimed that "diasporic Chinese are in effect 'sleepers' to be activated by some remote, cryptic and mythical code."[110] This situation brings a lot of pressure on members of the Chinese diaspora, in terms of identity and allegiance. In particular, it makes it challenging for them to be accepted and trusted by the local community in the place they live.

Overall, the situation is more nuanced and complex than some mainstream media discourses tend to present it. It is important to remember that identity is not frozen in the mists of time; instead, it is an object of constant struggle, change, proclamation, and mobilisation.[111] Those complex engagements over questions of identity never have a predetermined outcome.[112] The expression of identity varies from country to country, and from person to person.

Various studies have pointed out that diasporic Chinese communities have followed distinct paths of development and acquired identities that are different from each other.[113] In renowned historian Wang Gungwu's study of Southeast Asian Chinese, he found the copresence of multiple identities, including a local national identity, a communal identity, an ethnic identity, a nationalist identity, a past-oriented historical identity, a cultural identity, and a class identity.[114] The claim that the Chinese diaspora is an integrated part of the CCP apparatus set on exporting its ideology and influence thus appears simplistic and misguided. The

---

[107] Cao (2022).
[108] Zhuang (2021).
[109] Wong (2003).
[110] Ibid.
[111] Ibid.
[112] Ibid.
[113] Ibid.
[114] Wang (1991).

reality is, numerous Chinese diasporas can independently, objectively, and constructively engage with their homeland, informed by nuance gained during their time overseas.

Taiwan—A Cultural Perspective

The discussion of how Chinese culture is at the core of its soft power projection abroad and unification at home opens a possibility to better understand the delicate relationship between China and Taiwan.

While Western nations frequently question the legitimacy of the CCP, virtually none dispute the legitimacy of China as a highly respected culture and civilisation with many revolutionary technological and intellectual accomplishments in history. This acknowledgement serves as a potent shield for the CCP as it governs mainland China, the cradle of this great culture and civilisation. Therefore, when the CCP consistently asserts that Taiwan is central to China's core interests and that it will not accept an independent Taiwan, from a cultural perspective, it could mean the existence of an alternative centre of Chinese culture and civilisation is deemed unacceptable because it could threaten the CCP's position as the guardian and inheritor of this culture. Nevertheless, on this specific matter, a subtle trend is emerging.

In April 2021, 21 Republican members of Congress called on the U.S. Department of Education to consider using an educational programme developed with Taiwan as an alternative to the Chinese language and culture learning programme offered by the Confucius Institute prevalent in U.S. colleges.[115] They acknowledged the high demand among American students for learning about Chinese culture, history, and language, but questioned the adequacy of lessons provided by China's CCP-affiliated Confucius Institutes. These concerns arose amid increasing evidence of the Confucius Institutes suppressing academic freedom to avoid content perceived as harmful to China's national interests.[116] These Republicans suggested Taiwan to offer a censorship-free alternative for those interested in Chinese culture and history.[117] Countries like Australia, the United Kingdom, Canada, Sweden, and France have expressed similar concerns and have taken various actions to reduce the influence of Confucius Institutes.

In addition, there are arguments that the Chinese culture preserved by Taiwan is more 'authentic' and 'complete' because the CCP 'damaged' traditional Chinese culture during the Cultural Revolution, which sought to eliminate ideas, customs, habits, and culture that were deemed old. A commonly proposed piece of evidence to back this claim is that mainland China switched to using simplified characters for writing, while Taiwan has maintained the use of traditional script. As culture is an ever-evolving construct, the notion of authenticity or completeness is itself

---

[115] Taipei Times (2021).
[116] Ibid.
[117] Aspinwall (2021).

culturally constructed. However, perceived legitimate heredity is a pertinent element of soft power, making this an important matter.

Furthermore, instead of framing Taiwan as the true heir and protector of authentic Chinese culture, some views suggest that Taiwan could be in the early stages of a transition akin to that of Japan, South Korea, or Vietnam.[118] Each of these countries has been deeply influenced by Chinese culture historically, yet they have each cultivated their unique cultural identities.[119] Japanese culture, for instance, is substantially influenced by the Tang dynasty. The resulting cultural sophistication, coupled with economic advancement, subsequently offered Japan an edge. It even opened up the possibility for Japan to position itself as the new epicentre of civilisation, a status that China had long maintained. It also offered an alternative for other smaller states, who could join the Japanese civilisation and a Japan-dominated tributary system, hence shaking the Pax Sinica order dominated by China. This situation historically posed a significant challenge to China's economic and security standing, leading to many conflicts between the two nations. From this viewpoint, whether Taiwan positions itself as a direct rival to mainland China, claiming to be the 'true heir' of Chinese culture, or embarks on a transformation similar to Japan, both scenarios could potentially impede the CCP's ability to use Chinese culture as a tool of soft power for global influence.

A Clash of World Orders?

Thinking of the future, are we heading towards a clash between communism and liberalism? Or is it between the Chinese Tianxia order versus the Westphalian order? It could be argued that the era in which worldviews acted as the driving force and stimulus for great-power conflicts has ended.[120] In its place, the diverse values and models championed by China and the West are aimed at forging internal identities, legitimising power, and externally reinforcing each side's soft power capabilities.[121]

The first step towards making informed perspectives about how China will use its soft power to exert global influence, and potentially reshape the world order, is to comprehend China on its own terms. There is a common tendency to assume that the rules, institutions, and norms evolved from the European system over the past centuries, and the U.S.-led rules-based global order of recent decades, are natural and inevitable. Such assumptions suggest that all international systems should abide by the guiding principles of these models and predict China's future through these lenses. This perspective calls for a deeper understanding of China's extensive history and inherent logic of governance. The common proposition—that individuals from

---

[118] Cui (2011).
[119] Ibid.
[120] Sven (2021).
[121] Ibid.

abroad should invest more effort in understanding China—makes sense in general. However, when it comes to its practical implementation, there are a lot of challenges.

First, people's cognitive capacities are limited—whether among ordinary people or political and business leaders. Today's complex world often leaves us feeling overwhelmed and fatigued, as there appears to be far more to comprehend than ever before. While we have a surplus of data and information on China at our disposal, what we lack are reliable tools for making sense of it all. Therefore, there is a clear deficit in our collective ability to interpret China accurately.

A significant reason for this deficiency is the substantial disparity in global familiarity between the United States and China. American personalities, landscapes, institutions, histories, and values are much more widely recognised worldwide, via popular culture, cinema, media narratives, and education, compared to their Chinese counterparts. The result is a general cognitive and emotional distance from Chinese perspectives. While there is a strong emphasis on 'the West' to enhance their comprehension of China, it is equally crucial for China to help break down those cognitive and emotional barriers. China must provide tools to make its perspectives familiar and its intentions clear. To accomplish this objective, relying on the creation and spread of propaganda narratives is insufficient and counterproductive. Instead, it requires greater transparency of information, complemented by explanations of intent that are presented in a manner that is easily comprehensible beyond China's borders.

Secondly, to understand China's intentions and influence, it is essential to perceive them through the lens of the radical transformations that people are currently experiencing collectively. In other words, it is insufficient to concentrate narrowly on China alone and disregard the interrelated macro-trends, from globalisation to technological disruptions and ecological challenges. Although we all have lived in a globalised world for decades, our default thinking mode tends to remain national. This means that we are closely attuned to potential threats posed by China to the national interest, while its potential positive contribution to the global good is less readily perceived.

On this matter, one impediment is that the current economic models have not yet progressed adequately to accurately assess social and environmental value, let alone on a worldwide level. Additionally, these models fail to account for the value of avoided catastrophic risks, particularly environmental ones. In the absence of such tools and models, it is difficult to realise the role and value that China could contribute on a global scale. Any sense-making tools to help us understand China, therefore, would need the added value of helping us make sense of our changing global situation.

In conclusion, this chapter argues that China's principal soft power tools for managing foreign relations and extending its global influence are grounded in economic benefits and cultural impact. The chapter also underlines that China's military strength is used to create a deterrent effect, thus enabling China to focus predominantly on the use of soft power tools. However, in a rapidly changing global landscape, this approach presents immediate limitations. From a short-term perspective, political and business leaders must recognise the risks and implications associated with China's soft power tactics to broaden its global sway, as examined in this chapter. They need to carry out comprehensive risk evaluations and strategic analyses to develop an effective strategy to counter China's influence.

In a longer-term perspective, with no readily available solution to shared global challenges, a different view may be adopted. Rather than looking at China and the West as two systems in contradiction, it could be possible to think of them as an experiment that history is running for us: two parallel labs where future paradigms are actively being researched. Such a frame would allow us to look at the formal features of governance systems not as givens—as we tend to do—but choices, eventually revealing better possible structures that would enable more effective multilateralism as well as a more stable and just world order. From this perspective, we must consider one crucial variable: namely, the role played by Xi Jinping, the leader of China, whose personal approach will be a factor of major importance in the country's future evolution. He will be the focus of the next chapter.

References

Allison G (2017) Destined for war: Can America and China escape Thucydides's trap? Scribe Publications Pty Ltd., Melbourne, p.21.
Amer R (1993) Sino—Vietnamese relations and Southeast Asian security. Contemporary Southeast Asia 14(4):314–331.
Aspinwall N (2021) US asks Taiwan to fill void as Confucius Institutes close. In: Nikkei Asia. Available at: https://asia.nikkei.com/Business/Education/US-asks-Taiwan-to-fill-void-as-Confucius-Institutes-close. Accessed 10 October 2021.
Ban G (2003) Han Shu (The book of Han). Zhongzhou Guji Press, Zhengzhou.
Bewick A (2009) Silencing the silk road: China's language policy in the Xinjiang Uyghur Autonomous Region. San Diego International Law Journal 11:135–170.
Blackwill RD, Harris JM (2016) War by other means: Geoeconomics and statecraft. Harvard University Press, Cambridge.
Brzezinski Z (1998) The grand chessboard: American primacy and its geostrategic imperatives. Basis Books, New York.
Callahan WA (2008) Chinese visions of world order: Post-hegemonic or a new hegemony? International Studies Review 10(4):749–761.
Cao DS (2022) United front work key to development of nation. In: China daily. Available at: https://global.chinadaily.com.cn/a/202207/30/WS62e4728da310fd2b29e6f3e1.html. Accessed 10 November 2022.
Cui C (2011) Keeping traditional Chinese culture alive. In: BBC. Available at: https://www.bbc.com/news/world-radio-and-tv-15153707. Accessed 17 October 2021.
Da silva DL et al (2021) Trends in world military expenditure, 2020. In: Stockholm International Peace Research Institute. Available at: https://www.sipri.org/sites/default/files/2021-04/fs_2104_milex_0.pdf. Accessed 1 May 2021.
Fairbank JK (1969) China's foreign policy in historical perspective. Foreign Affairs 47(3):449–463.
Fairbank JK, Goldman M (1998) China: A new history. Oxford University Press, Oxford.
Fairbank JK (1968) A preliminary framework. In: The Chinese world order: Traditional China's foreign relations. Harvard University Press, Cambridge, p.2.
Frahar J, Mathieson R (2016) Arms spending spree in Southeast Asia has Singapore worries. In: Bloomberg. Available at: https://www.bloomberg.com/news/articles/2016-03-24/arms-spending-spree-in-southeast-asia-has-singapore-worried. Accessed 12 March 2021.
Guo YZ (2021) In depth: Can China overtake U.S. to become world's top consumer? In: Caixin Global. Available at: https://www.caixinglobal.com/2021-04-13/in-depth-can-china-overtake-us-to-become-worlds-top-consumer-101690571.html. Accessed 22 May 2021.

Harding H (1993) The concept of "Greater China": Themes, variations and reservations. The China Quarterly 136:660–686.
Hayton B (2020) The invention of China. Yale University Press, New Haven.
Ho K, et al (2004) Manifestations of ethnic prejudice: Japanese occupation of Korea and Taiwan- The Asian vs. The Asian-American experiences. In: The edge by Stanford University. Available at: https://web.stanford.edu/class/e297a/Japanese%20Occupation%20of%20Korea%20and%20Taiwan%20-%20The%20Asian%20vs%20The%20Asian-%20American%20Experiencea.doc.
Jervis R (1978) Cooperation under the security dilemma. World Politics 30(2):167–214, pp.178-179.
Jia SH, Han SM (eds) (2009) Liao jin shilunji. China Social Sciences Press, Beijing.
Kang D (2010) East Asia before the West: Five centuries of trade and tribute. Columbia University Press, New York, p.2.
Kissinger H (2011) On China. Penguin Books Ltd., New York, p.529.
Kumar M (2023) India raises defence budget to $72.6 bln amid tensions with China. In: Reuters. Available at: https://www.reuters.com/world/india/india-raises-defence-budget-726-bln-amid-tensions-with-china-2023-02-01/. Accessed 12 February 2023.
Lee JY (2017) China's hegemony: Four hundred years of East Asian domination. Columbia University Press, New York.
Lehr AK, Bechrakis EK (2020) Combatting human rights abuses in Xinjiang. In: Center for Strategic & International Studies. Available at: https://www.csis.org/analysis/combatting-human-rights-abuses-xinjiang. Accessed 2 February 2021.
Liu X et al (eds) (2017) Lie zhuan. In: Jiu tang shu (the old book of Tang). National Library of China Publishing House, Beijing.
Lu BW et al (eds) (2022) Lushi chunqiu (The spring and autumn annals of master lu). Zhonghua Book Company, Beijing.
McDonagh N (2021) Putting "values" into value chains in an era of system. In: The University of Adelaide, Institute for International Trade. Available at: https://iit.adelaide.edu.au/news/list/2021/04/09/putting-values-into-value-chains-in-an-era-of-system-rivalry. Accessed 22 May 2021.
McLaughlin R (2016) The Roman Empire and the silk routes: The ancient world economy & the Empires of Parthia, Central Asia & Han China. Pen & Sword Books Ltd., Barnsley.
Ouyang X et al (eds) (2015) Zaixiang shixi biao (the genealogy table of prime ministers). In: Xin tang shu (the new book of Tang). Zhonghua Book Company, Beijing.
Ren GC (1995) Shiwen shibashiji qingwenhua dui chaoxian de yingxiang. The Qing History Journal (4):28–39
Repnikova M (2017) Media politics in China: Improvising power under authoritarianism. Cambridge University Press, Cambridge, p.3.
Reynolds I (2022) Japan begins defense upgrade with 26 percent spending increase for 2023. In: Bloomberg. Available at: https://www.bloomberg.com/news/articles/2022-12-23/japan-begins-defense-upgrade-with-26-spending-increase-for-2023. Accessed 17 January 2023.
Schuman M (2020) Superpower interrupted: The Chinese history of the world. Public Affairs, New York.
Shinobu S (1982) Riben jindai zhengzhishi. Shanghai Translation Publishing House, Shanghai.
Sima Q (2011) Shiji (Records of the Grand Historian). Zhonghua Book Company, Beijing.
Sven B (2021) Grand strategy in 10 words: A guide to great power politics in the 21st century. Bristol University Press, Bristol.
The Economist (2016) The upper Han. Available at: https://www.economist.com/briefing/2016/11/19/the-upper-han. Accessed 22 May 2021.
The Economist (2017) China is spending billions to make the world love it. Available at: https://www.economist.com/china/2017/03/23/china-is-spending-billions-to-make-the-world-love-it. Accessed 28 May 2021.

References

The National Development and Reform Commission (2021) Zhonghua renmin gongheguo guomin jingji he shehui fazhan di shisige wunian guihua he 2035nian yuanjing mubiao gangyao. Available at: https://www.ndrc.gov.cn/xxgk/zcfb/ghwb/202103/t20210323_1270124.html?code=&state=123. Accessed 25 March 2021.

Taipei Times (2021) Taiwan can replace Confucius Institutes: US legislators. Available at: https://www.taipeitimes.com/News/taiwan/archives/2021/04/10/2003755423. Accessed 10 October 2021.

Wang YS (1979) Liushinian zhongguo yu riben. SDX Joint Publishing Company, Beijing.

Wang GW (1991) China and the Chinese overseas. Times Academic Press, Singapore.

Wang GW (2013) Early Ming relations with Southeast Asia: A background essay. In: The Chinese World Order. Harvard University Press, Cambridge.

Wong L (2003) Belonging and diaspora: The Chinese and the internet. First Monday 8(4). https://doi.org/10.5210/fm.v8i4.1045.

Xinhua News Agency (2018) Shijie gedi yiyou 548 zuo kongzi xueyuan. Available at: http://www.xinhuanet.com/world/2018-12/05/c_1210009045.htm. Accessed 22 January 2020.

Ye ZC (2005) Zhongguo waojiao de qiyuan. Studies of International Politics 1:9–22.

Zhang YJ, Buzan B (2012) The tributary system as international society in theory and practice. The Chinese Journal of International Politics 5:3–36.

Zhou FY (2011) Equilibrium analysis of the tributary system. Chinese Journal of International Politics 4:147–178.

Zhao TY (2004) Tianxia tixi: Shijie zhi du zhexue daolun. Jiangsu jiaoyu chubanshe, Nanjing.

Zhuang GT (2021) The overseas Chinese: A long history. In: The UNESCO Courier. Available: https://en.unesco.org/courier/2021-4/overseas-chinese-long-history. Accessed 27 December 2022.

Chapter 9
The Man and the Times: Xi Jinping and the Intricate Dance of History

> *"Xi is driven by a deep sense of personal integrity, personal destiny and the decisive role that he is to play in bringing about two historical missions for his country: first, national rejuvenation… and second, saving the Communist Party itself from the cancer of corruption."* (Rudd, 2015)
> —Kevin Rudd, the 26th Prime Minister of Australia

Abstract Throughout China's extensive history, the country's leader has invariably played a pivotal role in determining its fate. As we look towards the future, the question arises: How will Xi Jinping influence China's path and its position within the global order? This chapter argues that Xi Jinping's ascent to power and his highly concentrated personal authority were not an accident or just a temporary phenomenon. The chapter emphasises the crucial role that the inherent inertia of the Party system plays, and the policies and strategic paths set by past leaders. These factors have profoundly influenced China over the years, thereby significantly constraining and shaping the range of options and decisions available to Xi Jinping today. To facilitate a better understanding of Xi Jinping's decision-making, the chapter proposes a lens of Xi Jinping's 'founder' mentality. This viewpoint, stemming from the author's personal observations of Xi Jinping, aims to offer fresh perspectives on his actions and decisions.

The Longer Telegram

On 28 January 2021, a paper titled "The Longer Telegram: Towards a New American China Strategy" was published. Authored anonymously by a former high-ranking U.S. government official, this paper arrived 77 years subsequent to the renowned 'Long Telegram'. The 'Long Telegram' was penned by George Kennan, a former U.S. diplomat, from Moscow amidst the Cold War era, offering an analysis of the weakness of the Soviet System.

Focused on Xi Jinping, the 'Longer Telegram' introduced a new expression, "the pre-Xi strategic status quo".[1] The main message is that the goal of the United States'

---
[1] Anonymous (2021).

China strategy should be to see China return to its pre-2013 path, before Xi Jinping took power.[2] The reasoning was that "under all five of its post-Mao leaders prior to Xi Jinping, [China] was able to work with the United States. Under them, China aimed to join the existing international order, not to remake it in China's own image."[3] Implied is the notion that Xi Jinping's leadership marks an inflection point in China's global attitude. From then on, the country is no longer a willing participant in the U.S.-led system and advocate of the status quo. The suggestion seems to be that if Xi Jinping were no longer in power, the geopolitical challenges presented by China would be resolved, and global relations could revert to the non-confrontational status quo that existed before 2013. However, to what extent is this true and realistic?

At the end of the Second World War, Franklin Roosevelt envisioned for a postwar world order, the 'Four Policemen'—consisting of the United States, the United Kingdom, the Soviet Union, and China—aimed at maintaining global peace and preventing future world wars.[4] However, the intensifying geopolitical tensions between the United States and the Soviet Union inevitably challenged this vision.[5] The emergence of the Cold War as a result of these tensions added complexity to international relations, necessitating a reassessment of strategies in Washington. Washington therefore faced a critical strategic question: Was Soviet intransigence merely a passing phase which Washington could wait out?[6] A similar question arises today in the context of Xi Jinping. Is Xi Jinping a temporary phenomenon that Washington could wait out? Or does he represent a deeper trend, suggesting that China's global interactions are unlikely to undergo significant changes, even with potential new leadership in the future?

'Founder' Versus 'CEO'

The first time I found myself in the same room as Xi Jinping and heard him outline his vision for China's future was at a private reception in Sydney during his state visit to Australia in 2014. At the time, I had been engaged in developing a Tasmania-Shaanxi Memorandum of Understanding for modern agricultural collaboration. As a result of this work, I was invited to attend this reception alongside select individuals, including Australians of Chinese background and Chinese citizens residing in Australia, in acknowledgement of the positive contributions to the bilateral relationship. The meeting room was not large, and Xi Jinping addressed the room in a slow and gentle tone. The first image I had of him was that of a kindly elder, an image somewhat reminiscent of his Chinese nickname, 'Xi Da Da'—'Uncle Xi'.

---

[2] Ibid.
[3] Ibid. p. 7.
[4] Kissinger (1994).
[5] Ibid.
[6] Ibid.

However, despite his kindly tone, Xi Jinping spoke with a strong sense of emotion, responsibility, belief, and 'ownership'.

I remember thinking that I had never heard any of his predecessors (Jiang Zemin and Hu Jintao, whom I have a direct memory of) speak about China in the same way. A number of years have passed, and though I cannot recall all the details of his talk, a deep impression lingers. Over the years since 2014, I have had the opportunity to listen to Xi Jinping on multiple occasions while participating in various high-profile conferences both in China and abroad, and each encounter reinforced this impression. Looking back, if I try to make sense of my impressions and triangulate them with the rest of Xi Jinping's behaviour and statements, my sense is that Xi Jinping is showing a 'founder' mentality. In that, he is very different from his predecessors Jiang Zemin and Hu Jintao, whose mentalities were was arguably closer to that of a 'CEO'.

Typically, a founder possesses a long-term perspective for their business, demonstrating a readiness to embrace risks and even effect substantial directional changes during crucial periods, while paying less attention to short-term concerns or immediate personal gains. By contrast, a CEO is more closely aware of their accountability to the board and shareholders, and therefore more focused on short- to medium-term performance, and more likely to be risk-averse. Furthermore, they are more prone to be swayed by their immediate personal interests, partly because their professional identity and interests are not as intricately linked to the long-term success of the company.

Arguably, Xi Jinping's 'founder' mentality can be traced to his family background and personal experience. Xi Jinping's father, Xi Zhongxun, was one of the giants of the communist revolution and a comrade-in-arms of both Mao Zedong and Deng Xiaoping. He made significant contributions to the Chinese communist revolution and the development of the PRC, from the founding of communist guerrilla bases in northwestern China in the 1930s to the leading of early economic liberalisation in southern China in the 1980s.[7] Xi Zhongxun also held a pivotal political and military role in the Sino-Japanese War and the Chinese Civil War.[8] Yet, during the Cultural Revolution, he faced several imprisonments and purges, leading to Xi Jinping's exile from Beijing and his assignment to work in rural areas. Given his family's significant contributions and sacrifices for the country's establishment and growth, it is likely that Xi Jinping embraced a profound sense of 'ownership' and emotional connection to the nation. His sentiments towards China are thus reminiscent of those held by Mao Zedong, who viewed himself as a 'founding father'—or at the very least, the heir of a 'founding family'. I suggest here that this heritage, and associated emotions, might have driven Xi Jinping to aspire towards not just a materially powerful China, but a nation that carries itself with pride and commands international respect.

---

[7] Central Government of People's Republic of China (2008).
[8] Ibid.

Playing Chess

Historical evidence suggests that the personal experiences and established beliefs of a strong leader often play a significant role when navigating the complexity of decision-making processes. The fundamental difference in mentality between Xi Jinping and his immediate predecessors may offer an additional angle to understand his vision and future actions. There are two important implications, namely urgency and control.

Xi Jinping's 'founder' mentality may prompt a sense of urgency in his actions. In that regard, he is very different from his predecessors. To make better sense of this point, let us use the analogy of two strategic board games: chess and go (or in Mandarin, 'Weiqi', which directly translates as 'game of surrounding pieces'). Both games require strategic insights, but the goals are different. Chess is about cornering the king to win a decisive victory.[9] Go is about controlling space on the board to gain relative advantages.[10] In other words, chess is a decisive battle, while go is a protracted battle.[11] Chinese leaders have traditionally thought and acted in a more patient way, aligned with playing go. They have traditionally acknowledged that not every problem can be solved, and that overemphasising complete control over specific events may disrupt the overall balance of the situation.[12]

However, Xi Jinping seems to be playing chess. He seems to have an unprecedented sense of urgency, displays less patience than his predecessors, and sets to achieve decisive victories on many fronts at once. One explanation could be that, pressed by his 'founder' mentality, Xi Jinping resents the way that China has missed an opportunity for its strategic development in recent history, while the Party has allowed heavy corruption and mistrust to spread, threatening its legitimacy. Consequently, he must not only lead the growth of China and revitalise the Party, but also make up for time lost by his predecessors. In this regard, Xi Jinping is very much like Emperor Hongwu, the founder of the Ming dynasty, who presented his new dynasty as a revival of Chinese rule after a century of humiliation under the Mongols.[13] Xi Jinping, in the same manner, characterises himself as the champion of the Chinese nation, after a century of humiliation by Western imperialists.[14]

Such a narrative instils a sense of urgency around Xi Jinping's own 'mandate of heaven' to accomplish the pledged 'rejuvenation'. To better understand this, let us use another analogy. Mao Zedong's China can be compared to a company in a start-up phase. Mao Zedong's primary task was to lay a solid foundation for the long-term development on all aspects of this 'new China', including establishing core beliefs, culture, and social structures. Deng Xiaoping, Jiang Zemin, and Hu Jintao led China during a period of rapid growth. Their key responsibility was to establish conditions

---

[9] Kissinger (2011).
[10] Ibid.
[11] Ibid.
[12] Ibid.
[13] Schuman (2020).
[14] Ibid.

and extend opportunities to sustain China's continual growth and swift expansion. However, China has now transitioned into a mature phase. Drawing parallels with the business world, a company in its mature stage often risks decline if its engines of growth and innovation are insufficient. Consequently, one could argue that Xi Jinping's fundamental task diverges from his predecessors, as it involves preventing a potential decline of China.

In the corporate sphere, to prevent a mature company from declining, the leadership's initial response can involve propelling the company into new growth cycles. This can be achieved by identifying fresh markets, creating innovative offerings, and implementing significant changes that enable the emergence of new growth opportunities. Xi Jinping has adopted a comparable strategy, significantly shaking up the established order. Indeed, he has embarked on an incredibly ambitious trajectory, rapidly progressing on four almost parallel fronts: invigorating the Party, reinvigorating Chinese nationalism, initiating profound economic reforms, and overhauling China's military.[15] And he has achieved success in almost all of these endeavours. His sense of urgency made people realise that expecting a tranquil environment under his leadership is far from realistic.[16] Instead, continual shake-ups have become the new norm. It appears that Xi Jinping is a risk-taker, yet his risks are calculated, not reckless. The risks he has taken were meticulously gauged within the boundaries of his power and the support he could muster, stemming from the undercurrents within the Party and the nation. This brings us to the second implication of his 'founder' mindset: the concentration of power and control.

Did the Man Make the Times?

Xi Jinping can arguably be considered as one of the most influential figures globally at present. This stature arises from his leadership of a China that boasts the world's second-largest economy, as well as his own personal power within the country. Domestically, Xi Jinping has attained an unprecedented level of authority, comparable to Mao Zedong and Deng Xiaoping, surpassing that of most Western leaders in their respective nations. His command over every facet of China's progress is so extensive that foreign analysts have dubbed him the 'chairman of everything'. In this respect, he also operates akin to a CEO, exerting influence over all aspects of the country's governance.

Xi Jinping's rise and power are in part a matter of inheritance. He enjoys the privileges that come with being a 'princeling' of the CCP. As mentioned earlier, his father was a top-ranking official among the first generation of Chinese leadership. On the basis of this legacy, Xi Jinping's career was an expedited road to success and power. From the age of 46, he started occupying leading political roles—by Chinese standards, this is a relatively young age. In particular, he was given the opportunity

---

[15] Allison (2019).

[16] Rudd (2015).

to lead internationally minded and economically progressive regions, notably Fujian and Zhejiang provinces, as well as Shanghai. This experience served as valuable preparation for pursuing policy measures that foster the growth of the private sector, encourage foreign investment and trade, as well as promote financial liberalisation. Throughout this period, Xi Jinping garnered considerable public support from the urban middle class and opinion leaders, thereby reinforcing his perceived 'mandate of heaven'.

Further, Xi Jinping's elite pedigree and his career in affluent coastal areas have allowed him to forge connections with a number of factions within the Party. In a political system largely based on consensus, this gave Xi Jinping an excellent position in the factional game as the best available compromise among competing factions within the Party. In addition, Xi Jinping's previously unassuming and discreet style made him a safer choice among other candidates.

What is more important, Xi Jinping's strong faith in the Party as the best vehicle for China's greatness made him a desirable candidate for the country's top job. Xi Jinping's ideological stance differs from that of his predecessors. While Deng Xiaoping and Jiang Zemin both pursued education abroad and were fluent in foreign languages, Xi Jinping, in contrast, is a Mandarin-speaking monolingual. His educational background at Tsinghua University focused on chemical engineering, Marxist theory, and ideological education. Prior to assuming the highest leadership position, he had limited experiences outside of China. As a result, his worldview has been significantly influenced by Maoism and the Yan'an spirit inherited from his family and his work engagements in a Yan'an village during his youth, rather than by extensive international exposure.[17]

In his book *CEO, China: Rise of Xi Jinping*, British political scientist Kerry Brown used Pope Francis as an analogy to explain Xi Jinping's faith and commitment to the CCP. The basis for the analogy is that both are newly installed leaders of almost a billion people—Chinese and Catholics respectively—and that they share a similar challenge.[18] Pope Francis is attempting to "instil a renewed sense of mission into a Church that has lost touch with its spiritual roots, tarnished its legitimacy and become consumed by material power"—a situation not unlike that faced by Xi Jinping.[19] Moreover, both are somehow the incarnation of the organisation they lead. Kerry Brown summarised : "Looking into the eyes of Xi Jinping, you look into the eyes of the Party itself—the personification of its ambition and spirit, its most faithful and truest servant, and someone like Pope Francis, who, for all his outward exemplification of influence, persuasion, and force, would almost certainly object to the claim that he is pursuing his own interests and indulging the narcissism of power."[20]

Last but not least, Xi Jinping's unprecedented access to concentrated power also comes from his own proactive efforts at grabbing it and keeping hold of it. As Lee

---

[17] Brown (2016).

[18] Ibid.

[19] Ibid. p. 275.

[20] Ibid. p. 280.

Kuan Yew stated, "A nation's leader must paint his vision of their future to his people, translate that vision into policies which he must convince the people are worth supporting, and finally galvanise them to help him in their implementation."[21] In the Chinese context, Mao Zedong used the vision of founding a glorious new China to win the support of the people. Deng Xiaoping used determination to overcome the backwardness of the country, together with a promising economic outlook, to unite and inspire his people. Xi Jinping is using the grand mission of 'rejuvenating China' to bring people along with him.

Like Emperor Taizong of the Tang dynasty, Xi Jinping is capitalising on the successes of his predecessors to promote an expanded influence of China's worldview globally.[22] Like Emperor Wu of the Han dynasty, Xi Jinping is "confronting global challenges by strengthening his state, as well as his own position at home and abroad".[23] And, like Emperor Hongwu of the Ming dynasty, Xi Jinping has pledged to lead the country towards a renewed future following a century of humiliation. However, accomplishing these tasks cannot be done lightly and quickly. A key tool for Xi Jinping to achieve this goal is through the extension of his tenure.

Many people, both in China and abroad, only started to take Xi Jinping seriously in early 2018, when he abolished term limits on the presidency, removing a major obstacle to remain in power for longer than the usual two terms. The extension of Xi Jinping's mandate has been widely commented on internationally, as there has been no precedent since the foundation of the PRC. This was seen as a big challenge to the norms set by Deng Xiaoping. Looking back, if we consider this extension of term limits from the perspective of a 'founder' mentality, it may not appear particularly surprising.

A more optimistic viewpoint suggests that Xi Jinping's actions may be strategically aimed at consolidating his power and facilitating the implementation of long-term policy goals, rather than merely reflecting a wish to retain his position indefinitely. This could be because his colleagues might hesitate to confront vested interests and commit to the anti-corruption initiative if they were sure of Xi Jinping's exit after a decade. If this were the case, during his second term, his supporters and allies would have been preoccupied with avoiding future retaliation from adversaries, leaving few fully supporting his policies, especially those targeting corruption and vested interests. Essentially, without the term extension, Xi Jinping would only have his first five-year term to achieve his policy objectives. With his tenure extended with no definitive end date to his powerful position, arguably, Party elites who align with his vision and the bureaucratic system are more incentivised to actively assist him in fulfilling his ambitions.

However, the abolition of term limits has also raised serious concerns. Critics argue that the centralisation of power in the hands of a single leader could pose risks to China's political stability in the long term, and they worry about the potential for increased authoritarian rule. Furthermore, some argue that this move undermines

---

[21] Allison (2019).

[22] Schuman (2020).

[23] Ibid. p. 310.

the institutional norms established to prevent the excesses of power seen in the era of Mao Zedong. Paradoxically, the prolongation of Xi Jinping's incumbency may inversely intensify, rather than mitigate, potential instability. The reason being that aspirants for power might experience a sense of constraint, leading to the gradual cultivation of oppositional sentiment within the Party.

Did the Times Make the Man?

Based on the above analysis, Xi Jinping appears to be the right man who fulfilled several crucial criteria and proactively shaped the course of events. However, there is more to the story. Xi Jinping's concentration of power, beyond his own personal ambition, also stems from a rare historical opportunity, whereby the Party has allowed and enabled the present situation to emerge.

Many China watchers have stated their belief that Xi Jinping's concentration of power has come at the expense of the Party.[24] It is important to note, however, that the seeds of Xi Jinping's ascension were sown well in advance of him taking office.[25] Over the period of Xi Jinping's rise to power, the CCP leadership has expressed a preference for centralising and consolidating power by reducing the Politburo Standing Committee from nine to seven members, giving each of them more power in proportion.[26] In addition, it was anticipated that five of those would be too old to stay on past the 19th CCP National Congress, giving Xi Jinping room to promote his allies into China's top governance body.[27] To understand this paradox of the CCP allowing such concentrated power, we need to roll the tape back a little further, and understand the underlying trends that have resulted in the preference for a strong leader.

When Mao Zedong came to power in 1949, China was in a state of economic and military weakness. Mao Zedong's goal was to remake China from the ground up. In his own words: "we want to change the China which is being kept ignorant and backward under the sway of the old culture into an enlightened and progressive China under the sway of a new culture."[28] This process changed China's weak power status, but also brought about a state of chaos, epitomised by the turmoil of the Cultural Revolution. After the death of Mao Zedong, his successor Deng Xiaoping found China in a state of unrest: confusion, exhaustion, anger, and disappointment prevailed among ordinary Chinese people.[29] The country was still backward, and the desire for order and prosperity was at its peak among the people and the leadership.

---

[24] Gueorguiev (2018).
[25] Ibid.
[26] Ibid.
[27] Ibid.
[28] Schell and Delury (2013).
[29] Ibid.

Deng Xiaoping played a critical role in the history of contemporary China, as the first leader to come after the founder. When Deng Xiaoping took the reins in 1978, against the backdrop of the Cultural Revolution and staggered economic growth, he initiated the famous 'reform and opening up' policy shift. Since then, according to the International Monetary Fund (IMF), China's annual growth rate rose from an average of five percent a year in 1960–1977 to ten percent a year in 1978–2011.[30] Also, IMF estimates show that from 1980 to 2017, China's GDP grew from USD 305 billion to USD 11 trillion.[31] As a result, China escaped the poverty trap in 1998 and became an upper-middle-income country in 2010.[32]

Deng Xiaoping's leadership may one day be seen in the same way that historians have come to view France under the leadership of Jean-Baptiste Colbert, the early stages of Frederick the Great's reign in Prussia, or Japan in the post-Meiji Restoration decades.[33] Those historical periods saw "a country straining to develop its power (in all senses of that word) by every pragmatic means, balancing the desire to encourage enterprise and initiative and change with an étatiste determination to direct events so that the national goals are achieved as swiftly and smoothly as possible".[34] During the reform process, Deng Xiaoping took the pragmatic road of borrowing extensively from the West, including capitalist theory, advanced management systems, financial sector reform, participation in international organisations, and more. Yet, one thing he did not borrow from the West was its liberal democratic political model.[35] Instead, Deng Xiaoping "dreamed of a post-political age in which economic development could proceed undisturbed by either Maoist mass politics or individualistic liberal democracy".[36] However, along with China's economic miracle, social disparities and deteriorating political conflicts emerged.

The trends set by Deng Xiaoping continued under his successors. When Jiang Zemin came to power in 1989, China was already emerging as a major global player based on its spectacular economic growth. At the time, China also showed a general sense of comfort with the international order that it had joined. Jiang Zemin recognised that, in the rapid modernisation process, key factors to sustain economic growth, such as technology, private economy, and globalisation, were gaining prominence and needed to be incorporated into the CCP agenda.[37] As a result, during Jiang Zemin's speech to celebrate the 80th anniversary of the CCP on 1 July 2001, he proposed a new ideological theory, known as the 'Three Represents'.

The 'Three Represents' theory redefined who the Party represents, namely advanced productive forces (the new business elite), advanced culture (Confucian culture of social harmony and respect of authority and social order), and fundamental

---

[30] Zhong (2017).

[31] Ibid.

[32] Ibid.

[33] Kennedy (2017).

[34] Ibid. p. 448.

[35] Schell and Delury (2013).

[36] Ibid. p. 260.

[37] Fewsmith (2002).

interests (the new social constituencies).[38] This new theory marked a profound shift in the way that the CCP expressed its class nature and the sources of its political legitimacy. As China's sole ruling party, the constitution of the CCP professes to represent all Chinese people. According to traditional communist ideology, this is interpreted as representing only Chinese workers, both rural and urban. The introduction of the 'Three Represents' signified a significant shift in the Party's class representation and accountability, moving from a sole focus on the rights of the working class to a more balanced approach among capital, state bureaucracy, and workers.

Deng Xiaoping's reforms had already broadened freedoms for the private sector, but the 'Three Represents' deeply embedded this shift within Party ideology. Further, in a speech in 2001, Jiang Zemin advocated for the integration of private sectors and other elite groups into the Party. Effectively, this theory evolved the Party into a more inclusive organisation, which in this context implies greater receptivity to capitalist principles. The impact of this ideological reform was significant. The changing interactions between the state, private economy, and civil society, coupled with significant societal transformations and the deterioration of the social welfare system, led to increased tensions and risks.[39] The rise of a capitalist class and the breakdown of the 'iron rice bowl' exacerbated the growing disparities among social classes, between urban and rural regions, and between coastal and interior areas. The social issues arising from an excessive focus on economic growth and wealth accumulation sparked unease and resentment among the Chinese populace. This, in turn, triggered a rising wave of pro-democracy movements and popular unrest, particularly among rural and working-class individuals, which challenged both the Party's legitimacy and country's stability.

According to Chinese government figures, the number of mass incidents grew from 8,700 to 60,000 between 1993 and 2003.[40] These figures kept increasing and reached 90,000 in 2006.[41] Not only did the volume of mass incidents grow significantly, but so did the scale. As per the Chinese expert's research, the total number of individuals involved in mass incidents increased from 73,000 to 3.07 million people.[42] The majority of the participants in these incidents were from the grassroots level, specifically individuals from the working class and rural areas.

The circumstances did not improve significantly during Hu Jintao's term (2002–2012). Both Jiang Zemin and Hu Jintao were widely regarded as bearers and executors of Deng Xiaoping's policies, acting as consensus leaders during periods of collective leadership. Among them, Hu Jintao had significantly less power than Jiang Zemin. In fact, he is often considered the weakest leader in China since 1949. It is well known that throughout his term, the real control was held by Jiang Zemin's loyalists.

Moreover, amid China's domestic unrest and societal divide, even the Party itself was not well positioned to reverse the situation. It was ensnared in factional disputes

---

[38] Li (2017).
[39] Ibid.
[40] Liu (2011).
[41] Ibid.
[42] Ibid.

and faced the danger of losing its legitimacy because of severe corruption.[43] A primary source of corruption was the leasing or selling of government-owned land. As per official Chinese data, the income from local land transfers in 1998 was 50.7 billion yuan (USD 6.1 billion).[44] This figure soared to 8.4 trillion yuan (USD 1.22 billion) in 2020, marking an increase of approximately 165 times.[45] Moreover, such conduct was permissible, because Deng Xiaoping's 'reform and opening up' policy included profit-sharing within the bureaucracy.[46] The phenomenon stemmed from a major shift in the responsibilities of Chinese officials. While their primary role previously involved planning and commanding, economic liberalisation and market reforms had bestowed them with additional economic duties.[47] Those functions included "attracting high-stakes investment projects, borrowing and lending capital, leasing and selling of land, as well as demolishing and building at a frenzied pace".[48] In summary, public officials have been able to personally benefit from capitalism as long as they stayed loyal to the CCP.[49]

Corruption is a substantial political challenge for the CCP because the public expects the government, to whom they entrust decision-making powers and a degree of their personal freedom, to act in the public's best interest, not in favour of their self-interest or that of a select group. Surveys conducted during Hu Jintao's administration consistently showed that 'addressing corruption' was the area causing the greatest public dissatisfaction.[50] In spite of stringent media control, public discontent became apparent and was extensively debated in public spaces.

Furthermore, during the era of 'reform and opening up', vested interest groups had emerged in almost every area of society, ranging from railway systems to telecommunications or finance. One outcome of this is that China's developmental momentum has become more stagnated. To comprehend this viewpoint, let us employ another analogy. Chinese economy can be compared to a two-stage rocket.[51] In the early stage of its development, it relied on an export-driven and cheap labour booster that transformed it from an impoverished rural country into a prosperous urbanised giant.[52] In the more mature stage, China needs to gradually discard the old booster and shift from imitation to innovation, moving up to higher levels of global supply chains.[53] This implies that China's economy and society must undergo a painful process of reform and readjustment, which includes shaking up vested interest groups and changing the prevailing equilibrium of wealth and resource distribution.

---

[43] Gueorguiev (2018).
[44] Chen (2021).
[45] Ibid.
[46] Ang (2021).
[47] Ibid.
[48] Ibid.
[49] Ibid.
[50] Saich (2020).
[51] Goldman (2020).
[52] Ibid.
[53] Ibid.

Even though many were hopeful that liberal reforms could serve as a solution to corruption and economic challenges, the prospect of choosing a strong leader to enact changes seemed more enticing. As discussed in Chap. 3, when the CCP faces substantial challenges, the dilemma often arises whether to opt for a stronger system or a stronger leadership. The tendency leans towards the latter, primarily due to concerns over losing control and power.

Against this background, Xi Jinping was off to a good start as China's new leader. For one, he enjoyed a majority of the Politburo Standing Committee advocating for more centralised power, and assumed office with genuine power.[54] Unlike Jiang Zemin, who stayed on for two extra years as Chairman of the Central Military Commission after leaving his role as President (and so, continued to hold real power over the country), Hu Jintao handed over all key leadership positions to Xi Jinping in one clean transfer.[55] This transition enabled Xi Jinping to establish real authority and begin consolidating personal power from the very first day of his tenure. Over time, Xi Jinping has shown a far greater aptitude and ability to consolidate personal power than his peers had anticipated, but he was the strongman that the Party had asked for.[56]

From the above discussion, it is evident that the story is not merely about 'the man made the times' but also 'the times made the man'. The CCP system tends to select particular types of leaders based on the most crucial challenge that needs to be overcome. For Mao Zedong, this centred on the existential struggle with the Kuomintang. For Deng Xiaoping, he addressed the country's economic backwardness. For Xi Jinping, he needs to revitalise the Party and its legitimacy.

At the beginning, Xi Jinping's heavy concentration of power combined with a strong personality did result in successful reforms and shake-ups. Those include anti-corruption campaigns and economic reforms that greatly improved people's confidence in the CCP. However, as time passed, people began to question the actual intentions behind a protracted anti-corruption process, with decisions increasingly seeming to be influenced more by the leader's personal ambitions than by a rational evaluation of the actual situation.

History has shown that after a strongman's risky actions get repeatedly confirmed without severe consequences, he will be more convinced that a highly concentrated power and strong control are the only path forward. There are many cases in history—to quote only three recent examples, Margaret Thatcher, Recep Tayyip Erdogan, and Vladimir Putin. In this context, external risks are amplified when Xi Jinping is under pressure to act. His track record of facing minimal backlash for addressing risky matters, ones his predecessors may never have dared to, likely enhanced his confidence and solidified his chosen course, including taking bold and risky actions.[57] In such circumstances, China, under Xi Jinping's leadership, is anticipated to persist in challenging the existing order, potentially escalating the competition between the

---

[54] Li (2013).

[55] Gueorguiev (2018).

[56] Ibid.

[57] Erickson and Collins (2021).

A Strategic Crossroad: What Does Xi Jinping Want?

United States and China. As previously mentioned, the CCP selects its leader based on specific challenges it needs to address at a particular point in history. With the Sino-U.S. rivalry now emerging as the new primary challenge for the CCP, a key question arises: How will the system reassess and decide on the kind of leader it needs?

A Strategic Crossroad: What Does Xi Jinping Want?

With unparalleled levels of influence and control, Xi Jinping's vision and personality have significantly impacted China's future course. Hence, the crucial question we must ask is: what does Xi Jinping want?

In 2012, after visiting the *Road to Revival* exhibition at the National Museum—about the journey of an emerging new China since Western powers invaded the declining Qing empire—Xi Jinping articulated a bold long-term vision. He circulated this vision under the term 'Chinese Dream'. Later, at the 19th CCP National Congress in October 2017, Xi Jinping outlined a two-stage development plan to fulfil this 'Chinese Dream'. The first stage unfolds from 2020 to 2035, by which time China aims to become a modernised innovative leader with greater soft power, improved social governance, and a better ecological environment.[58] The second stage is from 2035–2050, by which time China aims to become a great modernised socialist country that is "prosperous, strong, democratic, culturally advanced, harmonious and beautiful".[59] And with advancement in all aspects of society and enhanced comprehensive national power, "the Chinese nation will stand among the nations of the world with a more high-spirited attitude".[60]

The term 'Chinese Dream' has been widely circulated in the international media, but its origin is not well understood. Many seem to think that Xi Jinping's personal vision is the direct source of this ambitious plan. However, the 'Chinese Dream' vision had long been set, before Xi Jinping arrived at the top rung of power.

Henry Kissinger once said that Chinese leaders think in centuries. In 1961, when Mao Zedong received British Field Marshal Bernard Montgomery, he indicated that it would take more than 100 years to fulfil his vision for China to become a strong socialist economy that could catch up with the most advanced capitalist countries.[61] This implies this task, having started in 1949, would come to maturity around 2050.

Later, when Deng Xiaoping met with the Deputy General Secretary of the Spanish Socialist Workers' Party Alfonso Guerra on 30 April 1987, he shared a comprehensive vision of China's economic modernisation by 2050.[62] Deng Xiaoping explained that for China to withstand the pressure of Western hegemony and power politics, it was

---

[58] Xi (2017).
[59] Ibid.
[60] Ibid.
[61] Leng (2013).
[62] Lu (2022).

crucial for the country to achieve rapid economic growth.[63] He further proposed three steps to achieve this goal, known as the 'Three-Step Development Strategy'. The first step was to double China's per capita gross national product (GNP) from USD 250 in 1980 to USD 500 by 1990, so as to "ensure that the people have adequate food and clothing".[64] The second stage was to quadruple the 1980 per capita GNP to USD 1,000 by the end of the twentieth century, at which time China would "have shaken off poverty and achieved comparative prosperity".[65] The third stage was to complete China's industrialisation, and increase its per capita GNP to USD 4,000 to match moderately developed countries by 2050.[66] Deng Xiaoping's articulation was formally captured and expanded in the report of the 13th CCP National Congress in October 1987. Retrospectively, the first step was attained by 1988 while the second was achieved in 1995, five years ahead of schedule.[67]

When Xi Jinping took the reins, he was standing just over the middle of Mao Zedong's century-long vision for China, to build a strong socialist economy and catch up with the most advanced capitalist countries. He was also early into the third stage of Deng Xiaoping's 'Three-Step Development Strategy'. The 'Chinese Dream' may thus be described both as part of a tradition for Chinese leaders to articulate ambitious long-term plans with multiple steps, and as a more specific contemporary blueprint set by Xi Jinping for the later stages of long-term plans articulated by Mao Zedong and Deng Xiaoping.

The question is, however, whether Xi Jinping will be able to carry forward the implementation of his vision, and in particular, whether the international environment will allow him to do so. It is important to remember that the first two stages of Deng Xiaoping's 'Three-Step Development Strategy' were completed in an environment of increasing globalisation, integration, and cooperation. Facing increasing pressure from the United States and the West to de-risk, will Xi Jinping choose to isolate or integrate, confront or cooperate? And what precedents in the Party's tradition will be guiding this choice?

A Period of Strategic Opportunities

To answer the questions above, it is important to understand an expression commonly used by the CCP, 'period of strategic opportunities'. The concept was articulated by Deng Xiaoping in a meeting with Chinese diplomats in Beijing in July 1979: "Now we have to fight for a relatively long period of peace, and we must use this time and grab this time to build up our own country. This time must not be lost. If it is one year, we seize one year. If it is five years, we seize five years. If it is 20 years, that is even

---

[63] Ibid.
[64] Chang (1996). p. 386.
[65] Ibid. p. 386.
[66] Ibid.
[67] Ibid.

better. By that time, our goal will be achieved, and we will not be afraid of war."[68] The meaning of this speech has two implications. First, it makes clear that one of the core missions of the Party was to seize an opportunity and create favourable conditions to allow China a period of predictable and sustained rise—in terms of national strength, international competitiveness, and influence. Second, it implies that Chinese leaders had to come to terms with an uneasy truth. To maintain such a peaceful environment for its own build-up, China may need to make short-term concessions, like deferring the resolution of territorial and border conflicts, and wait to resolve those conflicts until it had more strength and capabilities.[69]

Deng Xiaoping's speech has served as a core principle to guide China's sustained growth within the constraints of a U.S.-dominated unipolar international environment. In November 2002, Jiang Zemin further initiated a doctrine of '20-year period of strategic opportunities', emphasising that the first 20 years of the twenty-first century (2000–2020) would matter significantly to China's future prosperity.[70] This doctrine recognised that China's priorities should be domestic and, crucially, that it should avoid strategic confrontation with the United States.[71]

During the 'period of strategic opportunities', China has been actively cultivating bilateral and multilateral ties in Asia and beyond. It also has been heavily participating in international organisations and supporting globalisation and multilateralism. In this manner, China's economy has continued to grow, and international cooperation platforms reduced international fears of a fast-growing Chinese power. In short, this concept of 'period of strategic opportunities' has had a long-term and critical impact on China's rise.

Gone Is the Favourable External Environment

In his 2005 article 'A Grand Chessboard', Ashley Tellis wrote that China's peaceful rise would lead to a future where "it becomes a true rival of the United States. At that point, China will face another strategic crossroads".[72] This is where Xi Jinping finds himself today. After China's rapid build-up of comprehensive national power over the last decades, in 2017, for the first time, the U.S. government labelled China a 'strategic competitor' that "challenges American power, influence, and interests, attempting to erode American security and prosperity".[73] On 10 January 2023, the U.S. House of Representatives formed the Committee for Competition with China,

---

[68] Leng and Wang (eds.) (2004).

[69] David (2007).

[70] Jiang (2002).

[71] David (2007).

[72] Tellis (2005).

[73] White House Archive (2017).

with overwhelming bipartisan support.[74] In such circumstances, China has changed its stance on the perception of 'period of strategic opportunities'.

At the 20th CCP National Congress in 2022, Xi Jinping rejected the 2017 Congress assessment that the country still enjoys a favourable external environment for its development. Instead, Xi Jinping articulated, "Risks and challenges are concurrent and uncertainties and unforeseen factors are rising." Later, in a speech delivered at the second collective study of the Politburo of the CCP on 2 February 2023, he further emphasised that China must strengthen its viability, competitiveness, development, and sustainability against all kinds of "foreseeable and unforeseen storms and turbulent waves", to ensure that the great rejuvenation process of the Chinese nation would not be delayed or even interrupted.[75] He called for a 'great struggle' under new historical characteristics. Meaning, China's political system is now actively asserting China's rights to growth and prosperity in a changing international environment.

This change in assessment of external environment has two implications. Firstly, to respond to this changing and uncertain global environment, Chinese leadership has been proactively reviving nationalism as an ideological tool to stand against external pressure. As argued by British military historian Correlli Barnett, "The power of a nation-state by no means consists only in its armed forces, but also in its economic and technological resources … It consists most of all in the nation itself, the people, their skills, energy, ambition, discipline, initiative, their beliefs, myths and illusions."[76] Historically, countries around the world, including those in the West, have harnessed nationalism as an ideological tool to achieve national objectives, including military ones. Notably, the era following the French Revolution and Napoleon's rule saw the rise of mass armies fuelled by nationalist sentiments, an organisational innovation that had profound implications for future conflicts and the course of national development.[77] Chinese leaders also use nationalism to unite the people behind harsh reprisals, demonstrating its toughness abroad, and blaming Western hostile forces for China's challenges, especially as China becomes more insecure under mounting pressure from the West.

Garnering nationalistic fervour is not a difficult task. As China's comprehensive national power has grown, so has its confidence as a great nation on a global stage. Historical precedents suggest that when a nation feels it has been unjustly relegated by other nations that took advantage of its temporary weakness, it is likely to have the will and means to change the status quo once it grows in strength.[78] For instance, when Athens' power grew over the fifth century BCE, so did its sense of entitlement.[79] Similarly, when the German empire emerged as a major power in Europe in the late nineteenth century, following triumphant wars against Austria (1866) and France (1870–1871), Germany "was no longer the object of other people's history but the

---

[74] Congress.Gov (2023).
[75] Xi (2023).
[76] Kennedy (2017).
[77] Fearon (1997).
[78] Allison (2019).
[79] Ibid.

subject of its own story of national greatness".[80] While these examples are not an inevitable outcome of a nation's ascension, and are indeed heavily influenced by their specific historical backgrounds, they offer a lens through which to understand the historical sentiments that might be driving China's actions today.

The second implication is a rise in assertive or even aggressive behaviours from Chinese officials, which is perceived as an essential part of the 'great struggle' to deter external aggression. The result is a new 'Chinese assertiveness' meme circulating in the Western media. In the age of social media, narratives are created and spread at unprecedented speed—forming a sort of discursive tidal wave.[81] In this social media landscape, participants in policy debates have very limited time (and incentives) to conduct rigorous comparative analysis prior to participation.[82] The 'assertiveness' narrative, based on filtered headlines, may therefore narrow the range of interpretative lenses through which Chinese foreign policy is understood abroad.[83] This in turn affects global public perception of China, and from then on, the policy options available to the Western media, think tanks, and political elites. On the other hand, the story of China's assertiveness, amplified by the Western media, may well work as a self-fulfilling prophecy, putting pressure on governments to adopt foreign policy settings that are tougher towards China—leading in turn to greater assertiveness from China.

Not a Temporary Phenomenon

In conclusion, when examining how Xi Jinping will shape China's future, the focus cannot solely rest on Xi Jinping himself. It is essential not to ignore the inertia of the Party system itself, as well as the long-term policies and directions set by Xi Jinping's predecessors, which have profoundly influenced China's trajectory over the last decades. Those factors have significantly shaped the landscape of possibilities and decisions available to Xi Jinping today. The danger of perceiving Xi Jinping as an isolated factor lies in mistaking an underlying trend for a transient phenomenon, leading to misinterpretation of signs and ineffective strategies.

Moreover, as it did for Deng Xiaoping, after a period of highly centralised personal power and authority-building, Xi Jinping's successor is less likely to have enough authority to quickly change the direction that Xi Jinping has set for China. Instead, he may mainly carry forward and further implement Xi Jinping's vision. This is due to the fact that Xi Jinping is likely to endorse a candidate who is committed to his vision. Also, prior to the power transition, he might curtail his successor's personal power and revert to a style of collective leadership. This means Xi Jinping's vision is likely to continue to influence the next generations of Chinese leaders.

---

[80] Ibid. p. 63.
[81] Johnston (2013).
[82] Ibid.
[83] Ibid.

With this conclusion, I want to reiterate a crucial argument made at the beginning of the book—the pressing need to keep the channels of influence open, encouraging China towards a more constructive role on the world stage. If China were to veer towards an inward-focused and aggressive stance, it could take an entire generation to realign towards a more positive trajectory. In the process, crucial time for unified action to address pressing challenges—environmental, social, and technological—could be lost. It is a daunting task, and it may even seem implausible or unattainable. Given the few opportunities to ignite internal transformations within China, it becomes indispensable to champion external shifts, specifically paradigm shifts that might stimulate China to evolve for the better. Such efforts will require open-mindedness, empathy, and the courage to transcend cognitive boundaries. They will demand shrewd engagement from all major stakeholders. In the concluding section of this book, I will explore some of the foremost emerging trends poised to direct the future of China's progress, and suggest several mechanisms that various sectors of the global community can harness to encourage China's constructive future path.

References

Allison G (2019) Destined for War: Can America and China escape Thucydides's trap? Scribe Publications Pty Ltd., Melbourne, p.121.

Ang YY (2021) The robber barons of Beijing: Can China survive its Gilded Age? In: Foreign Affairs. Available at: https://www.foreignaffairs.com/articles/asia/2021-06-22/robber-barons-beijing. Accessed 18 September 2021.

Anonymous (2021) The longer telegram: Toward a new American China strategy. In: Atlantic Council. Available at: https://www.atlanticcouncil.org/content-series/atlantic-council-strategy-paper-series/the-longer-telegram/. Accessed 20 February 2021.

Brown K (2016) CEO, China: The rise of Xi Jinping. I.B. Tauris & Co. Ltd., London.

Central Government of People's Republic of China (2008) Xi Zhongxun. Available at: http://www.gov.cn/gjjg/2008-10/21/content_1126629.htm. Accessed 12 March 2020.

Chang MH (1996) The thought of Deng Xiaoping. Communist and Post-Communist Studies 29(4):377–394.

Chen YK (2021) 20 yunian tudi churang shouru: cong 500duoyi zengzhi 8.4 wanyi yuan. In: Yicai. https://www.yicai.com/news/101079337.html. Accessed 18 September 2021.

Congress.Gov (2023) H.Res.11-Establishing the select committee on the strategic competition between the United States and the Chinese Communist Party. Available at: https://www.congress.gov/bill/118th-congress/house-resolution/11. Accessed 2 February 2023.

David S (2007) China stands up: The PRC and the international system. Routledge, New York.

Erickson AS, Collins GB (2021) A dangerous decade of Chinese power is here. In: Foreign Policy. Available at: https://foreignpolicy.com/2021/10/18/china-danger-military-missile-taiwan/. Accessed 27 December 2021.

Fearon JD (1997) The offense-defense balance and war since 1648 (draft paper). In: The University of Stanford. Available at: https://web.stanford.edu/group/fearon-research/cgi-bin/wordpress/wp-content/uploads/2013/10/The-Offense-Defense-Balance-and-War-Since-1648.pdf. Accessed 20 February 2019.

Fewsmith J (2002) Rethinking the role of the CCP: Explicating Jiang Zemin's party anniversary speech. China Leadership Monitor 1(2).

References

Goldman DP (2020) The Chinese challenge: America has never faced such an adversary. In: Claremont Review of Books. Available at: https://claremontreviewofbooks.com/the-chinese-challenge/. Accessed 27 December 2020.

Gueorguiev DD (2018) Dictator's shadow: Chinese elite politics under Xi Jinping. China Perspective 1–2:17–26. https://doi.org/10.4000/chinaperspectives.7569.

Jiang ZM (2002) Jiang Zemin tongzhi zai dangde shiliuda shang suozuo baogao quanwen. In: China daily. Available at: http://www.chinadaily.com.cn/dfpd/18da/2012-08/28/content_15820005.htm. Accessed 8 February 2020.

Johnston A (2013) How new and assertive is China's new assertiveness? International Security 37(4):7–48.

Kennedy P (2017) The rise and fall of the great powers: Economic change and military conflict from 1500 to 2000. Harper Collins Publishers Ltd., London, p.202.

Kissinger H (1994) Diplomacy. Simon & Schuster Paperbacks, New York.

Kissinger H (2011) On China. Penguin Books Ltd., New York.

Leng R, Wang ZL (eds.) (2004) Deng Xiaoping nianpu (1975–1997), Vol 1. Central Party Literature Press, Beijing, p.533.

Leng R (2013) Shenme shi zhongguomeng, zenyang lijie zhongguomeng. In: People's Daily. Available at: http://opinion.people.com.cn/n/2013/0426/c1003-21285328.html. Accessed 12 October 2019.

Li C (2013) Rule of the princelings. In: Brookings. Available at: https://www.brookings.edu/articles/rule-of-the-princelings/. Accessed 19 January 2020.

Li X (2017) The endgame or resilience of the Chinese Communist Party's rule in China: A Gramscian approach. Journal of Chinese Political Science 23(1):83–104.

Liu N (2011) Dangdai zhongguo de qunti shijian: xingxiang diwei bianqian he fenlei kaungjia zaigou. Journal of Jiangsu Administration Institute 2:53–59.

Lu J (2022) Deng xiaoping yu zhongguoshi xiandaihua daolu. In: Research Institute of Party History and Documents of the Central Committee of the Communist Party of China. Available at: https://www.dswxyjy.org.cn/n1/2022/1008/c423730-32540670.html. Accessed 1 February 2023.

Rudd K (2015) U.S.-China 21: The future of U.S.-China relations under Xi Jinping. In: Belfer Center for Science and International Affairs. Available at: https://www.belfercenter.org/sites/default/files/legacy/files/Summary%20Report%20US-China%2021.pdf. Accessed 21 September 2022, p.10.

Saich A (2020) Testimony before the U.S.-China economic and security review commission: Year in review. In: U.S.-China Economic and Security Review Commission. Available at: https://www.uscc.gov/sites/default/files/2020-09/Saich_Testimony.pdf. Accessed 19 December 2020.

Schell O, Delury J (2013) Wealth and power: China's long march to the twenty-first century. Little, Brown Book Group, London, p.252.

Schuman M (2020) Superpower interrupted: The Chinese history of the world. Public Affairs, New York.

Tellis A (2005) A Grand Chessboard. In: Carnegie Endowment for International Peace. Available at: https://carnegieendowment.org/2005/01/01/grand-chessboard-pub-16540. Accessed 22 July 2020.

White House Archive (2017) National security strategy of the United States of America. Available at: https://trumpwhitehouse.archives.gov/wp-content/uploads/2017/12/NSS-Final-12-18-2017-0905.pdf. Accessed 8 May 2019, p.2.

Xi JP (2017) Juesheng quanmian jiancheng xiaokang shehui duoqu xinshidai zhongguo tese shehui zhuyi weida shengli. In: Central Government of People's Republic of China. Available at: http://www.gov.cn/zhuanti/2017-10/27/content_5234876.htm. Accessed 18 June 2019.

Xi JP (2023) Xi Jinping zhuchi zhonggong zhongyang zhengzhiju dierci jiti xuexi bing fabiao zhongyao jianghua. In: Government of People's Republic of China. Available at: http://www.gov.cn/xinwen/2023-02/01/content_5739555.htm. Accessed 2 February 2023.

Zhong FT (2017) China's grand strategy in a new era. East Asia Forum Quarterly 9(4):29–30.

Part III
A Possible Way Forward

Chapter 10
A World at Stake: Competition, Destruction, or Cooperation?

> *"The empire long divided must unite and long united must divide. Thus it has ever been."* (Luo and Brewitt-Taylor, 2002)
> —Luo Guanzhong, Romance of the Three Kingdoms

Abstract This chapter aims to open a discussion on how China is likely to impact the future of the world in a context of unprecedented historical change. It is structured around two topics. First, it aims to present fresh perspectives on the central dynamics driving geopolitical, environmental, and technological change, and their intersection with China's evolution, employing a cyclical view of history. The argument is that the present global uncertainty and instability are due to a transitional phase in human development at the intersection of two long cycles: the cycle of great-power rivalry, and the cycle of technological revolution. Second, it seeks to bring together two typically disparate analyses: exploring both the opportunities and challenges stemming from geopolitical, environmental, and technological shifts, and those emerging from China's rise. It argues that China acts as an ambivalent power and proposes three pairs of scenarios to further dissect its ambivalence. This chapter concludes by introducing the key concept of 'rivalry partners', emphasising that in this new epoch of consecutive and intertwined disruptions, nations should not forego competition. Positive and healthy competition can drive innovation and prosperity if there are clear frameworks to guide diverse political systems to be increasingly competitive without being confrontational.

Part I and Part II of the book probe into the ways that China's geographical features, history and traditional philosophy have shaped its logic of governance, as well as its means of exerting influence on the international stage. Those first two parts underscore the persistent constraints and adaptability inherent within the Chinese system. This analysis aims to guide readers in distinguishing between fleeting changes and substantial evolutions in Chinese statecraft that will likely have enduring impacts. Building on those insights, we are now in a position to discuss how China is likely to impact the future of the world. Obviously, any such discussion must be made against the current background of unprecedented historical change. Those changes range from the accelerating drumbeat of extreme weather events and the contested battle over critical resources; the deep societal changes brought by the rapid development of technology, including its applications to cyber and armed weaponry; the intensified geopolitical environment, with escalated risks of conflicts or even wars; and amplified frustrations over inequalities, leading to far-right movements, extremism, and terrorism.

In addition, these changes and challenges have grown into a rising tide of mutually reinforcing and interlocking crises, which are likely to manifest more frequently and intensely in almost every region and country, causing widespread strains on societies and catastrophic shocks.[1] Some observers have characterised the current period as a "new era of successive and interconnected disruptions".[2] Therefore, a permanent sense of crisis has become the new normal.[3]

So, how will China's future trajectory shape these evolving challenges? This is arguably the most pivotal question of our era, yet there are no definitive answers. The chapter does not aim to predict the future, but instead provokes thought and dialogue about the massive transformations and challenges characterising today's world, as well as potential global trajectories that will likely be influenced by China in the next one or two decades.

To achieve this objective, this chapter will focus on two topics. Firstly, it intends to offer novel insights into the core dynamics propelling geopolitical, environmental, and technological transformations, and their interplay with China's rise, using a cyclical perspective of history. The argument put forth is that the present global uncertainty and instability are due to a transitional phase in human development at the intersection of two long cycles: the cycle of great-power rivalry, and the cycle of technological revolution.

Secondly, the chapter proposes to bring together two strands of analysis that are typically kept separate: concurrently examining the opportunities and risks arising from geopolitical, environmental, and technological shifts, as well as those emerging from China's rise. If the analysis on China is primarily framed in terms of China's ascent and obstacles to it—whether discussions of this ascent and associated obstacles are tinted with hope or concern—rather than matters of common concern, it would result in a one-dimensional view of China that is overly focused on its power dynamics. To establish the context, I will begin by offering a brief discussion of the cyclical view of history and its impact on our understanding of China and the global circumstances we inhabit.

---

[1] The National Intelligence Council (2021).
[2] Bunde et al. (2022). p. 14.
[3] Ibid.

A Cyclical View of History

In today's highly interconnected world, the answer to how China's evolution will shape our transforming world cannot be solely found by examining China in isolation. Instead, a primary step is to comprehend our current position within the broader context of global history. In this manner, we can better reflect upon and participate in the transformation of our common past, present, and future. Assessing the question of 'where we are' cannot be naively taken as a matter of universal agreement, if only because many various 'we' coexist. Yet we can attempt a high-level synthesis of converging understandings.

A prevailing strand of discourse among commentators and analysts from developed countries—echoed in fiction and film—describes the present situation in terms of radical rupture and catastrophic potential. From this lens, this is the age of the singularity, where humanity might fuse with machines. This is the age of the Anthropocene, a new geological age where humans are transforming the very fabric of the natural world. Also, it is the age of global disruption, with media hammering on about the possibility of a second 'fall of Rome', a new dark age, civil wars, or a third world war.[4] In summary, this age is riddled with dangers that pervade both our homelands and the global stage, seemingly suggesting that disorder has claimed dominion over the world.

As a counterpart to this catastrophic view of history, some voices like to put forward the towering achievements of the contemporary world. From Steven Pinker to Hans Rosling, they turn our attention to the material comforts of our world, inviting people to celebrate the present as the best time to be alive.

A third discourse, somewhat answering the first as a mirror, can be heard from 'the rest', 'the developing world', or minorities in 'the West'. This discourse underlines that the 'worlds' of indigenous and colonised peoples have been radically upturned. Therefore, whatever crisis is experienced today by 'us all' has been experienced by colonised peoples for centuries: The 'Anthropocene', in that perspective, is the label used when the destruction wreaked on dominated, colonised and coloured peoples start reaching into the territories of the dominant white people.[5] In short, the present moment is but the culmination of a crisis that has been centuries in the making.

Those different interpretations of 'where we are' are all derived from well-established facts. Yet, the decision to take certain facts into consideration and overlook others, as well as the method used to make meaning from those facts, depends on the model of history that people hold. Thus reading history through a different lens could yield a different understanding of past and present situations, even from the same set of facts.

Most readers of this book are likely used to taking a linear view of history, which represents history as sloping upward into greater and greater progress. Human history is thus understood as a series of 'accelerations', beginning about 30,000 years ago with the transition from the Lower to the Upper Palaeolithic. History then took

---

[4] Petty (2018).
[5] Yusoff (2019).

successive 'great leaps forward', with the invention of agriculture, the dawn of urban civilisation, and the progressive harnessing of the titanic physical forces held in fossil fuels. This very advancement, marked by increasingly rapid evolution, is now the root of our predicament. The 'Great Acceleration' graphs, commonly seen in many presentations and keynote speeches addressing the current crisis, visually represent historical challenges as interpreted through the lens of a linear understanding of time. In the commentary that accompanies those graphs, the present times are understood as 'unprecedented', and a critical moment of inflection. Therefore, there has never been a more important moment where what we do right now will define the entire future trajectory of humanity, and there is no clear historical precedent to learn from.

Traditional Chinese understanding of history offers a precious alternative model to understand the present historical moment, and its associated challenges. To quote the famous opening of Luo Guanzhong's classic book *Romance of the Three Kingdoms*: "The empire long divided must unite and long united must divide. Thus it has ever been."[6] In line with this classic, the default Chinese reading of history adopts a cyclical view. It means that history is understood as a cyclical alternation between periods of stable unity and periods of relative chaos.

Chinese leaders have traditionally recognised this cyclical understanding as integral to their own progression. A time of prosperity—such as the affluence brought to an agrarian society through political unity and peace—deteriorates into a disorder when the burden of military defence becomes too hefty for a non-mechanised economy to support. In this phase, the unified state fragments—only to reunite after an extended period of time, heralding the beginning of another cycle. These intervals of chaos between periods of stability are unlike the 'brief crisis' that have commonly characterised the developing world over the past century. Instead, they may persist for a whole generation, ultimately spawning a new world—a fresh phase of stability with unique attributes, which will endure until the onset of the next chaotic period. This perspective is anchored in a deep and original tradition of Chinese historiography that has remained relevant.

A cyclical view of history prompts Chinese policy makers to view the present transition period as a new strategic environment, necessitating timely adjustment and adaptation. From this perspective, they contend that by comprehending the essence of historical cycles, identifying the interconnected causalities that drive them, determining their place within the cycle, and anticipating potential outcomes, transitions can be managed in a harmonious manner, avoiding the escalation to conflict.[7]

Before I close this section, I must make it clear that both linear and cyclical conceptions of time exist in China and the rest of the world. China has adopted the Western/Christian calendar and is influenced by globalised Euro-American culture. Together with the adoption of Marxism, this means that Chinese leaders have been influenced by linear conceptions of history. Therefore, the argument put forward here is that cyclical models of history are more prevalent in China than in the United States or Europe—and therefore exert more influence in the reading of events. Engaging

---

[6] Luo and Brewitt-Taylor (trans.) (2002).
[7] Dalio (2021).

in this intellectual effort of understanding the Chinese cyclical view may shed some light on the way that Chinese leaders are likely to read present situations. It may also cast a fresh light on the present crisis, in the hope of suggesting new areas for solutions or mitigation. In the following section, I will delve into understanding the present global conditions through a cyclical perspective. Later in this chapter, I will revisit the implications of this cyclical viewpoint on the decision-making processes of Chinese leaders, and its broader impact on the world.

Polycrisis: The Most Dangerous Decade

Looking at today's geopolitics, it is easy to argue that humanity is experiencing a polycrisis—a complex web of interrelated crises that amplify each other, breeding a sense of unease and insecurity among the populace.[8] Through the lens of a cyclical interpretation of history, this can be understood as human development being at the transition stage between two extensive cycles: the cycle of great-power rivalry and the cycle of technological revolution.

The long cycle of global politics is the product of two intertwined factors: firstly, the collective desire to establish a renewed global system, and secondly, the unique features and constraints inherent to each global system that have been established thus far, which shape their effectiveness and lifespan.[9] When the driving force behind an existing order starts to wane, the preeminent position of global power lures competitors. Consequently, power rivalries grow fiercer, assuming the characteristics of oligopolistic competition.[10] There are countless examples in history, ranging from the alternation of power between the Chinese Song dynasty and the Mongol Empire, the Ming dynasty and the Manchu's Qing dynasty, or the wars between Athens and Sparta. As Graham Allison explains in his book *Destined for War*, as the gap in comprehensive national power narrows between rising power and predominant power, conflict is likely to occur.[11] While this viewpoint has been subject to critique and its accuracy is broadly contested, it markedly influences the interpretation of events in both the United States and China. In essence, the accuracy of the historical model is less important than its capacity to guide and influence the choices of leaders.

In this case, we are approaching a dangerous point in time. In 2022, China's GDP, amounting to approximately 121 trillion yuan (USD18.1 trillion), constituted about 71% of U.S. GDP (USD25.46 trillion).[12] Some analyses projected that China's economy would overtake that of the United States by around 2030.[13] This 2030

---

[8] Bunde et al. (2022).
[9] Modelski (1978).
[10] Ibid.
[11] Allison (2019a, b).
[12] The Central People's Government of the People's Republic of China (2023).
[13] Chen (2021).

milestone is important for two reasons: it is close at hand, and its impact is significant.[14] Over the course of the century following the United States surpassing the United Kingdom in GDP in 1894, the world witnessed major events such as two world wars, the Cold War, the collapse of the Soviet Union, the war on terror, and various regional wars and economic downturns.[15] Despite these events, the dominant economic status of the U.S. was never seriously threatened. At its peak, the Soviet planned economy was about 40% the size of the U.S. economy, while, in the late 1900s, Japan's economy reached a peak of around 70% that of the United States.[16] Nonetheless, neither country was able to challenge and surpass the United States: one disintegrated, and the other stagnated.[17]

Although the idea of a rising Chinese economy is based on questionable assumptions and projections, China presently appears as the only country with the genuine potential to threaten the status of the United States as the world's leading economy. Some U.S. scholars argue that, since China's economic power is about to reach parity with or even exceed the United States in the next few years, thus threatening U.S. dominance, the United States needs to "do whatever remains possible to 'peak' for deterrent competition against China by the mid-to-late 2020s, and accept whatever trade-offs for doing so".[18] They emphasised that no hypothetical accomplishment in 2035 or later is worth pursuing if it means sacrificing attainable capabilities that the United States could realistically achieve by the mid-to-late 2020s, especially when it comes to credibility in the eyes of China.[19] While these voices may seem somewhat radical, they largely echo a consensus critical of China that has emerged in Washington over the past decade. This consensus spans both major political parties and a wide range of economic and societal stakeholders, all promoting a more sceptical and cautious stance towards China.[20] In a similar vein, a consensus critical of the United States has also taken shape in China, narrowing the scope for diplomatic manoeuvring in both nations.

Moreover, other compounding factors beyond economic rivalry enter into play, such as the stark divergence in values, persistent tensions including disputes over Taiwan, rivalry for dominance in Asia, and the influence of a potent U.S. lobbying system advocating for augmented defence spending against China. There are views in both China and the United States that suggest a conflict between the two nations is inevitable. More dangerously, neither China nor the United States is content with the status quo, and both believe that time is on their side.[21] Thus, as a result, hard-security challenges intensify, giving rise to the classic security dilemma.[22]

---

[14] Ibid.
[15] Ibid.
[16] Ibid.
[17] Ibid.
[18] Ibid.
[19] Ibid.
[20] Erickson and Collins (2021).
[21] Anderson (2018).
[22] Ibid.

The rivalry between the United States and China is a bilateral conflict, and to some extent plays out as such, but its impact is felt globally.[23] As the strategic rivalry between the United States and China consolidates into a lasting global conflict constellation, it could set in motion a kind of deglobalisation. This is where we seem to be right now, and this circumstance has a crucial implication.

In contrast to the peak of globalisation, when leading nations focused on fostering collaboration and establishing new shared objectives and purposes, in a world where globalisation is waning, great powers are seeking to weaken their rivals' stance and deplete their strategic resources.[24] The dominant power, in particular, will take every possible action to maintain its dominant position and shift its strategic focus from preserving the stability of the global system to suppressing its primary rival.[25] In other words, against the background of great-power rivalry, when faced with the choice between upholding the international order and preserving its own dominant position, the dominant power typically opts for the latter.[26] This viewpoint underscores the key danger inherent in the present global state of affairs: failure or refusal to acknowledge the changing dynamics of globalisation and genuine conflicts arising from it, camouflaging them instead as ideological clashes. Such a course can only culminate in excessive conservatism and misdirected problem-solving efforts.

Interlocking Crisis: The Historical Cycle of Technological Revolution

What renders the current global environment particularly complex is the intertwining of the cycle of great-power rivalry with what could be termed the historical cycle of technological revolution. From a technological standpoint, it could be argued that we are now nearing the end of the third industrial revolution. The productivity boost facilitated by the third industrial revolution is starting to taper off. The onset of the fourth industrial revolution, marked by machine learning, quantum technology, and new materials, is still on the horizon.

At a more profound level, we are concluding a prolonged technological cycle that began with the first industrial revolution, fuelled by the discovery and utilisation of novel energy sources (which in turn heavily relied on ground-breaking technological advancements). We are currently exhausting the benefits accrued from the exceptional and relentless exploitation of fossil fuels during the nineteenth and twentieth centuries. Emerging renewable energy sources like solar, hydro, wind, and controllable nuclear fusion/fission power are not yet primed to fully realise their potential. And as we navigate from one industrial-economic-energy cycle to another, we are confronted with the catastrophic risk of climate change and ecological deterioration.

---

[23] Earth et al. (2021).

[24] Feng (2020).

[25] Ibid.

[26] Ibid.

The interlocking of the cycles of great-power rivalry and the long technology revolution, both in their chaotic phase, signals a 'special moment' and calls for great caution. For the foreseeable future, our world will likely be characterised more by rivalry and conflict over the allocation of dwindling resources, rather than collaboration to expand the economic pie. This is likely to happen all the more so as people worry about there not being enough wealth, creativity, and inventiveness to transform the world for the better. This fragility often triggers the adoption of populist and protectionist policies.[27] It is no surprise that phrases like 'take back control', 'America first', and 'European sovereignty' have become prevalent in today's political discourse.[28] Populism and nationalism have often triggered lost confidence, disintegration of authority, and the unrestrained assertion of narrow interests that amplify revolutions and wars demanding wealth redistribution, resulting in changes to the world order.[29]

In his whimsical essay *Perpetual Peace*, published in 1795, Immanuel Kant theorised that the attainment of global peace could be realised through either the establishment of a moral consensus or the progression of wars characterised by escalating levels of violence, ultimately leading to the incapacity of major powers.[30] During Immanuel Kant's era, technological limitations meant that even though war was destructive, the extent of damage was still contained enough for him to envision humanity enduring cycles of wars and conflicts, followed by periods of healing and recovery. Historical examples show that the Europeans managed to establish the Treaty of Westphalia, which provided innovative ideas and institutions for a stable and equitable international order, after enduring the Thirty Years' War. Meanwhile, the ancient Chinese succeeded in creating the first unified Qin dynasty after a brutal 200-year war. However, this conventional wisdom is being challenged in our era.

Today, state leaders act as if they have the option of competing for hegemony over addressing shared global challenges and revitalising the international order. But what if they actually do not have such a choice? Some hawks in both China and the West even advocate for war as a 'reset' towards the next cycle of growth, sometimes even putting forward the argument that wars stimulate technological innovation through the military. However, they miss a major point: the possible cost of war has grown to a point of no return. This means that the cost of modern wars has increased to a point where it is no longer an acceptable or feasible option for restarting the cycle of global growth. This has been true at least since the development of the atomic bomb. The potential consequences of a full-scale nuclear war are dire and far-reaching. Beyond the immediate loss of lives and destruction of cities and infrastructure, the ash and radioactive fall-out from the war could lead to global famine.[31] The risks posed by biological and chemical warfare, as well as the environmental costs of war, could herald human extinction—or at least an end to civilisation as we know it, and

---

[27] Ibid.

[28] Bunde et al. (2022).

[29] Dalio (2021).

[30] Kissinger (1956).

[31] Leyre (ed.) (2018).

an environment so degraded that surviving humans may never regain the advanced civilisation we have now.[32]

Furthermore, as technology and science continue to develop, destructive inventions such as autonomous weapon systems—or even powerful artificial intelligence (AI) with misaligned goals—will only make wars more destructive and increase the existential threat to humanity. Therefore, against the background of interlocking catastrophic risks, to get out of this disruptive and chaotic phase, wars may not be something we can afford. Or if it is a risk that leaders are willing to take, the risk should be considered with great lucidity.

In this regard, it is critical to discuss how China is likely to affect the future trajectory of the world in regard to emerging catastrophic risk categories: weapons of mass destruction, AI risk, and environmental and climate risks.

Overall, China seems to present as an ambivalent power. It is not immediately clear whether China is 'good' or 'bad' for the world, nor whether a future with a rising China is 'promising' or 'concerning', even if we were able to articulate clear criteria for any of those categories. It is unclear whether China is a 'peace stabiliser' or a 'geopolitical troublemaker', whether it is birthing digital global public goods or digital totalitarianism, and whether it is the catalyst of an ecological civilisation, or an aggressive resource exploiter. The following section will review those various areas of ambivalence in more detail.

An Ambivalent Power

- **'Peace stabiliser' versus 'Geopolitical troublemaker'**

The catastrophic risks associated with weapons of mass destruction have long been a subject of concern. However, with the emergence of AI technology, their potential for severe intensity and destructiveness has been heightened, making them particularly pertinent in today's global landscape. In this section, I will delve into the topic of weapons of mass destruction, examining it from both traditional viewpoints and through the lens of AI technology.

The resurgence of great-power rivalry, following decades of uncontested U.S. supremacy, has ushered in new challenges and risks, fostering a conflict-ridden geopolitical environment and arms races, including nuclear proliferation. Nevertheless, as Washington's leadership on this issue may be constrained by financial stress and domestic division, the necessity for collective strategic methods to maintain global stability intensifies, especially in relation to nuclear concerns.

As explored in Chap. 6, China's geography-derived interest in maintaining stability could position it as a key player in this task. In particular, with its economic

---

[32] Ibid.

sway over countries like North Korea and Iran, China could serve as both mediator and guarantor, leveraging a shared aspiration for global stability.[33] A notable example is the decade-long Iranian nuclear issue, where Beijing played an important role during the final leg of nuclear negotiations in 2013–2015, exerting effective leverage to bring Tehran back to compliance on the Joint Comprehensive Plan of Action.[34] China's economic might is integral for enforcing nuclear non-proliferation. Its economic scale means it cannot be excluded from international sanctions, especially those targeting energy exports, and its non-participation could significantly weaken international efforts to sanction or isolate Tehran.[35]

On the flip side, China's swiftly expanding military has exacerbated the threat of nuclear proliferation. For instance, Japan has seen a surge in demand for nuclear weapon development as a response to China's military prowess. Japan's advanced nuclear technologies and expertise in the field of civilian nuclear energy position it as a 'nuclear threshold' state, intensifying the urgency of the situation.[36] Another example is the establishment of the AUKUS pact, permitting Australia to possess nuclear-powered submarines as a counteractive measure to China's sway in the Indo-Pacific region. To counterbalance those pressures, Beijing may intensify its implicit backing of North Korea's missile capabilities, inducing Japan and South Korea to reconsider their U.S. alliances due to increased costs. In this case, Beijing's complicity in nuclear proliferation poses considerable risks to humanity.

Apart from the risk of nuclear proliferation, the heightened threat posed by weapons of mass destruction due to advancements in AI is deeply alarming. Progress in autonomous and AI-enabled weapons, such as AI-driven hypersonic missiles, escalates the destructiveness of warfare and provides a substantial upper hand to the party initiating the attack.[37] Driven by concerns about falling behind Russian and U.S. military innovation, the Chinese defence industry have been pursuing significant investments in robotics, unmanned systems, machine learning, and other applications of AI technology.[38] In 2016, Beijing established a new agency, the Military Science Research Steering Committee, which is modelled on the U.S. Defense Advanced Research Projects Agency, to supercharge the development of cutting-edge military technologies.[39] The estimated spending is more than USD 1.6 billion each year on AI-enabled weapons and military systems, putting China on a par with the Pentagon.[40]

U.S. President Ronald Reagan reminded us that "a nuclear war cannot be won and must never be fought". Similarly, an AI arms race would have no winners. The most extreme scenarios could involve using AI to manipulate autonomous weapons, such

---

[33] Johanson et al. (2019).
[34] Scita (2021), Zhao (2016).
[35] Almond (2016).
[36] Zhao (2016).
[37] The National Intelligence Council (2021).
[38] Kania (2020).
[39] Ni (2017).
[40] Fedasiuk (2021).

as those responsible for nuclear launches. Such instances could potentially trigger an apocalyptic conflict. The proliferation of AI weapons, the potential for their falling into the hands of non-state actors or terrorists, and the risk of accidental launch due to miscalculation or misunderstanding are all significant concerns. This concern is especially pronounced from the perspective of China. Given its vast manufacturing capacity, China could potentially produce large-scale inexpensive AI tools, such as AI-powered drones and robotics, which could be easily procured and manipulated by terrorists to execute deadly attacks.

Globally, there is still a lack of consensus on handling the legal, ethical, and arms control challenges that come with the development of AI weapons.[41] Despite China initiating several important governance measures for AI, it seems to share the reluctance of other major powers in limiting its own capabilities in autonomous weapon systems.[42] With no clear international legal boundaries, these powers feel pressured to invest in such technologies, assuming others are doing the same. This escalation, driven by the geopolitics of fear, increases the risk of dangerous misjudgements and miscalculations in warfare.

- **'Digital public goods catalyst' versus 'Digital totalitarianism'**

Digital technology significantly boosts productivity. However, the rapid adoption of new technologies can lead to uneven progress among nations, potentially widening disparities.[43] From a positive perspective, China's heavy investment of information and communications technology (ICT) in developing countries, especially in Africa, aids in reducing this inequality. Studies show there is a significant positive relationship between teledensity and economic growth in Africa.[44] Chinese companies such as Huawei and Xiaomi have provided easy and affordable smartphones and broadband to African countries, significantly increasing the teledensity of the region.[45]

China's digital power could thus turn the country into a global public goods catalyst that helps bridge emerging technological inequality and empowers the developing world. Yet critics have raised concern over the possibility that China could take advantage of its globally networked sensors and ample data to further strengthen its authoritarian regime, evolving into an extreme form of digital authoritarianism. By the end of 2020, China had the world's largest optical fibre network and 70% of the global 5G base stations (916,000 5G base stations).[46] Projections suggest that by 2030, eight billion devices within China will be interconnected via the Internet of Things, forming a powerful network of internet-connected objects.[47] This

---

[41] Asaro (2020).

[42] Kania (2020).

[43] The National Intelligence Council (2021).

[44] Minges (2016).

[45] The South African Institute of International Affairs (2021).

[46] Ibid.

[47] Oikawa and Shimono (2021).

system is further enhanced by China's quantum-enabled satellite.[48] These devices could enable extensive surveillance of China's citizens through facial recognition, predictive policing, and widespread internet censorship, leading to allegations of digital totalitarianism.

Moreover, Beijing's ability to harness robust AI systems and big data certainly brings unique considerations. Domestically, there is a risk that AI systems could unintentionally reinforce existing biases, or be deliberately misused for political suppression, particularly against opposition and marginalised groups. The latter would be a misuse of AI's promise of 'neutrality' and unbiased decision-making. Internationally, powerful AI systems could become instruments in cognitive warfare, involving information dissemination, ideological confrontations, and propaganda campaigns. These technologies' potential misuse raises concerns about maintaining international peace and stability.

Furthermore, it is possible that sophisticated AI systems could escalate tensions and potentially contribute to a cyber conflict between countries like China and the United States. The most extreme scenario could involve the complete wipe-out of the internet, precipitating a catastrophic situation for the digital industry and potentially leading to the collapse of economies and societies that are heavily dependent on the internet.

These challenges are not exclusive to China. They reflect global concerns in the realm of AI ethics. That said, given China's significant AI development capabilities and vast data resources, it certainly holds a prominent position in these discussions.

One important factor to consider here is the Whole Nation System which plays a critical role in driving China's technological development in history. The Whole Nation System is a government-led strategy concentrating resources on specific scientific innovations. China's ground-breaking accomplishment of the 'Two Bombs and One Satellite' projects between 1964 and 1970, serves as a prime example of the system's capability to meet particular objectives, even under severe conditions. Amid escalating Sino-U.S. technology competition, Xi Jinping is reinvigorating this system for technological self-reliance, particularly in areas of chips, AI, and aerospace.[49] The debate remains whether China can still leverage its Whole Nation System for technology breakthroughs, as it did in the early PRC days. While it can hasten progress in targeted sectors by directing resources and coordinating efforts, recent collapses of high-end Chinese chip companies seem to highlight the system's inefficiencies. These include overinvestment, lack of competition, and stifled innovation due to limited private sector initiatives.

It is crucial to recognise that a significant shift has occurred in the underlying dynamic of the Whole Nation System. In the early days of the PRC, with Chinese technological development starting from scratch, the system incentivised unity and coordination of resources towards a singular goal. However, after decades of technological industrial development, entrenched interest groups have formed within the

---

[48] Jia et al. (2021).
[49] Wang (2022).

technology industry. As policy incentives push in one direction, these groups sometimes steer efforts in different directions based on their varying interests, challenging the fundamental premise of a unified 'whole nation' effort.

- **'Ecological civilisation catalyst' versus 'Aggressive resource exploiter'**

Technology is not the only grave global risk inseparably tied to global divides. The climate and environmental crisis, and associated need for a global energy transition, are arguably more pressing. Lower-income countries are more likely to be exposed to climate hazards, yet they lack the capital, knowledge, and technology to pursue decarbonisation and leapfrog to renewable energy. China's investment into power-storage systems as well as extensive grid upgrades provide those countries with critical infrastructure to transition into green electricity. China's increasingly connected wind turbine and solar panel technologies are enabling massive and lower-cost projects worldwide, enabling developing countries to take advantage of renewable energy.[50]

In addition, China's own actions towards carbon reduction are promising. These actions on their own could wield substantial influence globally, given that China accounts for 18% of the world's population, contributes 18.6% to the global GDP, and produces approximately 30% of worldwide manufacturing output. In 2020, China achieved a 48.4% reduction in carbon intensity compared to 2005, which led to the prevention of 5.8 billion tonnes of carbon dioxide emissions.[51] Concurrently, the nation's GDP quadrupled during this timeframe, and almost 100 million rural inhabitants successfully rose above the poverty line.[52] Although the magnitude of its efforts is insufficient to fully address the challenge of climate change, this means China has embarked on a path of decarbonisation that can coordinate relatively well with its economic and social development.

In recent years, China has ventured into geoengineering, a contentious but potentially transformative technology. By 2025, China aims to control weather modification over an area exceeding 5.5 million square kilometres, more than 20 times the size of the United Kingdom.[53] In 2021, China also launched its 'artificial sun', a project aiming to harness infinite clean energy through controlled nuclear fusion.[54] While these technologies might help combat climate change, they also raise serious concerns due to their global implications, inherent uncertainty, and potential geopolitical tension, particularly if launched unilaterally. As for nuclear fusion, the potential to deploy it as a large-scale energy source—or any timeline to do so—remains uncertain for now.

Furthermore, China's investment in renewable energy has ranked first in the world for many years, with the aim to increase non-fossil energy consumption to around

---

[50] The National Intelligence Council (2021).
[51] Xinhua News Agency (2021).
[52] Ibid.
[53] The State Council of The People's Republic of China (2020).
[54] Ibid.

80% by 2060 from a current base of less than 20%.[55] As the leading global producer of electric vehicles and batteries, the country is set to continue this trend, with projections indicating that by 2030, 40% of vehicles sold in China will be electric.[56] Additionally, significant investments are being made in nanotechnology and quantum research for the development of future electric vehicle batteries and renewable energy technologies.

China's vast renewable energy transition is likely to significantly alter geopolitics, mirroring America's rise as a global power in the early twentieth century. This shift will particularly impact developing countries, potentially emerging as China's primary suppliers for crucial minerals like cobalt, lithium, and rare earth elements, essential for batteries and electric motors.[57] As various state actors strive to advance renewable energy technology over the next two decades, Beijing is likely to concentrate its diplomatic efforts on countries that provide these critical minerals, such as the Democratic Republic of the Congo and Bolivia.[58] China's energy transition could therefore prompt a rebalancing of global wealth, benefiting countries that have been relatively marginalised, though the scenario might also heighten geopolitical tensions.

On the flip side, investments in African metal mining for green technologies may introduce local and regional instability, given the challenges these countries face in managing corruption risks brought by gigantic metal export windfalls, as well as other associated risks such as factional rivalries over riches, inequality, and debt challenges.[59] Additionally, competition over critical materials might push China to secure long-term deals with countries like Afghanistan, potentially strengthening ties with the Taliban and providing them with strong economic backing.[60] Lastly, China's energy security will continue to depend on sea lanes, with supply routes through the South China Sea and the Indian Ocean remaining significant security flashpoints in the Indo-Pacific region.[61]

Another important perspective is that, as discussed earlier, the developed world and the Global South generally view the world differently. The state of mind of the Global South could be summarised as 'more justice, less power'. Meaning, most countries in the developing world consider themselves entitled to 'justice', in terms of sharing resources and allowing carbon emissions to fast-track their economic development. The rationale here is that the developed world made their wealth at the expense of the developing world. The latter are therefore entitled to compensations. Yet, compared with the Western establishment, their international leverage and power to safeguard their interests are limited. This might lead to a resentful attitude, whereby the developing world is less willing to cooperate or make any

---

[55] Xinhua News Agency (2021).
[56] Stauffer (2021).
[57] The National Intelligence Council (2021).
[58] Ibid.
[59] The Economist (2022).
[60] Mohseni-Cheraghlou and Graham (2021).
[61] Yergin (2020).

concessions to Western countries in climate negotiations—which could lead to a collapse of the whole system. This is more likely to happen in the current chaotic international environment, where competition over scarce resources is the dominant mode of thinking.

This risk of resentful refusal of cooperation extends to China. When criticised for its emissions exceeding all developed nations combined, Chinese policy makers have claimed that China is unfairly 'contained' by carbon tariffs on imports, and view this as developed countries enforcing a stealth form of trade protection through low-carbon development. However, unlike other developing countries, China does have greater power and agency to act on the global system. With this comes the potential for disruption, for better or worse.

How Does the Cyclical View of History Affect Chinese Decision-Making?

The above analysis highlights China's ambivalence. To comprehend this, it is essential to reflect on important insights drawn from the cyclical view of history, and how this understanding of history influences the way that Chinese leaders read present situations. There are three primary perspectives to consider.

- **Maintaining strategic options**

Firstly, a cyclical view of history urges leaders to tailor their strategies depending on whether they are leading in a period of stability or turbulence. This approach encourages them to be more realistic and pragmatic regarding the prevailing constraints and potential manoeuvres to accomplish their objectives. To give one example, faced with an unstable political, military, and economic environment, many Chinese emperors resolutely chose to move the capital to places with better conditions in order to gain the opportunity to start a new political rule.

From this perspective, the current global state is predominantly seen as a chaotic transition. This transition is perceived as turbulent, uncertain, and laden with risks. In such times, all actors, including China, are likely to display more unpredictable and ambiguous behaviour, complicating the interpretation of their actions. In this context, China has not clearly decided which game it is playing—whether it is playing the Warring States in a game of global hegemony, or acting as a collaborative player to build a multipolar world bound by new shared values. Its actions, in fact, aim at least in part to maintain multiple options.

In the event that hegemony becomes the sole objective, the available choice is to either act as a predator or become the prey. It is important to note that authoritarian leaders often prefer to be remembered as dominant predators. In this case, China is likely to engage in a hegemonic game while the rest of the world is fighting ground. It means China would be more likely to resort to the ruthless ideology of Legalism, where anything goes to attain power, control, and dominance. In this context, the international community does not want to see China echo the aggressive forms of fascist Germany or militaristic Japan from the Second World War. Similarly, the world does not want China to emulate the United States, leading to either a new Cold War with two hegemonic powers or a world where China replaces U.S. hegemony, sustaining the current imbalanced global order.

However, if multipolarity, with its checks and balances, was to appear as a viable option, China might offer a new approach to understanding and generating public goods, inspired by Confucian virtues and rituals. Ironically, the United States is itself an ambivalent power. In a multipolar world, the United States might even resume its long-standing values of non-interference, tolerance, and morally driven leadership. If that was the case, joint values may emerge.

- **Managing the 'Warring States period'**

Secondly, a cyclical view of history suggests that the upcoming era, while vastly different from our recent experiences, is likely to reflect aspects of deep history at comparable stages in the cycle. This means a crucial element in our interpretation of the current reality is how we draw guidance from history. From the cyclical view of history, we should expect the future we encounter in our lifetime to diverge from our recent past: relevant patterns lie in more distant and deep history rather than our immediate recollections.

While many Western scholars read the current state of the world using the First World War or Second World War as points of comparison, many Chinese scholars tend to view it from the longer perspective of Chinese history, and compare it with the Warring States period from 475 BCE. As discussed earlier, the Warring States period was a chaotic era where the Chinese plains were divided into a number of small states. It was characterised by near-continuous interstate conflicts, where the leaders of independent states vied for dominance.[62] At a deeper level, this was a world where the fundamental arrangement of great-power relations was uncertain, and rising powers sought to compete for new sources of influence to form new norms, rules, and institutions.

There are crucial differences between the analogy of the Warring States period and that of the First or Second World War. The world wars epitomise extreme conflicts over a fairly brief time span, involving two primary factions, eventually resolved through military battle. By contrast, the Warring States period was an extended period of turmoil and competition, with multiple participants influencing the formation of a new order. During this era, diplomatic strategies for reestablishing the balance of power among players were abundant, and conflicts were often resolved through alternatives to warfare. The choice of interpretative lens will thus focus attention on different factors in the situation—and offer different options to best navigate it.

Arguably, our current world more closely mirrors the dynamics of the Chinese Warring States period than those of the two world wars. One reason is that the current international environment, with the credible deterrence of mutually assured destruction provided by nuclear weapons, is less likely to turn into a full-scale war

---

[62] Lewis (1999).

than a longer period of power competition and rebalancing. In addition, despite the primary focus being on the competition between China and the United States, other established and rising powers are attempting to test and reestablish their influence amid a weakening global order. These include Russia, Japan, and India.

As the 'Warring States period' mindset reemerges, nations prioritise power struggles over collaborative problem-solving for shared challenges, promoting a geopolitical climate susceptible to conflict. This shift threatens long-standing norms and institutions, and diminishes the capacity and determination of state leaders to confront collective global threats. As a result, countries show a growing preference for domestic remedies to address international issues, yet the limitations of narrowly national actions render the prospects for substantial solutions disheartening. This trend could potentially intensify the disruptions of shared challenges and prolong the era of power struggle and rebalance, reflecting the dynamics seen during the Warring States period.

As discussed earlier, the historical experience of the extensive Warring States period also offers hope for diplomatic efforts to manage conflicts. While the Warring States period saw continuous large-scale military conflagrations, it also witnessed persistent diplomatic manoeuvring to manage a delicate balance of power among ever-changing coalitions. The central figures of this era were the diplomats who moved from state to state, promising their dukes to secure their interests through the alliances that they could obtain through their persuasive skills.[63] The regular meetings of dukes and visits by embassies established a routine of diplomatic exchange between competing states to help manage conflict and regulate wars.[64] This could serve as crucial reminders of the need to reemphasise diplomacy as a vital instrument to navigate the existing uncertainties of our time.

- **Unlearn helplessness**

Third, although Chinese history documents moments of depression and pain, it also shows that those disruptive periods, like cleansing storms, eliminate weaknesses and excesses. It also provides an opportunity for a fresh start by returning to the fundamentals on a sounder footing.[65] In other words, Chinese leaders trained in the cyclical view of Chinese history understand periods of chaos as periods where a new order is being negotiated.

Looking back at the Warring States period, dukes competed to prove their 'mandate of heaven' by striving to enhance their agricultural advancement. This led to the spread of iron farming tools and large-scale irrigation systems, resulting in a plentiful grain yield. They also focused on attracting top talents for philosophical and strategic advancements. Through continuous experimentation and learning from mistakes, the Chinese developed sophisticated governance systems and philosophical doctrines comparable to the level of refinement achieved by ancient Greek civilisation during the same period—the inception of Western philosophy. These advancements,

---

[63] Ibid.
[64] Ibid.
[65] Dalio (2021).

born of disruptive transformations, laid a robust foundation for China's prosperity that has lasted for more than 2,000 years.

The 2022 Munich Security Report identified a "collective helplessness" pervading the West as it grapples with a series of interconnected global challenges.[66] This frustration over the lack of consensus and progress has given rise to populist leaders whose radical and politically extreme policies only amplify societal divisions and fragmentation, thereby posing a threat to democracy. The danger is that this feeling of crisis fatigue, loss of control, and the perceived collective helplessness, mean that despite resources, strategies, and instruments available to address key global challenges, the world will not be able to do so.[67] This line of thinking is extremely perilous as it has the potential to become a self-fulfilling prophecy.

In contrast, the Munich Security Report revealed that China shows more optimism and confidence when confronting global challenges. The cyclical view of history may offer some explanation to the Chinese optimism. To unlearn 'helplessness', people need to believe that they can effect change in their environment and that they can exert a measure of control over their surroundings. When the flow of time is not held to be a back-and-forth tide, but a one-way flow, it is conceived of as having a beginning, and perhaps an end. And so, the approach of the climax is anticipated with a combination of fear and intensity. A cyclical view of history, by contrast, shows that healthy competition and reform to overcome weaknesses in the current system can lead to a new cycle of growth, reducing both the fear and the sense of intensity attached to the perception of chaos.

Rivalry Partners—The Chanyuan Treaty

To encapsulate our entire discussion in this chapter, I would like to introduce a historically insightful concept that could help address the current challenges we are facing—that of 'rivalry partners'.

As discussed earlier, the adoption of a cyclical view of history tends to make the Chinese leadership more inclined to adopt a pragmatic strategy for shaping a future global order. They view it as a natural and organic process of states and powers collaborating or dissolving as part of a cyclical evolution within the broader global system. In this process, diverse states and cultures learn from and influence one another, creating more or less open and interconnected economic, political, and cultural spaces across varying geographical regions. Within such a framework, states do not act based on a single faultline of ideological alignment.

The concept of 'rivalry partners' emerged more than 1,000 years ago in the Northern Song dynasty (960–1127). As discussed in Chap. 3, China has a long tradition of considering the unity of opposites in situations that seem characterised by contradiction. The term 'rivalry partners' appears as a contradiction, but it offers

---

[66] Bunde et al. (2022).

[67] Ibid.

a dialectical approach to reach a golden mean by finding a dynamic balance between cooperation and competition, therefore avoiding any radical results.

The 'rivalry partners' concept is derived from the Chanyuan Treaty in 1005. This was a peace treaty between the Northern Song dynasty and the Liao dynasty (916–1125), a Khitan-led regime on China's northern border. Acknowledging that neither side possessed absolute advantage to decisively defeat the other, and neither side could not eliminate the other without self-destruction, the Northern Song and Liao regimes adopted a pragmatic approach. They crafted an agreement that fostered a stable and lasting peace spanning over a century, established on the bedrock of equality.[68] Under this treaty, the Northern Song and the Liao agreed to both compete fiercely and collaborate intensely across various domains.[69] For example, they maintained competition in a military capacity while concurrently cooperating on trade.

As discussed in Chap. 8, there is a considerable latitude of flexibility within the tributary system. The Northern Song regime utilised this flexibility, and made regular tribute payments to the Liao, as a way to maintain stability. This provided the Liao with a dependable revenue stream and enabled trade with neighbouring countries. Perhaps even more noteworthy is the fact that the peace and trade opportunities sustained under this treaty stimulated the growth of prosperous international trade along the Northern Song-Liao border, thereby fuelling the economic expansion of the Northern Song regime and contributing to a cultural renaissance in arts and education.[70] Chinese historians often refer to this era as the golden age.

To maintain this rivalry partnership, it was essential to handle recurring challenges and adapt to changing circumstances. Despite having conflicting interests and differing values, the Northern Song and the Liao found common ground and facilitated the inauguration of various diplomatic institutions, regulations, and practices dealing with various matters, such as borderland issues, espionage, trade, and more. The execution of these strategies enabled the Northern Song and Liao dynasties to mitigate differences through institutional means, thus deescalating their militaristic expansion which was a significant strain on their economies. Consequently, they both could focus on addressing their internal challenges.

One important lesson from the Chanyuan Treaty is that positive and healthy competition can drive innovation and enhance prosperity if there are clear frameworks to guide diverse political systems to be increasingly competitive without being confrontational. In this context, could leaders from the United States and China find a modern equivalent to the Chanyuan Treaty in the twenty-first century?

The wisdom of the Chanyuan Treaty goes beyond Chinese history. During a 2009 interview, former Soviet Union leader Mikhail Gorbachev disclosed that former U.S. President Ronald Reagan, during a private walk at the Geneva Summit in 1985, directly posed the question to him whether they could set aside their differences in

---

[68] Wan (2017).

[69] Allison (2019a, b).

[70] Ibid.

the case of an invasion from outer space.[71] The intention behind this question was to highlight the shared fundamental interests that unite otherwise hostile adversaries.

Additionally, U.S. Secretary of State Antony Blinken outlined that the U.S. policy towards China will be "competitive when it should be, collaborative when it can be and adversarial when it must be".[72] The pivotal question that arises then is: What kind of frameworks or institutions can leaders from the United States and China construct that would allow them simultaneously to compete and cooperate? More importantly, how can these institutions provide them with the latitude needed to diminish the intensity of the arms race and address essential internal reforms?

Today, the world is at a dangerous transition phase, where stagnating economic growth, trade protectionism, and global catastrophic risks compound with global governance deficit and diminishing government authority and action. Developed and developing countries both have fragilities they need to tackle. Developed countries are more at risk of collapse from the inside because of political polarisation, extreme inequalities, and the surge of populism. The developing world is more at risk of collapse from outside systemic risks, ranging from climate risk to energy and food security. In order to move beyond this dangerous phase, the world needs a 'triple revolution', across the global level, in developed countries, and in developing countries. The question is whether state leaders can face our shared challenges honestly and adapt to meet them.

Adopting a cyclical view of history does not mean adopting a purely deterministic reading of history. It is not about accepting *fatum* with a brave heart, or naively stating that 'things will get better on their own'. Periods of chaos in historical cycles are notoriously dangerous. They can cause considerable harm while they last, and if handled badly, the next iteration of the order would be somewhat less prosperous than it would otherwise be. The discussion offered in this chapter will hopefully invite a shift in the question we raise, from 'Could it be true that history is doomed to repeat the same formulas?' or 'Are civilisations destined to collapse?' to 'How can we minimise harm as we go through this earth-shattering moment?' or 'What mistakes can we correct to reformulate a more ecologically sustainable and spiritually healthy future?' In the next chapter, I will focus on how external entities can influence China and collaboratively take positive steps to address these shared challenges.

References

Allison G (2019a) Destined for War: Can America and China escape Thucydides's trap? Scribe Publications Pty Ltd., Melbourne.
Allison G (2019b) Could the United States and China be rivalry partners? In: The National Interest. Available at: https://nationalinterest.org/feature/could-united-states-and-china-be-rivalry-partners-65661. Accessed 12 May 2021.

---

[71] Lewis (2015).
[72] Wadhams (2021).

References

Almond RG (2016) China and the Iran nuclear deal. In: The Diplomat. Available at: https://thediplomat.com/2016/03/china-and-the-iran-nuclear-deal/. Accessed 18 June 2020.

Anderson P (2018) 21shiji dedaguo xietiao. Beijing Cultural Review (1):20–29.

Asaro P (2020) Autonomous weapons and the ethics of artificial intelligence. In: Liao SM (eds) Ethics of Artificial Intelligence. Oxford Academic, New York. DOI: https://doi.org/10.1093/oso/9780190905033.003.0008.

Bunde T et al (2022) Munich security report 2022: Turning the tide - unlearning helplessness. In: Munich Security Conference. Available at: https://securityconference.org/publikationen/munich-security-report-2022/. Accessed 12 December 2022.

Chen Y (2021) Zhongguo jingji 10niannei jiang chao meiguo 'daguo zhengzhi de beiju' huifou chongyan. In: BBC. Available at: https://www.bbc.com/zhongwen/simp/world-56194990. Accessed 1 July 2022.

Dalio R (2021) Principles for dealing with the changing world order: Why nations succeed or fail. Simon & Schuster, New York; Liu H (eds.) (2013) Liangci quanqiu daweiji de bijiao yanjiu. China Economic Publishing House, Beijing.

Dalio R (2021) Principles for dealing with the changing world order: Why nations succeed or fail. Simon & Schuster, New York.

Earth TR et al (2021) China's quest for global primacy: An analysis of Chinese international and defense strategies to outcompete the United States. In: Rand Corporation. Available at: https://www.rand.org/pubs/research_reports/RRA447-1.html. Accessed 2 January 2022.

The Economist (2022) The transition to clean energy will mint new commodity superpowers. Available at: https://www.economist.com/finance-and-economics/2022/03/26/the-transition-to-clean-energy-will-mint-new-commodity-superpowers. Accessed 2 April 2022.

Erickson AS, Collins GB (2021) A dangerous decade of Chinese power is here. In: Foreign Policy. https://foreignpolicy.com/2021/10/18/china-danger-military-missile-taiwan/. Accessed 27 December 2021.

Fedasiuk R (2021) Harnessed lightning: How the Chinese military is adopting artificial intelligence. Center for security and emerging technology. DOI: https://doi.org/10.51593/20200089.

Feng S (2020) Cyclical globalization and China's strategic options. China Quarterly of International Strategic Studies 6(3):355–370. DOI: https://doi.org/10.1142/S2377740020500207.

Jia HP et al (2021) Towards new frontiers. Nature Index 593:24–27.

Johanson D et al (2019) New perspectives on China's relations with the world: National, transnational and international. E-international relations publishing, Bristol.

Kania EB (2020) "AI weapons" in Chinese military innovation. In: Brookings. Available at: https://www.brookings.edu/research/ai-weapons-in-chinas-military-innovation/. Accessed 20 October 2021.

Kissinger H (1956) Force and diplomacy in the nuclear age. Foreign Affairs 34(3):349–366.

Lewis M (1999) Warring States political history. In: The Cambridge history of ancient China: From the origins of civilization to 221 BC. Cambridge: Cambridge University Press, Cambridge.

Lewis D (2015) Reagan and Gorbachev agreed to pause the Cold War in case of an alien invasion. In: Smithsonian Institution. Available at: https://www.smithsonianmag.com/smart-news/reagan-and-gorbachev-agreed-pause-cold-war-case-alien-invasion-180957402/. Accessed 19 October 2022.

Leyre J (ed) (2018) Global catastrophic risks 2018. In: The Global Challenges Foundation. Available at: https://globalchallenges.org/wp-content/uploads/GCF-Annual-report-2018-1.pdf. Accessed 12 March 2020.

Luo GZ, Brewitt-Taylor CH (trans) (2002) Romance of the Three Kingdoms. Tuttle Publishing, Boston, p.1.

Minges M (2016) Digital dividends: Exploring the relationship between broadband and economic growth. In: The World Bank. https://documents1.worldbank.org/curated/en/178701467988875888/pdf/102955-WP-Box394845B-PUBLIC-WDR16-BP-Exploring-the-Relationship-between-Broadband-and-Economic-Growth-Minges.pdf. Accessed 12 December 2020.

Modelski G (1978) The long cycle of global politics and the nation-state. Comparative Studies in Society and History 20(2):214–35.

Mohseni-Cheraghlou A, Graham N (2021) Could China become the Taliban's new benefactor? In: Atlantic Council. Available at: https://www.atlanticcouncil.org/blogs/new-atlanticist/could-china-become-the-talibans-new-benefactor/. Accessed 19 October 2022.

Ni A (2017) China reveals new military technology agency. In: The Diplomat. Available at: https://thediplomat.com/2017/07/china-reveals-new-military-technology-agency/. Accessed 20 August 2020.

Oikawa A, Shimono Y (2021) China overtakes US in AI research. In: Nikkei Asia. Available at: https://asia.nikkei.com/Spotlight/Datawatch/China-overtakes-US-in-AI-research. Accessed 3 January 2022.

Petty HJ (2018) History and society: How we view the past reveals much about our future. In: Medium. Available at: https://harold-j-petty.medium.com/history-and-society-2b376e2952e3. Accessed 19 May 2020.

Scita J (2021) China is the real barometer of the state of Iran nuclear talks in Vienna. In: Atalantic Council. Available at: https://www.atlanticcouncil.org/blogs/iransource/china-is-the-real-barometer-of-the-state-of-iran-nuclear-talks-in-vienna/. Accessed 19 November 2021

Stauffer NW (2021) China's transition to electric vehicles. In: MIT News. Available at: https://news.mit.edu/2021/chinas-transition-electric-vehicles-0429. Accessed 9 June 2022.

The Central People's Government of the People's Republic of China (2023) 2022nian woguo GDP tupo 120wanyi zengzhang 3%. Available at: http://www.gov.cn/xinwen/2023-01/17/content_5 737514.htm. Accessed 7 February 2023.

The National Intelligence Council (2021) Global trends 2040: A more contested world. Available at: https://www.dni.gov/files/ODNI/documents/assessments/GlobalTrends_2040.pdf. Accessed 11 June 2021.

The South African Institute of International Affairs (2021) China-powered ICT Infrastructure: Lessons from Tanzania and Cambodia. Available at: https://saiia.org.za/research/china-powered-ict-infrastructure-lessons-from-tanzania-and-cambodia/. Accessed 2 January 2022.

The State Council of The People's Republic of China (2020) China to forge ahead with weather modification service. Available at: https://english.www.gov.cn/policies/latestreleases/202012/02/content_WS5fc76218c6d0f7257694125e.html. Accessed 12 February 2022.

Wadhams N (2021) Blinken says only China can truly challenge global system. In: Bloomberg. Available at: https://www.bloomberg.com/news/articles/2021-03-03/blinken-calls-china-competition-a-key-challenge-for-the-u-s. Accessed 10 July 2022.

Wan X (2017)Chaogong de mingshi yu chaogong zhiwai de dongya: fenlei kuangjia, anli juyu yu yanjiu jianyi. Quaterly journal of international politics 2(3):63–104.

Wang K (2022) Xi tells nation to mobilize for 'core technology' breakthrough. In: Caixin Global. Available at: https://www.caixinglobal.com/2022-09-07/xi-tells-nation-to-mobilize-for-core-technology-breakthrough-101937109.html. Accessed 12 October 2022.

Xinhua News Agency (2021) China contributes to global carbon emissions reduction. Available at: http://www.news.cn/english/2021-11/09/c_1310300766.htm. Accessed 2 February 2022.

Yergin D (2020) The new map: Energy, climate, and the clash of nations. Penguin Books Ltd., London.

Yusoff K (2019) A billion black Anthropocene or none. University of Minnesota Press, Minneapolis.

Zhao T (2016) Zhongguo yu guoji hezhixu de yanhua. Quarterly Journal of International Politics 1(1):1181–148. 101393D-2016-1-006.

Chapter 11
Navigating an Uncertain Future: Redefining Growth and Security

"History doesn't repeat itself, but it often rhymes."
—Mark Twain

Abstract In light of the world's efforts to seek a new equilibrium that incorporates the disruptions brought by China, as well as its inevitable influence on almost all global issues, this final chapter endeavours to spark thought and debate on the pivotal question: What is the optimal approach for an external party to impact China in a manner that increases the likelihood of it becoming a beneficial contributor to our shared future? This chapter modestly proposes a potential way forward, requiring two major tasks to be handled concurrently—navigating the present period of transition and uncertainty, and inventing a new future by shifting the paradigm. For the first task, this chapter discusses the central concept of 'dynamic constraints'. It explores the structural limitations that restrict China's actions, thereby forcing it to make compromises. Further, it highlights the inherent flexibility within the Chinese system that would be utilised to expand strategic options to influence China to act more positively. Regarding the second task, this chapter proposes a novel reconceptualisation of two core concepts—growth and security—aiming to encourage new thought patterns and models for addressing 'the China challenge' more prudently and effectively. It concludes by posing three key questions for readers to reflect upon and take further actions on their own.

A Possible Way Forward: Two Key Tasks

Chapter 10 delved into the dangerous transitional phase that the world is currently in, whereby a multitude of interlinked challenges place immense strain on nations and communities. These challenges encompass environmental and climate issues, geostrategic threats, and the disturbances brought by artificial intelligence. In such a volatile setting, any sudden shock could have catastrophic consequences. Against this unstable scenario, the expanding economic influence and military growth of

China bring added complexity, exacerbating the vulnerability of our interconnected world and testing the resilience of established global norms.

A crucial question to consider is whether 'the China challenge' should primarily be perceived as an additional threat jeopardising the delicate balance of global order, or if, in this moment of global reinvention, China could serve as a positive catalyst for worldwide change. Should the latter be true, what models or methods do we have to enhance China's positive global role. The intent of this concluding chapter is to stimulate discussion and reflection on this subject. More specifically, on how this can be accomplished with maximum safety and effectiveness.

I must admit from the outset that I do not possess a straightforward and immediate solution to this query as of now. However, what I intend to present is a set of thought-provoking points, hopefully inciting contemplation and debate on how to better tackle the issue. In this endeavour, as a guiding principle, I would like to propose that two distinct matters need to be assessed simultaneously: one is about navigating the current period of transition and uncertainty, and the other is imagining and building a radically different future by enabling a paradigm shift. Let us begin by discussing the first—how to best navigate the current period of transition.

Navigating Uncertainty

- **Keeping the window open**

As discussed in Chap. 10, the world is in a transition phase that we can anticipate to be tumultuous, challenging, and risky. During this period, all actors are likely to display ambiguous and inconsistent behaviour in response to the surrounding chaos, making it more difficult to anticipate or interpret their actions. In this context, it is paramount to preserve open channels for dialogue and engagement, aiming to minimise misinterpretations and miscalculations. 'Keeping the window open' implies establishing effective feedback systems in both bilateral and multilateral engagements through a diplomatic approach. This will allow all stakeholders to grasp each other's intentions more profoundly and understand interconnected impacts within a shared system, thereby enabling a systematic approach to the complex task of navigating the current uncertainty. Such a model, based on strong feedback loops, will make it easier for countries to adapt actions based on feedback and to synchronise efforts. In particular, one primary focus should be directed towards negative feedback loops, i.e. mechanisms designed to find balance between opposing ideas or directions and avoid a very rapid devolution towards extreme outcomes. This approach, which correlates to the Chinese 'Yin-yang' principle, is discussed in Chap. 3.

Nevertheless, the window to engage and influence China is narrowing. As discussed in Chaps. 6 and 7, China is currently grappling with an intense feeling of insecurity, stemming from Western security pressures and economic decoupling. In Beijing, there is an increasing perception that regardless of its conduct, China will be unfavourably perceived and face negative interactions from the United States and the West. As a result, China's own security concerns come to strongly dominate, while enthusiasm and openness towards engagement with the West diminish. This situation has three implications.

Firstly, an escalating trend of nationalism is apparent within China, generating anti-Western sentiment. Increasingly, any action by the West is viewed as an attempt to 'contain' China's growth and prosperity. This rising trend notably restricts the chances for Western societies to interact with the Chinese population in meaningful people-to-people exchanges, such as through culture, sports, and arts. These exchanges play a pivotal role in fostering understanding and trust, and frequently serve as an effective tool to diffuse conflicts during escalating tensions.

Secondly, in grappling with the mounting pressures of economic and technological decoupling, China has steered its policies towards cultivating technological self-reliance and bolstering internal economic circulation within its domestic sphere. This approach inadvertently curtails the opportunities once available for the global business community to collaborate and engage with their Chinese counterparts, thereby restricting the capacity of business professionals to foster confidence in their respective countries.

Thirdly, in order to strengthen domestic unity to withstand external disruptions, a trend is emerging within the Chinese bureaucratic system that favours individuals with strong personalities and significant ideological alignment with the Party. These individuals, by their very nature, tend to be less open to international engagement and less proficient at managing it, which presents additional challenges for foreign parties attempting to engage with various levels of the Chinese government.

These three factors significantly contribute to China's internal feedback loops, potentially leading to a self-feeding negative spiral. The negative spiral could propel China to strengthen its ties with anti-Western nations such as Russia. This shift would further narrow the perspectives through which foreign observers understand Chinese foreign policy, diminishing the trust and willingness of the West and China to mutually engage.

The dwindling opportunities for engagement are precipitating a dangerous 'mutually reinforcing cycle of fear and helplessness'. On the one hand, China feels compelled to project confidence and ambition. Yet, as it puts forth this image, it finds itself overextended and vulnerable as maintaining an assertive posture requires substantial resources. Essentially, the more assertive or even aggressive China appears externally, the more it grapples with its own internal fragility and vulnerability. While a confident China is a cause for concern, a vulnerable China raises far more serious worries. A vulnerable China is less cooperative and less competent. It is also less inclined and less equipped to find solutions for global challenges. Paradoxically, a more vulnerable China is more likely to resort to aggressive actions, especially towards Taiwan, as it becomes more self-serving and less concerned about the international community's opinion. Should China decide to move towards a more inward and regressive path, it could take up to a generation to reverse course. This delay would waste valuable time that could be better spent on coordinating efforts to address pressing global challenges.

On the other hand, with a narrowing opportunity to engage with China, Western countries may increasingly feel that they have no other option but to adopt a hostile stance towards China. Many in the West perceive that attempts to 'engage with China' have been made and have failed. This 'mutually reinforcing cycle of fear and helplessness' is inherently perilous and could potentially lead to a prolonged stalemate. In light of these developments, immediate actions must be taken by the heads of states around the world, especially leaders of the West. They must make an effort to uphold direct communications with Xi Jinping to extend the opportunities for dialogue and allow the infusion of diverse perspectives into his leadership realm.

- **Putting fear into perspective**

The second requisite step to successfully manoeuvre through this uncertain transitional phase is to address genuine challenges with focused and effective strategies. This requires distinguishing between 'imaginary fears'—perceived threats that China poses stemming from its statements or actions—and 'legitimate fears'—genuine challenges that China's rise presents to our collective future, stemming from its core interests. Let us begin with the discussion of those legitimate fears.

Legitimate fears about China's future trajectory are typically rooted in three key areas: security, economics, and ideology. First, security concerns stem from China's exceptional military growth, which could potentially trigger far-reaching conflict in Asia, particularly over Taiwan. As Chap. 6 explains, China's inherent geographical vulnerability drives its quest for survival and strategic security. This manifests in extensive resources allocated to military modernisation. Chapter 6 also highlights that severe external threats may provoke China into offensive actions, such as in a situation where Taiwan declares independence, posing a real threat to regional and global stability.

Additionally, economic anxieties arise from China's heightened economic cohesion, potential disruption to established market norms, possible unilateral dominance over maritime routes and resources, exploitation of data and technology for unfair economic advantage, as well as negative environmental impact. These concerns are reasonably founded. As outlined in Chap. 2, given China's persistent food security challenges stemming from its geographical features, citizens have developed pragmatic expectations of their government. This has led to a form of 'performance legitimacy' intrinsically linked to the government's ability to safeguard citizens' material welfare. Consequently, the CCP's primary interest in pursuing economic security and prosperity through growth could result in alterations to market regulations in its own favour, escalating tensions around the South China Sea and the larger Indo-Pacific region, as well as exploiting resources in regions where those are abundant. As highlighted in Chap. 8, China's long-standing practice of geoeconomic statecraft suggests the potential use of economic leverage to exert pressure on dissenting views.

The third point of legitimate fear has to do with China's ideology and its clash with Western liberal democracies. This specific concern holds validity within the Western perspective, and it unfolds in the following three aspects. A primary concern is that the Chinese communist ideology undermines the universal applicability of Western liberal democratic principles. This worry is valid for the West, as the universalism of their principles justifies its global predominance and domestic appeal. China's resistance to liberal democracy challenges the universality of Western norms and systems, reducing them to merely one of many, dependent on specific contexts rather than an inevitable human advancement. The West, therefore, faces the unsettling prospect of a world where their values are not destined to be globally accepted.

On a second level, this fear escalates as China extends its ideological influence beyond the Western regions to areas like Africa and the Middle East. This development could further limit the universal claims of Western liberal democracy, along with the narrative of its inevitable global spread as a symbol of modernity and worldwide emancipation for humanity. Finally, there is also fear relating to China's potential infiltration into Western nations through political manipulation and propaganda, posing a threat to their liberal democratic principles from within. This could ultimately signal the downfall of democracy and the loss of freedom.

The above discussion highlights legitimate fears linked to China's future evolution. However, contrasted with these legitimate fears, there also exist imaginary fears. These fears often stem from subjective perceptions, bias, misinformation, and anxieties about the unknown, potentially leading to bleak worst-case-scenario mindsets and a magnified perception of probability. Those imaginary fears often encompass a concept of China's global dominance—the idea that as China's economy and military power expand, China will take over the world. Many imagine a Chinese government resembling the dark Empire from the *Star Wars*, imposing mindless submission on the entire globe.

More specifically, from the security perspective, there is a concern that China's growing military may trigger large-scale direct conflicts with the West, especially the United States, or even result in a Chinese invasion of other countries like Australia. On the ideological front, the fear that China aims to infiltrate Western democracies in order to transform them into authoritarian regimes also qualifies as an imaginary fear. China often employs conventional tactics overseas, such as corruption, propaganda, and espionage, to assert influence and promote its national interests. However, the objective is primarily to secure better deals or enhance its positive image, not to alter the political regime.

These imaginary fears require careful contextualisation as they often bring more noise than nuance, fuelling undue tensions, misdirecting policy, obscuring critical strategic focus, and inducing aggressive behaviour from both China and the West. The crux of the argument here is that imaginary fears should be put into perspective, while legitimate fears need to be addressed by pinpointing effective points of influence.

To further unpack this argument, I would like to introduce the concept of 'dynamic constraints'. This concept aims to highlight the limitations and flexibility in Chinese decision-making. 'Constraints' refers to the persistent structural limitations emanating from China's geography and extensive history that restrict its actions, necessitating compromises. On the other hand, 'dynamic' pertains to the components of China's tradition and material conditions that facilitate a more open-ended approach to decision-making. When it comes to conceptualising imaginary fears, it is pivotal to understand the inherent constraints in China's actions, and the trade-offs it must make. This perspective assists in framing imagined fears more constructively while finding key priorities to tackle genuine challenges. In short, there are two primary constraints compelling China to moderate its actions: geographical constraints and structural constraints. I will start by discussing how to conceptualise imagined fears from the perspective of geographical constraints.

Prisoner of Geography

As discussed in Chap. 6, although Beijing has an ambitious vision for China's future trajectory, its grand strategy is not just a long list of heterogeneous goals, but a clearly-ordered list, with priorities and trade-offs defined by a range of enduring constraints.

On the security front, as discussed in Chap. 6, China's vulnerable border security constrains the possibility of global dominance. As China develops into a strong land and sea power, it starts to face a two-front security threat—squeezed between rivals on land and at sea. Historical lessons remind the country that it must avoid the potentially existential risk of picking two fights at the same time. Chapter 6 also highlighted that contingencies among neighbouring countries could pose significant threats to China's land borders, potentially drawing it into prolonged and costly land-based commitments. Over China's long history, this situation has consistently forced it to make trade-offs between landward security and maritime ambition. This geographical reality means that Beijing is likely to maintain a priority focus on its security endeavours around its immediate borders and cautiously balance its maritime ambitions, instead of aspiring for global dominance.

In the economic sphere, as highlighted in Chap. 7, China's historical shift in gravity towards coastal cities in Southeast China has fostered extensive maritime trade and economic interactions with the rest of the world. The nation's sea-borne trade constitutes 95% of its total trade and 45% of the national GDP. This economic structure has consequently woven China intricately into the fabric of the world's imports, exports, investments, and supply chains. Such interdependence implies that any pursuit of economic dominance would likely result in considerable self-inflicted harm, making it largely implausible. Asserting such dominance invites economic retaliation and sanctions from other countries, disrupts China's own established supply chain, and impedes the unobstructed exchange of goods that China's economy heavily relies on. Unlike Russia or North Korea, which can afford a more isolationist stance or economic sanctions due to limited global economic ties, China does not have this luxury. Conversely, China has deeply entrenched global economic ties. Hence, China's geographical circumstances coupled with its economic interdependence function as a self-check mechanism, limiting its pursuit of global economic dominance.

Moreover, to cement the CCP's performance legitimacy, Beijing must secure its position within the global trade system and sustain geopolitical stability. A key strategy to achieve this is by maintaining influence in multilateral forums. This necessitates China being perceived as a responsible global actor by the international community and taking corresponding actions. Hence, Beijing must strike a delicate balance between geopolitical assertiveness, including potential aspirations for dominance, and the ongoing need to attract foreign investment and trade by adhering to international regulations concerning trade, intellectual property, and environmental standards.

Regarding ideological matters, geographical proximity shapes China's endeavours towards ideological alignment. As explored in Chap. 8, China's traditional concentric circle model suggests that the country seeks to exert ideological dominance within its own territory. However, for nations beyond its borders, the objective is not dominant but rather to cultivate positive international impressions, with the intent to ward off challenges to the Chinese ideology. Furthermore, historical examples, presented in Chap. 6, also show that exerting control over diverse ethnic groups or pursuing colonisation requires substantial resources, ultimately weakening central power and threatening internal stability. Hence, China's extensive assimilation efforts in regions like Xinjiang and Tibet should not be misconstrued as reflective of its global ambitions. While these actions certainly call for significant attention to human rights issues, they should be understood as distinct strategies aimed at regions within the country that hold vital geostrategic significance for China.

Regarding ideological concerns, which are inherently intricate, I would like to add two points supplementing the geographical perspective. First of all, there is mounting evidence suggesting that as China seeks to enhance its international reputation, it utilises tactics of soft power, encompassing cultural assimilation, media propaganda, and political interference. Nevertheless, these attempts at direct influence have so far remained relatively restrained. One reason is that Western nations can effectively insulate themselves from Chinese influence by implementing laws to counteract political interference, which should assuage prevailing concerns. In addition, China has diverged significantly from the version of communism practised during the reign of the Soviet Union. Notably, there is no direct affiliation between the CCP and any communist parties in Western countries, despite potential ideological similarities. This is different from the situation seen in several countries, including France and Italy, during much of the twentieth century, where communist parties maintained direct connections with Moscow. The CCP has no documented history of systematically organising class action in a foreign country based on shared communist ideologies—such as large-scale infiltration of union movements or sponsorship of general strikes. Consequently, the communist ideological influence led by CCP today is considerably less than it was under the Soviet Union.

A second perspective worth considering involves placing concerns about Chinese ideology challenging Western universalism within a broader historical context. During the Enlightenment era, when Western liberal democratic principles were under debate, China was not only a point of keen interest, but also of considerable admiration. A literary example of this can be found in a famous scene of Voltaire's *Zadig*. During a philosophical debate about the deep structures of the world gathering representatives from across Eurasia, the protagonist extols the viewpoint of the 'man from Cathay' (that is, the Chinese man) as the most rational. By delving further into the history of Western liberal democracy and examining it in greater detail, we might discover many intersections and parallels with the Chinese models. This could help reinterpret these Chinese models not as fundamentally alien, but as variations of Western liberal democracy. Consequently, this understanding can help better conceptualise imaginary fears.

The Impossible Trinity

In addition to geographical constraints discussed earlier, it is also important to take into account China's structural constraints to gain a balanced perspective on imagined fears. These structural constraints could be described as the 'impossible trinity', which means that China faces a trade-off among its geopolitical, economic, and ideological interests and cannot advance all three objectives simultaneously. China finds itself navigating a landscape where advancement in one area could provoke pushback in another, illuminating the intricate dynamics of its global position.

In the era when China's military strength was relatively modest, the world seemed more accommodating to its economic and ideological influence, as it was not viewed as a real threat, particularly to Western democracies. However, we have since moved beyond that era, given China's accelerated military expansion over the past decade. Today, China's enhanced military power not only positions it as a top rival to the United States, but also foregrounds security as the paramount concern in global interactions with China. China's amplified military strength, when leveraged to extend economic influence, gives rise to escalating fear and opposition to China's ideological initiatives. Further, when China aims to bolster its ideological impact, coupled by assertive military posturing, this in turn triggers efforts at economic decoupling to mitigate global dependency on China. The trend is evident in many places, including Australia and the European Union. These structural constraints significantly limit China's capacity to concurrently exert military, economic, and ideological influence, engendering a complex balancing act.

By identifying and better understanding the constraints faced by the Chinese leadership, concerned policy makers and citizens in the international community can be more specific about the nature and extent of the threat they face, and take actions to address it, instead of letting a fearful imagination run loose. Now, I will close the argument on China's dynamic constraints by exploring one final provocation: What if we were to imagine 'the end of China'?

Imagining 'the End of China'

The above discussion on legitimate and imaginary fears about China as well as China's dynamic constraints are based on the presumption that China continues to exist as a one-party, CCP-led, and centralised state. However, beyond all that has been discussed, there is one radical option which involves 'the end of China'. In this hypothetical situation, 'the China challenge' would be alleviated by the breakdown of China, and the entire logic discussed in this book would somehow vanish. Now a new question arises: From a global perspective, does 'the end of China' scenario paint a desirable future state of the world, and could it therefore be a valid option to consider—or even a goal to pursue?

This provocative discussion involves two different 'revolutions', which should be carefully distinguished. One is 'the decomposition of China' as a centralised state. Effectively, this scenario suggests that today's China breaks apart and ceases to exist, in a somewhat fast or catastrophic way. This would most likely start with Tibet and Xinjiang, maybe Hong Kong or Macau, then possibly extend to other provinces, up to a complete partition or considerable increase in autonomy for, say, Guangdong, Dongbei, or Shanghai. The other scenario is 'the end of the CCP'. In this scenario, China would remain united within its existing boundaries, but would suddenly be run on a different operating system, as a republican or democratic China. Both scenarios are extreme but not unimaginable. Let us begin the discussion with the scenario of 'the end of the CCP'.

It is not beyond the realm of possibility to envision a regime change beyond the CCP. There is no denying that within China, there exist diverse and debated perspectives concerning the Party's legitimacy and its governance model. However, in the near to intermediate future, the lack of a robust and reliable substitute presents a major obstacle to this scenario. There are four distinct aspects to consider in this regard.

Firstly, there is a noticeable absence of a powerful, organised, alternative leadership. Despite China housing eight major democratic parties, which wield their influence through the Chinese People's Political Consultative Conference, these parties essentially act as a facade, given their lack of substantive power and leadership. These democratic parties differ fundamentally from the opposition parties found in Western democracies. Their primary objective is to collaborate with the CCP, adhering to principles of "long-term coexistence, mutual supervision, treating each other with full sincerity, and sharing weal and woe".[1] This means they review policy proposals, pose questions to refine these proposals, and occasionally propose alternatives, but they hold no decision-making authority, nor any possibility of rising to power within the current framework. Thus, these parties are more accurately seen as components of the CCP consultative apparatus.

Secondly, there is no powerful substitute for the CCP-cultivated elite force. As discussed in Chap. 5, a large number of the best talents nationwide are actively participating in the CCP, by joining the Party as well as passing the National Civil Service Exam, and seizing job opportunities within the system. The CCP has been instrumental in harmonising and standardising all bureaucratic entities within China while establishing common standards of conduct, norms, and values. These have become deeply entrenched in the majority of China's elite class. Those who hold power today have risen by adhering to these standards and norms, which predisposes

---

[1] Central Government of People's Republic of China (2020).

them to support the system, seeking enhancements and reforms from within rather than attempting to overthrow it.

Thirdly, there are no reliable alternative armed forces. As discussed in Chap. 5, 'the Party directs the Guns', meaning the military is fully controlled by the CCP. Given the long tradition of centralisation in China's military power and the CCP's tight control over the police force, the probability that they will betray the CCP and suddenly start a revolution is relatively remote. A more plausible scenario, in the event of ongoing and profound dissatisfaction, would be for them to compel a change in the top leadership rather than dismantle the entire system. Also, given Beijing's control over gun ownership—even knives—among ordinary citizens, and with strict surveillance measures, it is extremely difficult for ordinary citizens to form a sizeable armed force.

Last but not least, there is no formidable domestic opposition to the CCP. Despite increasing dissatisfaction with the CCP, a significant number of Chinese citizens firmly believe that dismantling the Party immediately would lead to chaos and the fragmentation of China, which they view as an unfavourable outcome. The basis for this belief extends beyond the patriotic education and propaganda propagated by the CCP. As discussed in Chap. 2, it also stems from the 'implicit contract' between the citizens and the CCP. Under this arrangement, the public supports the regime as long as they continue providing improved living standards. Overall, although imagining 'the end of the CCP' scenario is possible, the birth of an alternative force would be vital for a successful transition. At present, such forces are not in sight and would need time to materialise.

Now, let us turn to the scenario of 'the decomposition of China'. Chinese history has witnessed some significant periods of decomposition, particularly during the Warring States period. Mainstream historical narratives often associate these times with chaos and suffering, fostering a sense of fear and dismissal towards the idea of fragmentation among people. Nevertheless, determining the complete accuracy of this perception is challenging. As underscored in Chap. 1, our grasp of reality during these decomposition eras is constrained due to the paucity of evidence, in stark contrast with the plentiful records from unified periods. In light of pressing global issues that require collective action—climate change, nuclear proliferation, and the regulation of artificial intelligence—if China was to transition to a realm of independent and highly autonomous provinces, a new question would need to be raised. Could a fragmented China be capable of offering coordinated and robust responses to these critical global matters, or would fragmentation merely introduce further complexities?

In reality, the prospect of China disintegrating in a rapid or 'catastrophic' manner is unlikely given the present circumstances, which are notably different from historical periods of fragmentation. There is a lack of powerful separatist movements within the country, including in provinces like Guangdong, Yunnan, or Sichuan. The most significant fragmentation risk lies with Xinjiang and Tibet. This prompts us to contemplate whether a potential independence of Xinjiang and Tibet could be a desirable outcome in the foreseeable future, with regards to shared global challenges.

On the one hand, an independent Xinjiang and Tibet could potentially ease geopolitical tensions over contested resources, such as water, mineral resources, and renewable energy. On the other hand, as highlighted in Chap. 6, Xinjiang and Tibet's critical geostrategic importance attracts not only China's desire for control, but potentially that of other nations too. The only practical alternative to Chinese control would be neutrality. The crucial issue is whether the current uncertain international landscape would permit these regions to maintain their independence and neutrality, or whether a power vacuum would trigger severe power disputes, thereby amplifying global geopolitical uncertainties.

As former U.S. President Richard Nixon reminded us, coming to grips with the reality of China "means distinguishing carefully between long-range and short-range policies, and fashioning short-range programs so as to advance our long-range goals".[2] While both scenarios mentioned above are conceivable, albeit extreme—namely the replacement of the CCP with a different regime or the fragmentation of China—the current conditions do not seem ripe for their occurrence. Consequently, counting on them as primary options to address 'the China challenge' appears unrealistic.

Viewed from the 'dynamic constraints' perspective, it is crucial to acknowledge enduring limitations, such as China's geography and historical norms. However, it is equally important to understand that these constraints possess inherent dynamics. These flexible dynamics provide a realistic starting point when evaluating potential lines of action, their feasibility, necessary efforts, and success likelihood. Shifting perspectives in this manner can widen the spectrum of strategic options, enhancing the pool of possible lines of action and thus offering a pathway to reclaim agency and influence.

Points of Influence: Increase Strategic Options

To uncover the flexible dynamics within the Chinese system, it is essential to grasp the intricacies of the country's institutional power structures. As explained in Chap. 1, China's geography has fostered a durable centralisation of power, which is reinforced by a comprehensive political institutional framework and a meritocratic system for cultivating government officials to safeguard it. These measures are designed to uphold a unified governance system throughout the nation, imposing constraints on the Chinese leadership. Nevertheless, there are also flexibilities within the system. In fact, three key mechanisms can be leveraged to advantageous effect in this domain.

Firstly, as elaborated in Chap. 5, there is an active power dynamic between the Chinese central and local governments, which greatly shapes Beijing's decision-making. The flexibility of local implementation across different levels of government, from provincial to township level, makes it possible to trial new projects or create counter-powers to influence the central government, without challenging

---

[2] Nixon (1969).

the underlying centralised one-party system. If local officials stand to gain from a joint project with foreign partners, they could become local 'agents', advocating for domestic engagement with the West to fulfil economic targets and performance indicators. Successful local projects can create confidence and know-how, prompting a self-reinforcing positive loop. They can also be used as successful case studies to create spillover to other provinces and promote a bottom-up approach to influence the central level.

Secondly, as discussed in Chap. 4, the Chinese governance system can be seen as a fusion of the rule of ritual, the rule of law (Legalism), and the rule of virtue. A persistent constraint within this model is that, despite the emphasis on a well-established 'rule of law', it remains susceptible to shortcomings stemming from the 'rule of man'. This constraint reflects a challenge for external parties to engage China in a systemic and transparent way. However, strong personal features in decision-making mean flexibility to impact the people in power on a personal level through direct connections and/or by identifying their individual priorities. As mentioned earlier, these efforts should be focused particularly on engaging directly with Xi Jinping, considering his unparalleled control over every facet of China's governance.

Thirdly, as discussed in Chap. 5, the stringent one-party system significantly constrains China's decision-making process, often resulting in concerns over irrational decisions. Despite the inherent challenges for external parties to influence a decision before it is finalised, or attempt to reverse it after it has been made, opportunities remain to shape a decision by directing the specifics of its execution. This is particularly viable, given that China's standard approach involves making fairly general policy decisions initially, with the finer details worked out during the execution phase through various consultative processes. Such a method provides flexibility to adjust the plan in response to evolving circumstances anticipated over time. This approach also allows flexibility from external sources to shape the direction and outcomes of the decision at the implementation stage. For example, China has committed to the Paris Agreement and has set its sights on becoming carbon neutral by 2060. While the broad policy of reducing carbon emissions is set, the details of how this is achieved are flexible. International partners could engage with China on developing green technologies, offering technical expertise, or financial mechanisms, thereby influencing the specifics of China's transition to a green economy.

The approach proposed above should be acknowledged as being neither excessively audacious nor bold. Instead, it is predominantly centred on the principle of 'doing small things'. Navigating the uncertain transition period involves a paradox at the core: it calls for both boldness and caution. In an age of interlinked human security threats, we need a bold agenda to match the magnitude of the challenges at stake, put forward with humility in the face of the unknown. Meanwhile, we must also tread softly, and take careful steps to manage the current transition phase, in a context of radical uncertainty.

Invent the Future: Solving the China Challenge in a Global Context

- **Reconceptualising growth and security**

The previous discussions were focused on managing the present transitional phase. The subsequent discussion will delve into the second mission at hand: inventing the future. I would like to humbly suggest the possibility of a new approach, if only as a provocation. I would term this 'solving the China challenge in a global context' by instigating a paradigm shift. I would go as far as proposing this paradigm shift as the key action that needs to be taken if we are to imagine and build a positive new future.

This approach of 'solving the China challenge in a global context' implies that the primary goal of U.S. or Western policy on China should focus on shaping the environment into which China emerges, rather than seeking to contain its growth.[3] It suggests that this effort should extend beyond just shaping China's immediate geopolitical and security surroundings by applying stricter controls like augmenting military presence around China or intensifying trade sanctions. While such tactics could establish a credible deterrent, they also risk being perceived by Beijing as external powers exploiting China's geographical limitations to take bolder military actions. It may also encourage China into retreating by cutting off connections with the developed liberal world.

The approach of 'solving the China challenge in a global context' suggests that the effort to shape China's external environment should also be aligned with responses to emerging systemic issues shared by all, rather than concentrating solely on the actions of individual actors. Given China's deep integration into the global ecosystem, tackling China as an isolated problem, without addressing concurrent global issues, could potentially lead to counterproductive results. The possible repercussions could be severe, from environmental degradation and displacement of climate refugees to proliferation of weapons empowered by artificial intelligence. Such circumstances call for global paradigm shifts, fostering the emergence of innovative thinking and new models.

To unpack the essence of this approach, let us start by reviewing why the global paradigm needs to be shifted. Arguably, at the root of the various global challenges we face today are two phenomena. The first has to do with what is known variously as the Anthropocene, the environmental crisis, or climate change. The other factor relates to the emergence and impact of artificial intelligence and technological disruption. These developments bring forth challenges to fundamental concepts underpinning contemporary multilateralism: growth and security.

From the perspective of growth, over the past two centuries, the long-term trajectory of economic output has been unequivocally positive, leading to unprecedented job creation, investment, and wealth. However, the unprecedented level of globalisation has challenged the underlying assumption behind economic growth, as measured

---

[3] Burns (2019).

by GDP. GDP's foundational assumption posits that the economy is an independent network that connects autonomous individuals, organisations, and states through temporary contractual agreements. This view neglects to consider the significant and immeasurable exchanges that occur among interdependent individuals, countries, and ecosystems in our globalised age. Further, GDP alone does not offer a complete view of sustainability, as it does not adequately evaluate whether our current lifestyle is sustainable or whether we are guaranteeing an adequate quantity and quality of resources for the well-being of future generations.[4]

Economic policies focusing solely on GDP growth could compromise societal stability over time and potentially escalate geopolitical tensions. This is especially crucial in the context of climate change and environmental risks that have not only exacerbated social divisions and inequalities but also intensified geopolitical conflicts among nations vying for limited natural resources, including fresh water, arable land, and energy sources.

From the perspective of security, it is essential to shift the focus of security strategy from geopolitical rivalry towards future-readiness. The notion of peace is currently challenged in two respects. On the one hand, we are witnessing intensified military, technological, and political competition. Major global and regional players are increasingly engaging in military deterrence, hindering cooperation on global issues. On the other hand, emerging existential security risks, such as environmental risks and artificial intelligence disruption, are insufficiently addressed by existing international multilateral institutions and legal arrangements.

These challenges hold two significant implications. Firstly, the rise of non-traditional security threats necessitates integrating forward-thinking elements into the concept of security, moving past the traditional notion of a state's military defence against external threats.[5] Secondly, the transformation of security risks—characterised by their global, systemic, and interconnected nature—has redefined the interplay between nations. This change challenges the long-established Westphalian model, whereby the world is composed of separate nation-states, each possessing distinct independence and autonomy.[6] This shift towards a more global perspective on security also calls for a reassessment of geographical considerations, making the idea of 'siloed security' obsolete. Put simply, in our profoundly interconnected world, the security of one nation is inextricably tied to the security of other nations, as well as to overall global security.

Therefore, national and international security policies can only be effective when they reflect the global interconnectedness of the security landscape. However, security issues are often categorised and handled in silos, disregarding the possibility of unintended consequences and exacerbating other problems.[7] For example, policies intended to bolster national security can spark arms races and hegemonic endeavours,

---

[4] Stiglitz et al. (2010).
[5] Australian Security Leaders Climate Group (2021).
[6] Tapia et al. (2022).
[7] Ibid.

which not only escalate the military's carbon footprint but can also divert resources from human necessities and environmental conservation.[8]

Similarly, efforts to secure economic security through stricter control over resources like energy, oil, and water can intensify resource rivalry and escalate state conflicts, further undermining the development prospects of developing nations and accelerating to instability in unexpected ways. Furthermore, policies centred on food security can inadvertently exacerbate climate change, pollution, and biodiversity loss, particularly through deforestation and the adoption of single-crop agricultural practices.[9] Hence, it is critically essential to adopt the notion of human security and implement a broad collective security measure that goes beyond conventional defence expenditure. This approach should consider the interrelatedness among individuals, along with the complex links between people, the environment, and technology.[10]

- **The growth and security nexus**

It is crucial to understand the interconnected nature of these two concepts—growth and security. As long as growth remains materially oriented, it requires secure access to resources and unimpeded transit across land and sea routes. This inevitably breeds security concerns, leaving resource-rich areas and those adjacent to crucial access points, such as Xinjiang, Taiwan, or the South China Sea, vulnerable to potential conflict. Conversely, if security is equated with increased military deployments and weaponry to protect national territories, it demands more funding and resources to support the costs of soldiers, tanks, planes, and submarines. This scenario creates a 'spiral of doom', where growth is necessary to finance the military, and the military is crucial to maintain the conditions for growth.

In today's fiercely competitive global landscape, it is clear that the logic of military-economic competition has resurfaced as a significant motivator for many nations, diverting resources away from societal, environmental, and human-focused sectors. These trends are skewing economic globalisation and encouraging the exploitation of interdependence for economic leverage and hybrid warfare. Consequently, regional and global military build-up is on the rise, while arms control and non-proliferation systems are on the decline, leaving key players ill-equipped to lessen the risks of military escalation.

In light of the above discussion, it is evident that shaping the environment to guide China's future trajectory—rather than treating China as the sole problem—through a multilateral approach and within a shared global risk context might prove more advantageous. This strategy offers more prudence, could temper bilateral reactions, and might encourage China to give more serious consideration to international perspectives when responding to perceived threats. Moreover, it could widen the strategic alternatives available to China, thereby diminishing the allure of isolation, and instead encourage China to remain part of a global consensus, yielding benefits for all parties involved.

---

[8] Ibid.

[9] Ibid.

[10] Australian Security Leaders Climate Group (2021).

Let us explore how this approach may appear in practice. As elaborated in Chap. 4 Confucianism places the principle of reciprocity at the core of its governance philosophy. This suggests that China's actions are driven not only by its own ambitions and interests but also by the evolving dynamics of the outside world and its interactions with it. On the economic front, a collective and global reenvisioning of new economic models would instigate a normative transition and prompt China to adapt its legitimacy benchmarks. The affirmation of the CCP's legitimacy has largely hinged on economic prosperity, underlining the need to achieve various yearly key performance indicators (KPIs) in the Government Work Report. In the early days of the PRC, the Government Work Report primarily focused on GDP growth. However, in line with China's domestic evolution and global shifts, other elements have been incorporated over the years, such as advancements in higher education, biodiversity preservation, and innovation competitiveness. In light of the global focus on climate change in recent years, Chinese leaders have also adjusted their stance on the issue. They have been integrating considerations such as carbon emissions, carbon offsets, and strategies for achieving peak carbon emissions by 2030 into their Government Work Report since 2021. This action offers hope that global paradigm shifts can effectively influence China's strategy and priorities.

Similarly, and more ambitiously, if the world collectively reconceptualises a future-proof security concept and enables a paradigm shift on shared security risks, it is even possible to envision China establishing connections between its internal (national) and external (international) security policies in the Government Work Report, encompassing areas like climate, terrorism, energy, technology, cybersecurity, and food security. Going one step further, could we foresee China extending its security KPIs beyond defence expenditure to include contributions to regional stability and nuclear proliferation prevention? To enable this development, the message to China should be that the West is not trying to counter China's growing influence out of fear, but rather welcomes China's expanding contributions to address shared global challenges. In this context, the West should strive to persuade China that embracing a robust paradigm shift serves its best interests in achieving its goal of national rejuvenation, rather than viewing such paradigm shifts, like climate change, as geopolitical tools to counter Western influence.

Why Paradigm Shifts Are Difficult

While it is easy to talk about shifting paradigms—or consider the benefits of doing so—actually undoing any model that people have long grown used to is serious hard work in the best of times. There are three primary challenges.

Lack of know-how. The world currently finds itself in unprecedented situations, defining a new and complex reality—a period of transition and chaos. A notable hurdle is our limited comprehension of possible chains of causation—taking the form of uncertainty as to what events might trigger what specific outcomes and with what probability.[11] Further, there is also a lack of clear, tested, consensus-based strategies or models to discern variables and indicators that could meaningfully reshape security and growth, especially those taking into account the global context and future implications. Consequently, clear policy insights or frameworks that dissect and unpack the complex dynamics at play, aid leaders in prioritising different actions, or even pinpoint the initial steps required, are scarce.[12] In the case of enabling a paradigm shift in engaging with China, one of the hurdles is limited models for accurately assessing China's global role and contributions, for example, quantifying the value of avoided catastrophic risks. Therefore, it becomes challenging to calibrate our responses appropriately to China's development.

Limited cognitive capacities. There is little indication that a new paradigm can be put in place without a major overhaul of deeply held beliefs. Accumulated expertise and deeply internalised thought patterns all stand in the way. One critical cognitive limitation is that, although we have lived in a globalised world for decades, our mode of thinking tends to remain national by default. This means that people outside of China are closely attuned to potential threats posed by China to the national interest, while its potential contribution to the global good—positive or negative—is less readily perceived. At the same time, whether among ordinary people or political and business leaders, people in all positions are all too often overwhelmed and exhausted, because there is so much more to consider today than there seems to have ever been before. There is an abundance of data and information available, yet we lack reliable sense-making tools, and we certainly lack the widespread capacity to interpret situations accurately. This holds true for China, as it does for critical shared challenges.

Political expediency/incentives. There is a trade-off between the incentive to please the domestic audience, and efforts to drive important multilateral changes. In democratic countries, the election system is not properly incentivised to drive the latter, which tends to be less well understood and yields fewer electoral benefits. In other words, leaders are generally constrained by their local mandate. Additionally, the election cycle limits their capacity to formulate and commit to a long-term strategy. Their incentives are skewed towards concentrating on the upcoming budget cycle rather than addressing crucial issues that span decades. Consequently, they often opt to confront China assertively to score domestic political points, rather than investing efforts in fostering a long-term paradigm shift externally that would cultivate a more positive contribution from China.

Adding to this complexity, there is mounting evidence indicating a growing tendency for individuals to lack trust in governmental institutions, especially in regard to their capacity to interpret information and make responsible decisions. As a result, institutions may excessively prescribe conduct, worsening the issue of mistrust.[13] Under such circumstances, it appears that effective leadership is also

---

[11] Kagan (2022).
[12] Ibid.
[13] Tapia et al. (2022).

urgently required to instigate a paradigm shift—although it is uncertain what form this leadership should take. On this note, I would like to propose the following questions as the final provocations and points of reflection.

- Does a possible reconceptualising of sustainable and durable growth create new opportunities to escape the current zero-sum blame game model? And how do we build global consensus around it?
- Does a possible reenvisioning of a future-proof security create new opportunities to escape the current 'destined for war' rhetoric? And how do we do this concretely?
- How can we create a system that motivates political leaders to be responsible for and invest in a common collaborative future rather than just focusing on the present?

These questions highlight that new leadership competencies and capabilities are required, and upskilling is urgent in the context of shared global challenges. It may also be useful to recall the concept of 'rivalry partners' derived from the Chanyuan Treaty as discussed in Chap. 10. In the context of enabling a necessary paradigm shift to tackle shared global challenges, China and the United States could collaborate on the collective endeavour to identify existing know-how, unpack the complex dynamics at play, and develop clear priorities for courses of action, while maintaining healthy competition on their respective competency- and capacity-building.

How Will History Remember Our Century?

Many commentators emphasise the specific challenges of the current times. The discourse of the Anthropocene presents our generation's historical situation as unique and existentially critical. What we do in the coming years may define the entire future trajectory of our species—even its very survival. It is easy to feel overwhelmed when so much rests on our shoulders and give up.

I am not questioning the magnitude of those challenges, nor the historical significance of today. Yet engaging with deep history may invite a somewhat calmer approach to the challenge by prompting acknowledgement that historical responsibility is a human constant. Human history has long been an alternation between peace and war, periods of chaos and order. As Mark Twain reminded us, "History doesn't repeat itself, but it often rhymes." Greater awareness of those patterns may help us negotiate our dire straits, minimise harm, and maintain the possibility of future greatness.

To gain the momentum and drive for this, a useful shift is to adopt a historical perspective, and raise the bold question: How will history remember our century?

I hope that, when future historians write about our century, they will call it a 'golden age'. A golden age not derived from conflicts and destruction that promote military innovation and philosophical thinking, like the Warring States period or seventeenth-century Europe. Rather, a golden age built by courage and wisdom, that can transcend our own limitations to explore the full range of possibilities offered by the future. The key to this golden age is how we choose to influence the future of China. This book, I hope, will invite its readers to think hard on the question, and nurture hope that peaceful solutions can be found.

References

Australian Security Leaders Climate Group (2021) Missing in action: Responding to Australia's climate & security failure. Available at: https://www.aslcg.org/wp-content/uploads/2021/09/ASLCG_MIA_Report.pdf. Accessed 28 February 2022.

Burns W (2019) William J. Burns, "The Back Channel." In: Politics and Prose. Available at: https://www.youtube.com/watch?v=y9ILXTbVO7Q. Accessed 22 July 2022.

Central Government of People's Republic of China (2020) Bada mingzhu dangpai. Available at: http://www.gov.cn/guoqing/2017-12/31/content_5269697.htm. Accessed 20 April 2021.

Kagan R (2022) The price of hegemony, can America learn to use its power? In: Foreign Affairs. Available at: https://www.foreignaffairs.com/articles/ukraine/2022-04-06/russia-ukraine-war-price-hegemony. Accessed 10 December 2022.

Nixon R (1969) Congressional record: Proceedings and debate of the 91st Congress. Vol 115. United States Government Printing Office, Washington D.C. p.2384.

Stiglitz J et al (2010) Mismeasuring our lives: Why GDP doesn't add up. The New Press, New York.

Tapia H et al (2022) New threats to human security in the anthropocene: Demanding greater solidarity. UNDP, New York.

Index

A

Abe no Nakamaro, 176
Academic freedom, 184
Academics, 6, 88. *See also* intellectuals
Acheson, Dean, 146
Activism, 137
Aden, 130
Advanced management systems, 199
Advanced manufacturing, 43
Aerospace, 42, 76, 224
Aerospace Group/Cosmic Club, 76
Afghanistan, 111, 115, 116, 226
African metal mining, 226
Ageing population, 28
Age of Exploration, 135
Aggressive stance/action, 28, 121, 123, 208, 237
Agrarian (society), 6–9, 21, 40, 98, 216
Agriculture, 5, 8–10, 18, 21, 22, 39, 40, 98, 99, 216
Aircraft carrier, 116, 140, 141, 144, 146, 147
Air Defence Identification Zone (ADIZ), 142
Airstrips, 151
Alcohol, 42
Aleutian Islands, 143
Alibaba Group, 37
Alipay, 37
All-China Federation of Industry and Commerce, 77
Alliances, 5, 11, 30, 73, 104, 107, 119, 121, 139, 149, 154, 155, 165, 222, 229
Allocation of resources, 42, 44
Ambassadors, 170
Ambivalence, 171, 213, 221, 227

Amphibious warfare, 140, 141
Anatolia, 106
Angola, 117
An Lushan Rebellion, 78
Annam, 176, 182
Annamese Range, 103
Antagonistic, 123, 154
Antarctica, 114
Ant financial, 36, 37
Ant Group, 36–38
Anthropocene, 215, 247, 252
Anti-Access/Area Denial, 139, 143, 144
Anti-ballistic missile defence system, 118
Anti-corruption campaign, 28, 29, 202
Anti-extradition protests, 137
Anti-tradition, 65
Anti-Western sentiment, 237
Arabian Sea, 152
Arable land, 10, 11, 112, 132, 248
Arab region, 150
Arab Spring, 23
Arctic Ocean, 114, 128
Aristocracy/aristocrats, 62
Armed conflict, 107, 118, 147, 165
Arms race, 150, 158, 221, 222, 232, 248
Army/armed forces, 7, 77, 78, 101, 102, 106, 108, 117, 206, 244. *See also* People's Liberation Army
Arsenal, 115, 149
Art/arts, 104, 182, 231, 237
Artificial intelligence, 30, 67, 116, 158, 221, 235, 244, 247, 248
Artificial sun, 225
Asia, 54, 101, 110, 114, 117–121, 128, 132, 140, 145, 147, 148, 150–152, 164,

© The Editor(s) (if applicable) and The Author(s), under exclusive license to Springer Nature Singapore Pte Ltd. 2023
J. Dong, *Chinese Statecraft in a Changing World*,
https://doi.org/10.1007/978-981-99-6453-6

255

169, 172–174, 181, 182, 205, 218, 238
Asia Minor, 106
Assertiveness, 207, 241
Assimilation, 106, 175, 180, 181, 241
Assured retaliation, 115
Athens, 206, 217
Atlantic Ocean, 128, 131, 153
Atomic bomb, 220. *See also* nuclear power
AUKUS pact, 222
Australia, 10, 119, 165, 184, 192, 222, 239, 242
Austria, 113, 206
Authenticity, 184
Authoritarianism, 223
Authority, 20, 21, 36, 38, 40, 42, 47, 54, 57, 59, 72, 79, 81–86, 108, 122, 147, 167, 178, 191, 195, 199, 202, 207, 220, 232, 243
Autocracy, 71. *See also* despotism, dictatorship
Autonomous regions, 4, 12
Autonomous weapon systems, 221–223
Autonomy, 12, 22, 56, 82, 111, 112, 137, 146, 148, 166, 169, 171, 222, 243, 244, 248
Autumn Harvest Uprisings, 78

B

Balancing act, 156
Balkans, The, 115, 178
Bangladesh, 153
Banks, 37, 82, 128
Barbarians, 53, 102, 168, 175–177
Barley, 165
Barnett, Correlli, 206
Basic living conditions, 10, 21, 24, 25
Battleships, 133
Bay of Bengal, 153
Beef, 165
Beijing (place), 22, 24, 28, 47, 74, 75, 86, 90, 102, 109, 112, 114, 115, 118, 119, 121, 123, 132, 137, 139, 143, 146, 149, 151, 152, 155–157, 177, 193, 204, 222, 226, 236, 240, 241, 247
Beiyang fleet, 133
Belgium, 113
Belgrade, 116
Belt and Road Initiative, 111
Benevolence, 57, 61, 62
Bengal, 7

Berlin, 180
Bias, 224, 239
Big data, 224
Bilateral, 47, 109, 182, 192, 205, 219, 236, 249
Biological warfare, 220
Biotechnology, 76
Birdcage economy, 38
Birth rate, 27
Blinken, Anthony, 232
Blockade, 130, 135, 137, 139, 140, 142
Bolivia, 46, 226
Border markets, 164, 166
Border security, 102, 240
Bottom-up approach, 246
Boycott, 165. *See also* sanctions
Brahmaputra, 114
Brazil, 10
British, 135, 137, 196, 203, 206
(British) East India Company, 105, 132
British Houses of Parliament, 58
British India, 105
Broadband, 223
Bronze smelting, 102
Brother state, 170
Buffer states, 11, 100, 102, 111, 112, 121
Bureaucracy, 47, 63, 72, 74, 75, 77, 84, 85, 101, 105, 132, 133, 167, 200, 201
Bureaucrats, 29, 42, 60, 74, 76, 85, 91
Business leaders/businessmen, 35, 39–42, 66, 73, 86, 91, 98, 105, 132, 186, 251

C

Cadres, 63, 74, 75
Cai (kingdom), 62
Calendar, 57, 216
Cambodia, 105, 151
Canada, 10, 108, 181, 184
Cape of Good Hope, 152
Capital, 12, 36–38, 40–42, 44, 45, 59, 66, 100, 129, 132, 133, 177, 200, 201, 225, 227
Capitalism, 43, 201
Capitalists, 35, 39–42, 66, 67, 73, 105, 199, 200, 203, 204
Carbon emissions, 114, 226, 246, 250
Carbon footprint, 249
Carbon neutral, 114, 246
Carbon offsets, 250
Carbon tariffs, 227
Caribbean Sea, 152, 154
Carrots and sticks approach, 55

Index 257

Carthage, 128
Catholics, 196
Cattle, 7, 9, 40, 42, 101
CCP, alternative to, 28, 66, 244
CCP, economic accomplishments/
    achievements of, 22, 28
CCP General Secretary, 78
CCP National Congress, 25, 29, 64, 66, 75,
    86, 90, 121–123, 157, 198, 203, 204,
    206
Censorship, 56, 184, 224
Central Asia, 6, 109, 132
Central China, 56
Central Commission for Discipline
    Inspection of the CCP, 29
Central Committee of the CCP, 58
Central Economic Work Conference, 59
Centralisation/unification, 11, 12, 60, 71,
    78, 146–149, 156, 177–179, 184,
    197, 244, 245
Centralised power, 3, 13, 18, 35, 55, 57, 67,
    71, 72, 78, 79, 81, 83, 99, 106, 172,
    202, 207, 242, 243, 246
Central Military Commission, 77, 122, 202
Central planning system, 25, 38
Century of humiliation, 133, 136, 194, 197
CEO, 76, 192, 193, 195, 196
Changbai Mountains, 6
Chanyuan Treaty, 230, 231, 252
Chaos, 20, 35, 36, 58, 62, 65, 67, 87, 198,
    216, 229, 230, 232, 236, 244, 250,
    252
Charisma, 28, 29
Checks and balances, 60, 64, 75, 228
Chemical warfare, 220
Chengdu, 12
Chen (kingdom), 62
Chen, Yun, 38
Chess, 194
Chiang, Kai-shek, 113, 145
China National Chemical Corporation, 44
China National Petroleum, 43
China proper, 167, 175, 177, 178, 181
China's aspirations/ambitions, 118, 153,
    154, 157, 182
China's defence, 110
China's embassy, 116
China-US rivalry, 10, 154, 203, 219
Chinese Central Plains, 11, 100, 102, 103,
    121, 176–178
Chinese characters, 179, 180
Chinese Civil War, 193

Chinese Communist Party (CCP), 10, 17,
    21–25, 27–31, 35, 44, 47, 51, 56, 57,
    60, 63–67, 75–78, 84, 86–88, 108,
    111, 113, 122, 145–149, 157, 179,
    183–185, 195, 196, 198–204, 206,
    238, 240–245, 250
Chinese dream, 203, 204
Chinese ethnicity, 177
Chinese People's Political Consultative
    Conference, 243
Chinese Red Army, 77
Chinese traditions/customs, 40, 60, 63, 67
Chongqing model, 23
Christianity, 53
Chu (kingdom), 62
Cinnabar, 41
Civic rights, 53
Civil law, 59
Civil liberties, 137, 180
Civil servants, 74
Civil war, 78, 82, 147, 149, 215
Clans, 5, 130, 166, 167, 176
Class action, 241
Class conflict, 51, 66
Cleanliness, 75
Client states, 97, 154
Climate, 7, 101, 113, 128, 129, 152, 164,
    221, 225, 229, 232, 235, 250
Climate change, 10, 30, 67, 85, 90, 144,
    175, 219, 225, 244, 247–250
Climate negotiations, 227
Climate refugees, 247
Coal, 41, 42, 114, 165
Coastal areas, 196
Cobalt, 226
Cochabamba, 46
Coexistence, 44, 59, 97, 108, 169, 243
Cognitive warfare, 224
Cohesion, 122, 163, 169, 238
Colbert, Jean-Baptiste, 199
Cold war, 108, 115, 138, 150, 153, 157,
    191, 192, 218, 228
Collective action, 244
Collective duty, 53
Collective security, 3, 11, 12, 249
Collectivised land, 22
Colonised peoples, 215
Coloured people, 215
Columbus, 130, 131
Combat experience, 115, 121
Combat vessels, 130. *See also* battleships
Commerce, 5, 40, 78, 85, 86, 166, 173
Commercial laws, 41

Commodity trading, 105
Common prosperity, 23, 66
Communism, 185, 241
Comparative advantage, 22, 107
Compass, 102, 130
Competency, 75, 252
Competition, 30, 35, 46, 47, 54, 59, 71, 74, 85, 118, 119, 128, 134, 153, 154, 157, 181, 202, 205, 213, 217, 218, 224, 226–231, 248, 252
Computer chips, 116, 224
Concentric circle model, 241
Confederation, 166, 178
Conflict of interest, 85
Conflict resolution, 97
Conformity, 60, 65
Confrontation, 127, 205
Confucianism, 55, 56, 60–62, 64, 67, 250
Confucianism, criticism of, 74
Confucian scholars, 18
Confucius, 19, 55, 57, 60–62, 182, 184
Confucius Institutes, 182, 184
Consensus, 12, 20, 86, 87, 122, 181, 196, 200, 218, 220, 223, 230, 249, 251, 252
Consent, 82, 181
Conservative (worldview), 97, 99, 123
Construction projects, 86
Consultative process, 86, 89, 246
Consumption (of goods), 10, 52
Contradiction, 45, 47, 58, 66, 187, 230. *See also* paradox
Control, excessive, 47, 103
Convergence, 108, 169, 181
Cooperation, 5, 85, 91, 108, 110, 146, 164, 166, 169, 172, 173, 204, 205, 227, 231, 248
Copper, 41
Corn, 9
Corruption, 28, 29, 42, 194, 197, 201, 202, 226, 239
Counties, 13, 72, 79, 83, 84
COVID-19 pandemic, 25, 43, 84
Creativity, 220
Criminal law, 19, 59
Crops, 9, 22, 40, 249
Cuba, 153
Cultural appropriation, 28
Cultural exchanges, 12
Cultural influence, 163, 164, 175, 179, 182
Cultural revolution, 24, 30, 64, 65, 184, 193, 198, 199

Culture, 4, 11, 53, 57, 65–67, 98, 107, 137, 175–177, 179–186, 194, 198, 199, 216, 230, 237
Culture, as a construct, 184
Cybersecurity, 250
Cyberspace, 134
Cyberspace Administration of China, 38
Cyber warfare, 116
Cyclical view (of history), 213–216, 227–230, 232

D

Da Gama, Vasco, 131
Dance, 53
Darfur, 101
Data, 8, 43, 77, 111, 157, 174, 186, 201, 223, 224, 238, 251
D-Day, 141, 142
De Albuquerque, Afonso, 131
Deaths/fatalities, 7, 21, 59, 84, 104, 112, 131, 198
Debt, China's, 25, 26, 226
Decarbonisation, 225
Decentralisation, 78, 180
Decision-making, 12, 17, 35, 39, 51, 52, 64, 71, 74, 77, 79, 86–91, 98, 191, 194, 201, 217, 224, 227, 239, 243, 245, 246
Decline (of dynasty), 17, 57, 78
Decomposition of China, 243, 244
Decoupling (with China), 10, 28, 47, 121, 144, 236, 237, 242
Defence spending/expenditure/budget, China's, 25, 26, 28, 83, 102, 108, 110, 134, 148, 150, 157, 172, 174, 182, 218, 250
Defence spending, Japan's, 172, 173
Defence spending, US, 134
Deglobalisation, 219
Deliberation, 87
Democracy, 24, 54, 62, 66, 67, 86, 148, 230, 239, 241, 242
Democratic Progressive Party of Taiwan, 148
Democratic Republic of the Congo, 226
Demographic shift, 27
Deng, Xiaoping, 23, 30, 65, 89, 135, 193–205, 207
De-risking (with China), 28, 121
Descent, 171, 176
Despotism, 6, 53, 64
Deterrence, 107, 122, 123, 127, 166, 228, 248

Index 259

De Tocqueville, Alexis, 63
Developed nations, 10, 227
Developing countries, 10, 21, 223, 225–227, 232
Dialectical materialism, 67
Dialects, 178–180
Dialogue, 214, 236, 238
Diaspora, 55, 183, 184
Dictatorship, 21, 62. *See also* despotism
Didi (company), 38
Digital power, 223
Digital technology, 223
Digital totalitarianism, 221, 223, 224
Dikotter, Frank, 21
Dilemma, 46, 57, 58, 72, 147, 173, 202
Diligence, 75
Ding, Xuexiang, 76
Diplomacy, 54, 71, 88, 158, 229
Disaster relief, 19
Disruption, 8, 11, 25, 99, 103, 121, 132, 173, 186, 213–215, 227, 229, 235, 237, 238, 247, 248
Dissent, 47, 55, 137
Diversification, 21, 47, 151
Diversity, 66, 71
Division/fragmentation of power, 5, 12, 13, 78, 106, 113, 119, 221, 230, 248
Djibouti, 117, 153
Domestic demand, 43
Dongbei, 243
Dong, Zhongshu, 60
Droughts, 7, 12, 19, 99, 101, 102, 164
Dujiangyan Irrigation System, 6
Duke of Zhou, 166
Dukes, 229
Dutch, 21, 105, 132, 135, 148
Dutch East India Company, 105, 132
Dynasties, Chinese, 7, 9, 17, 18, 28, 40, 52, 76, 111, 112, 172, 176, 177, 231
Dzungar Khanate, 103, 132

E
East Africa, 130
East Asia, 101, 132, 147, 152, 164, 172, 182
East China Sea, 6, 116
Eastern Europe, 30
Ecology, 17, 29, 31
E-commerce, 36, 37
Economic downturn, 218
Economic/financial stability, 82
Economic governance, 35, 42, 45
Economic influence, 43, 117, 235, 242

Economic liberalisation, 193, 201
Economic reform, 43, 195, 202
Economic security, 135, 136, 151, 238, 249
Economic slowdown, 157
Education, 24, 25, 43, 60–62, 74, 157, 182, 184, 186, 196, 231, 244, 250
Efficiency, 20, 21, 29, 44, 46, 57, 65, 83
Egypt, 4, 7, 98, 99, 123
Eighth Route Army, 77
Elections, 45, 66, 86, 251
Electricity, 25, 42, 114
Electric vehicles, 175, 226
Electromagnetic space, 134
Electronic warfare, 149
Elite class, 23, 61, 62, 76, 196, 197, 199, 200, 207, 243
Emotions, 53, 63, 193
Emperor(s), 8, 9, 17–19, 28, 30, 39–41, 56–58, 60, 62, 72, 73, 76, 78, 79, 82, 83, 102, 106, 132, 156, 167, 169, 170, 197, 227
Employment, 8, 43, 86, 157
End-user interests, 46
Energy generation, 114
Energy resources, 114
Energy security, 226
Energy transition, 225, 226
Enfeoffment model, 166
Engagement with China, 28, 46, 90, 91, 157
English (language), 40
Entry barriers, 46
Environmental conservation, 249
Environmental degradation/impact, 24, 238, 247
Environmental science, 76
Envoy, 167, 176
Erdogan, Recep Tayyip, 202
Espionage, 231, 239
Ethiopia, 117
Ethnic conflict, 152
Ethnic groups, 78, 100, 105, 111, 178, 241
Euphrates (river), 4, 98
Eurasia, 60, 241
Eurocentrism, 169
Europe, 8, 11, 29, 40, 57, 73, 99, 105, 121, 127, 128, 132, 135, 148, 152, 169, 170, 172, 180, 206, 216, 252
European languages, 40
European union, 181, 242
Evergrande, 26
Exceptionalism, China's, 28, 182
Executive power, 20, 72
Exile, 145, 148, 193

Existential threat, 100, 109, 121, 144, 221
Expectations, people's, 24
Exponential growth, 45
Exports, 174, 201, 222, 226, 240
External pressure/threats, 28, 39, 107, 108, 110, 117, 129, 156, 165, 180, 206, 238, 248
Extremism, 214

F
Facebook, 45
Facial recognition, 224
Fairness, 47, 66, 67, 83
Family lineage, 73
Famine/hunger, 3, 6–9, 11, 12, 18, 21, 132, 220
Far East, 99. *See also* Southeast Asia
Farmers, 3, 8–10, 21, 22, 39, 40, 42, 101, 104, 112, 164
Farmland, 4, 10, 11, 98
Federal system, 180
Feedback, 47, 87, 89, 122, 236, 237
Ferghana, 120
Feudalism, 72
Feuerwerker, Albert, 8
Fighter planes, 140
Film/cinema, 182, 186, 215
Fines, 38, 59, 83
First industrial revolution, 219
First Sino-Japanese War, 133, 145
First World War, 123, 228
Fiscal capacity, 27
Fiscal deficit, 82
Five-Year Plan, 43, 79, 114, 182
Flashpoints, 123, 127, 145, 147, 150, 163, 226
Flexibility, 46, 58, 81, 83, 170, 231, 235, 239, 245, 246
Floating fortresses, 130
Floods, 3–7, 12, 18, 19, 40, 99, 132
Food production, 42
Food security, 8, 10, 17, 232, 238, 249, 250
Food shortages, 10, 21. *See also* famine
Food supply, 8, 21, 39
Foreign aid, 165
Foreign/external influence, 112, 172
Foreign policy, 4, 98, 109, 119, 122, 147, 154, 155, 170, 207, 237
Foreign trade, 43, 129
Forests, 7, 10, 11
Fortifications, 102, 139
Fossil fuels, 175, 216, 219

Four Books and Five Classics, 60
Four Policemen, 192
Fourth industrial revolution, 219
France, 113, 184, 199, 206, 241
Frederick the Great, 199
Freedom of expression/speech, 41, 137
Freedom of navigation, 135, 151
Freedom of the press, 137
Free market, 20, 22, 47
French Revolution, 206
Frigates, 153
Frontier lands, 112
Fujian, 196
Funan, 151
Fuzhou, 133

G
5G, 43, 174, 223
Game theory, 110
Gaozu (emperor), 103, 170
Gas, 46, 114, 153
General Administration of Market Supervision, 59
General Armaments Department, 116
General laws, 58–60
General strikes, 241
Geneva summit, 231
Genocide, 180
Geoeconomics, 164, 165, 238
Geoengineering, 225
Geographical constraints/limitations, 13, 155, 156, 182, 242, 247
Geography, China's, 3, 71, 91, 98, 221, 239, 245
Geography, Europe's, 11
Geopolitics, 165, 217, 226
Geopolitics of fear, 112, 114, 150, 223
Geostrategic, 105, 111, 112, 114, 127, 137, 144–147, 149, 157, 180, 235, 241, 245
Germany, 9, 113, 150, 157, 206, 228
Gifts, 57, 107, 131, 167
Global challenges/threats, 91, 187, 197, 220, 229, 230, 237, 244, 247, 250, 252
Global dominance, 128, 132, 239, 240
Global Financial Crisis (2008), 25, 26, 43, 45
Global influence, 97, 157, 163, 164, 185, 186
Globalisation, 3, 29, 150, 154, 174, 186, 199, 204, 205, 219, 247, 249

Index   261

Global power, 30, 118, 154, 156, 172, 217, 226
Global security, 158, 248
Global South, 226
Global trade, 151, 152, 240
Goguryeo (kingdom), 104, 121
Gold, 41, 99, 174
Gorbachev, Mikhail, 231
Governance, logic of, 4, 42, 45, 51, 52, 55, 60, 62, 64, 67, 98, 185, 213
Government-owned/state land, 201
Government Work Report, 250
Go/weiqi (game), 194
Grain, 8–10, 19, 22, 40, 131, 229
Granaries, 19
Gratitude, 52
Great Depression, 156
Great Leap Forward, 21, 64, 65
Great-power rivalry, 217, 219–221
Great Wall, 11, 12, 102, 164, 176
Greco-Roman era, 98
Greece, 54, 98
Green electricity, 225
Green technologies, 226, 246
Grey-zone, 142
Gridlocked (government), 20
Gross domestic product (GDP), 4, 8, 22, 25, 26, 43, 79, 86, 110, 130, 135, 156, 199, 217, 218, 225, 240, 248, 250
Gross national product (GNP), 204
Guam, 139, 140, 143, 144, 147
Guangdong, 178, 243, 244
Guangdong Model, 23
Guangzhou, 133
Guerra, Alfonso, 203
Guerrillas, 193
Gulf of Mexico, 128
Gulf War, 116
Gun ownership, 244
Gunpowder, 102
Guns, 77, 134, 244
Guotai Junan Securities, 43
Gwadar, 111

H

Habeas corpus, 41
Hakka people, 178
Han Chinese, 98, 100, 113, 137, 146, 177–179
Han dynasty, 8, 9, 40, 41, 52, 60, 73, 100, 102, 104, 111, 112, 129, 164, 197
Hangul, 180

Hangzhou, 38, 129
Harmonious society, 29
Hawaii, 144, 147
Hebei, 178
Hegemony, 31, 97, 99, 110, 128, 181, 203, 220, 227, 228
Henan, 4, 8
Hierarchy, 52–54, 61, 64, 169
High-speed rail network, 12
High-tech, 116
Highway system, 12
Himalayas, 6, 103, 111, 112
Hindu, 130
Historical humiliation, 28. *See also* Century of Humiliation
Hobbes's, Thomas, 55
Homogeneity, 67
Hong Kong, 38, 105, 136, 137, 243
Hongwu (emperor), 104, 105, 137, 194, 197
Honour, 64
Hormuz, 130
Hospitals, 44
Hostility, 157, 175
Household Responsibility System, 22
Housing, 24, 25, 54, 77, 157, 174, 243
Hua (tribe), 178
Huawei, 223
Hui (ethnic group), 179
Hu, Jintao, 29, 66, 193, 194, 200–202
Humanists, 60, 61
Humanities, 61, 62, 215–217, 220–222, 239
Human rights, 112–114, 137, 172, 241
Hunan, 132
Hundred Schools of Thought, 54, 55, 60
Hydraulic engineering, 5, 6
Hydroelectric dam, 114, 117
Hydropower, 114
Hypersonic weapons, 149

I

Identity, 3, 57, 91, 111, 148, 163, 175–181, 183, 185, 193
Ideological alignment, 76, 78, 230, 237, 241
Ideological clashes, 154, 219
Ideological confrontations, 224
Ideological influence, 239, 241, 242
Ideology, 51, 56, 60, 65–67, 86, 173, 179, 183, 200, 227, 238, 241
Image, China's, 182, 192, 237
Imaginary fears, 238, 239, 242
Imperial decrees, 58
Imperial examination system, 71–74, 76

Imperialism, 65, 99, 145
Imports, 98, 153, 174, 227, 240
Incense, 99
Income inequality, 23
India, 99, 105, 111, 112, 114, 118, 130, 132, 150, 153, 155, 180, 229
Indian Ocean, 118, 127, 130–132, 152–154, 226
Indian subcontinent, 6
India's defence budget, 172
Individual/personal freedom, 19, 20, 201
Indochina Peninsula, 152
Indonesia, 105, 138, 151
Indo-Pacific region, 153, 222, 226, 238
Indo-Pacific strategy, 153
Industrialisation, 9, 23, 29, 204
Industrial production, 43
Industrial Revolution, 8, 137, 219
Inequalities/disparity, 23, 28, 52, 84, 121, 174, 186, 199, 200, 223, 232, 248
Infiltration, 239, 241
Inflation, 82
Informal systems, 79, 81
Information and communications technology, 223
Information technology, 116
Infrastructure, 5, 13, 25, 26, 39, 46, 114, 117, 140, 151, 153, 220, 223, 225
Initial Public Offering, 36
Injustice, 20, 25
Innovation, 43, 59, 64, 65, 85, 87, 195, 201, 206, 213, 220, 224, 231, 250
Integrity, 52, 191
Intellectual property, 241
Intellectuals, 18, 54, 65, 66, 87, 177, 183, 184, 217
Interconnect, 7, 31, 45, 214–216, 223, 230, 236, 248, 249
Interdependence, 173, 240, 249
Interests of citizens, 46
Interference, 36, 85, 135, 171, 172, 241
International community, 44, 91, 114, 121, 123, 137, 180, 228, 237, 241, 242
International law, 151
International order, 30, 164, 192, 199, 219, 220
Internet, 36, 38, 182, 224
Internet of Things, 223
Invasion/invaders, 11, 12, 19, 97, 100, 103, 104, 107, 129, 130, 133, 140, 141, 149, 164, 176, 177, 232, 239
Investments, 25–28, 37, 39, 43, 46, 47, 85, 86, 104, 117, 119, 138, 150, 153, 155–157, 165, 173, 196, 201, 222, 223, 225, 226, 240, 241, 247
Iran, 222
Iraq, 115, 116
Iron, 41, 42, 200, 229
Irrigation, 6, 9, 229
Islamic, 130. *See also* Muslim
Island chains, 137, 138, 144
Israel, 123
Italy, 61, 241

J

Japan, 9, 65, 103, 105, 115, 118, 119, 133, 135, 138, 140, 141, 143, 145–148, 150, 154, 157, 167, 171, 172, 177, 180, 182, 185, 199, 218, 222, 228, 229
Japan Maritime Self-Defence Force, 141
Java, 138
Jervis, Robert, 110, 164, 173
Jiang, Zemin, 136, 193, 194, 196, 199, 200, 202, 205
Jin-class (Type 094) submarines, 143
Jing (emperor), 164
Jin regime, 171
Job creation, 247
Job prospects, 24
Joint Comprehensive Plan of Action, 222
Journalists, 88
Judicial power, 20
Junzi, 62
Jurchens, 129, 171
Justice, 17, 24, 67, 226

K

Kang, David, 172
Kanji, 179
Kant, Immanuel, 220
Kazakhstan, 111
Kennan, George, 191
Kenya, 117, 130
Khalkha Mongols, 103
Khitan, 231
King of Zhou, 166, 167
KMT military expenditure, 82
Know-how, 246, 250, 252
Kokand, 171
Korean Peninsula, 7, 155
Korean War, 109, 115, 121, 146
Korean Wave, 182
Kosovo, 116
Kowtow, 170

Index 263

Kuomintang, 30, 77, 82, 113, 145–148, 202
Kuril Islands, 138
Kyrgyzstan, 111

L
Labour, 8, 22, 39, 98, 103, 104, 166, 201
Land power, 128, 129
Land reclamation, 9
Land reform, 22
Land rent, 41
Landward security, 118, 155, 163, 240
Language, 3, 52, 61, 111, 176–180, 182, 184, 196
Language law, 179
Lanzhou, 12
Lanzhou–Xinjiang railway, 12
Law enforcement, 46
Law-policies, 58, 59
Le dynasty (Vietnam), 171
Lee, Kuan Yew, 13, 197
Legalism, 55–57, 61, 64, 227, 246
Legislative power, 20, 72
Legitimate fears, 238, 239
Leipzig, 180
Leninism, 65
Lesser Khingan Range, 6
Lhasa, 12, 171
Lhoba, 111
Liao dynasty, 231
Liberal democracy, 58, 74, 88, 180, 199. *See also* democracy
Liberties, 36. *See also* freedom
Libya, 115
Liechtenstein, 113
Linear view (of history), 215
Line Islands, 143
Li, Qiang, 75
Literature, 180, 182
Lithium, 226
Livelihood(s), 18, 19, 82, 101
Loans, 25, 37
Lobbying system, 218
Local constituencies, 73, 76
Local Government Financing Vehicles, 26
Local governments, 9, 25, 26, 71, 72, 76, 78, 79, 81–84, 86, 174, 245
London, 24
Longmen Mountains, 6
Long-range cruising ships, 130
Love, 52
Lower class, 73
Loyalty, 52, 75, 76, 78, 85, 90, 166, 182

Luoyang, 100
Luxembourg, 113

M
Machiavellianism, 56
Machine learning, 219, 222
Macroeconomics, 43
Maghreb, 99
Magistrates, 19
Mahan, Alfred, 128, 134, 152
Ma, Jack, 38
Major power, 118, 153, 154, 206, 220, 223
Malacca straits, 111, 152
Malaysia, 103, 151
Manchuria, 115, 145, 178
Manchus, 100, 103, 132, 176–179, 217
Mandarin (language), 177, 179, 182, 196
Mandate of Heaven, 18, 20, 25, 30, 194, 196, 229
Manila Trench, 152
Manufacturing, 9, 10, 25, 173, 223, 225
Maoism, 196
Mao, Zedong, 21, 30, 65, 77, 78, 90, 109, 133, 145, 155, 193–195, 197, 198, 202–204
Marginalised groups, 224
Maritime ambition, 155, 163, 240
Maritime Asia, 127
Maritime economic security, 135, 136
Maritime power, 130–132, 155
Maritime trade/commerce, 128–130, 132, 135, 151, 240
Market failures, 46
Market forces, 43, 44. *See also* free market
Marxism, 51, 65–67, 216
Marxism-Leninism, 51, 65
Masks, 44
Mass incidents, 200. *See also* protests
Material well-being/welfare, 19, 28
Mathematics, 98
McCarthyism, 148
Meat, 10
Media, 75, 87, 88, 183, 186, 201, 203, 207, 215, 241
Medical protective equipment, 44
Medical services, 25
Medicine, 84, 98
Mediterranean, The, 7, 98, 128, 151
Meiji Restoration, 199
Mekong (river), 114, 151
Mencius, 19, 60
Meritocracy, 75

Mesopotamia, 7
Micro-lenders, 37
Micro-lending, 37
Micronesia, 143
Middle class, 157, 196
Military bases, 139, 143, 144, 147
Military build-up, 97, 108, 110, 122, 249
Military-economic competition, 249
Military exercises, 118
Military innovation, 120, 121, 123, 222, 252
Military, modernisation of, 155, 238
Military power, 56, 78, 108–110, 122, 151, 156, 239, 242, 244
Military presence, 106, 111, 112, 139, 141, 247
Military Science Research Steering Committee, 222
Military service, 39
Military strategy, 97–99, 101, 102, 107, 108, 115, 116, 119, 121–123
Military technology, 117, 222
Millennials, 24
Mill, John Stuart, 63
Ming dynasty, 9, 73, 100, 104, 105, 130–132, 138, 165, 167, 194, 197, 217
Mining, 8
Ministry of Commerce, 59, 86
Ministry of Ecology and Environment, 85
Ministry of Foreign Affairs, 66, 85
Ministry of National Defense, China, 77
Minjiang River, 6
Minority groups, 179, 180
Misappropriation (of funds), 84
Miscalculations, 223, 236
Misinformation, 45, 239
Missiles, 116, 140, 141, 143, 151, 165, 222
Mistrust (against the private sector), 35, 39–41, 66, 73, 194, 251
Mixed ownership, 44
Mobility (social), 73, 84
Modernisation, 23, 54, 89, 116, 123, 134, 137, 199, 203
Monarch, 18, 64
Mongolia/Mongol, 4, 100, 103, 106, 111, 113, 121, 131, 132, 176, 178, 179, 194, 217
Monopoly, 41, 46, 59, 71, 72
Monpa, 111
Monsoon, 7, 101, 102, 164
Morals/morality, 18, 19, 52, 57, 60–64, 67, 74, 75, 147, 166, 170, 220

Moscow, 30, 149, 171, 191, 241
Mother tongue, 180
Mountain ranges, 6, 11, 103
Multilateral, 47, 181, 205, 223, 236, 240, 248, 249, 251
Multipolarity, 30, 228
Music, 53, 182
Muslim, 111
Mutiny, 78
Mutual Defense Treaty of 1954, 146
Myanmar, 153

N
Nanchang uprising, 78
Nanotechnology, 226
Napoleon, 4, 73, 120, 206
Narrative, 3, 4, 13, 28, 56, 65, 66, 75, 122, 136, 148, 178, 186, 194, 207, 239, 244
National boundaries, 30, 176
National Civil Service Exam, 60, 74, 75, 243
National Development and Reform Commission, 85, 182
Nationalism, 28, 108, 157, 173, 183, 195, 206, 220, 237
Nationalists, 25, 65, 156, 177, 179, 183, 206
National People's Congress (NPC), 58
National People's Congress, Standing Committee, 58
National Revolutionary Army, 77
National security, 110, 115, 137, 157, 174, 180, 248
National Security Law (Hong Kong), 137
National Social Security Fund, 44
Nation-building, 178–180
Natural barriers, 11, 12, 113
Natural disaster, 3, 5, 11, 19, 31, 39, 99, 132
Natural gas, 113, 114, 151
Natural resources, 114, 128, 248
Naval base, 130, 143
Naval presence, 118
Negative feedback loop, 35, 45, 47, 236
Neican, 88
Neolithic, 178
Netherlands, The, 113, 128
Neutrality, 224, 245
New Fourth Army, 77
Newspapers, 88
New World, 130, 216
New York Stock Exchange, 38
New Zealand, 10, 143

Index 265

Nicholas II, 150, 157
Nile, The, 3, 4, 98
Nine-dash line, 151
No. 1 central document, 10
No-first-use policy, 115
Nomads/nomadic, 9, 11, 100–103, 107, 112, 120, 121, 129, 131, 132, 164, 168, 176–178
Nonferrous metals, 42
Non-interference, 169–171, 228
Non-proliferation systems, 249
Non-traditional security threats, 248
Norms, 45, 52, 53, 62, 67, 71, 73, 74, 170, 181, 185, 195, 197, 198, 228, 229, 236, 238, 239, 243, 245. *See also* rules
Northeast Asia, 109
Northeast China, 7
Northern and Southern dynasties, 76
Northern Song dynasty, 230, 231
North Korea, 109, 172, 222, 240
Northwestern borders, 165
Nuclear deterrence, 143, 149, 151
Nuclear fusion/fission power, 219, 225
Nuclear parity, 115
Nuclear-powered submarine, 119, 143, 222
Nuclear proliferation, 221, 222, 244, 250
Nuclear warfare, 116, 142
Nuclear weapons, 108, 111, 115, 116, 140, 142, 149, 151, 152, 157, 163, 222, 228

O

Oasis States, 165
Obedience, 52–54, 61, 169, 171
Oceania, 109
Offence (military strategy), 52, 97, 101, 102, 117, 134
Oil, 10, 42, 46, 113, 114, 139, 151, 153, 249
Oligopoly, 46
Oman, 153
One Country, Two Systems, 137
One-party system, 75, 81, 246
Opening up (of China's economy), 22, 30, 36, 39, 65, 89, 90, 116, 135, 199, 201
Opposition, 25, 89, 120, 176, 224, 242–244
Optical fibre network, 223
Optimism, 88, 230
Organization Department, 84
Oriental aquamarine, 41
Ottoman Empire, 170
Outer China, 167, 175, 178, 181

Outer Mongolia, 9, 113, 145
Overcapacity (economy), 26
Over-the-horizon radars, 144

P

Pacific Ocean, 128, 132, 144, 153, 154
Pacifism, 141
Pakistan, 111, 153
Palaeolithic, 215
Palau, 139
Pamir Mountains, 6
Papua New Guinea, 143
Paracel Islands, 151
Paradigm shift, 47, 208, 236, 247, 250–252
Paradox, 81, 85, 87, 198, 246
Paramilitary organisation, 113
Paris Agreement, 246
Party branches, 76–78
Party discipline, 29, 66
Party Secretaries, 76
Pastoralism, 40, 53
Pax Romana, 128
Pax Sinica, 172, 185
PayPal, 37
Peace, 13, 99, 101, 102, 115, 117, 121, 142, 146, 149, 155, 170, 172, 173, 192, 204, 216, 220, 221, 224, 231, 248, 252
Peace talks, 164
Peanuts, 9
Pearl Harbor, 135
Peasant rebellion, 18, 23
Penghu, 113, 145
Pension system, 27, 28
Pentagon, 138, 143, 222
People's Liberation Army Navy (PLAN), 133, 134, 139, 141, 153
People's Liberation Army (PLA), 77–79, 108, 115–117, 122, 123, 134, 139, 142, 156
People's Republic of China, establishment of, 177
Performance legitimacy, 21–23, 27, 66, 238, 240
Period of transition, 235, 236, 250
Persian, 128, 176
Persian Gulf, 130
Personal interests, 53, 193
Petrarch, 60, 61
Petrochemicals, 114
PetroChina, 44, 114
Philip II, 150, 157

Philippines, The, 103, 138, 147, 151
Philosophers, 18, 52, 54, 55, 60, 61
Philosophical tradition/heritage, 51, 67, 166
Phoenicia, 128
Pirates, 131
Planned economy, 42, 218
Plato, 63
Polarisation, 232
Police force, 244
Policy-laws, 58–60
Politburo, CCP, 76, 198, 202, 206
Political consciousness, 23
Political equal, 170
Political factions, 196
Political institutional framework, 20, 71, 245
Political legitimacy, 200
Political philosophy, 17, 51, 52, 54, 55, 57, 61, 62, 64, 66, 67
Political rights, 19
Political stability, 37, 41, 82, 83, 197, 240
Political support, 10, 21
Political volatility, 173
Polycrisis, 217
Pope Francis, 196
Population dilution, 113. *See also* tuntian
Population growth, 9, 102, 104
Populism, 220, 232
Ports, 111, 117, 128, 135, 139
Portugal, 128
Positive feedback loop, 45, 46
Postal services, 46
Potatoes, 9
Poverty, 23, 199, 204, 225
Power, administrative, 73
Power, balance of, 12, 102, 140, 142, 144, 145, 149, 153, 154, 228, 229
Power, conception of, 3
Power, consolidation of, 122. *See also* centralised power
Power projection, 116, 151, 184
Power sharing, 79
Power-storage systems, 225
Power struggle, 30, 86, 229
Power vacuum, 153, 245
Pragmatism, 106
Precious metals, 99
Predictive policing, 224
Prefectures, 72, 83, 84
Premiership, 75
Presidency of China, 197
Prices, 22, 24, 38, 39, 41–43, 46, 59, 174
Prince Henry the Navigator, 131

Princess, 170
Privacy, 45
Private enterprises, 36, 38, 39, 77
Private sector, 23, 28, 35, 36, 38, 43, 44, 46, 65, 66, 74, 77, 196, 200, 224
Private tutoring, 36
Procedural laws, 59
Productivity, 10, 22, 104, 156, 219, 223
Propaganda, 186, 224, 239, 241, 244
Property rights, 137
Prosperity, 3, 5, 6, 8, 12, 13, 19–21, 28, 40, 44, 46, 90, 99, 100, 108, 113, 114, 128, 132, 135, 138, 151, 155, 157, 172, 175, 180, 198, 204–206, 213, 216, 230, 231, 237, 238, 250
Protectionism, 232
Protectorate of the Western Regions, 111
Protests, 25, 46, 110, 112, 137
Provinces, 4, 6–8, 12, 13, 27, 75, 76, 82–84, 111, 113, 177, 178, 196, 243, 244, 246
Provincial governors, 76
Prussia, 199
Public opinion, 87, 122
Public ownership, 66
Public services, 72, 74, 157, 174
Punishment, 19, 55, 56, 61
Punti, 178
Putin, Vladimir, 149, 202

Q

Qing dynasty, 6, 9, 19, 41, 65, 76, 82, 103, 111, 112, 121, 132, 167, 171, 172, 177, 178, 217
Qinghai, 4, 9, 113
Qin Shihuang, 9, 11, 12, 40, 57, 72
Quadrilateral Security Dialogue, 119
Quan Rong, 100
Quantum technology, 219
Quarantine, 84

R

Race/racial, 53, 85, 113, 177
Radar, 151
Raids, 101, 104, 164
Railway, 12, 42, 44, 113, 117, 134, 201
R&D, 46
Rare earth elements, 226
Rational actor, 71, 84, 85, 166
Raw materials, 98
Reagan, Ronald, 222, 231
Real estate sector, 26, 27

Index 267

Realpolitik, 136
Rebellions, 9, 78, 100, 105, 171. *See also* uprising, mutiny
Reciprocity, 61, 250
Redistribution, 83, 174
Red Sea, 152
Red tape, 84
Reeducation camps, 137
Reform and opening up, 22, 30, 36, 39, 65, 89, 90, 116, 201
Regional Comprehensive Economic Partnership, 154
Regional security, 120, 172, 173
Rejuvenation, China's, 117, 183, 206, 250
Religion, 169
Remote sensing assets, 144
Renaissance, 60, 61, 231
Renewable energy, 114, 219, 225, 226, 245
Republican Chinese Navy, 133
Republic of China/Republican era, 10, 12, 21–23, 28, 63, 65, 66, 77, 82, 100, 110, 113–117, 133, 146, 148, 177–179, 193, 217, 225
Resource rivalry, 249
Retirement age, 27
Retirement benefits, 25
Rewards, 9, 55, 131
Righteousness, 52, 61, 107
Right to food, 19
Rise of China, 153, 196, 205, 213, 214, 238
Rivalry partners, 213, 230, 231, 252
Rivers, 4, 7, 89, 90, 98, 114, 133
Road-building, 12
Robotics, 222, 223
Roman Empire, 60, 100, 106, 170
Rome, 98, 106, 128, 215
Rule of law, 29, 41, 51, 55, 56, 58, 64, 71, 246
Rule of man, 58, 246
Rule of ritual, 51–55, 61, 64, 67, 71, 246
Rule of virtue, 51, 57, 60, 61, 63, 64, 71, 74, 246. *See also* virtue
Ruling classes, 176
Rural, 10, 22, 26–28, 43, 193, 200, 201, 225
Russia, 105, 109, 111, 115, 116, 149, 150, 157, 172, 229, 237, 240
Russian Revolution of 1917, 65
Ryukyu Islands, 138
Ryukyu Kingdom, 167, 168

S
Sahel, 101

Salt, 41
Sanctions, 29, 149, 165, 180, 222, 240, 247
Satellites, 134, 144, 224
Saudi Aramco, 37
Savings, 28, 174, 191
Scarborough Shoal, 151
School of Literati, 60
Science, 75, 76, 119, 221
Sea lanes, 128, 129, 131, 151, 152, 226
Sea/naval power, 127–131, 133, 134, 136
Sea-trading, 98. *See also* maritime trade/commerce
Second Opium War, 133
Second Sino-Japanese War, 77
Second World War, 30, 133, 135, 140, 141, 143, 145, 150, 157, 192, 218, 228
Security dilemma, 110, 120, 164, 172, 173, 218
Security risks, 11, 248, 250
Self-reliance/self-sufficiency, 98, 121, 224, 237
Semiconductors, 43, 76, 174, 175
Seoul, 180
Separatist movements, 12, 111, 244
Shaanxi, 4, 192
Shandong, 4, 132
Shang dynasty, 18, 56, 166
Shanghai, 24, 133, 196, 243
Shanghai Clique, 64
Shang Yang, 55–58
Sherpa, 111
Shi (concept), 107
Shipbuilding, 130
Shipping lines, 128
Shu (kingdom), 11
Siberia, 103
Sichuan, 4, 6, 11, 113, 244
Sichuan–Tibet railway, 12
Silk, 8, 40, 99, 170
Silk Road, 9, 102, 120, 129
Silk road, 177
Silver, 41, 99
Simplified Mandarin characters, 179, 196
Singularity (theory), 215
Sinopec, 43
Slaves/slavery, 53, 65, 99
Smartphones, 223
Social benefits, 44
Social class, 73, 200
Social control, 24, 25
Socialism, 43, 65, 66
Social media, 25, 207

Social order, 25, 52, 64, 199. *See also* stability
Social stability, 35, 44, 45, 109
Social status, 40
Social unrest, 37, 46, 83, 84
Social welfare, 47, 200
Soft power, 123, 163–165, 174, 175, 179, 182, 184–186, 203, 241
Sogdian-Turkic, 78
Solar energy, 114
Soldiers, 78, 104, 109, 112, 120, 131, 249
Solomon Islands, 143
Song dynasty, 8, 41, 129, 130
South America, 9
South Asia, 6, 109
South China Sea, 111, 116, 118, 119, 127, 143, 147, 150–152, 154, 226, 238, 249
Southeast Asia, 6, 109, 135, 154, 173
Southern Caribbean Sea, 128
Southern Tibet/Arunachal Pradesh, 114
South Korea, 118, 140, 154, 165, 180, 182, 185, 222
South Pacific, 118, 143, 144
Southwest China, 153
Sovereignty, 118, 133, 135, 138, 146, 148, 151, 154, 169–172, 174, 220
Soybean, 10
Space cyber-attack, 140
Space (technology), 43
Spain, 7, 128, 150, 157
Spanish Socialist Workers' Party, 203
Sparta, 217
Special Education Bureau (Japan), 180
Spices, 41, 99
Sports, 182, 237
Spratly Islands, 151
Spring and Autumn Period, 5, 54
Stalemate, 238
Standardisation, 52, 179
State Council, 22, 23, 28, 58, 110
State/fiscal revenue, 40, 41, 82, 83, 104, 129
State/government intervention (economics), 35, 36, 44, 45, 47
State-owned Assets Supervision and Administration Commission, 42
State-Owned Enterprises (SOEs), 26, 28, 35, 36, 39, 42–47, 66, 76, 77
Status quo, 110, 148, 153, 157, 191, 192, 206, 218
Steam ships, 134
Steel, 42, 114
Strategic competition, 134

Strong leadership, 47, 198, 202
Structural constraints, 240, 242
Subjective perceptions, 239
Submarines, 119, 133, 141, 143, 146, 152, 249
Subsidies, 39, 59, 84
Sudden attacks, 140, 142
Suez Canal, 152
Sui dynasty, 73, 104
Sunflowers, 9
Sun Tzu, 107
Superpower, 118, 154
Supply chain, 10, 174, 201, 240
Surface combatants, 133
Surplus, 7–9, 21, 186
Surveillance, 137, 141, 143, 144, 224, 244
Sustainability, 206, 248
Sutlej, 114
Suzerain, 170
Sweden, 184
Sweet potato, 9
Switzerland, 113
Sydney, 192
Symbolic order, 169
Syria, 115, 123

T
Taiga, 6
Taiwan, 109, 113, 116, 118, 122, 123, 127, 134, 137–142, 145–150, 154, 156, 157, 163, 184, 185, 218, 237, 238, 249
Taiwan's democracy, 147
Taiwan Strait, 64, 119, 127, 140–142, 147, 150
Taizong (emperor), 197
Tajikistan, 111
Taliban, 226
Tamang, 111
Tang dynasty, 5, 78, 103, 105, 129, 176, 185, 197
Taobao, 37
Tarim Basin, 114, 120, 165
Tasmania, 192
Taxes, 22, 40, 41, 56, 82, 83, 99
Tax reform, 83, 174
Tax revenue, 9, 43, 82–84
Tax system, 82
Tea, 8
Technological inequality, 223
Technological revolution, 213, 214, 217, 219

Index 269

Technology, 30, 36, 37, 40, 43, 45, 75, 76, 90, 102, 113, 116, 134, 144, 175, 182, 199, 214, 219–226, 238, 249, 250
Technology companies, 45, 59
Tehran, 222
Telecommunications industry, 46
Teledensity, 223
Telegraphs, 134
Television, 53, 182
Tellis, Ashley, 205
Terminal High Altitude Area Defense (THAAD) system, 119, 165
Territorial conflicts, 108, 115, 152
Territorial conquest, 97
Territorial control, 103
Thailand, 151
Thatcher, Margaret, 202
Theatrical performances, 53
Third industrial revolution, 219
Third World War, 108, 215
Thirty Years' War, 220
Three Gorges Dam, 6, 114
Three Represents, The, 199, 200
Tianjin, 133
Tianxia, 57, 165–167, 169, 175, 177, 185
Tibet, 9, 12, 103, 111–114, 137, 167, 178, 241, 243–245
Tibetan Plateau, 6, 114
Tigris (river), 4, 98
TikTok, 45, 174
Tin, 41
Tobacco, 41, 42
Tokyo, 180
Tolerance, 24, 53, 228
Tonga, 143
Top-down approach, 79, 80
Tourism, 165
Tower Ship Navy, 129
Township, 79, 83, 84, 245
Toyotomi, Hideyoshi, 145, 167
Trade, 5, 7, 8, 10, 39, 47, 85, 97, 99, 119, 121, 128–130, 132, 135, 136, 139, 150, 151, 157, 165–167, 173, 196, 227, 231, 232, 240, 241, 247
Trade-off, 20, 155, 218, 240, 242, 251
Trade restrictions, 165, 174. *See also* sanctions
Traditional characters, 180
Transparency, 47, 186
Transportation, 38, 54, 135, 138, 139, 152, 182
Treaty of Shaoxing, 171

Treaty of Shimonoseki, 145
Treaty of Westphalia, 170, 220
Tribes, 5, 100, 103, 129–131, 176
Tributary system, 131, 163, 165–167, 169–173, 175, 182, 185, 231
Truman administration, 146, 148
Tsinghua University, 196
Tuntian, 112, 113
Turkic kingdoms, 111
Turkish (language), 111, 176
Turks, 103, 104, 121
Two-ocean power, 152–154
Two Sessions meeting, 87
Tyranny, 35

U
Ueda, Kazutoshi, 180
Ukraine, 115, 149
Umbrella Movement, 137
Uncertainty, 26, 67, 90, 121, 206, 213, 214, 225, 229, 235, 236, 245, 246, 250
Unification, 11, 12, 71, 78, 146–149, 177–179, 184
Unification with Taiwan, 156
Unilateral, 61, 174, 180, 238
Union movement, 241
Union of Soviet Socialist Republics (USSR), 30, 42, 241
Unipolarity, 205
United Kingdom, 113, 119, 128, 182, 184, 192, 218, 225
United Nations, 23, 109, 146, 172
Unity/unified, 3, 5, 8, 9, 11–13, 44, 47, 55, 57, 61, 71–73, 78, 112, 128, 176, 179, 208, 216, 220, 224, 225, 230, 237, 244, 245
Unmanned systems, 134, 222
Upper Palaeolithic, 215
Uprising, 18, 104. *See also* rebellion
Upward accountability, 84–86
Urban labour, 43
Ürümqi, 12
US. Congress, 58
US Defense Advanced Research Projects Agency, 222
US Department of Defense, 77, 115, 116, 123, 133, 139
US Joint Chiefs of Staff, 77
US Pacific Fleet, 143
US-Soviet rivalry, 30, 146
US supremacy, 221
Uyghurs, 113, 179, 180

V

Values, 3, 22, 24, 31, 36, 38, 40, 52, 61, 62, 64, 65, 71, 73, 90, 101, 102, 105, 136, 137, 147–149, 153, 154, 166, 167, 169, 171, 173, 174, 176, 177, 181, 182, 185, 186, 218, 227, 228, 231, 239, 243, 251
Vanuatu, 143, 144
Vassal states, 154
Vietnam, 103, 133, 138, 151, 168, 171, 172, 185
Virtue, 29, 61–64, 67, 73, 75, 101, 166, 176, 181, 228
Voltaire, 241

W

Wang, Gungwu, 183
Wang, Ming, 30
Warfare, 30, 54, 102, 103, 106, 115, 116, 121, 129, 133, 141, 156, 157, 222, 223, 228, 249
War games, 140
War horses, 101
War on terror, 218
Warring States period, 11, 39, 54, 61, 228, 229, 252
Warships, 134, 140. *See also* battleships
Watchdog model, 88
Water, 3, 5, 6, 12, 25, 40, 46, 61, 98, 101, 111, 114, 129, 135, 136, 151–153, 245, 248, 249
Wealth accumulation, 8, 200
Wealth redistribution, 41, 220
Weapons, 65, 102, 116, 134, 141, 172, 222, 247
Weapons of mass destruction, 221, 222
Weather, 3, 8, 21, 214, 225
Weights and measures, 57
Wei (kingdom), 62
West Africa, 131
West-East Gas Pipeline, 114
Western civilisation, 3, 7, 98
West Pacific, 139, 140, 144
Western Zhou dynasty, 52, 54, 56, 100
Westphalian model, 169, 172, 248
West, the, 6, 20, 28, 36, 44, 46, 54, 63, 65, 66, 88–91, 102, 103, 114, 132, 140, 143, 144, 152, 174, 181, 185–187, 199, 204, 206, 215, 220, 230, 237–239, 246, 250
White people, 215
Whole Nation System, 224

Wind energy, 114
Wine, 41, 165
Wittfogel, Karl, 6
Work outcomes, 75
Work points system, 22
World order, 120, 154, 164, 169, 185, 187, 192, 220. *See also* international order
World Trade Organization, 47
World wars, 192, 228
Written script, 57
Wu (emperor), 9, 41, 60, 120, 164, 165, 197

X

Xia dynasty, 5, 56
Xianbei, 176
Xiaomi, 223
Xiao, Pei, 29
Xi, Jinping, 10, 21, 23–25, 28, 29, 43, 44, 59, 64, 66, 75, 76, 78, 90, 91, 108, 117, 119, 121, 122, 149, 157, 182, 187, 191–198, 202–207, 224, 238, 246
Xinjiang, 12, 103, 111–114, 137, 145, 167, 178, 180, 181, 241, 243–245, 249
Xinjiang Production and Construction Corps (XPCC), 113
Xiongnu, 9, 100, 101–104, 120, 121, 129, 164, 165, 170, 171, 176
Xi, Zhongxun, 193
Xuanzong (emperor), 78
Xunfu, 76
Xun Zi, 61

Y

Yalu River, 109
Yan'an, 30, 196
Yan'an Rectification Movement, 30
Yangtze River, 5, 57, 114, 131
Yarlung Tsangpo River, 114
Yellow River, 3–6, 11, 12, 98, 114, 132, 178
Yellow Sea, 4, 6, 152
Yin-yang (concept), 35, 45
Yom Kippur War, 123
Yongzheng, 9
Youth League, 64
Yu, 5
Yuan dynasty, 132
Yuanmingyuan (Old Summer Palace), 133
Yue, 52
Yuezhi, 102
Yunnan, 244

Z

Zhejiang, 196
Zhenbao Island, 109
Zheng, He, 130, 131
Zhou dynasty, 18, 52, 61, 166

Made in United States
Cleveland, OH
02 November 2024